THE EUROPEAN ADMINISTRATIVE ELITE

JOHN A. ARMSTRONG

The European Administrative Elite

PRINCETON UNIVERSITY
PRESS

JF
1411
.A73

TO THE MEMORY OF

Philip Edward Mosely

THIS BOOK has been a long time in the making. During 1963-64 (with assistance from the American Council of Learned Societies and the University of Wisconsin) I was able to spend the academic year in Europe talking to seventy public administrators and private businessmen who had been in close contact with the Soviet administration. Little of the information from these interviews has been used directly in preparing this book, but personal acquaintance with contemporary administrators has made my study of their history much more meaningful. Most important were the striking differences in Europeans' observations of the same phenomenon—Soviet administration. It seemed to me that these differences were correlated not only to differences in nationality but to differences in educational background. This impression encouraged me to proceed with the idea of a study in chronological depth of differences in roles and the socialization patterns which produced them. I am very grateful, therefore, to these seventy informants who helped me at the start.

During 1967-68, with a Guggenheim Fellowship and a second University of Wisconsin Graduate School grant, I spent nearly a year consulting European colleagues and working in libraries. Most of the research was carried on in the Bibliothèque Nationale, a much maligned institution which, if one makes an effort to adapt to its schedule, is actually as efficient and cooperative as any I have encountered. The British Museum, the Cologne University Library, the Deutsches Industrie-Institut, the Hamburg Weltwirtschaftsinstitut, and the libraries of the Ecole des Ponts et Chaussées and the Paris Faculté de Droit, were also very helpful, as was, of course, my own university library.

It is impossible to list all the persons who aided me, but I must mention the invaluable assistance of Clémens Heller of the Sixième Section, Ecole des Hautes Etudes Pratiques, and Wilhelm Treue, professor of history at Göttingen University. In the United States, John E. Turner, professor of political science at the University of Minnesota; the group of outstanding administrators whom Alfred Diamant assembled at Indiana University in December 1970; and my University of Wisconsin colleagues from many disciplines have been very helpful. My research assistants, Brian Silver, James O'Connor, Virginia Parkum, Gregory Tewksbury, and Jerry Jansen, aided me immensely in preparatory statistical studies. I must, of course, take full responsibility for the factual accuracy as well as the interpretations of the completed work.

The Social Science Research Council provided a semester grant (1972) which enabled me to find the time for writing. But I should have been quite unable to get this done had it not been for the unfailing assistance of my wife, Annette Taylor Armstrong, who not only typed the entire manuscript, but edited it as only one long familiar with my idiosyncrasies could have done. Gregory L. Graf drew the finished versions of the line graphs.

Finally, I am very grateful to the staff of Princeton University Press, particularly Sanford G. Thatcher and Eve Hanle, who not only arranged a remarkably speedy evaluation of the manuscript but have carried out the unusually laborious task of editing meticulously and skillfully.

Madison, Wisconsin
July 1972

CONTENTS

THE EUROPEAN ADMINISTRATIVE ELITE

CHAPTER ONE

The Problem and the Analysis

Our times are fickle in their treatment of the high administrator. To-day, and the day before yesterday, he is a "bureaucrat," plodding and pettifogging, reproducing his kind faster than the population explosion. Yesterday, and perhaps tomorrow, he is the counterweight to private indulgence, the prime mover of "freedom under planning." Common to both sets of popular images is the focus on the institution, the vast, grey labyrinth of Kafka's castle. What matters in both these interpretations are laws, rules, organizational charts. Executors and client-victims alike are faceless, locked in a pattern that grew, somehow, of itself. Only occasionally does an individual portrait emerge as an anecdote of benevolence or bumbling.

This book is primarily concerned with the men who direct administrations, rather than with administrative institutions. It is a study of how high administrators themselves, and other elites closely associated with them, have perceived the administrator's role. The study seeks to do more than identify role perceptions, however; it explores the processes by which role definitions are acquired. As far as feasible, we shall try to relate changes in these processes to broader changes in the four European societies examined.

Because we are interested in the *evolution* of the administrative elite role, the study deals with a long period—for some purposes eighteenth-century and occasionally even seventeenth-century histories of administration are pertinent. On the other hand, the focus is narrow: it is not the administrative role in all its richness and ambiguity, but the special relation of the administrative role to economic development. We wish to learn how the administrator and those most closely related to him ("principal reference groups") have perceived his participation in economic development, i.e., the increase of material production.

We do not intend to identify the factors which caused European economic development. In recent years numerous impressive studies, notably Robert T. Holt and John E. Turner, *The Political Base of Economic Development*, have attempted this identification.[1] These studies are examinations of total societies, for determination of *necessary* factors in a general societal process like economic development entails

[1] Robert T. Holt and John E. Turner, *The Political Basis of Economic Development: An Exploration in Comparative Political Analysis* (Princeton, 1966).

scrutiny of all potentially relevant elements in the social system. Our aim is deliberately more restricted. We do not contend that the nature of high administrators' role definitions was a *necessary* condition for economic development in the four European societies studied. On the contrary, since it is generally recognized that all have attained roughly similar levels of economic development, variance in role definitions cannot have been decisive. In fact, an underlying assumption of this study is that other factors could adequately substitute (at least in earlier stages) for administrative participation in development. While we cannot fully explore the implications of this substitutability within the scope of this study, we shall discuss some of its aspects at various points, notably in Chapter Fourteen.

What is the use of exploring the elite administrative role in economic development if, in the long run, administrators have not decisively affected economic development? One answer, surely, is that the subject is historically interesting because of the way changing role definitions reflect the general position of the high administrator in his society and permit one to explore the impact of changing socialization processes. We think there is a more fundamental, or, if one prefers, a more practical response as well. For many reasons—changes in the international environment, technological progress, and the like—the mix of factors affecting economic growth changes over time. Factors like administrative intervention, which once were marginally important or even counter-productive, may become crucial, as Andrew Shonfield argues:

> The turn-round in British and American thinking about France and its economic methods is dramatic. It is worth asking how and why it occurred. . . . A conservative bureaucracy in a period of revolutionary technological change like the nineteenth century would clearly slow down the rate of progress. . . . But once the apparatus of government is directed to the exploitation of technological change and the men in charge are attuned to the expectation that this change will proceed at a high tempo, the balance of advantage could shift in favour of those who try to organize for change well ahead, and away from those who merely suffer it to happen.[2]

Our data will not permit us to settle the question of whether administrators have ever decisively affected the course of economic development. But our main concern is sufficiently close to this topic that we feel justified in pointing out suggestive evidence on the accomplishments as well as the attitudes of high administrators. In dealing with experiences spanning several centuries and involving four large so-

[2] Andrew Shonfield, *Modern Capitalism: The Changing Balance of Public and Private Power* (New York, 1965), pp. 73-75.

cieties, the purposes of analysis are best served, we believe, by a sharply defined, relatively narrow focus. Thus we shall concentrate on the major dependent variable of role definition and the intermediate variables of recruitment and socialization. We shall seek to identify a set of factors which have persistently produced positive definitions of the administrative role in relation to economic development. If such factors can be identified for the major European systems, we can hypothesize that they have a general significance for administrators in societies which are developing economically. Consequently, this is essentially an exploratory study. Our aim is not to *test* hypotheses (although we shall advance and examine numerous working hypotheses as guides to our exploration) but to distill hypotheses of potential nomothetic significance. In contrast to an investigation primarily concerned with verifying hypotheses, we must use a wide range of indicators (particularly in relation to the socialization process) not directly related to our major conclusions.

FOCUS AND SERENDIPITY

Setting a focus should be a device for concentrating light, not shutting it out by methodological blinders. The serendipitous potential of an exploratory study covering a wide span of time and space is considerable. Surprisingly, there is no really comprehensive history of even one of the four major national administrations. A real comparative history of European administration is hardly possible; and we certainly have no intention of contributing to what J. P. Nettl has called "a growing service industry—the writing of 'special' history predigested for sociologists, a sort of academic baby-food."[3] But this study ought to make some contribution toward an eventual comparative history. While most of the evidence we shall consider has already appeared in print, much has never been related to problems of administration even at the national level. Consequently, we present some of this evidence at greater length than is strictly necessary for our immediate purposes. The extensive notes and bibliography may also be useful. For certain major topics, sociological as well as historical, implications of the evidence outside our primary focus can at least be suggested.

As discussed above, we shall devote some attention to the actual impact of high administrators on economic growth, although we cannot treat the topic systematically. Another question which has preoccupied political scientists is administrative responsiveness. All philos-

[3] J. P. Nettl, *Political Mobilization: A Sociological Analysis of Methods and Concepts* (London, 1967), p. 21.

ophies of government must grapple with the dilemma arising from actual exercise by career administrators of extensive authority which the legitimizing principles of the social system nominally confer on others, such as hereditary monarchs or elected officials. The dilemma is not directly pertinent to this study, but our investigation of ideological arguments for administrative elite recruitment and socialization will involve some consideration of the legitimacy of administrative authority.

A whole series of questions relates to the concepts of "administration" as compared to "bureaucracy" and "organization." Surely administrative elite roles are significant only within organizational contexts; but as we are not mainly interested in organizations as such, most of the impressive body of organization theory will not apply to this study. The distinction between "administration" and "bureaucracy" deserves slightly more elaboration. To some extent, use of these terms has been a matter of disciplinary bias. Political scientists prefer to use administration to designate the formally nonpolitical activities of governments, while sociologists since Max Weber have preferred bureaucracy. But the distinction is surely more profound. It is not only that bureaucracy appears in many contexts other than governmental, and that even many strictly nonpolitical governmental activities (e.g., the judiciary in common-law countries) are hardly bureaucratic. More significant was Max Weber's *model* of bureaucracy, which posited a special type of rationalized organization. We have explored in previous works some empirical situations in which Weber's model can be evaluated; we do not intend to pursue this evaluation in the present study.[4] But the path laid out by Weber and broadened by more recent students of bureaucracy like Peter Blau and Michel Crozier is an enticing one. Our concentration on roles and the socialization which shapes them will inevitably lead to some attention to specific features of the bureaucratic model.

Roles, Values, and Ideology

In order to meet the minimal requirements of a far-ranging exploratory study, we must deal, at the beginning, with basic concepts of theory and method. The approach we use intrudes on many disciplines and, we hope, will attract readers of very different backgrounds. Some

[4] John A. Armstrong, *The Soviet Bureaucratic Elite: A Case Study of the Ukrainian Apparatus* (New York, 1959); John A. Armstrong, "Sources of Soviet Administrative Behavior: Some Soviet and Western European Comparisons," *American Political Science Review*, LIX (1965), 643-55; John A. Armstrong, "Old-Regime Governors: Bureaucratic and Patrimonial Attributes," *Comparative Studies in Society and History*, XIV (1972), 2-29.

may consider the sociological language an unnecessary complication. Perhaps a moment's reflection on the central concept of "role" will explain why we consider technical terminology to be indispensable. The term is often used in a metaphorical sense, but if it is to be useful as more than a passing stimulus to the imagination, "role" must be defined with reasonable precision. To undertake this definition without reference to the conceptual frameworks of social psychology in which the implications of "role" have been elaborated would be inexcusably wasteful. An *ad hoc* definition might seem to enable us to get on with the substance of the inquiry; ultimately, both the analysis and the reader's comprehension of it would suffer. Such is the case with other key concepts employed in this work. It is neither feasible nor desirable to define them all at once in a kind of primer of the social sciences. Many concepts, and a few assumptions, will appear in later chapters as they are required. There is, however, a basic conceptual framework which must be explicated at the start.

Before entering upon the more theoretical aspects of "role," let us begin by stating the assumption that the way high administrators perceive their roles represents learned responses to social stimuli. Certainly this assumption does not preclude a considerable element of rational choice by individuals. As will be discussed in Chapter Eleven, assimilation of values by adults, especially after they have entered the administrative organizations, is heavily influenced by rational calculation of the individual's chances for advancement. Social psychological theories of socialization to roles, however, do assume that basic values are learned in childhood and adolescence without conscious awareness of their significance, and that even much of the recombination of these values for role adaptation in later life is not consciously undertaken by the individuals involved.

An essential element of our approach is the search for genetic explanations of contemporary differences in role perceptions. Instead of treating variance in perceptions or attitudes as culturally determined, i.e., residual factors after other aspects of the contemporary social situation have been explained, the genetic approach seeks the origins of these differences in specific past behavior. At some moment in the past a formal institution was established, a behavior pattern adopted, a value acknowledged. Not infrequently each of these social phenomena was initiated by an identifiable individual or group of individuals. Identifying these origins as unique events is the work of historiography in the narrower sense. What is more important to the sociological perspective is determining how and why a pattern of social behavior became institutionalized, i.e., widely repeated and accepted in a segment of society. Even more important for the present study is the question of why some institutionalized patterns of behavior (which we may simply call "institutions" without implying that they necessarily have any formal legitimization) persist while numerous others disappear over a period of time. The question is similar to one which anthropologists have considered for many years: why are traits diffused to many cultures selectively adopted in some cultures but rejected by others?[5] At certain points this study, too, will discuss crosscultural diffusion in the proper sense of the term, but the main concern is with diffusion over time, i.e., selective *persistence*.

One solution is to try to find the societal function which the persistent institutions perform. Without attempting to assess impressive recent efforts to develop functional explanations of societal change, one may safely say that the functionalist approach is less readily adaptable to investigation of long historical periods involving drastic alterations in social systems than it is to instantaneous equilibrium situations. The structural functionalist concept posits system maintenance as the ultimate test of function performance, yet no generally accepted definition of system dissolution has been advanced. More specifically, the scope of our investigation embraces at least two catastrophic events (the French and the Russian revolutions) which *might* be considered terminal for the social systems involved. Unless one could determine whether or not the old-regime social systems were actually terminated —a matter far beyond the compass of this work—a functional approach would involve grave ambiguities.[6]

Conflict models, on the other hand, were generally developed precisely to explain societal dynamics over a period of several generations or more. Utilizing these conceptual approaches, one does not seek to explain the adoption or persistence of a structure by reference to its (essential) functional position in the total society, but by its utility to a specific societal segment.

The classic conflict model is Karl Marx's theory of social classes.

[5] Raul Naroll, "Two Solutions to Galton's Problem," *Philosophy of Science*, XXVIII (1961), 17; Everett M. Rogers, *Diffusion of Innovations* (New York, 1962), p. 135.

[6] The problem of functionalist interpretation obviously is far broader than one can treat here. See especially Carl G. Hempel, "The Logic of Functional Analysis" in Llewellyn Gross (ed.), *Symposium on Sociological Theory* (Evanston, Ill., 1959), p. 225; and Alvin W. Gouldner, "Reciprocity and Autonomy in Functional Theory" in *ibid.*, p. 243. We should, however, stress at this point that we follow Adam Przeworski and Henry Teune, *The Logic of Comparative Social Inquiry* (New York, 1970), p. 105, in holding that it is unnecessary to accept the functionalist explanation in order to employ the concept "system" in the sense of "any distinct set of interrelated elements." The crucial aspect of systemic interrelation of societal elements is the presence of feedback when one element affects another. The concept of feedback will be important throughout the study.

Anyone who attempts to utilize a conflict model is indebted to his insights, whatever one may think of his general interpretation of history. Two closely related concepts are particularly pertinent to this study. "False consciousness" was the first distinct formulation of the concept that the expressed reasons for social actions frequently mask (even for those giving the reasons) real motives related to group interests. "Ideology" for Marx was the form of false consciousness peculiar to a dominant social group. Even for the group itself, ideology legitimizes, by ostensibly universalist arguments, behavior actually directed toward preserving the group's particular interests. In employing "ideology" we shall retain the basic sense in which Marx used the term, i.e., an argument (more frequently an elaborate system of arguments) advanced to explain why an institution or value was introduced or maintained. Ideology will be distinguished from other types of arguments, theories, or doctrines by the considerable element of false consciousness which the ideological position contains, though an ideology, too, may contain many objectively true propositions. Conversely, other types of arguments, while possibly largely false or even deliberately deceptive, do not, on the whole, act as covers for group interests. Obviously an argument may be advanced on a nonideological basis and then become adopted as an ideology; more rarely the reverse process occurs.

It is apparent that the validity of this type of explanation depends on the assumption that social groups (or, as Amitai Etzioni calls them, "collectivities") possess emergent qualities. That is, the decisions these units make are more than the sum of the decisions of the individuals composing them.[7] While Etzioni and many others have presented cogent reasons why this is so, for our purposes the proposition can be taken simply as an assumption. It is equally apparent, however, that relating this proposition to the concept of ideology does not in itself advance one's analysis. As Karl Mannheim pointed out, Marx and his followers were prevented from elaborating a theory of the general relationship of ideology to group interests by their insistence on restrict-

[7] Amitai Etzioni, *The Active Society: A Theory of Societal and Political Processes* (London, 1968), pp. 45ff. When used as in the preceding paragraph, "ideology" resembles "latent function," in the broad sense in which the latter term was employed by Ralph Linton and Robert Merton. Both concepts are concerned with discovering the real content of a pattern of behavior which is legitimized by arguments or formulas which conceal rather than reveal this content. In both cases, persons involved in the pattern do not themselves understand the import of their behavior or the falsity of their arguments. "Ideology," however, is a more specialized concept in that it refers to arguments which conceal a partial (group) interest, while "latent function" *may* (although, in contrast to *structural* functionalism it *need* not) refer to systemic or holistic interests.

ing this relationship to the thought of their opponents.[8] Mannheim, in his impressive effort to elaborate such a theory of knowledge, is also restrictive. It is possible to accept his definition of ideology as applying only to conservative thought if one assumes that "conservative" applies to the defense of *any* group interest which has already been, at least to a considerable extent, established.

What is more dubious is Mannheim's adoption of Alfred Weber's formula of the "socially unattached intelligentsia." Mannheim elaborates this idea to mean, in effect, that intellectual groups have a unique opportunity to present relatively unideological arguments.[9] On the contrary, we assume that occupational groups consisting largely of intellectuals (such as secondary or higher school teachers and, in some societies, administrators) may be as prone to ideological argumentation as other social collectivities. Indeed, because of their facility in verbal presentation, one might well expect ideologies to be more frequently, though not more predominantly, characteristic of such occupational groups. If the concept of false consciousness, like the materialist conception of history, "is not to be compared to a cab that one can enter or alight from at will,"[10] then intellectuals, too, must take their chances with the rigidities of mass transportation.

Looked at in this way, the problem of ideology becomes one of empirical investigation rather than a priori assumption of the superior power of arguments presented by particular social groups or classes. Fortunately, an extended chronological treatment makes such an empirical inquiry more feasible, for often positions which at one point in time have been defended ideologically were originally bluntly advanced as group interests. A striking example was the establishment of the segregated Administrative and Executive Classes in the British civil service. Elaborate arguments (analyzed in Chapters Eight and Ten) have been presented throughout most of this century to justify this division. When it was first introduced (in 1870), on the other hand, the arguments advanced frankly asserted the unsuitability of lower-middle-class men for high administrative posts.[11]

---

[8] Karl Mannheim, *Ideology and Utopia: An Introduction to the Sociology of Knowledge* (New York, 1954), p. 249.

[9] *Ibid.*, p. 137.

[10] See Mannheim's reference to Max Weber's aphorism (in "Politics as a Vocation"), quoted in *ibid.*, p. 67.

[11] Roger K. Kelsall, *Higher Civil Servants in Britain from 1870 to the Present Day* (London, 1955), p. 35; see also Chapter Eight below. For an incisive application of ideological analysis to the arguments of the German academic spokesmen of the 1920's, see Fritz K. Ringer, *The Decline of the German Mandarins: The German Academic Community, 1890-1933* (Cambridge, Mass., 1969), p. 394.

ROLE DEFINITION

The excursus on group properties has been necessary because we are concerned not merely with the existence of roles but the way in which they originated. A brief examination of the meaning of the concept of "role" will indicate why this is true. Short as is the history of systematic efforts to define the concept, many divergent shades of meaning are already common.[12] For this study emphasis will be on the second element of the threefold division presented by Bruce J. Biddle: role as the sum of expectations. Since, however, we are dealing with organizations in which jobs or positions are formally defined, one can anticipate a fairly high congruence between these expectations and the codified official sum of tasks which Biddle posits as the third meaning of role. Conversely, role as the sum of behavior (Biddle's first meaning) will not be used in this study. When performance, as contrasted to expectation, is discussed, the distinction will be clearly specified.[13]

Norms and expectations of society in general (or at least of many persons in it) define the elite administrator's role, for it is a general social role, never a subculture role.[14] Societal groups salient for role definition, because individuals occupying the role are especially sensitive to their influence, are "reference groups." In our study most reference groups will be upper social strata or occupational elites. While roles are usually defined by general societal expectations, role definitions by the actors themselves may be expected to diverge significantly from the societal definition.[15] When the actors are members of an elite societal segment like the high administrators, one may expect these peculiar expectations, or self-perceptions, to be especially salient for role definition. The main thrust of this study is how elite administrators have, as groups, defined their own roles in relation to the particular task of economic development. In a sense to refer to this definition as "self-perception of the role" or as "the elite administrator's role perception" is redundant, for, as indicated above, the concept "role" contains the notion of expectation or perception. In order to distinguish expectations of the elite administrators from general societal expecta-

---

[12] See Anne-Marie Rocheblave-Spenlé, *La Notion de Rôle en Psychologie Sociale: Etude Historico-Critique*, 2nd ed. (Paris, 1969), pp. 53ff.

[13] Bruce J. Biddle, "Roles, Goals, and Value Structures in Organizations," in William W. Cooper, H. J. Leavitt, and M. W. Shelley II (eds.), *New Perspectives in Organization Research* (New York, 1964), p. 160.

[14] J. Milton Yinger, "Contraculture and Subculture," in David O. Arnold (ed.), *The Sociology of Subcultures* (Berkeley, 1970), p. 124.

[15] Biddle, in Cooper, p. 160.

tions defining their role, however, using the term "perception" as we have done seems justified.

Because they are contemporary, role studies commonly take the expectations and norms which define the roles as culturally determined, i.e., as given for the particular cross section of time to which the study applies. When one considers the evolution of roles over extended periods, however, the question of how these expectations and norms arose becomes critical. As indicated above, one can approach the question only by a conceptual framework which permits one to explain how latent interests and overt expression are related. The relationship between arguments, ideological and nonideological, and the norms and expectations which define the elite administrative role, is very complicated. One cannot even begin to consider the relationship until one has examined the meaning of the linkage concept, socialization. First, however, the actual development of literature on administrative elites requires one to examine certain special aspects of the role concept.

ROLE AND STATUS

Ralph Linton and many of the sociologists and anthropologists who acted as midwives for his seminal ideas considered role as twinned with the concept of social status. Put at its simplest, role was the dynamic aspect of a status, e.g., the expected performance in an occupation, as contrasted to the occupation itself.[16] Others have tended to see the relationship as much more complex. Michael Banton, for example, sees status as a reflection of the sum of roles, an "evaluation of an individual's claim to deference in respect of the prestige of the various roles he plays."[17] Other concepts replace "status" (except as a prestige category) entirely by "position." What all of these approaches agree on is the close but distinguishable relationship between an individual's expected participation in social activity and the place he is seen to occupy in the social structure.

The question just discussed would not directly concern this study except for the fact that the overwhelming concern of students of European elite administrators has been with their significance as a status group. This emphasis is partly due to the relative stability of the European social order. In contrast to the rapid role-change of the typical American, the European acquires most of his salient roles early in life.[18] As will be shown later in this chapter, European stability of so-

[16] Ralph Linton, "A Neglected Aspect of Social Organization," *American Journal of Sociology*, XLV (May 1940), 875; Rocheblave-Spenlé, pp. 53ff.

[17] Michael P. Banton, *Roles: An Introduction to the Study of Social Relations* (London, 1965), p. 37.

[18] Rocheblave-Spenlé, p. 93.

cial roles has a crucial importance for the kinds of topics and data considered in this study. For most investigators, however, the focus has been upon implications of the early acquisition of elite administrative status for status stratification in European societies. A typical emphasis has been on the "circulation of elites" as an indicator of social mobility or equality of opportunity. In his general treatment in his book, *Elites and Society*, for example, Thomas B. Bottomore is concerned with whether and why "there have been historical changes in the composition and cultural outlook of the elite, or in the relations between the elite and the masses."[19] He is particularly concerned with administrative elite status, as is Hans Rosenberg who, in his treatment of eighteenth-century Prussia, approaches the administrators as a "peculiar social and political status group" rather than as a "technical instrument of professional public administration."[20]

The latter phrase refers to (though it does not completely define) the area of our study: administrative elite role as a potentially active element in the process of development. Consequently, in relying (as is necessary) upon the numerous earlier studies, one must constantly bear in mind the essential difference between their purpose of relating the elite administration to social stratification, and the goal of establishing changing self-perceptions of roles. The large body of evidence accumulated on such factors as hierarchical positions, social origins, life chances, and social distance within administrations is intimately related to elite administrative roles and the process of socialization by which expectations defining these roles are established. This evidence constitutes, indeed, most of the data for this study. Formal position is, as indicated below, so closely associated with role definition that we shall often be obliged in practice to treat position as congruent with role. But such data are only *indicators*, that is, their relationship to role definition is inferential rather than direct. For a historical study one cannot resort to the most common way of establishing norms and expectations (or other more diffuse attitudes) by directly questioning the appropriate subject persons. Consequently (except in the rather infrequent instances when a source explicitly states role perceptions) one is reduced to less satisfactory operationalizing procedures. One assumes that expectations are reflected in behavior (which is also difficult to determine) or that an individual holds expectations because he has been subject to the same stimuli (e.g., occupation of a status) which gave rise to known expectations in others.[21] Inevitably these

[19] Thomas B. Bottomore, *Elites and Society* (London, 1964), pp. 53ff.
[20] Hans Rosenberg, *Bureaucracy, Aristocracy and Autocracy: The Prussian Experience 1660-1815* (Cambridge, Mass., 1958), p. viii.
[21] See Biddle, in Cooper, p. 151.

procedures involve a large measure of speculation even when data is abundant and reliable. For this reason, too, the results of the study must be considered as exploratory and hypothetical.

Divergence in focus of investigation is important not only for the relation between role and status, but for specifying the meaning of "elite." For most writers whose research findings will be used in this study, "elite" is primarily a stratification concept, i.e., an elite is a group of persons who enjoy superior status. As used in this study, on the contrary, "elite" refers (to use Etzioni's term) to roles in a societal control center. This usage rests simply on the assumption that some occupational roles are more crucial for society than others and that roles involving social control are especially crucial. Conceivably occupants of these roles could change very frequently, though, as will appear later, this is unlikely. Our concept of the elite assumes only that, at any given moment, a small proportion of the individuals comprising a society exercises very disproportionate authority in social control and allocation of resources. To this assumption we need merely add the specification that elite administrative roles are potentially crucial. Use of this minimal definition avoids (as Etzioni points out) the implication that a superior status *necessarily* accompanies the elite role. Ordinarily, to be sure, elite roles do imply high status, but in referring to the latter category alone we shall use such terms as "upper class" or "higher strata." On the other hand, we shall also use the term "elite" to refer to processes (especially education) which differentiately influence elite roles. Our definition also avoids the "elitist" assumption that occupancy of authoritative roles necessarily implies superior qualities.[22] Further, "elite" as used in this study does not assume cohesion of interests or attitudes among occupants of elite roles.[23] Certainly it is reasonable to anticipate that all of the characteristics frequently ascribed to elites will often be present in an administrative elite, particularly in Europe. The extent of their presence, however, remains a matter for investigation, not assumption.

Definition of the elite as a set of roles is appropriate for this study for an additional reason. A definition especially widespread in political science requires that the elite consist of persons who actually play a predominant part in decision-making. For many purposes such a definition is useful, but it is very difficult to apply, particularly for groups widely dispersed in time and space. For this study, the decision-making approach is unnecessary, for the main concern is not who in fact made decisions on economic development. At times, to be sure, partici-

[22] Etzioni, *The Active Society*, pp. 113ff.
[23] *Ibid.*

pation of elite administrators in decisions is an important *indicator* of their role perceptions. Throughout this study, however, the emphasis is on the perception rather than on behavior such as decision-making.

The point is crucial, for use of the role concept rather than decision-making makes reliance on official definitions more feasible. As indicated earlier, one way of looking at roles is through official job definitions. While not all aspects of even formal roles are officially defined, one thing that European administrative organizations nearly always provide is precise official definitions of superordinate and subordinate job *levels*. It is evident that not all occupants of roles associated with superordinate positions will in fact participate in major decisions, but official definitions ordinarily establish a role-defining expectation that they will. As an initial approximation, one may take the formal designation of superordinate positions as defining the hierarchical limits of the administrative elite. Accepting these designations as a starting point means that the administrative elite, including aspirants, numbers from the hundreds to the low thousands for those systems which provide a sharply defined career pattern. In no case do the men in top posts number more than one thousand. We are dealing therefore with groups which comprise a very small proportion of the populations of their societies, yet are large enough to make examination of group interactions rather than individual reactions the crucial matter.

SOCIALIZATION

The significance of socialization as the link between societal expectations and norms and administrators' role perceptions has already been noted. At this point, however, a definition which expresses the general linkage aspect of socialization is worth quoting. To Orville Brim socialization is:

a process of learning through which an individual is prepared, with varying degrees of success, to meet the requirements laid down by other members of society for his behavior in a variety of situations. These requirements are always attached to one or another of the recognized positions or statuses in this society. . . . The behavior required of a person in a given position or status is considered to be his prescribed role, and the requirements themselves can be called role prescriptions. . . . If socialization is role learning, it follows that socialization occurs throughout an individual's life.[24]

[24] Orville G. Brim, Jr., "Personality Development as Role-Learning," in Ira Iscoe and Harold W. Stevenson (eds.), *Personality Development in Children* (Austin, 1960), p. 128.

As Brim points out, socialization is a lifelong process; but most social psychologists have tended to see childhood—indeed early childhood—as the period of most significant socialization. It is possible, indeed, as Urie Bronfenbrenner has recently suggested, that subsequent periods (when peer-group influences become important) are more significant than Western psychology has generally recognized.[25] Nevertheless, Brim and Stanton Wheeler argue, what is learned in childhood is difficult to change because of 1) inertia of the basic personality established then; 2) frequency and intensity of early learning situations; and 3) the prevalence of partial reinforcement conditions. Adult socialization therefore focuses upon role-specific expectations, overt behavior, ability, and knowledge. To Robert Merton, adult socialization does include "acquisition of attitudes and values, of skills and behavior patterns making up social roles."[26] He might well agree, however, with the Brim and Wheeler position that, ordinarily, adult socialization creates new combinations of responses arising from the individual's basic values ("affect socialization") in order to enable him to fill specific roles.[27] Any effort to instill new basic values ("resocialization") is inordinately difficult if not impossible.

If this theoretical position is valid, the implications for studying an adult role like that of the elite administrator are profound. An effort limited to an examination of administrators' manifest perceptions of their roles would be superficial, for the responses learned as an adult would frequently conceal old responses not manifest at a conscious level.[28] Fortunately, some intuition of this principle has guided writers on the subject for generations. While attention has rarely been directed to the early years of childhood—which we therefore treat only in the most cursory fashion—literature on "school days" is abundant. The immediate problem is not to determine a cutoff point for proceeding backward in examining the socialization process, but to find out what specific kinds of socialization, within the range prevalent in a given society, are relevant for future administrative elites. In order to do this, we must establish a preliminary understanding not only of socialization, but of the process by which a system recruits its elite administrators.

Three abstract models are useful as a start toward determining the relevancy of different types of socialization. All three models contain

[25] Urie Bronfenbrenner, *Two Worlds of Childhood: U.S. and U.S.S.R.* (New York, 1970), p. 103.
[26] Robert Merton, *et al.*, *The Student-Physician: Introductory Studies in the Sociology of Medical Education* (Cambridge, Mass., 1957), p. 41.
[27] Orville G. Brim, Jr. and Stanton Wheeler, *Socialization after Childhood: Two Essays* (New York, 1966), pp. 22, 25.
[28] *Ibid.*, p. 22.

the fundamental elite assumption that the number of roles in a social system's control center is very small in proportion to the total number of adult roles, or to the total number of adults in the population. In practice, we may restrict the relevant population to adult males, for (in all the societies we examine) women have been excluded from elite administrative roles until very recently, when their entrance has been at the token level. We may envisage a typical male population cohort as in the hundred thousands. Since the number of top posts available per year is a very small fraction of that cohort, it is convenient to draw the abscissa of our model graph on a logarithmic scale, for a natural scale would make it impossible to depict the fraction attaining top positions. On the ordinate representing age of attainment, natural scale intervals are convenient. As will be shown empirically in Chapter Twelve, with a few exceptions the age level for attaining *top* administrative posts has fallen between the early forties and early fifties.

Model 1, which we call the Maximum Deferred Achievement Model, assumes that no selection is made among the male cohort until its members reach the appropriate age level for high administrative posts. At that point, the required number of men are selected by some

FIGURE 1. Maximum Deferred Achievement Model

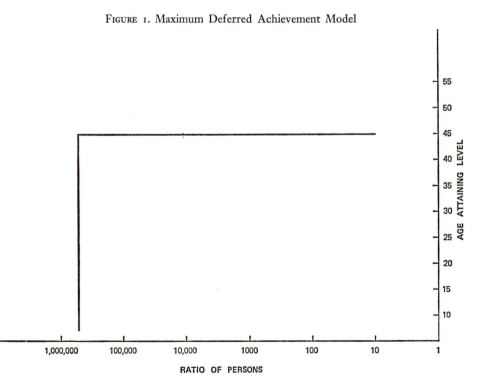

process which gives all—as far as discernible social characteristics go —equal access. By definition, therefore, their prior socialization is identical to that of a random sample of the male cohort. Consequently, the only relevant socialization process would be: 1) socialization after attainment of top posts; and 2) the mass socialization prevailing in the society during the four to five decades when the cohort was attaining the age required for selection for top administrative posts.

Probably no society has ever followed Model 1 in recruiting any major elite segment. The nearest approach seems to have been transitory elite recruitment arrangements during periods of extreme social upheaval, as symbolized by the French Revolutionary dictum that "every soldier carried a marshal's baton in his knapsack." Under similar circumstances Lenin momentarily advocated filling top administrative posts by random selection: "through the device of rotation in office, everyone would get his chance to be a bureaucrat for a while," as Alfred G. Meyer summarizes the proposal.[29] If the Soviet regime had in fact pursued this method of selecting personnel, socialization of elite administrators-for-a-day would necessarily have mirrored that of the general population, or at least of the urban proletariat. In fact, the Soviet administrative elite has been recruited overwhelmingly from workers and peasants. But, as will appear shortly, the method of selection is such as to provide *partial* socialization differing sharply from the mass experience.

Model 2, which we call the Maximum Ascriptive Model, is the opposite of Model 1. At an early age a very small portion of the male cohort is selected to occupy the top administrative posts when the individuals attain the required age. In principle, any characteristic can be used for selection. It is said that the Lamaist Buddhist leaders of Tibet were selected solely because their moment of birth coincided with the instant of death of their predecessors. However, heredity is the usual basis for selection in the sacral societies which have resorted to infantile elite recruitment. Given the high death rates in such societies, a considerably larger number is selected from each cohort than will actually be required to fill posts at maturity. Consequently, the vertical line segment in the graph of Model 2 might be slightly inclined to the left; but the polar characteristics of Models 1 and 2 are best brought out by simplified vertical representation.

Model 2 involves one further assumption: that the group chosen in infancy is segregated for socialization purposes throughout its life span. For the sacral societies this assumption is probably quite realistic. As a result, the student of a Model 2 administrative elite (assuming

[29] Alfred G. Meyer, *Leninism* (Cambridge, Mass., 1957), p. 190.

FIGURE 2. Maximum Ascriptive Model

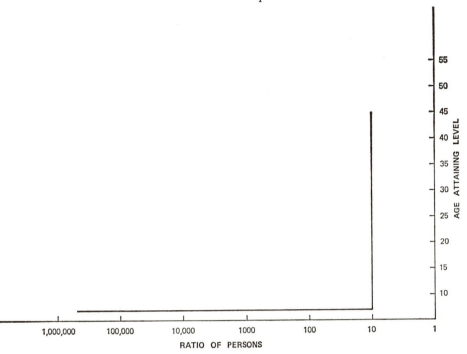

that such a specialized elite category exists in such a society) can con-centrate entirely on the special elite socialization process.

Probably no complex European society in recent centuries has ap-proached Model 2 very closely. As the empirically derived curves pre-sented in Chapter Eleven show, however, most of the systems we ex-amine do tend toward this model. Were it not for the properties of the logarithmic abscissa, the closeness of the fit would be even more ap-parent to a cursory inspection.

As later chapters will show, the reasons why European elite selec-tion tends to approach the Maximum Ascriptive Model are complex. It must be recognized, however, that socialization theory implies sub-stantial societal economies in this method of selection. If—as noted above—affect socialization is completed fairly early, a social system re-duces its need for investment in socialization by early selection of in-dividuals possessing basic values and motivations which require the least recombination.[30] When anticipatory socialization, i.e., conformity in advance to the expected adult role, is intense, virtually no resocial-ization may be required.[31] Segregation of future elites permits, though

[30] Brim and Wheeler, p. 27.   [31] *Ibid.*, p. 83.

it does not ensure, the presence of structures which induce such intense anticipatory socialization (see Chapters Six and Seven). Equally important is the potential for an uninterrupted line of *reinforcing* socializing experiences from infancy to attainment of top positions.

On the other hand, there are equally obvious disadvantages, even from the standpoint of societal efficiency. In principle, random infants could be removed from their natural families for complete socialization by societal agencies. In practice (in Europe and nearly everywhere else) boys destined for elite roles have been selected by *family*, i.e., ascriptively, according to parental status. While ascriptive selection for even a single elite segment is quite different from patrimonial inheritance of specific offices, the particularistic features of the ascriptive principle may (as discussed in Chapters Four and Twelve) contribute to a patrimonial "regression." Such a trend has serious consequences for national integration, which is a major avowed goal of administrative elites. Complete ascription also tends to reduce achievement motivation and may thereby lower the potential for administrative initiative in areas like economic development. Even if one does not assume that talent based on individual psychological and physical characteristics is randomly distributed, extremely high ascriptive selection will eliminate a large portion of the talent pool available in a given population. Finally, ascriptive recruitment has increasingly offended overtly universalist philosophical principles in modern European societies.

Two hypotheses can be derived from the prevalence of Model 2 in Western European systems:

1) Early stages of socialization peculiar to elites are particularly significant for future role definition;
2) Actual recruitment for elite roles at early age levels will be increasingly justified by ideological arguments.

Taken together, rather than constituting substantive hypotheses for testing, these hypotheses point the direction for investigation. As guides the hypotheses are significant because they show that (in contrast to studies of administrative elites in countries like the United States) an entire elite socialization process, including special educational institutions, must be studied to understand specific administrative elite roles.

For this study, Model 3 (Progressive Equal Attrition Model) is the deviant case. Approaches to the model are sufficiently common, however, for it to merit close attention. The model assumes that at each of several equal time intervals the same proportion of the male cohort is eliminated from eligibility for top administrative posts, until just the

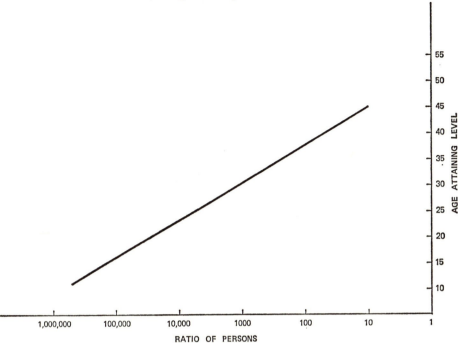

FIGURE 3. Progressive Equal Attrition Model

RATIO OF PERSONS

requisite number to fill available posts remains when the appropriate age level is attained. Mathematically, this model may be represented by the familiar formula for geometric progressions:

$$a_n = a_1 r^{n-1}$$

when a_n is the male cohort and a_1 the annual number of top positions open; r may vary. Graphically, if the abscissa were a normal-number scale, the curve would be exponential, thus approaching in appearance Model 2. With a logarithmic scale abscissa, however, the curve becomes a diagonal line, as shown in Figure 3. The steepness of the slope is proportionate to the ratio of the annual number of top openings to the male cohort.

If (as always occurs in practice) a comparatively small number (n) of time intervals are used as selection stages, the implications for investigating socialization are interesting. Since no attrition has occurred in early childhood, any study of this phase must deal with the mass socialization characteristic of the population. Adolescent socialization, on the other hand, while embracing an enormously larger number of boys than will eventually find administrative elite posts, does leave

out a notable portion of the cohort which is less favored or less qualified. Early adult socialization concerns a further reduced proportion;
for groups in their late twenties or thirties the proportion undergoing
the appropriate socialization experiences is so small as to approach
similar age categories in Model 2. Consequently, one must examine the
mass socialization characteristic of the society he is investigating to
determine the basic values and norms acquired by the administrative
elite. To determine how these basic elements are recombined to affect
role perceptions, on the other hand, one must examine adult socialization of an elite or semi-elite nature, commonly within administrative
organizations themselves.

A glance at the graphs in Chapter Eleven will show that the Soviet
experience closely approaches Model 3, while earlier Russian experiences and that of the German Federal Republic, though more complicated, bear some resemblance to it as compared to other Western European administrative elite experiences. While we have not attempted
to represent the recruitment patterns of the United States Federal civil
service graphically, in some respects they also come close to Model 3.
At this point, a few remarks on the general socialization problems associated with Model 3 will suffice. Clearly its achievement characteristics tend to satisfy universalist or egalitarian principles more than
Model 2, for progressive attrition can be made to provide protracted
equality of opportunity in a way which ascription by definition cannot. Whether in fact selection mechanisms do provide such opportunities, or tap a major portion of the society's pool of talent, is an empirical question. One would normally anticipate that Model 3 would go
further in these directions than Model 2. If opportunities to attain the
next stage are perceived by each level of individuals selected, their
achievement motivation may be heightened. While particularistic
tendencies of an ethnic nature (for example) are not precluded, the
low ascriptive element virtually eliminates the patrimonial regression
threat to national integration.

On the other side of the ledger, Model 3 implies heavy societal costs.
Some systems will resort to considerable resocialization (particularly
the Soviet, as discussed in Chapter Eleven). The American Federal
service is (from this point of view) anomalous because it relies so
heavily on lateral entry at various levels to government service and has
no clearly identifiable career route to top positions. Very large numbers of personnel are inducted at lower levels and no systematic resocialization is carried out at any level. Successive stages of elimination
from competition for higher positions of civil servants leave a residue
of the more adaptable; but lower administrative personnel with strong
achievement motivation, possibly lacking other requirements, sharply

resent their inability to realize their perceived potential. Some other negative effects of this pattern of recruitment will be discussed briefly later.

Identifying "Elite Administrators"

So far, the discussion has assumed that "administrators" are readily identifiable. In fact, one problem associated with using the relatively highly reified category under investigation is that it is difficult to set conceptually defensible boundaries. In establishing the boundaries for the level of the administrative elite, one is able to rely heavily on official definitions because (in the European systems considered) hierarchical distinctions are relatively stable and are salient to the administrators' perceptions. Formal designations are also an essential starting point for delimiting the administrative elite from other elite segments, but many more difficulties arise. Official designations tend to classify together all persons with legal status as higher civil servants. In some cases these classifications (e.g., the Administrative Class in Great Britain) provide reasonably accurate indexes to the kind of administrator we are interested in, but in other instances official classifications require much reworking. In general, European definitions tend to limit the administrator category to positions which constitute part of a lifelong career pattern. Usually we too shall concentrate on such career pattern positions, but (as indicated in the discussion of Model 3) for some systems a broader definition is indispensable.

In examining the available aggregate data, one cannot be wholly consistent in adhering to any clearly defined boundaries, for the data has been collected according to varying criteria. It is important, nevertheless, to indicate the range of positions we have tried to establish. The guiding criterion is whether the positions are indicators of roles which have a high *potential* for participation in decisions significantly affecting major resource mobilization and allocation for the national social system. As indicated in the discussion of the significance of "elite," this study does not try, as a rule, to determine whether holders of positions actually participated in decision-making. Unless, however, the roles administrators occupy potentially provide access to such decision-making, their self-perception of participation in economic development is irrelevant. Since we are interested, moreover, in anticipatory socialization, administrative positions too low for access to significant decision-making, but which provide strong chances of attaining such higher positions, are important for the investigation.

The criteria just presented enable one to exclude several important categories of officials who occupy nonadministrative elite roles. Except in special circumstances, diplomats, police officials, military officers, and judges are not part of our subject. It is more difficult to delineate the boundary between high administrators and political officials. We shall follow the usual convention by excluding officials (mostly parliament members) elected in genuine interparty contests even when they devote several years to major resource mobilization and allocation tasks. Conversely, appointed cabinet ministers must be considered a part of the administrative elite when their appointment (as was commonly the case in monarchical regimes other than Britain) represented a normal administrative career phase.

A more serious problem, because they have been so significant in defining the elite administrator's role, are the prefectural governors. As discussed in Chapter Twelve, this body of officials has been crucial not only in France and Tsarist Russia, but (despite sharp formal distinctions) in the USSR. An examination of the political involvement of the typical group, the French prefect, is important, therefore, to elucidate the reasons why we consider it essential to include prefectural governors among the administrative elite.

The prefectural corps recruited by Napoleon included few professional administrators. Instead, lawyers, professors, and especially military officers were utilized. Terms varied sharply and there were no clear promotion prospects for those entering at the sub-prefect level.[32] Nevertheless, a considerable number remained at their posts through the violent transition from the First Empire to the Restoration. By that time many prefects already regarded themselves as *fonctionnaires*, custodians of administrative continuity obliged to remain at their posts regardless of political affiliations or risks. It is significant that Louis XVIII retained most of the prefectural corps, especially at the sub-prefect level.[33] Subsequent periods of political instability down to the Liberation of 1944 resulted in more severe turnover in the prefectural group, with a massive influx of men from partisan political careers, journalism, and the like. But the career principle was generally weak in mid-nineteenth-century French office-holding, even in the judiciary.[34] "Purges" of the prefects were distinguished only in degree from dismissals or compulsory retirements in such incontestably elite administrative bodies as the Council of State, which experienced one-

[32] Brian Chapman, *The Prefects and Provincial France* (London, 1955), p. 25; Jean Savant, *Les Préfets de Napoléon* (Paris, 1958), pp. 94ff.; Pierre-Henry, *Histoire des Préfets: Cent Cinquante Ans d'Administration Provinciale 1800-1950* (Paris, 1950), p. 21.

[33] *Ibid.*, p. 93.

[34] Jean Lhomme, *La Grande Bourgeoisie au Pouvoir (1830-1880): Essai sur l'Histoire Sociale de la France* (Paris, 1960), p. 86.

fifth turnover both when the Third Republic was "refounded" as a real republican regime in 1879 and when the Vichy regime was overthrown.[35] To be sure, the prefectural corps has a range of duties which makes its political loyalty essential. Increasingly in recent decades, however, these duties have been interpreted to stress maintenance of regime stability through preservation of public order rather than (as in the nineteenth century) election manipulation and other distinctly partisan tactics. The prefectural corps retains—as Jeanne Siwek-Pouydesseau rightly points out—a mixed political-bureaucratic character.[36] On the whole it is closer to the administrative elite boundary than corresponding bodies of officials in Old-Regime France, Russia, or Prussia and therefore can serve as the limiting case for our analysis.

The territorial governing administrator is especially significant because he stands out as a generalist, coordinating several types of more specialized officials. This aspect of his role almost invariably involves him (as discussed in Chapter Twelve) in economic development decisions. In general, we can hypothesize at this point that "line" administrators, i.e., those concerned with overall problems of coordination and direction, rather than the performance of specialized tasks, have a high potential for perceiving their roles to include development initiative. However, as it has developed historically, the "generalist" role identification has certain peculiar characteristics which may lead in exactly the opposite direction. As we shall elaborate later, the British Administrative Class, while embracing a "generalist myth," has reinterpreted the term to mean *avoidance* of direction and coordination, particularly in the area of economic management. Instead, this administrative elite (at least until very recently) has restricted its activity primarily to formulation of policy or, as the formal definition runs, "policy advice" to ministers.[37] In the usual terminology of administrative analysis, in other words, this elite has redefined its "generalist" role to mean essentially a staff rather than a line role.

Some types of staff roles may, on the other hand, contain significant potential for development participation. This is specifically true of official roles explicitly concerned with financial and economic tasks. Financial specialists have constituted a basic category in European administrations since the preindustrial era, beginning with the partial separation (as in the Ferme Générale in France) of official roles from the semi-official private bankers ("court financiers"). More recently

[35] Charles E. Freedeman, *The Conseil d'Etat in Modern France* (New York, 1961), p. 47.

[36] Jeanne Siwek-Pouydesseau, *Le Corps Préfectoral sous la Troisième et la Quatrième République* (Paris, 1969), p. 19.

[37] Kelsall, p. 35.

some of the administrative elites have included high officials explicitly charged with economic planning, though other elites have excluded this category as such.

Finally, there is the difficult question of managers of industrial or construction establishments. Management of industrial plants by government administrators is a relatively new phenomenon, but construction of the transportation infrastructure has been a major concern in some systems for centuries. As will appear later, this area of administrative activity has been crucially important for the evolution of administrators' role perception. Consequently, it would fatally limit the study to omit consideration of technical officials directly involved in construction. Since the same type of official (often the same individual) is frequently employed in state industrial direction, managers of large state enterprises are also included. The fundamental criterion, followed to the extent that the available data make it practicable, is whether the managerial role is a part of a broader career pattern involving general participation in resource mobilization or allocation.

This criterion leads to the apparent conceptual anomaly of including, say, the director of the nationalized Renault automobile factory while excluding the manager of Citroën, a private firm. However, as just indicated, the Renault director would be included only if his post was normally part of a *career* (such as that actually pursued in the great French technical corps) including a *number* of varied high administrative roles. Nevertheless, since the role of professional manager was established (about a century ago), this private-sector elite has constituted an outside reference group of particular importance in defining the elite administrative role. Consequently, while this study will not attempt to examine the private managerial elite in detail, considerable comparative data will be presented on managers.

CHAPTER TWO

The Comparative Method

THE ultimate purpose of this study is not merely to explain a historical phenomenon but to suggest ways in which modern administrative
elites generally may relate to economic development. Is it at all realistic to hope to discover these patterns in a comparative study limited
to four societies? Part of the answer has already been given, when we
cautioned that this is an exploratory investigation rather than an attempt to demonstrate propositions. Surely any generalizations derived
from a limited segment of human experience require further testing
under different conditions. When the number of cases is very small the
inevitable absence of statistical tests, even for propositions established
as valid for each system, demands further efforts at verification. Even
if confined to a very few systems, "variable analysis" may be useful to
show how correlation of data derived from a single system may be
spurious.[1] In fact, we shall encounter numerous propositions (whether
derived from quantitative correlations or not) based on studies of administrations in one European system—or the United States—which
immediately appear spurious when contrasted to other systems. The
approach is far more valuable when more complex phenomena are
considered. A striking instance is the assertion, common in German
treatises, that extensive legal training *and* experience are indispensable
for high administrators in systems which have accepted Roman law.
A comparison with France—certainly no less a Roman-law country
than Germany—demonstrates that, despite superficial indications,
such a requirement has not been mandatory either now or in the past
century and a half. As we shall attempt to show later, the German
argument has been a crucial element in an ideology which utilizes certain legal institutions to further administrative elite interests. If an institutional complex favors the material interests or status of a group;
if members of the group persistently advance superficially coherent
arguments for the institutional complex; if these arguments seek to
legitimize the institutions by appealing to societal traditions or interests but do not admit special group interests; if, in other times and
places, these arguments are readily recognized as dubious; if the arguments (and possibly the institutions themselves) are abandoned when

[1] Howard A. Scarrow, "The Scope of Comparative Analysis," *Journal of Politics*, xxv (1963), 573.

they no longer accord with the group interests; then the institutional complex is being used ideologically. It is extremely difficult, if not impossible, to apply this analysis, which is central to our approach, to a single time and place. The comparative method is nearly indispensable.

SCALE AND HOMOGENEITY OF SOCIETIES

There are particular reasons for selecting the societies to be compared. Though few in number, France, Germany, Great Britain, and Russia constitute a quasi-universe of immense significance: large social systems in which industrialization has been successfully accomplished. By any of the customary economic indicators, there are only two other members of this select group—the United States and Japan. Mainly because of the peculiarities of its administrative organization, American experience has not been treated in detail. Indirectly, it is drawn upon frequently, for many of the conceptual propositions were ultimately derived from American experience in areas like socialization. We have been able to present occasional summary comparisons of some aspects of American and European administrative phenomena. Unfortunately, our data could not be related even summarily to Japanese experience. Material in European languages is simply too sparse; without a deep knowledge of the Japanese cultural context we could not interpret what is available.

Certainly the six systems just listed do not constitute the universe of industrialized societies. But the question of scale is vitally important. Small societies unquestionably have distinctive experiences, but in areas like economic development and administration much of their evolution is derivative. Comparability in scale and autonomy of experience are particularly significant because our study involves extended longitudinal as well as cross-national comparison. For many purposes (as will appear shortly) the number of cases is extended by chronological subdivision from four to thirteen. Given the brevity of American and Japanese experience, full consideration of these cases would only increase the universe by three or four.

Ethnic homogeneity of the administrative elites is also an important factor which reduces the range of variance and thus the complexity of our investigation. While we shall often, as is customary, refer to the "British," it is not misleading to use "English" to denote the national administrative elite of Great Britain and the institutions associated with it. The minor territorial change entailed by independence for Ireland did not significantly alter the boundaries relevant to our study, since only the Anglo-Irish did or do contribute notably to the British administrative elite. Scotland is nearly always an exception to what is said about the British system. Two examples will suffice. The Ministry for Scottish Affairs does not regularly employ Administrative Class officials *in Scotland*. H. M. Inspectors of Schools have been a powerful force in establishing the public boarding school as a model for English secondary education. But one of H. M. Inspectors of Schools *for Scotland* told us—with a noticeable burr in his voice—that he would not think of sending his son to a public school.

At first sight there seems to be little continuity between eighteenth-century Prussia and contemporary West Germany. Indeed, territorial continuity is obviously greater between Prussia and the German Democratic Republic. As yet, however, the latter's administrative system is so derivative (from the USSR) that it would not be very useful to examine it. On the other hand, the considerable difference in territory between Prussia and the German Federal Republic conceals continuities much more basic than the latter's legal claim to be Prussia's successor state. By 1800 the swollen Prussian monarchy had a dominantly Slavic population, but the overwhelmingly German composition of the administrative elite was bolstered by a steady flow of recruits from Western Germany. By 1800 they constituted one-tenth of the justice officials and—more significant for our concerns—one-fifth of the finance officials.[2] The process by which the present West German system arose is in a sense only the culmination of a long westward shift in the center of gravity of the Prussian state. This shift began with the acquisition of the Rhineland and adjoining territories as compensation for renunciation of most Polish territories in 1815. As we shall see (Chapter Twelve), however, certain western provinces (Mark and Cleves) had a special significance even for late eighteenth-century Prussian administration. The nineteenth-century incorporation of the cradles of German industrialization greatly enhanced this significance. Moreover, Prussian administrative models gradually penetrated much German practice, both in private organizations and in non-Prussian state administrations.

Under the Second Reich and the Weimar Republic, Prussians constituted about two-thirds of top state officials (because the Prussian state had nearly two-thirds of the total population) and probably a slightly larger share of the relatively small Reich apparatus. Despite territorial changes, the same proportion of "Prussians" appears in at least the older component of the German Federal Republic administrative elite. To begin with, about half of the present Federal Repub-

[2] Henning von Bonin, "Adel und Bürgertum in der höheren Beamtenschaft der preussischen Monarchie, 1794-1806," *Jahrbuch für die Geschichte Mittel- und Ostdeutschlands*, xv (1966), 173.

lic was formally Prussian from at least 1866 on. In addition, a very large component of the administrative elites—much larger than of the general population in West Germany—consists of persons born in other parts of what was Prussia. In 1959 about 12 per cent of the highest *Federal* officials had been born in the Soviet occupation zone (most of which had been Prussian for centuries) or Berlin, and 27 per cent in "eastern lands," most of which had also been Prussian.[3] Southern states of the Federal Republic had smaller proportions of "easterners" among their officials. The populous northern states which had been part of Prussia before 1933 had administrative elites composed, on the other hand, almost entirely of Prussians by birth. A much more significant problem—as we have already noted in passing—is the apparent discontinuity in definition of elite levels. In part this difficulty arises from our consolidation of Federal and state administrative elites, in contrast to examination of the Prussian administrative elites (and the few Reich top administrators) for earlier periods. Unfortunately, available data, which is generally unsatisfactory, appears to permit no alternative.[4] Whereas Reich officials (1870-1933) were predominantly drawn by lateral transfer from a single state (Prussia), German Federal officials are drawn (at top and middle levels) from all the state services. In addition, there is considerable interchange (particularly for upwardly mobile officials) among state services.

As a result, a nationally homogeneous administrative elite exists to a greater extent now than it did for the Reich as a whole, although to a much smaller extent than was the case for the Reich and the Prussian services taken apart from the lesser states of 1870-1933. Examination of the Reich administrative elites, to the exclusion of the Prussian elite which provided its recruits and which even at higher levels performed most of the tasks which concern this study, would be utterly unsatisfactory as a basis for comparison with the unitary systems of the other European countries. The activities of the central administration under the German Federal administration are somewhat broader than under the Second Reich, but many key tasks are still prerogatives of the state administrations.

Problems of continuity and homogeneity in Russia arise on quite a different basis. The formal federal structure of the USSR is not a significant complication. In fact, the post-1938 administrative elite (which is the only Soviet generation we shall examine in detail) is far more homogeneous ethnically than the Tsarist elite. While numerous formal positions are occupied by non-Slavs (who comprise about one-fourth

[3] "Landsmannschaftliche Herkunft der Bundesbeamten," *Bulletin des Presse- und Informationsamtes der Bundesregierung*, December 2, 1961.

[4] Wolfgang Zapf (ed.), *Beiträge zur Analyse der deutschen Oberschicht* (Munich, 1965), p. 87.

of the total population), nine-tenths of the real administrative elite posts are occupied by Russians, Ukrainians, and Belorussians.[5] Our evidence indicates that elite administrators from the latter two Slavic groups are very heavily Russian in cultural socialization. In contrast, Erik Amburger estimates that East Slavs constituted only 62 per cent of his large sample extending over two centuries.[6] Nearly all of the remaining officials were of Western European ethnic origin, although frequently born to families which had resided in the Russian Empire for generations. A minimum of 18 per cent were ethnic Germans. Another estimate puts the number of Germans in the Tsarist administrative elite at certain periods at over one-third.[7]

Reliance on an ethnic minority to staff such a large share of a system's elite administrative posts usually is an indication of an early stage of administrative development.[8] Prussia drew on other German states for its best administrators until well into the nineteenth century, and even resorted (as discussed in Chapter Twelve) to massive non-German recruitment for special purposes.

It is scarcely surprising that for the period we consider France has had the most ethnically homogeneous administrative elite, although persons of foreign origin who are thoroughly Gallicized have been generally acceptable. Again, we point out these circumstances not to evaluate recruitment practices in terms either of basic values or of societal stability (religious and partisan cleavages in the French administrative elite have been as serious as ethnic cleavages in other systems), but to indicate the restricted importance of the ethnic factor for our study. The low salience of ethnic division is particularly significant in considering socialization, where ethnic differences often complicate examination of stratification factors. Moreover, in "layered" societies where different ethnic groups fill specific types of elite roles, identifying reference groups which define these roles becomes excessively complicated.

CHRONOLOGICAL LIMITS

Since we are interested in tracing the origins of social patterns associated with the administration, the starting points must be sufficiently remote to permit the maximum practical investigation. The search

[5] John A. Armstrong, *Ideology, Politics, and Government in the Soviet Union: An Introduction*, rev. ed. (New York, 1967), pp. 142-43.

[6] Based on Erik Amburger, *Geschichte der Behördenorganisation Russlands von Peter dem Grossen bis 1917* (Leiden, 1966), p. 517.

[7] Walter Görlitz, *Die Junker: Adel und Bauer im deutschen Osten* (Bluchsburg am Ostsee, 1957), p. 259.

[8] See our discussion in Erich Goldhagen (ed.), *Ethnic Minorities in the Soviet Union* (New York, 1968), pp. 3ff.

for remote origins, like monarchs tracing their family trees back to the Garden of Eden, lends itself to caricature. Many studies of formal administrative institutions do not hesitate to trace them to Babylon or Media. If the definition of formal institutions is sufficiently precise and consistent over time and place (as Roman law endeavored to ensure), such comparison may be meaningful. Sociological categories obviously have not been subjects of uniform formal definition. Our conceptual framework requires that each pattern be examined within the context of its social system to determine feedback relations with other relevant aspects, before the pattern is compared to formally homologous patterns in other systems. "If social phenomena are treated as components of systems . . . the behavior of any component in a system is determined by factors intrinsic to the system and is relatively isolated from influences outside of the system."[9] Przeworski and Teune go on to point out that "A second implication of treating social phenomena as components of systems is that specific observations must be interpreted within the context of specific systems."[10] In order to know, therefore, whether an element in an earlier social system was actually the origin of an element in one of our social systems, we would have to study in detail related aspects of the earlier system and probably intervening social systems as well. Even assuming that the evidence was available for remote periods, the encyclopedic requirements would utterly transcend the limits of this study.

Because of these considerations, the chronological limit is placed at the point where stable, formally recognized administrative systems with characteristics at least superficially resembling those of the present day appeared. We then analyze system relationships for the earliest periods as fully as more recent ones. For the Continent, as Shmuel Eisenstadt points out, establishment of "modern" administrations represented a major aspect of monarchs' efforts to mobilize economic and manpower resources to maintain political control and to undermine the particularistic nobility.[11] It was, in other words, a basic feature of national integration rather than of economic development per se, though mobilization of resources was an important secondary factor in the origin of stable administrations.

While scholars identify significant precursors of strong central administration under Richelieu, under Henry IV, and even under Louis XI, there is a broad consensus on 1661 (when J. B. Colbert stabilized

[9] Przeworski and Teune, p. 12.
[10] *Ibid.*, p. 13.
[11] Shmuel N. Eisenstadt, *The Political System of Empires* (Glencoe, Ill., 1963), pp. 121ff.

government after the Fronde) as the initial date for a stable French administrative elite.[12] For our purposes, the single most important consideration in identifying a "modern" administrative elite is the regularity of the administrative career. Without elaborating on this characteristic at present, we can accept Vivian Gruder's conclusion that (from the seventeenth century on) "beneath the indeterminateness and inconstancy of the ancien régime's practice was a pattern of recruitment that revealed a rational procedure for preparing and selecting" [salient elite administrators].[13] For Prussia scholarly consensus is not quite so clear, but a career administrative elite hardly existed when Frederick William I began his reign (1713). At his death the nucleus of the permanent Prussian higher administration had been constituted. For our purposes, the end of his reign (1740) is sufficiently accurate. For Russia the situation is more complicated because of the extended period of disorder following Peter I's ambitious effort to emulate Western European administrations.[14] While the outstanding American authority would not place the beginning of a regular bureaucratic administration until after 1800, the principal Soviet study and an impressive examination recently published in Germany agree on the beginning year (1762) of Catherine II's reign.[15]

Neither the reasons for the establishment of a modern administration in Great Britain, nor the timing, correspond to the Continental experience. A slightly more detailed examination of the generally accepted interpretations can be useful as an initial clarification of what is meant by establishment of a "modern" administration. A recent English comparative history, *The Ancien Régime in Europe*, presents a fundamental reason why administrations developed at different times:

> The same waters protected England from foreign invasion. . . . It was not the result of national character, nor of God "revealing himself first to His Englishmen" (to use Milton's words). It was simply a piece of luck that England could afford the luxury of being lightly administered. While Continental states could not survive outside the

[12] E.g., Georges Pages, *La Monarchie d'Ancien Régime en France (de Henri IV à Louis XIV)* (Paris, 1928), p. 159; A. Chéruel, *Histoire de l'Administration Monarchique en France depuis l'Avénement de Phillippe-Auguste jusqu'à la Mort de Louis XIV* (Paris, 1855), I, vii.

[13] Vivian R. Gruder, *The Royal Provincial Intendants: A Governing Elite in Eighteenth Century France* (Ithaca, 1968), p. 10.

[14] Iurii Got'e, *Istoriia Oblastnogo Upravleniia v Rossii ot Petra I do Ekateriny II*, Vol. I (Moscow, 1913), 36ff.

[15] Marc Raeff, "The Russian Autocracy and Its Officials," *Harvard Slavic Studies*, IV (1957), 80; N. F. Demidova, "Biurokratizatsiia Gosudarstvennogo Absoliutizma v XVII-XVIII vv.," in *Absoliutizm v Rossii (XVII-XVIIIvv.)* (Moscow, 1964), p. 209.

iron lung of absolute rule, Englishmen could stretch themselves under a bureaucratic framework as light as gossamer.[16]

The natural protective barriers which permitted Britain to postpone a "modern" administration so long paradoxically facilitated tentative administrative developments earlier than on the Continent. After the Norman Conquest, central administrative organs were effective to a degree scarcely known elsewhere in Western Europe. Four centuries later the Tudors had an administrative mechanism better than other monarchs'. Quite possibly—though we must be very hesitant in treating a period so remote from our direct concern—it was precisely the easy attainment of national integration in the essential "heartland" of England and Wales which made aristocratic regression so effective in the seventeenth and eighteenth centuries. As Eisenstadt shows (and as we shall discuss in more detail later), aristocratic regression to particularistic or patrimonial office-holding is a cyclical characteristic of preindustrial administrations. On the Continent, these cycles were shortened by intense efforts at national defense and integration. In sheltered England, such pressures were minimal; hence the embryonic central administrations atrophied. Especially significant was the lack of a territorial officer dependent on the center. Instead, the justice of the peace system, dominant until well into the nineteenth century, represented particularistic local interests.[17]

The vestigial central administration retained (in the seventeenth century) some bureaucratic features, such as avoidance of sinecurism, considerable emphasis on legal training, hierarchy, and departmental subdivision. As G. E. Aylmer's analysis shows, however, a very small minority (one-eighth) of the office-holders could be considered professional administrators according to the criteria of 1) performance of administrative tasks as contrasted to other specialized work; 2) a "full-time," "serious approach"; 3) dependence on the administrative career for their income and status. Most posts were filled by "sub-infeudation," i.e., appointments were the particularistic prerogative of great Crown officers.[18]

After the seventeenth century, administration as a career declined still further. The breakup of the system of Crown "placemen" in the last decades of George III, carried out by the Whigs on the grounds of economy, was effective in destroying monarchical ability to manip-

[16] E. N. Williams, *The Ancien Régime in Europe: Government and Society in the Major States, 1648-1789* (London, 1970), p. 451.

[17] See especially Fritz Morstein-Marx, "Berufsbeamtentum in England," *Zeitschrift für die Gesamte Staatswissenschaft*, LXXXIX (1930), 456.

[18] G. E. Aylmer, *The King's Servants: The Civil Service of Charles I 1625-1642* (New York, 1961), pp. 70, 89, 94, 159, 282, 461.

ulate (through patronage) Parliamentary elections.[19] But decentralization of patronage apparently carried the deterioration of the central administration a step further. Since patronage was delegated to departments, administrative coordination was undermined. Elimination of Crown patronage also left appointments more than ever at the discretion of local interests, including members of Parliament who frequently nominated men of low status and qualifications. After the electoral reforms of the 1830's patronage declined, but retention of promotion almost exclusively by seniority continued virtually to preclude a higher administrative career pattern, even if individual agencies were reasonably effective.[20] How a "modern" administration did finally take form in Britain in 1870—two centuries after the French administrative elite originated and at least a century later than our other Continental examples—will appear in subsequent chapters. Here we need only note that it was a response (though an ambiguous one) to industrialization rather than a factor in its accomplishment.

PERIODIZATION AND COMPARISON

Setting outer limits is only the first step in periodization. To quote Przeworski and Teune again:

> One of the main problems in generalizing across spatio-temporal parameters stems from the fact that social phenomena are either "functionally interdependent" or "interrelated in syndromes" that have specific historical localization. Therefore a change in one element of these syndromes would bring about not only a change in the other elements, but a change in the entire pattern.[21]

Whether "syndromes," or patterns, are comparable between periods of the same society is essentially a matter for empirical determination —which we shall attempt at appropriate points in the substantive analysis. Even for qualitative comparisons, however, some preliminary delineation of time periods in which one can expect generally stable pattern relationships is useful, provided one does not let the initial framework act as a strait jacket preventing ascertainment of significant shifts in pattern relationships *within* periods.

Except in the USSR, historians have devoted little attention to pe-

---

[19] Archibald S. Foord, "The Waning of 'The Influence of the Crown,' " *English Historical Review*, LXII (1947), 497-99.

[20] Emmeline W. Cohen, *The Growth of the British Civil Service, 1780-1939* (London, 1941), pp. 24, 98-99; Edward Hughes, "Civil Service Reform 1853-55" *History*, XXVII (1942), 53, 58.

[21] Przeworski and Teune, p. 29.

riodization.[22] As Gordon Leff has recently pointed out, however, there is no way to organize the diverse events of a chronological period into phases of the same institution or epoch except by having a mental notion to begin with which is ideal and comparative.[23]

For quantitative comparisons, periodization is essential. No doubt in some branches of economic history, or in historical election studies, periodization can be avoided initially because the natural time intervals for which data is available are short and uniform. Cutoff points dividing time periods of theoretical interest can then be established empirically by finding discontinuities in the curves plotted. Unfortunately, data on administrative elites is too sparse and too unstandardized to permit recourse to such procedures. For a few time intervals we have generated data by aggregating individual biographical information. Since this expensive procedure could be used only sparingly, the intervals had to be chosen because they appeared significant theoretically. Most of the aggregate data we have utilized refers to intervals too far apart to permit plotting meaningful curves. Generally speaking, the best results that could be expected by either procedure were quantitative indicators summing up, in a very approximate way, relationships typical of a conventional generation (for a graphic example, see Figure 4). Specific procedures used for the more complex bodies of quantitative data are summarized in the Appendix. At many points throughout the text, other data which can be explained more succinctly is presented. In nearly every case the initial basis for selection has been the preliminary determination of appropriate periods, each fairly long, in which in-system stability of interrelationships affecting the data can be shown.

As Przeworski and Teune emphasize in the passages quoted earlier, determination of in-system stability for pattern relationships is an essential prerequisite for intersystem (cross-national) comparisons. The usual approach to cross-national comparisons employs strictly contemporary data. It is assumed, for example, that it is useful and practical to compare attitudes on political competence in India and Canada during the late 1950's. Given the fact that most categories of social data, particularly if derived from surveys, are confined to the last few decades, this approach is unavoidable for most subjects. Inevitably, it entails comparing societies in sharply different stages of development (whatever the criteria for "development" in a particular theoretical framework may be). Our extended longitudinal approach has the advantage of permitting comparison of conceptually congruent periods of different societies. We call this "asynchronous" comparison

---

[22] Gordon Leff, *History and Social Theory* (University, Ala., 1969), p. 136.
[23] *Ibid.*, p. 135.

as contrasted to the usual synchronic cross-national comparisons or the diachronic comparison, discussed above, of periods within the same society.

Obviously preliminary periodization is even more essential for asynchronous comparison than for diachronic comparison. The principle is well illustrated by Figure 4. Reduced to essentials, the line graph

FIGURE 4. Old-Regime Governors' Terms

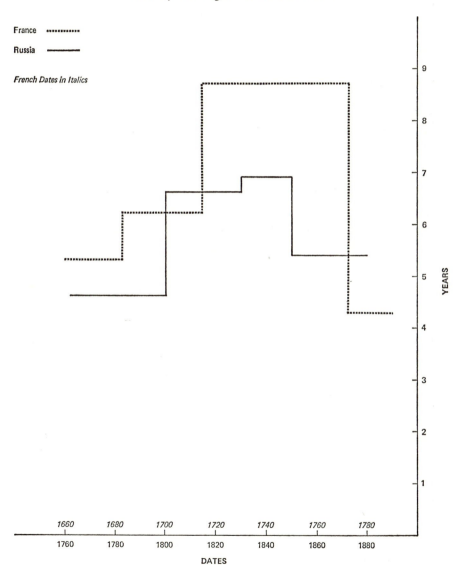

shows the rates of turnover in office of three generations of French governors and three of Russian governors. A glance at the figure shows a rather striking fit of these discontinuous lines, though they relate to periods approximately a century apart. From the methodological standpoint, one must ask: how can such a fit be discovered, even when categories are as simple and data as precise as that used here? Conceivably one could have calculated turnover rates for every generation of French and Russian governors from 1660 to the present. Practically speaking (leaving aside evidence availability) the task would have been impossible within the scope of this investigation. Consequently a preliminary conceptual ("theoretical" would be a pretentious adjective for our simple reasoning) decision on appropriate periods for asynchronous intersystem comparison was required. For the more complicated consideration of masses of disparate data, prior periodization is much more important.

The problem, then, is to divide the extended time segment between the starting dates already established and the present into conceptually meaningful intervals. We have already determined that data paucity makes any interval smaller than a generation (say twenty to forty years) impracticable. This factor sets the lower limit for our periodization. In itself, the natural generation (as discussed below) has considerable conceptual significance. Since, however, the theme of this study is the elite administrator's perception of his role in economic development, we should prefer to relate the generation boundaries to economic change.

For the present, we shall define economic development fairly narrowly to mean increase in the material output of a society. We therefore definitely exclude such developments as increased educational levels, even though they may indirectly influence subsequent production. We are not concerned with measures designed solely to redistribute to individual consumers a fixed societal output, even if these include welfare measures which may influence subsequent output. Increases in agricultural production may be pertinent in certain circumstances, but they have usually been secondary and unanticipated in modern Europe. As noted earlier, construction of a transportation infrastructure is a key element of our definition, and actual increase in industrial output is even more central. We are concerned with efforts to mobilize, from a limited stock, resources for a societal purpose, if this mobilization has a potential for eventual output increase. This is the case even when the dominant immediate purpose of resource mobilization is an unproductive activity like war, though we shall note the implicit contradictions in such efforts to increase output.

Our definition of economic development is identical, or nearly so, to the usual definition of "industrialization." Consequently, we can resort to the impressive body of analyses of European industrialization for help in periodization. Certainly we can expect that societal definition of elite administrators' roles, and their own perceptions, will be affected in some manner by the actual state of industrialization, although the nature of this effect may vary widely. In a preindustrial society, for example, it was simply impossible for observers to define the elite administrative role in development the way Shonfield does in the quotation in Chapter One. The greater the actual participation of *some* high administrators in industrialization initiatives, the higher the feedback effect (conceivably in a negative direction) on role perceptions in other administrative segments. Industrialization also produces new reference groups (first entrepreneurs, later managers) to whom elite administrators react in ways which drastically affect their own role perceptions.

Since Walt W. Rostow presented his theory of stages of economic growth,[24] an elaborate debate on the timing of industrialization has gone on. For our purposes, the simplest division which appears to be supported by a general consensus is best. Consequently, we shall omit Rostow's period of "drive to mature industrialization." We are left with four periods: preindustrial, "take-off," industrial, and postindustrial. The *preindustrial* period may be defined simply as the period when capital accumulation and industrial output had not noticeably accelerated, and when overall industrial production was a small portion of the national product. All of the administrations we treat except the British were established long before this period ended. For France, Rostow's generally accepted terminal date (1830) conveniently coincides with the overthrow of the restored Old Regime of the Bourbons. For Germany, Rostow sets the terminal date at 1850; a recent historian of Prussia sets its terminal date at 1846.[25] Falling as they do on both sides of the 1848 revolution, these dates are not clearly associated with a regime change marking a dividing point in our data. Simon Kuznets' growth series appear to justify a somewhat earlier termination date (1840) for the preindustrial period.[26] This modification seems in accord with recent economic history trends to consider industrialization a rather more extended process.

[24] Walt W. Rostow, *The Economics of Take-Off into Sustained Growth* (New York, 1963).

[25] Ulrich P. Ritter, *Die Rolle des Staates in den Frühstadien der Industrialisierung: Die preussische Industrieförderung in der ersten Hälfte des 19. Jahrhunderts* (Berlin, 1961), p. 162; cf. W. O. Henderson, *The Industrial Revolution on the Continent: Germany, France, Russia 1800-1914* (London, 1961), p. 4, who generally agrees with Rostow's periodization.

[26] Simon Kuznets, *Six Lectures on Economic Growth* (Glencoe, Ill., 1959), p. 20.

The Russian situation is somewhat more complicated because of the slow, uneven rate of Russia's industrialization.[27] According to Roger Portal, machine technology was not dominant in textiles until the 1870's and in metallurgy until the 1880's.[28] Kuznets' series appear to justify a date as early as 1870. Because of the considerable regime changes during the reform period of Alexander II, we shall set the date slightly earlier—at 1865. For Great Britain there is no doubt that the preindustrial period ended in the eighteenth century. The precise date (Rostow uses 1783) is not material to our concern. The same general considerations apply to the United States, where industrialization certainly began long before a regular administration was established.

As indicated above, recent economic history has questioned whether there was a distinct *take-off* period of rapid accumulation of capital and a sharp upturn of industrial growth. Robert W. Fogel in particular considers Rostow's limits of the American take-off (1843-60) or the English (1783-1802) much too abbreviated.[29] No doubt similar criticism could be directed at the Continental periodization which is more pertinent to this study. Still, there does seem to be a period of approximately a generation when growth and technological innovation, even if not greatly accelerated physically, made a spectacular impression on contemporaries. This consideration leads us, for the rather limited purposes which we have, to regard the British take-off as extending to 1840. For the Continental countries, the best solution seems to be to accept elastic definitions roughly consonant with the opinions of economic historians yet convenient for our data divisions. By these criteria, the French take-off, commonly regarded as terminated by about 1860, can be extended to the end of the Second Empire (1870). The Prussian take-off can be considered ended at the same time (the foundation of the Second Reich). Kuznets' data suggests that date, Rostow uses 1873, Rithter 1861, and David S. Landes would put German industrial maturity as late as the 1890's.[30]

For Russia, 1895 seems to be acceptable. Some economists would extend the period of attainment of "industrial maturity" virtually to the

[27] Josef Kulischer, "Die kapitalistischen Unternehmer in Russland (inbesondere die Bauern als Unternehmer) in den Anfangsstadien des Kapitalismus," *Archiv für Sozialwissenschaft und Sozialpolitik*, LXV (1931), 318; Alexander Gerschenkron, *Economic Backwardness in Historical Perspective* (Cambridge, Mass., 1962), pp. 17ff., 125.

[28] Roger Portal, "Das Problem einer industriellen Revolution in Russland in 19. Jahrhundert," *Forschungen zur Osteuropäischen Geschichte*, I (1954), 208.

[29] Robert W. Fogel, *Railroads and American Economic Growth: Essays in Econometric History* (Baltimore, 1964), pp. 228-29.

[30] David S. Landes, *The Unbound Prometheus: Technological Change and Industrial Development in Western Europe from 1750 to the Present* (Cambridge, England, 1969), p. 229.

start of World War I.[31] However, the interwar period was marked by sharp economic fluctuations and certain years of stagnation even in the USSR. Consequently, we shall consider the whole interval from the end of the take-off until the end of the 1940's as a single period of *industrial* society.

Beginning with the completion of recovery from World War II in the early 1950's (some years earlier in the United States), the major Western European societies have, according to a general consensus, entered a new period sometimes designated *postindustrial*. For convenience in considering the aggregate data, we shall consider the postindustrial period as starting a little earlier, in 1946. While much of the postindustrial distinction from earlier periods is determined by changes in consumption rather than production patterns, sustained growth rates (though lower in Britain than in France and West Germany), high investment, and rapid technological innovation have prevailed. There is no question but that the changes have affected Western European administrative elites' roles, though in sharply different ways.

The situation in postwar Soviet Union is much less clear. Certainly all the characteristics just mentioned have been present in the Soviet economy, but this economy started (in 1950) at a much lower level than those of Western Europe. Even leaving aside consumer satisfaction, there is little doubt that industrial complexity and *overall* introduction of new technologies did not characterize the Soviet economy until the 1960's. The fact that pressures for change in economic elite roles were not considerable until shortly before then is another indicator—discussed in subsequent chapters—that the USSR did not enter the postindustrial period until very recently. For convenience, we shall consider the industrial period in the USSR as extending until the overthrow of N. S. Khrushchev (1964). Since the remaining time span is so short, our investigation will be limited in assessing the impact of this development for the USSR.

Our periodization is summarized in Table I. As it shows, synchronic comparison is appropriate for the Western European societies (and the United States) for the postindustrial period. For most purposes synchronic comparison is feasible also for these four societies during the industrial period. France and Prussia may be fairly readily compared in simultaneous take-off periods. Except for a portion of the preindustrial period, it is difficult to compare Russia synchronically with any of the other societies. At first glance it would seem quite feasible to compare Russia and the Western European societies for the industrial period.

[31] David E. Novack and Robert Lekachman (eds.), *Development and Society: The Dynamics of Economic Change* (New York, 1964), p. 48.

However, the Russian pre-World War I interval is truncated, with very sparse data collected and analyzed as yet on many aspects of the administrative elite. Then came a generation of revolutionary upheaval (until the end of the Great Purge, 1938) in which a stable administrative elite did not exist. Consequently, for many purposes the Russian administrative elite in an industrial society must be compared with Western European administrators prior to World War II and even World War I.

In discussing periodization, we have not hesitated to point out the necessity of adjusting to the practical limitations of aggregate data available. Apart from the need to adjust the periods (or even to leave out decades) in accordance with sharp changes in regimes, it is important that each period be at least thirty years long. As the Appendix indicates, in most administrations men enter elite career patterns in

TABLE I. PERIODIZATION

	Preindustrial	Take-Off	Industrial	Postindustrial
Great Britain	(-1782)[a]	(1783-1840)	1841-1945	1946-1972
France	1661-1830	1831-1870	1871-1945	1946-1972
Prussia	1740-1840	1841-1870	1871-1945	1946-1972[b]
Russia	1762-1865	1866-1895	1896-1964	(1965-1972)

[a] Intervals in parentheses not relevant for direct examination of administrative elites.
[b] German Federal Republic.

their early twenties and attain top posts (if successful at all) on the average in their late forties. Since these posts are held until approximately sixty, thirty years is a very rough approximation (comparable to the conventional "generation") of the time required for a given age cohort of administrators to become the median age group in top posts. Given the importance of preentry socialization—at least back to adolescence—we should prefer a forty-year interval. Thus one could examine changes at every age level correlated with the changed features of each period. But, as admitted earlier, the aggregate data is usually too sparse to permit such refined correlation (whether quantitatively or qualitatively). More often, we shall have to deal with imprecise averages or "typical" situations. This is especially true where— even apart from regime changes—extensive organizational alterations or redefinitions of data categories intervene in a period.

Given these considerations, there are few options for subdividing the periods established by stages of economic development. Take-off periods (except the British, which is only marginally relevant) barely reach our desired length and postindustrial periods are even shorter. Preindustrial periods do permit extensive subdivision. For some purposes this can be done very fruitfully, as Figure 4 and preliminary publications based on our investigation are intended to demonstrate.[32] In all three Continental countries highly significant differences appear in regimes and administrative elites between the last eighteenth-century generation (taken in a very approximate sense) and the first nineteenth-century generation influenced directly or indirectly by the French Revolution and its sequel. While data is not always adequate to treat these differences fully, they will be noted at many points later in this book.

One might infer that a similar major distinction separates the pre-World War I and postwar generations in the Western European administrative elites. For most features data is adequate for making fairly exact comparisons. At some point these can be introduced usefully in our general analysis. As the discussion in the Appendix indicates, however, differences between the two intervals are for most purposes too insignificant to require analytic distinction.

EVIDENCE, QUANTITATIVE AND CONSENSUAL

"Generalizations are implicitly quantitative in character, even though this may not always be clearly brought out."[33] William O. Aydelotte points out that this remark applies just as much to a historical study like our investigation as to contemporary research. We have tried, therefore, to use quantitative data where it was feasible to do so. Some of the complicated and necessarily uncertain methods employed are discussed in the Appendix. Here we need only stress the fact that most of our quantitative evidence consists of aggregate data, i.e., of statistics collected and tabulated for other purposes. Fortunately, as Erwin Scheuch has pointed out, European aggregate data is much better, especially for earlier periods, than American.[34] For most topics, nevertheless, quantitative evidence has not been available, either because materials are wholly lacking or because the costs of generating quantitative data (e.g., by content analysis) are far too great for our resources. Our main reliance has therefore necessarily been the converging evidence of secondary sources. Our sensitivity to the pervasiveness of ideological reasoning leads us to be especially suspicious of convergence of opinion by persons of the same background. Even when the observers are professional researchers (for example, a homogeneous group of literary historians), the danger of "group subjectiv-

[32] Armstrong, "Old-Regime Governors."

[33] William O. Aydelotte, "Quantification in History," *American Historical Review*, LXXI (1966), 804.

[34] Erwin A. Scheuch, "Cross National Comparisons Using Aggregate Data," in Stein Rokkan and Richard L. Merritt (eds.), *Comparing Nations: The Use of Quantitative Data in Cross-National Research* (New Haven, 1966), pp. 132-33.

ity" is high.[35] The danger is greater when reliance is placed on the consensus of members of a rather closed organization. For example, the oral tradition of the French Council of State has maintained that members were often seconded to outside administrative posts. A recent quantitative examination shows, however, that this is a considerable exaggeration.[36]

Faute de mieux we must rely on consensual evidence for most important examinations of administrative elite perceptions, particularly overall evaluations of responses to challenges in Chapter Twelve. In fact, these episodes (particularly the crucial Prussian responses) were selected partly because the expert consensus is unusually convincing. Both the response to railroad construction and the response to World War I economic demands have been studied exhaustively. Observers include contemporaries and retrospective scholars starting from an extraordinary range of presuppositions: Nazis, conservative officials, laissez-faire liberals, and Marxist-Leninists. Their sources—direct participation and documentation—are at least partly independent and their arguments are internally coherent.

In the final analysis, as Lynton K. Caldwell has pointed out, the value of the surviving historical evidence on administrative evolution depends as much on the tools and methods of research as on the records themselves.[37] No reader will accept all the propositions advanced in the following chapters. Whether he considers the interpretation valid depends on his evaluation of the general conceptual framework and method presented in these two chapters.

In trying to present as coherent a substantive comparison as possible, we have rejected a country-by-country approach. We also reject a period-by-period approach, which would have some advantages for a study of administrative evolution, because we wish to focus on social-psychological categories. It would have been possible to take as the expository framework the alternative model aspects presented in the concluding chapter. Complete detachment of fragments of evidence from their social and historical context would have led, however, to enormous repetition if the evidence were to be made intelligible to readers inexpert in any of the numerous subjects treated. Consequently, an approach has been utilized which offers a compromise between contextual description and pure analysis. The overall responses analyzed in Chapter Twelve and the development doctrines discussed in

[35] Folke Dvoring, *History as a Social Science: An Essay on the Nature and Purpose of Historical Studies* (The Hague, 1960), p. 16.

[36] Marie-Christine Kessler, *Le Conseil d'Etat* (Paris, 1968), p. 268.

[37] Lynton K. Caldwell, "The Relevance of Administrative History," *Revue Internationale des Sciences Administratives*, xxi (1955), 455.

Chapter Three lend themselves to a generally chronological treatment. For the core of the investigation, consideration of socialization as the linkage variable, the treatment follows the successive stages experienced by the individual. Within each stage, exposition varies according to the requirements of the subject. For some topics, extended discussion of a single complex pattern (e.g., Prussian legal training) appears essential. For others, factor-by-factor comparison across time and space is feasible.

CHAPTER THREE

Diffusion of Development Doctrines

There is no real substitute for ideological fervor. A country or at least a significant portion of the elite has got to want economic achievement badly enough to give it priority over other desires.[1]

We have defined economic development as growth, especially in industrial output. This is an effective, minimal definition for relating this investigation to the wealth of economic historiography. But there is another side to the concept. Even relatively sophisticated men like elite administrators could not, until very recent decades, perceive their roles in formal economic terms. If they thought of development at all, their thinking was more likely to move in philosophical channels, to question human ability to modify the world in a substantial and sustained manner. These philosophical assumptions were challenged by new ideas which were, as David C. McClelland suggests in the above quotation, advanced with fervor. We shall call them "doctrines" rather than "ideology" because we reserve the latter term (as discussed in Chapter One) for arguments which constitute "false consciousness," defenses of group interests. Development doctrines can become ideologies—they are more likely to acquire an ideological character years after they have been introduced—but may remain neutral. We take "doctrine" to mean something more than a single idea or a slogan; it is an articulated, coherent, and at least superficially consistent set of ideas. The actual doctrines we examine contain many ideas which, either analytically or historically, are not integrally related to *economic* development, however. Except when it is essential to consider the whole doctrinal complex to understand the impact of the development content, we shall confine our attention to the latter.

The most sweeping contention that development doctrines are causally related to economic growth is presented by the eminent economic historian, Alexander Gerschenkron:

To break through the barriers of stagnation in a backward country, to ignite the imagination of men, and to place their energies in the service of economic development, a stronger medicine is needed

[1] David C. McClelland, *The Achieving Society* (Princeton, 1961), p. 430.

than the promise of better allocation of resources or even of the lower price of bread. Under such conditions even the businessman, even the classical daring and innovating entrepreneur, needs a more powerful stimulus than the prospect of high profits. What is needed to remove the mountains of routine and prejudice is faith—faith in the words of Saint-Simon, that the golden age lies not behind but ahead of mankind.[2]

In another work Gerschenkron asserts that the "intensity of the industrialization ideology used to vary [in nineteenth-century Europe] with the degree of backwardness."[3] Thus the steady industrialization which England experienced at an early date required only a low-key doctrine, whereas protracted Russian efforts ultimately demanded intense doctrinal stimulation.[4]

While reserving evaluation of Gerschenkron's direct association of doctrine and development, we can see at once that it is highly suggestive for our examination. We shall be concerned in subsequent chapters not just with the process of socialization, but its content. Especially in earlier centuries, explicit doctrinal content has nearly always been more important in the kinds of elite socialization which will be our main subject than in mass socialization. In order to understand socialization aspects which we treat, a minimal acquaintance with the development component of prevalent doctrines is required.

The adjective "prevalent" should be stressed. This survey is not an essay in intellectual history. It would not be useful to analyze in detail the writings of the authors of the doctrines, for our interest is not intellectual history but cultural influence. Consequently, we are more interested in widely diffused Benthamite doctrines than in Jeremy Bentham's formulations, more concerned with Saint-Simonism than the Count de Saint-Simon.

The question of diffusion is particularly important. If the diffusion process was effective, the general prescriptions of a doctrine must have been available to all societies shortly after the doctrine was originated. If that was the case, one may assume that differential receptivity rather than unavailability of the development value pattern accounts for administrative elites' variance in adopting development values. Since values are acquired through socialization, we should (and do) examine this process comparatively to determine synchronic receptivity differences. If, however, as Gerschenkron suggests, later development

[2] Gerschenkron, *Economic Backwardness*, p. 24.
[3] Alexander Gerschenkron, *Europe in the Russian Mirror: Four Lectures in Economic History* (Cambridge, Mass., 1970), p. 115.
[4] *Ibid.*; Gerschenkron, *Economic Backwardness*, p. 24.

doctrines were more intense, such comparisons made asynchronously would be misleading. In that case, stronger development values among administrative elites might be due entirely to the availability of more intense doctrinal stimulation. We shall therefore need to examine doctrinal intensity closely.

In contrast to the analyses advanced by Gerschenkron and McClelland, our focus requires that we distinguish doctrines which encourage *individual* economic activity from those which favor administrative intervention. Role concepts are useful in making this distinction. A given role (sometimes called a "focal role" or "role set") is defined, in each aspect, by a set of "counter-roles" held by other individuals.[5] The concept of counter-role does not imply antagonism between role occupants, but merely that one role (e.g., patient) is defined in one aspect (being healed) by another role (physician). Counter-role differs from reference group in that the role occupant may not be directly influenced by counter-role occupants' expectations concerning his own role. In our approach we look both for counter-roles which will enable society and the individual elite administrator to define his role in economic development and for reference groups which are salient in making this definition.

As long as conscious efforts to expand the economic product were inconceivable, such counter-roles were also meaningless. When doctrines envisaging any kind of economic development became available, on the other hand, a choice of counter-roles was present. The administrative elite role could be identified with traditional roles (notably, as we shall see, of the particularistic aristocracy), which (perhaps tacitly) accepted the idea of a static economy. In this case the counter-role necessarily consisted of an elite role (such as the private entrepreneur's) outside the governmental framework. Obviously doctrines emphasizing individual economic achievement provided the values incorporated in this kind of counter-role. If the administrative elite did not reject the development values *for society in general*, the elite administrator himself would adopt a passive role definition; i.e., he would not perceive his role as interventionist in economic matters. Conversely, if the administrative elite rejected individualist economic achievement values, the elite administrator might retain an interventionist role definition acquired in earlier periods. In that case, the administrative elite would be hostile to development.

[5] Rocheblave-Spenlé, p. 177. "Counter-role" as we employ the term resembles "alter-role" and "complementary role" sometimes used in sociological writings, but "counter-role" perhaps conveys the concept of alternative roles more distinctly.

As we shall see, such simple role definitions were uncommon because of the complicating effects of ideological positions. The analysis does suggest, however, that in order for the administrative elite to define its role as interventionist, it was important that *both* the traditional particularistic elite role *and* the new entrepreneurial role be perceived as salient counter-roles. Consequently, it was very significant for administrative elite role definition not only that development doctrines be widely diffused, but that they contain an explicitly interventionist element calling for a considerable measure of centralized initiative and planning in mobilizing and increasing economic resources.

INDIVIDUAL ACHIEVEMENT AND SOCIETAL RESOURCES

The usual obstacle to any type of development doctrine is not an explicitly antidevelopment idea—although, as discussed later, such arguments appear as ideologies after development is underway—but the general assumptions of traditional society. The possibility of deliberate, sustained increase of societal material resources is ignored rather than rejected as undesirable or immoral. To be sure, efforts to attain such increase might well be ranked lower in a traditional (or, for that matter, a modern) scale of values than spiritual or aesthetic achievement. However, as long as it is tacitly assumed that deliberate increase is impossible, no such conscious rank-ordering occurs.

The point is simple, but is often misunderstood in considering Max Weber's famous thesis relating the rise of capitalism to Calvinism. There is little doubt that Calvinist ideas (and related Pietist doctrines in Germany) were significant stimuli for entrepreneurial activity which ultimately had a major, possibly dominant, part in economic growth. Calvinist doctrines, however, were not concerned in any direct sense with increasing societal resources, for their teaching was the need for individual achievement in one's calling as a sign of spiritual election.[6] The doctrine was not strongly anti-interventionist; state and community enterprise were significant in Holland. The general effect of Calvinist-type doctrines, however, was to justify intense individual efforts to achieve material success as the *dominant* form of economic activity.

Certainly *this* stress differed sharply from traditional Christian emphases, whether Roman Catholic, Jansenist, Eastern Orthodox, Anglican, or Lutheran. All deprecated individual concentration on attaining material rewards mainly (as, for example, R. H. Tawney has pointed

[6] Max Weber, *The Protestant Ethic and the Spirit of Capitalism* (New York, 1958), pp. 53ff., 108-109, 115.

out) because in the fixed resource situation traditionally assumed, such achievement would be at the expense of others.[7]

Whether the traditional Christian outlook would have been altered by a basic understanding of the growth potentials of technological innovation and changed economic organization can never be known. The considerable effort of the churches to mobilize scarce societal resources for wide-ranging welfare purposes suggests that concern for just distribution might have led, in favorable circumstances, to acceptance of innovations which were likely to increase total resources available for *societal* as contrasted to individual purposes. There was no lack of *communal* economic innovation in ecclesiastical institutions like monasteries. On the other hand, many institutional patterns had become legitimized on the assumption that economic resources were fixed. Like all institutions, these became identified with group interests; the latter produced ideologies to defend the status quo. Inevitably some of these ideologies attempted to utilize traditional Christian doctrine, although others (like the legal ideologies of sixteenth- and seventeenth-century France) had no essential relation to Christianity.[8]

By the seventeenth century, traditional assumptions were being challenged not only by Calvinist justifications of individual achievement, but by doctrines which suggested—however tentatively—that societal resources could be increased by deliberate, centrally directed efforts. Unlike Calvinism, the economic aspects of these doctrines were not opposed per se to traditional values. From the conservative viewpoint of the churches, other aspects of the doctrines appeared suspicious; these suspicions provided levers for ideological opposition to innovation. The tension this situation produced is clear in the spread of Cartesianism in France. Some clerical bodies opposed the new doctrine strongly. René Descartes and the founder of the Oratorian order, Pierre de Bérulle, had been friends, however; by the eighteenth century, Cartesianism was widely accepted in the Oratorian schools which constituted the vanguard of elite education.[9] A generation earlier, according to James E. King, Louis XIV and Colbert had virtually adopted Cartesianism as their official doctrine.[10] While the ideas of Descartes and his followers did not directly call for economic devel-

---

[7] R. H. Tawney, *Religion and the Rise of Capitalism: A Historical Study* (New York, 1947), especially pp. 34ff.; Ernst W. Eschmann, *Die Führungsschichten Frankreichs*, Vol. 1 (Berlin, 1943), 176. On Jansenism, see Elinor Barber, *The Bourgeoisie in 18th Century France* (Princeton, 1955), p. 44.

[8] Tom Kemp, *Economic Forces in French History* (London, 1971), p. 60.

[9] H. C. Barnard, *The French Tradition in Education: Ramus to Mme. Necker de Saussure* (Cambridge, England, 1970), pp. 166, 174.

[10] James E. King, *Science and Rationalism in the Government of Louis XIV 1661-1687* (Baltimore, 1949), p. 85.

opment, their rejection of the "Gothic past" in itself undermined the traditional barrier. Cartesian emphases on reason, the use of science for practical purposes, and mechanics as the governing principle of the universe strongly suggested that the physical environment could be significantly altered for human purposes.[11]

LIMITATIONS OF MERCANTILISM

Mercantilism, the actual "policy science" of late seventeenth- and eighteenth-century governments, strongly favored state intervention but was more ambiguous on economic development. As Gerschenkron points out, for mercantilism throughout Europe, "it is power policies and subordination of economic policies to the exigencies of power that provide the common denominator; the economic policies centering on economic development in general, and industrial development in particular."[12] Though pragmatic, mercantilism amounted to more than *ad hoc* policy recommendations. In France it constituted an important element of the "administrative mysteries" passed on by Colbert (see Chapter Eleven). In Germany (as well as in Italy) it was a regular university subject.[13] Three factors worked against its becoming a vigorous development doctrine.

1) In Western Europe vested interests were still too powerful to be overcome by a doctrine which was essentially confined to small circles in the royal courts and administrations.

2) The principal goal indicated by mercantilist doctrine was strengthening the monarchical state. This was the same goal that sovereigns and their ministers had pursued for several centuries by national integration and defense. Consequently, although mercantilism was innovative in emphasizing the economic bases of power, there was a severe strain between the need to use military power immediately (thus consuming the scarce resources which had been accumulated) and the effort to mobilize resources for sustained increase in economic capability. Since long-range planning was rarely feasible, mercantilist administrators were usually reduced to extracting for military purposes a larger share of a fixed amount of societal economic resources.

3) Economic methods were not sufficiently advanced to provide a basis for complex planning for societal economies. The extreme concern for favorable trade balances and accumulation of precious metals (more pronounced in Western Europe than in Russia) was counterproductive. Moreover, this concern tended to reinforce the lingering

[11] *Ibid.*, pp. 17, 20.   [12] Gerschenkron, *Europe*, p. 86.
[13] Anton Felix Napp-Zinn, *Johann Friedrich von Pfeiffer und die Kameral-wissenschaften an der Universität Mainz* (Wiesbaden, 1955), p. 12.

traditional assumption of a fixed resource base. Wholly inadequate statistics (many French provincial officials simply made guesses when asked to report) fostered this preconception and made national planning highly problematic. It can even be argued that the basic weakness of mercantilism was its obsession with macro-economics in a period when the eclectic concepts which passed for economic theory were as apt as not to prescribe wrong intervention at the societal level. Conversely, when local administrators were inspired by mercantilist presuppositions to intervene in narrow-range problems which they could grasp by common sense observation, results were often highly productive.

Ascendancy of Anti-Interventionist Doctrines

In the second half of the eighteenth century the obvious weaknesses of mercantilism made the advance of anti-interventionist doctrines easier. It is significant that two currents, by no means compatible with one another, helped undermine mercantilism. In France (and to a much more restricted degree in the other Continental countries) the physiocrats were dominant. Although A.R.J. Turgot was not a thoroughgoing physiocrat, his ascendancy marks the height of the influence of the *Economistes*, who were then able to suppress most of their critics' pamphlets. Physiocratic doctrine ("To govern better one must govern less") urged the removal of both the cumbersome body of central regulations built up since Colbert, and particularistic restrictions on trade. While vigorous statesmen like Turgot resisted the aristocratic reaction of the late eighteenth century, physiocratic doctrines were not entirely antiparticularist. Dismantling central intervention often meant a relative gain for local interests, for local self-government was favored.[14] Moreover, the emphasis on agriculture as the essential base of a healthy society coincided with provincial interests. In extreme forms the agrarian populist element of physiocracy actually became an anti-industrial, hence antidevelopment doctrine.

Adam Smith's doctrines (generally known as laissez faire) were equally anti-interventionist. Lacking the agrarian bias of the physiocrats, however, they were favorable to industrialization. Though Adam Smith himself was a contemporary of Turgot, the triumph of laissez faire—far greater than that of any previous development doctrine—did not come until the second quarter of the nineteenth century.

---

[14] Heinrich Heffter, *Die deutsche Selbstverwaltung im 19. Jahrhundert: Geschichte der Ideen und Institutionen* (Stuttgart, 1950), p. 50; Léon Wueleresse, "Les Physiocrates sous le Ministère de Turgot," *Revue d'Histoire Economique et Sociale*, XIII (1925), 315-23.

Smith's ideas had begun to spread in Prussia and Russia a half-century earlier, however, and played a notable part in undermining mercantilism. A key element was the demand for disclosures of the "financial mysteries" which administrators from Colbert to Frederick II's time had utilized as a way of safeguarding their operations. Like the physiocrats, laissez-faire advocates were vehement in attacking the whole web of state controls, including those inherited from traditional particularistic institutions and those superimposed by mercantilist policies. In contrast to the physiocrats on the one hand and Calvinism on the other, the "invisible hand" theory of laissez faire insisted not only that individual achievement was best left alone, but that pursuit of private advantage unfailingly resulted in maximum societal good.

Laissez-faire doctrine thus "solved" the problem of planned mobilization and allocation of resources which baffled mercantilism by declaring that the problem did not exist. In addition, laissez faire provided a secular legitimization for the strong achievement motivations which Calvinism had fostered by asserting that there was no inherent contradiction between individual success and societal economic progress. We cannot determine the extent to which the advance of laissez faire actually facilitated the spectacular economic growth which proceeded while the doctrine was being propagated. It is easy to see, however, why laissez-faire thinking enjoyed enormous prestige for over a century.

In practice, laissez-faire doctrines became increasingly rigid in the late nineteenth century when they were reinforced by the strongly individualist bias of social Darwinism. As Karl Polyani's famous book points out, by then English businessmen believed that market economics as they knew it contained all the theoretical principles needed. Anyone who advocated sweeping "social engineering" was regarded as a crank, or worse.[15] Their American contemporaries even considered discussion of business motivation as visionary.[16] As will appear later, Continental opinion was never so uniformly anti-interventionist. Nevertheless, from the 1830's to the 1930's the general elite economic doctrine almost everywhere was laissez faire, consequently anti-interventionist. In a sense, for the century embracing the take-off and industrial society periods we shall not be studying the competition of interventionist and noninterventionist development doctrines to determine administrative elite roles. *Insofar as economic development values prevailed*, the counter-role of the entrepreneur was almost unassailable. Vestigial interventionist values from earlier periods, the

[15] Karl Polanyi, *The Great Transformation* (New York, 1944), pp. 120-21.
[16] Edward C. Kirkland, *Dream and Thought in the Business Community, 1860-1900* (Ithaca, 1956), p. 162.

receptivity of particular elite socialization processes to new interventionist doctrines, and special administrative elite experiences provided limited alternatives to the dominant counter-roles. These alternatives could have a significant impact on role definition only in special circumstances when tension between the dominant laissez-faire doctrine and ideological rejection of development values by other elites left room for an administrative elite role which rejected both extreme positions.

FREEMASONRY AND THE DIFFUSION OF DEVELOPMENT DOCTRINES

Before considering the development interventionist alternatives, it is useful to devote attention to a special aspect of the diffusion process in European societies, not because it worked uniformly to spread any particular type of doctrine, but because the differences in receptivity themselves provide a significant link to differences in socialization. Freemasonry has been little examined in this context, no doubt because as a vehicle for spreading particular doctrines it is ambiguous. When Masonic associations developed in early eighteenth-century Britain, the saliency of development was not high. As discussed above, Calvinism had already done much of the work of instilling individual entrepreneurial motivation. To upper-middle-class and aristocratic strata attracted to the lodges, general notions of social progress, brotherhood, and freedom were more important than economic emphases. The association with Enlightenment ideas was even closer a generation later when Freemasonry spread rapidly in France. Within a few decades, the democratic elements of Masonry were attenuated there and in Prussia, where Frederick II sponsored Masonic lodges, especially in the army. Instead the newer, complicated Scottish rite and the mysteries of lodge initiation, while bringing the upper bourgeoisie and the aristocracy together, tended to strengthen barriers between the elites and lower strata.[17] Lawyers, officials, and especially the high magistracy predominated in France.[18] What is most significant from our standpoint is the degree to which French Freemasonry contributed to an openness of general elite milieus to ideas of technical and social progress. For example, the intendant of Franche-Comté, himself a Mason, was so impressed by the philanthropy of the Besançon lodge

[17] Ferdinand Josef Schneider, *Die Freimauerei und ihr Einfluss auf die geistliche Kultur in Deutschland am Ende des XVIII. Jahrhunderts: Prologomena zu einer Geschichte der deutschen Romantik* (Prague, 1909), pp. 25, 42; Paul V. Aubry, *Monge, le Savant Ami de Napoléon Bonaparte 1746-1818* (Paris, 1954), p. 32.
[18] Louis Amiable, *La Franc-Maçonnerie et la Magistrature en France à la Veille de la Révolution* (Aix, 1894), pp. 13, 16, 46, 50ff.

that he held its rites in the official residence. In Paris literary lions were important figures in Masonic meetings.[19] Real technological innovators like the great engineers J. R. Perronet and Gaspard Monge could not (as we shall see) aspire to membership in the Old-Regime administrative elite.[20] But through their Masonic membership both were able to associate with the general elites. As will appear a bit later, there is a direct connection between the pre-Revolutionary Masonic membership of such figures and the spread of development doctrines in the nineteenth century.

The contrast to German Masonry is instructive. There, too, initial influences (especially in the northwest) were English; they were welcomed as an offset to French cultural dominance in the mid-eighteenth century. The Prussian nobility, however, welcomed the French practice of restricting the pseudo-feudal symbols of Masonic "knighthood" to nobles. Later (see Chapter Six) these symbols, much exaggerated, became central elements of elite socialization.[21] For the eighteenth century, the anti-Enlightenment tendencies of Prussian Masonry were much more significant. In his brief but excellent comparative examination, Henri Brunschwig writes that both French and German lodges of the early eighteenth century "of deist tendency, are striking in their utilitarian conception of morality and their faith in technical progress, which they trace from the origins of the world." In Germany, however, "these seedbeds of the Enlightenment where the future elites grew up by the cold light of reason were very quickly invaded by bad seed"— namely the obscurantist and occultist Rosicrucians.[22] Instead of the openness to real technological progress which characterized French lodges, the Rosicrucian lodges opposed the "secular sciences" of Priestley, Lavoisier, and Newton in favor of alchemy and other medieval fantasies. As the historian of German Masonry, Ferdinand Schneider, writes, the German secret societies of the end of the eighteenth century kept their country in a "somnambulant dream condition."[23] Perhaps the clearest example of the retrograde influence of the Rosicrucians was Frederick William II's minister of religion, a "renegade" Lutheran pastor named Johann von Wöllner, who blocked internal

[19] Roger de Lurion, "M. [Charles-André] de Lacoré, Intendant de Franche-Comté (1761-1784)," *Académie des Sciences, Belles-Lettres et Arts de Besançon: Procès-Verbaux et Mémoires*, 1897, p. 248.

[20] Jean Petot, *Histoire de l'Administration des Ponts et Chaussées, 1599-1815* (Paris, 1958), p. 185; Aubry, p. 32.

[21] Schneider, pp. 25, 42, 144.

[22] Henri Brunschwig, *La Crise de l'Etat Prussien à la Fin du XVIIIe Siècle et la Genèse de la Mentalité Romantique* (Paris, 1947), p. 222.

[23] Schneider, pp. 120, 174.

improvements proposed by Baron Heinrich vom Stein, the future leader of Prussian reform, when he was endeavoring to facilitate the embryonic industrialization in the key province of Westphalia.[24]

German influence was very strong in Russian Freemasonry. Under Catherine II about one-third of the lodge members were Germans; as late as 1811 the chief minister, Michael Speransky, was apparently inducted into a German lodge in St. Petersburg.[25] But many of the German Masons in the capital were merchants, who seem to have imported the early, rationalist outlook of the northwest German lodges.[26] As in France and Prussia, nobles were privileged. Lower classes were explicitly excluded from full membership, and even merchants and priests were rare in higher grades. By the end of Catherine's reign, about one-third of all high central officials were Masons.[27] As one of the few meeting places of any kind tolerated by the regime, the lodges probably played a greater part in social communication than in other European capitals. Until about the turn of the century, Russian Freemasonry acted as a vehicle for Voltairian ideas, natural law, and rationalism. The lodge meetings brought officials in contact with physicians, educators, and even French engineers.[28] Gradually, though, mystic tendencies resembling those in Prussia turned some members from institutional reform to "internal regeneration."[29] After 1822, when Alexander I turned from encouragement to hostility, some Freemasons moved in a diametrically opposite direction, to conspiratorial revolutionary politics.[30] Russian Masonry ceased to be a significant carrier of Western European ideas of any type by the 1830's; but by then other vehicles were available.

[24] Guy Stanton Ford, *Stein and the Era of Reform in Prussia, 1807-1815* (Princeton, 1922), p. 39.

[25] A. N. Pypin, *Russkoe Masonstvo: XVIII i Pervaia Chetvert' XIX. V.*, ed. by G. V. Vernadsky (Petrograd, 1916), p. 388; George V. Vernadsky, *Russkoe Masonstvo v Tsarstvovanie Ekateriny II* (Petrograd, 1917), p. 12.

[26] Marc Raeff, *Origins of the Russian Intelligentsia: The Eighteenth Century Nobility* (New York, 1966), pp. 161-65; A. Lentin (ed. and trans.), *Prince M. M. Shcherbatov: On the Corruption of Morals in Russia* (Cambridge, England, 1969), editor's introduction, p. 20.

[27] Vernadsky, p. 86.

[28] *Ibid.*, pp. 91ff., 211; Sidney Monas, *The Third Section: Police and Society in Russia under Nicholas I* (Cambridge, Mass., 1961), p. 51; T. Sokolovskaia, *Russkoe Masonstvo i Ego Znachenie v Istorii Obshchestvennago Dvizheniia (XVIII i Pervaia Chetvert XIX Stoletiia)* (St. Petersburg, n.d.), pp. 133, 168.

[29] Pypin, p. 180; Richard Pipes, *Karamzin's Memoir on Ancient and Modern Russia: A Translation and Analysis* (Cambridge, Mass., 1959), editor's introduction, p. 27.

[30] Hans Joachim Torke, "Das russische Beamtentum in der ersten Hälfte des 19. Jahrhunderts," *Forschungen zur Osteuropäische Geschichte*, XIII (1967), 207.

SAINT-SIMONISM AS DEVELOPMENT DOCTRINE

For the concerns of this study, Saint-Simonism is much the most important nineteenth-century development doctrine. Its direct links to eighteenth-century Enlightenment concepts are numerous. Soon after the Revolution, Monge went to Paris to become director of the newly founded Polytechnique. Though Saint-Simon himself was not entirely enthusiastic about the "algebraists" of the Polytechnique, he knew Monge and his school well. The Polytechnique became a seminary for Saint-Simonians, including the most famous disciple, Auguste Comte. Through Comte, whose positivism was virtually accepted as the official doctrine of mid-nineteenth-century French Freemasonry, the circle of influence in France was completed.[31] As we shall see, the dual institutional channels of Masonry and the Polytechnique were also crucial for spreading Saint-Simonism to Russia.

Like Masonry itself, Saint-Simonism had a tendency to dissolve into a mystic cult. The absurdities of the "Saint-Simonian religion" propagated by disciples like B. P. Enfantin need not concern us except to recall that the development aspects of the doctrine were only one side, whether in Saint-Simon's original concept or the more influential elaborations of his followers. Taken as a development doctrine, however, Saint-Simonism was far more intense in its appeal than the eighteenth-century ideas just examined. Not only did the doctrine completely reject the assumption of fixed societal resources, it taught that the era of abundance could be attained certainly and quickly. The guaranteed means were application of science and technology to unrestricted mastery of nature.[32] The basic utilitarian precept advanced by Saint-Simon of the greatest good for the greatest number implied, in contrast to strict individualism, a concern for societal economic growth:

It cannot be repeated too often, the only useful action exercised by man is the action of man on things. The action of man on man is always, in itself, injurious to the species because of the dual destruction of energies which it entails. It becomes useful only insofar as it is secondary and conduces to exercizing a greater action on nature.[33]

[31] Albert Lantoine, *Histoire de la Franc-Maçonnerie Française: La Franc-Maçonnerie dans l'Etat* (Paris, 1935), p. 324.

[32] Georg G. Iggers, *The Cult of Authority: The Political Philosophy of the Saint-Simonians, A Chapter in the Intellectual History of Totalitarianism* (The Hague, 1958), p. 10.

[33] Quoted in Werner Leendertz, *Die industrielle Gesellschaft als Ziel und Grundlage der Sozialreform: Eine systematische Darstellung der Ideen Saint-Simons und seiner Schüler* (Dissertation, Cologne University, Economics and Social Science Faculty) (Emsdetten, 1938), p. 9.

As the above passage indicates, Saint-Simon's original doctrine rejected, in principle, strong social control agencies. At the same time, Saint-Simonism regarded science as capable of solving societal problems by social engineering. One criticism that Saint-Simonists directed against laissez faire was that it left selection of social leaders to chance.[34] Most students of Saint-Simon believe that an "elitist" strain was inherent in his ideas, although his followers (especially Comte) carried this element much further than the founder. Moreover, they envisaged a special kind of elite preparation vastly different from that of traditional European elites. Michel Chevalier, for example, remarked that it would soon be as ridiculous to appoint a prefect who had no industrial management experience as it would be to appoint a bishop to command a regiment.[35]

Despite these radical proposals, Saint-Simonism was not as unambiguously for *state* administrative intervention as it was for development. Apart from their abhorrence of the chance elements of laissez faire, Saint-Simonians feared the "waste" of competition. But they also feared government waste and rigidity. The solution was the "omnium," a great bank-holding company which Saint-Simon conceived through personal contacts with bankers, and which, like so many other elements, his followers elaborated. The omnium was to mobilize and allocate economic resources through central planning by nonpolitical "industrials," constantly working for societal purposes and avoiding private speculation.[36] In effect, it would be a state within the state, far more important than the vestigial legal order.

In practice, of course, this grand scheme could not be implemented. The Crédit Mobilier of the strongly Saint-Simonist Péreire brothers always faced severe competition from other financial houses (particularly the Rothschilds) as well as state restriction. In fact, it was essential to secure state as well as para-state centralized intervention to cope with the difficult conditions of French industrialization. The Péreires themselves advocated close relations between the bank and the state. Many Saint-Simonists saw Napoleon III (in the 1850's) as the ideal sovereign who would facilitate mobilization of resources as well as assure international peace, another of Saint-Simon's basic prescriptions.[37]

[34] Iggers, pp. 137ff., 188.

[35] Jean Meynaud, *Technocratie et Politique* (Lausanne, 1960), pp. 53ff.

[36] Rondo E. Cameron, *France and the Economic Development of Europe, 1800-1914: Conquests of Peace and Seeds of War* (Princeton, 1961), p. 114; Bruce Mazlish (ed.), *The Railroad and the Space Program: An Exploration in Historical Analogy* (Cambridge, Mass., 1965), p. 30.

[37] Iggers, pp. 137ff., 146, 188; Maurice Wallon, *Les Saint-Simoniens et les*

By offering the option of a semi-private central economic administration (the bank), however, Saint-Simonism dampened the drive for state intervention per se. In particular, the prospect of utilizing a superior type of economic administrator (in practice, engineers) outside the confines of the administration lessened the demand for a thorough restructuring of the administrative elite itself.

Among the countries we consider, apart from France, Saint-Simonian influence was strongest in Russia. The Russian experience of Saint-Simonian engineers had an important feedback effect (after they were expelled by Nicholas I in 1832) on their planning French railroads along lines originally envisaged for Russia.[38] As indicated earlier, Masonic influences prepared the ground for the reception of Saint-Simonism in Russia, including many personal contacts for his followers. Admiration for the Polytechnique was important, especially for Alexander I, who called it the "finest institution which man had ever made."[39] Nevertheless, as a general and lasting influence on Russian elites, Saint-Simonism was very limited. For liberals, the rather simple, unilinear ideas of Saint-Simon were assimilated to those of Comte and the English historian Henry Buckle.[40] The conservative Baron Haxthausen, influential at court under Nicholas I, was also an admirer of Saint-Simon. But Haxthausen completely neglected the development aspect, twisting Saint-Simon's doctrine to justify preservation of the agricultural commune (*mir*) and the autocracy. These institutions, Haxthausen argued, reflected Saint-Simonian socialism "purified" by relation to the Orthodox Christian monarchy.[41] The lasting achievement of French Saint-Simonists in Russia was the creation of the Transport Institute, an elite school highly important in the second half of the century. By then its Russian students who had risen to power were highly critical of any foreign influence (including the Crédit Mobilier's Russian activities). On the other hand, Saint-Simonism provided a legitimization for engineering manipulation of resources which (as we shall see) helped this aspect of the elite administrator's role, generally so alien to preindustrial elites, to become quickly established in Russia.

Chemins de Fer (Dissertation, University of Paris, Faculté de Droit) (Paris, 1908), p. 145.

[38] G. Lamé, B.P.E. Clapeyron, and Stéphane and Eugène Flachat, *Vues Politiques et Pratiques sur les Travaux Publics de France* (Paris, 1852).

[39] Gaston Pinet, *Histoire de l'Ecole Polytechnique* (Paris, 1887).

[40] Gerschenkron, *Economic Backwardness*, pp. 180, 185; W.H.G. Armytage, *The Rise of the Technocrats: A Social History* (London, 1965), p. 148.

[41] Baron von Haxthausen, *The Russian Empire: Its People, Institutions, and Resources*, Vol. 1 (London, 1856), 132-35; Mikhail Tugan-Baranovsky, *Geschichte der russischen Fabrik* (Berlin, 1900), p. 355.

PRUSSIA—UNIQUE DEVELOPMENT ROLE OF THE ENTREPRENEUR

Saint-Simonism was influential among the first generation of Rhineland entrepreneurs. To Gustav Mevissen, Saint-Simon was a "Columbus who had discovered a new sea of life."[42] Saint-Simonism provided these men with a doctrine which emphasized societal interests, even when they were struggling against the rigidities of Prussian administration. Ludolf Camphausen regarded his railroad company as a means of serving state interests in progress. Others influenced by Saint-Simon saw their railroads and industrial enterprises as exemplification of brotherhood and Christian renewal. Speculation as a means of maximizing private profits was, therefore, at least nominally repugnant to them.

A whole list of economic theorists and practitioners tried to use Saint-Simonism as a basis for finding feasible routes [to industrial development]. Just as in France the Péreires encountered the opposition of the Rothschilds and their associates, this internal contradiction [of private enterprise] appeared in Germany in the struggle between Camphausen, Hansemann and even Mevissen against the "bankers."[43]

There is no doubt that the transitory impact of these Saint-Simonist ideas prepared the ground for Ferdinand List's doctrine. In contrast to Saint-Simon, however, List stressed national interest. This element made List's doctrine more explicitly anti-laissez faire than its precursor, for List believed that strict adherence to Smith's doctrine would handicap Germany in trading with more industrialized Britain and France. Here List was influenced by his encounter with Hamiltonian protectionism during his stay in the United States. List was also influenced by Hamiltonian advocacy of state support for a transportation infrastructure to promote economic development, although the American railroads which List tried to emulate in Germany had been privately built.[44]

What List was doing, in a sense, was providing a more impressive economic rationale for the coalescence of national integration and eco-

---

[42] Werner Suhge, *Saint-Simonismus und junges Deutschland: Das Saint-Simonistische System in der deutschen Literatur der ersten Hälfte des 19. Jahrhunderts* (Berlin, 1935), pp. 60-61.

[43] Mathieu Schwann, *Ludolf Camphausen*, Vol. 1 (Essen, 1915), 121.

[44] Edwin Kech, *Geschichte der deutschen Eisenbahnpolitik* (Leipzig, 1911), p. 37; Hans Gehrig, *Friedrich List und Deutschlands politisch-ökonomische Einheit* (Leipzig, 1956), pp. 137, 192, 200; Roger Portal, *La Russie Industrielle de 1881 à 1927* (Paris, n.d.), p. 46; Napp-Zinn, *Johann Friedrich von Pfeiffer*, p. 3.

nomic development interests which mercantilism had sought to obtain. Like all nineteenth-century economics, List's doctrine was theoretically inadequate as a basis for systematic administrative intervention. Nevertheless, one might assume that it would have had a powerful appeal as a legitimization of administrative elite economic initiatives. In fact, this was not the case. Apart from certain individual top administrators and politicians, List's doctrines appealed mainly to entrepreneurs and managers. His doctrine served to strengthen the Saint-Simonian legitimization of private entrepreneurs who saw themselves as serving societal interests rather than purely private achievement. In terms of our role analysis, the entrepreneurial role was redefined in a way which enabled it to acquire an extraordinarily strong position as the *only* development role in Prussia. For ideological reasons, elite administrators tended to accept the entrepreneurial role as the only counter-role of their own, which was therefore defined as anti-development.

AMBIVALENCE OF BENTHAMISM

Superficially, British doctrinal evolution was quite different. For a single generation it appeared as if laissez faire would be challenged in Britain as well as on the Continent. Jeremy Bentham and Saint-Simon were contemporaries, though the former's ideas were well advanced before the French writer appeared in print. There was considerable cross-influence between the two thinkers' followers, however, because the impact of Bentham's radical ideas was slowed by British reaction to the French Revolution.[45] Outside Great Britain, Bentham's doctrine tended to reinforce the impact of Saint-Simon's. His book, available in St. Petersburg (it was quoted at length by Speransky), probably smoothed the way of the French Saint-Simonist engineers.[46]

When Bentham's work first appeared in Great Britain, on the other hand, the take-off was well underway. By the time that he and his followers had acquired a significant influence, the initial stage of industrialization was almost accomplished, and laissez faire took full credit for it. In contrast, therefore, to Saint-Simon's or List's doctrines, Benthamism was in the position not of stimulating the industrial take-off as much as questioning comfortable laissez-faire assumptions con-

[45] Josef Redlich, *Englische Lokalverwaltung: Darstellung der inneren Verwaltung Englands in ihrer geschichtlichen Entwicklung und ihrer gegenwärtigen Gestalt* (Leipzig, 1901), pp. 6, 7ff.
[46] Alexander Vucinich, *Science in Russian Culture*, Vol. 1 (Stanford, 1963), 187; Marc Raeff, *Michael Speransky, Statesman of Imperial Russia, 1772-1839* (The Hague, 1957), pp. 130ff.

cerning automatic progress. The Benthamites, as reformers rather than stimulators, remained a sect, though temporarily an influential one.[47]

In itself, the famous utilitarian calculus did not contradict laissez faire—as long as one accepted the notion of the invisible hand. Reforms might be incremental, as contrasted to the putative system-wide planning of the Saint-Simonians. Nevertheless, "the view of the utilitarian theorists that increasing government intervention was necessary to reconcile and harmonize diverging interests" ran counter to the increasingly self-confident and rigid laissez-faire views dominant in England after Bentham's death.[48] Joseph Schumpeter did not hesitate to identify utilitarianism as "socialist" rather than capitalist.[49] A more nuanced interpretation is that Bentham desired an "administrative state to be active and useful, but not despotic," because balanced by local-central division of powers and laissez faire.[50]

It is scarcely surprising that Benthamites after Bentham went in divergent directions. Some were essentially individualists, distrusting French administrative models and strong government. Others, especially Edwin Chadwick, pushed the element of systemic planning in Bentham's thought much further. English historians have in fact seen Chadwick as "unique" among prominent Englishmen in glorifying the public official.[51] Significantly, he looked to a strong, efficient central administration rather than to Parliamentary enactments to overcome the abuses of industrialization and protect societal interests.[52]

Three significant factors limited the impact of Benthamism even at its height in the 1840's. Chadwick and his associates never acquired high authority. Perhaps, as one author puts it, the "centralized bureaucracy which his [Bentham's] disciples, Chadwick and Southwood Smith, were to fashion from the Poor Law Commission and Local Government Board" did express an "authoritarian" bent, but these institutions possessed little authority in the total elite complex.[53] Some historians have argued that (in institutions like the Railroad Board discussed in Chapter Thirteen) the crucial officials, if not a majority of the officials, were Benthamites.[54] Others contend that even

[47] Eric Stokes, *The English Utilitarians and India* (Oxford, 1959), pp. 52, 58.
[48] Asa Briggs, *The Age of Improvement* (London, 1959), pp. 274-75.
[49] Joseph A. Schumpeter, *Imperialism and Social Classes* (New York, 1951), p. 92.
[50] David Roberts, "Jeremy Bentham and the Victorian Administrative State," *Victorian Studies*, II (1958-59), 194.
[51] Samuel E. Finer, *The Life and Times of Sir Edwin Chadwick* (London, 1952), pp. 17, 91, 475.
[52] Polyani, pp. 117, 139, 146. [53] Stokes, p. 60.
[54] Henry Parris, "The Nineteenth Century Revolution in Government: A Reappraisal Reappraised," *The Historical Journal*, III (1960), 27.

Chadwick's accomplishments represented merely a "conjunction of Chadwick's mind and Tory interests." In this view, industrialization had made abuses so visible and amenable to correction that the "Benthamite" measures were obvious palliatives any regime would have carried out.[55]

While the incremental impact of these reforms was lasting, their effect as part of an interventionist doctrine was transitory at best. For it must be recognized that very few of the Benthamite reforms even envisaged economic regulation, much less planning, as contrasted to social amelioration.[56]

The third way in which Benthamism drastically differed from Saint-Simonism was that "social not technical invention was [for the Benthamites] the intellectual mainspring of the Industrial Revolution."[57] Like Saint-Simon, Bentham had envisaged a mechanical model of social progress, but he did little to relate his societal concepts to actual technological or natural scientific advances. As will appear in Chapter Nine, Benthamism, unlike Saint-Simonism in France or Russia, could not act as a stimulus for new professional groups in science and technology to redefine the administrative role.

AMBIVALENCE OF MARXISM

So far there is little to suggest that the intensity of development doctrines increased during the nineteenth century. Instead (for complex reasons which we have only begun to explore), the important differentiating factor appears to be the receptivity of the European societies. Gerschenkron, however, bases his argument for the late appearance of extraordinarily intense development doctrines primarily on the rise of Marxist economism ("legal Marxism") in late nineteenth-century Russia.

Despite a rather widespread opinion to the contrary, Marx's ideas themselves are not in any fundamental sense development doctrines. They are certainly strongly interventionist; but Marx and Engels envisaged administrative intervention as a means for redirecting production and particularly for the redistribution which they considered essential to transform human nature. Basically, the work of industrialization, of mobilizing and vastly increasing societal resources,

[55] Oliver MacDonagh, "The Nineteenth-Century Revolution in Government: A Reappraisal," *The Historical Journal*, 1 (1958), 65; Oliver MacDonagh, *A Pattern of Government Growth, 1800-60: The Passenger Acts and Their Enforcement* (London, 1961), p. 226; David Roberts, *Victorian Origins of the British Welfare State* (New Haven, 1960), pp. 95, 102, 113.

[56] *Ibid.*, p. 113.

[57] Polyani, p. 119.

would have been accomplished *by capitalism* before the proletarian revolution.[58]

It is hardly surprising that the rather sporadic impact of Marxism in Russia produced—like Saint-Simonism—diametrically different viewpoints concerning state intervention in an economy which was obviously far distant from the capitalist plenty which Marx had envisaged. In fact, brief comments by Marx and Engels themselves on Russian conditions gave comfort to those "populist" elements who opposed industrial development. Utilization, in the 1890's, of Marxist theory to argue for rapid industrialization with massive state support was a late Russian improvisation rather than a direct result of the diffusion of Marxism.[59]

One can, of course, argue (as Gerschenkron appears to do) that conditions of backwardness call forth ideas designed to overcome them. Whether ideas as such are unique creations of individuals or responses to social conditions is a perennial question which we regard as insoluble on purely empirical grounds. For practical purposes, differential receptivity—which can, at least in principle, be determined empirically—appears sufficient to explain intensity of development doctrines in Russia as elsewhere. Regardless of how Marxism became a development doctrine in the 1890's, earlier in the century Russian elite culture generally was not able to receive a readily available development doctrine like Saint-Simonism. By the 1880's, on the contrary, the elite was receptive to other development doctrines besides Marxist economism. Indeed, there are strong grounds for agreeing with Theodore Von Laue that the most powerful legitimization for elite administrative intervention during the whole period between 1885 and 1910 was Sergei Witte's adaptation of List's doctrine.[60] Several years before becoming finance minister, Witte studied List's doctrine intensively and argued strongly for its validity. Not only was Witte impressed by List's national-interest emphasis, but by his personal experience and advocacy of railroad construction. Like List, Witte preferred private enterprise as the "true creators." However, he argued that historically in Russia administrative bureaucrats had been the introducers of progressive reforms and were still necessary for direct mobilization of re-

[58] See especially Robert C. Tucker, *The Marxian Revolutionary Idea* (New York, 1969), p. 103.

[59] See Arthur P. Mendel, *Dilemmas of Progress in Tsarist Russia: Legal Marxism and Legal Populism* (Cambridge, Mass., 1961), pp. 123, 145.

[60] See Bertram D. Wolfe, "Backwardness and Industrialization in Russian History and Thought," *Slavic Review*, XXVI (1967), 192-96, who generally agrees with Gerschenkron on the importance of Marxist economics, but points out that effective pressure for industrialization came from above (i.e., from the regime and the administrative elite).

sources and organization of the transportation infrastructure for industrialization.[61]

RATHENAU—AT THE THRESHOLD OF INTENSE DEVELOPMENT INTERVENTIONISM

The real qualitative increase in the intensity of development interventionist doctrines appears to coincide with the last years of World War I—i.e., near the midpoint of the industrial period. The direct effect of the war experience on administrative elite role definitions examined in Chapter Thirteen, while very important for our purposes, was surely marginal for societal opinion in general. Much more fundamental was the shattering effect on laissez-faire assumptions. Only a few aspects of this enormous theme can be treated here.

The development doctrine most directly influenced by war experience is Walther Rathenau's, though he and his associates had begun to advance their ideas a few years earlier. For us, Rathenau's doctrine is particularly interesting, not only because we can later examine how it evolved in direct conflict with Prussian administrative elite ideologies, but because Rathenau's ideas resemble Saint-Simonism. Rathenau (in contrast to List) was no theoretical economist.

> In Germany, a country of specialists, it was this man's versatility that damned him most of all. The industrialists regarded him as only half a writer and the literary world saw in him only half a director of companies and banks.[62]

An engineer by training, Rathenau's preference was for "productivists" who closely resembled Saint-Simon's technologically oriented "industrialists." Unhappy experiences with bankers led Rathenau to reject the "omnium" type of organization. Like the Saint-Simonists, however, Rathenau and his followers preferred to bypass formal administrative elites by relying on para-state devices like an "economic General Staff." Success of the wartime innovation of semi-private planning organizations equipped with legal sanctions constituted, in a sense, a practical application of Saint-Simon doctrine. So did the notion of "little parlia-

[61] Theodore H. von Laue, *Sergei Witte and the Industrialization of Russia* (New York, 1963), pp. 56, 61; Theodore H. von Laue, "The Industrialization of Russia in the Writings of Sergei Witte," *American Slavic and East European Review*, x (1951), 175; Portal, *La Russie*, pp. 46, 50.

[62] Hans Fürstenberg (ed.), *Carl Fürstenberg*, p. 380, as quoted in W. O. Henderson, "Walther Rathenau: A Pioneer of the Planned Economy," *The Economic History Review*, second series, IV (1951-52), 100; cf. Charles-Georges Mohnen, *La Sociologie Economique de Walther Rathenau* (Dissertation, University of Nancy, Faculté de Droit) (Paris, 1932), p. 255.

ments" at territorial as well as central ministerial levels to impart initiative to the bureaucracy.[63]

Like Saint-Simonism, Rathenau's ideas had elements such as pacifism, moral regeneration, and the like which have no direct relation to development interventionism. Though Rathenau's followers scarcely constituted a "church," they may have had more influence in noneconomic affairs than Saint-Simon's.[64] Certainly Rathenau's stress on determinism and biological analogies, his belief in the natural self-selection of leaders, and the corporatist aspects of the organizational structure he proposed contributed something to antidemocratic trends in the interwar period. More pertinent for our consideration was the impact of Rathenau's development doctrine in other countries. In France it was a significant factor in the "neo-Saint-Simonism" of writers like Bertrand de Juvenel and Henri Fayol. In Russia, the influence was more practical; Rathenau's wartime industrial organization and its expansion under military control constituted a kind of model for Lenin and his followers.

LENINISM—A CULMINATION OF DEVELOPMENT INTERVENTIONISM IN THE EAST

Whether Lenin himself really endorsed "socialism in one country" need not be settled here. What he certainly did was to change the emphasis of Marxism from a critique of capitalist development to a legitimization of extreme state intervention in the economic development process. In fact, long before Lenin was ready to urge Marxist revolutionaries to seize power *before* capitalism had carried out its historic mission of industrialization, his faction had a special attraction for persons influenced by technology. Leaders of the group of illegal Marxists formed in 1887 at the St. Petersburg Technological Institute eventually became "core members" of the Bolshevik faction. The most prominent, L. B. Krasin, regarded conditions at the technological institute as more favorable than in the universities. As Arthur P. Mendel remarks, "their occupational activities [as engineers] involved closer and more frequent contacts with workers, and their professional interests found direct expression and application in the worker propaganda circles, where they praised the 'gigantic industrial undertakings in Europe and America' and criticized the Tsarist government for holding back

---

[63] *Ibid.*, pp. 203ff.; Henderson, "Walther Rathenau," pp. 101ff.

[64] Eugene Weinberger, *L'Economie Sociale de W. Rathenau* (Dissertation, University of Paris, Faculté de Droit) (Paris, 1924), pp. 279ff.; C. J. Gignoux, "L'Industrialisme de Saint-Simon à Walther Rathenau," *Revue d'Histoire Economique et Sociale*, XI (1923), 202-207.

Russian industrial development."[65] Later Lenin himself wrote that
their "science" brought technologists to the Revolution.[66] It is equally
apparent that his social engineering emphasis was much more in tune
with their interests than the more abstract approach of Marx or the
emotionalism of the populists. Indeed, Leninists have always had considerable respect for Saint-Simonism, rejecting its "utopian socialist"
but not its technological elite features.[67]

Immediately after the Revolution, as Merle Fainsod graphically
wrote:

> Consciously or unconsciously, willingly or unwillingly, the Bol-
> shevik leadership found itself thrust into the role of an industrializ-
> ing elite. From the beginning, Lenin provided the lead. As early as
> April 1918 we find him urging the adoption of the Taylor system in
> Soviet industry and proclaiming, "The Soviet Republic must at all
> costs adopt all that is valuable in the achievements of science and
> technology in this field. The possibility of building Socialism will be
> determined precisely by our success in combining the Soviet govern-
> ment and the Soviet organization of administration with the modern
> achievements of capitalism."[68]

It would be hard to imagine a clearer formulation of the basic elements of development interventionist doctrine. Yet (as we argue elsewhere) Marxism-Leninism is much more than a development doctrine.

The primary nature of Marxism-Leninism as a doctrine of unrestricted social control for transforming human nature explains why, in
our opinion, its impact has been so uneven. There is no need to recount
Leninism's appeal in societies where desperate economic and social
conditions are combined with fragile attachment even to minimal individual values of the Western type. Conversely, Leninism has never
really penetrated the general elites of the Western European societies
we consider. Even for the marginal Communist counter-elites of Weimar Germany and post-World War II France, Marxism-Leninism has
represented intensification of anticapitalist protest rather than a realistic appraisal of the potential for development interventionism. It is
said that Labour planners immediately after World War II kept
analyses of Soviet planning out of sight in their desk drawers. If that
is true, the subterfuge was singularly ineffective. It could hardly have

[65] Mendel, p. 124.

[66] S. A. Fediukin, *Sovetskaia Vlast' i Burzhuaznye Spetsialisty* (Moscow, 1965),
p. 16.

[67] Iggers, p. 64.

[68] Merle Fainsod, "Bureaucracy and Modernization: The Russian and Soviet
Case," in Joseph LaPalombara (ed.), *Bureaucracy and Political Development*
(Princeton, 1963), pp. 251-52.

been otherwise in view of the immense distance between Labour and Leninist presuppositions, as well as the paucity of information then available on the highly eclectic procedures of the first three Five Year Plans. French planners a decade later found much to sympathize with in Soviet planning, but had little doubt about the superiority of their own doctrine.

THE KEYNESIAN CULMINATION IN THE WEST

Although many elements from French history (including Saint-Simonism) shaped contemporary French doctrine, the basic element was Keynesian.[69] In a curious way the evolution of John Maynard Keynes' critique of laissez-faire capitalism parallels Marx's. To be sure, Keynes wrote to reinvigorate the basic capitalist system rather than to replace it. Nevertheless, the basic point of his critique, like Marx's, was that drastic intervention is required to overcome the distributive mal-functioning of capitalism. On the other hand, both doctrines initially assumed that the production aspect of laissez faire had been generally adequate as a development doctrine. As we have seen, it took more than a half-century for Marxism to be transformed into a development interventionist doctrine. Keynesian doctrines recapitulated the process in less than two decades.

Like List's doctrines and the practical import (if not the long-range intention) of Leninism, Keynes' teachings concentrated on macro-economic effects within a single national system. Consequently, planning for resource mobilization and allocation were important elements. Though the problem was more complex in the advanced industrial societies that were his first concern, statistical data and methods were vastly advanced over those available in the nineteenth century, to say nothing of the mercantilists'. Keynes himself supplied part of the theoretical apparatus required to utilize them. He considered that "the almost total obliteration of Malthus' line of approach and the complete domination of Ricardo's for a period of a hundred years has been a disaster to the progress of economics."[70]

Apart from opposing laissez faire, Keynes was ambiguous in his attitude toward the entrepreneur. Certainly he did not want to eliminate him. Nevertheless, he regarded the businessman's "secretiveness" and

[69] Alfred Sauvy, *Histoire Economique de la France entre les Deux Guerres, I: De l'Armistice à la Dévaluation de la Livre* (Paris, 1965), p. 110; Jean-François Kesler, "Les Ancien Elèves de l'Ecole Nationale d'Administration," *Revue Française de Science Politique*, XIV (1964), p. 263; Frederick F. Ridley and Jean Blondel, *Public Administration in France* (London, 1964), pp. 200-201.

[70] Seymour Harris, *John Maynard Keynes: Economist and Policy Maker* (New York, 1955), p. 30.

"nepotism" as unsuitable to the "modern age of progress and retrogression."[71] Like Rathenau and List, Keynes was especially critical of bankers. The effect of these critiques for elite administrators who subscribed to Keynesianism was to legitimize their own role redefinition both by convincing them that they possessed the theoretical basis for efficacious intervention in the economy and by undermining the prestige of the entrepreneurial counter-role.

As in the case of Marxism-Leninism, much of the appeal of Keynesian interventionism was to underdeveloped societies. Very likely it is significant that Keynes himself became converted to interventionism after his experience in India, although he remained a liberal advocate of international specialization while serving there.[72] There was a fundamentally optimistic bias in favor of economic expansion even in Keynes' original concept. As Keynesian doctrines were absorbed in France in the 1950's and by the British Treasury staff in the 1960's, they became a force for planned, continuous growth. At the same time, unlike Leninism or even some of the nineteenth-century doctrines, Keynesian thinking—as its official acceptance by American Republican leaders suggests—did not represent a revolutionary challenge to the basic values of the Western societies.[73] Just as traditional Christianity's value assumptions required the rejection of Calvinism, but could adapt to Cartesian and mercantilist doctrines stressing societal goals, the drastic revision advocated by Keynes was, perhaps, ultimately compatible with restrained individualism, private property, and social pluralism. In both historical instances, to be sure, ideological interests were, for long periods, more significant in influencing the absorption of values through the socialization process than were rational calculations of value compatibility. The contemporary cultural environment is complicated by the persistence of value patterns derived from traditional Christianity as well as the exaggerated individualism of laissez faire. Whether, in these circumstances, Keynesianism can indeed provide the development interventionist synthesis which evaded earlier periods remains to be seen.

The above survey (summarized in Figure 5) appears to justify the conclusion that strong development interventionist doctrines were available in all four societies in the century between 1830 and 1930. Not until approximately the latter date did distinctly more intense doctrines (Leninism and Keynesianism) become available. One may,

[71] *Ibid.*, pp. 196-202.

[72] Frédéric Clairmonte, *Le Liberalisme Economique et les Pays Sous-Developpés: Etudes sur l'Evolution d'une Idée* (Geneva, 1958), p. 147.

[73] Gottfried Haberler, "The General Theory," in Robert Lekachman (ed.), *Keynes' General Theory: Reports of Three Decades* (New York, 1964), pp. 285, 295.

therefore, infer that the varying influence of development interventionist doctrines was a matter of differential receptivity during the century of take-off to industrialization and industrial society. To discover the factors influencing receptivity of development values in elite administrators' role definition, one must turn to the socialization process. On the other hand, for the end of the industrial period and the postindustrial period we can expect that differences in socialization do not provide the whole answer; redefinition of roles was due, at least partly, to the decline of laissez faire and the rise of stronger, more coherent interventionism.

FIGURE 5. GENERAL SCHEME OF DEVELOPMENT
AND INTERVENTIONIST ELEMENTS IN DOCTRINES

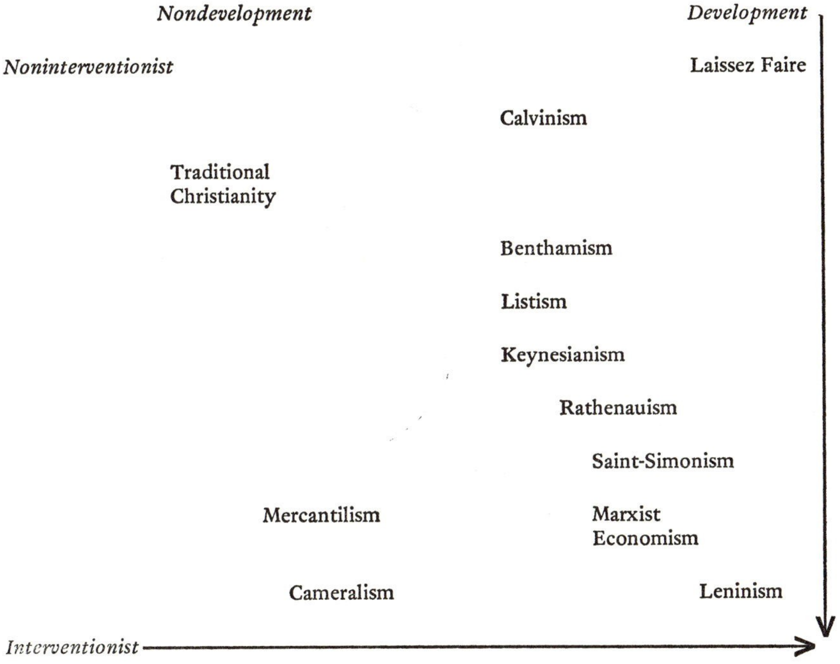

Nondevelopment   *Development*

Noninterventionist   Laissez Faire

                                         Calvinism

                    Traditional
                    Christianity

                                         Benthamism

                                         Listism

                                         Keynesianism

                                            Rathenauism

                                               Saint-Simonism

                    Mercantilism   Marxist
                                              Economism

                    Cameralism   Leninism

Interventionist ⟶

CHAPTER FOUR

Recruitment and Class Role Model

THE dominant model of recruitment for European administrative elites, as was explained earlier, tends toward ascription. In effect, this means upper-class boys are the main source of recruits. We use "class" both as a stratification concept (i.e., as defined by differences in wealth and privilege) and a matter of societal consensus. In Europe in recent centuries, the two definitions have, for the broad purposes we use them, nearly coincided. Given these circumstances, transmission of privilege by upper-class families is virtually certain. It is true that certain segments even of the higher classes may not be recruited heavily for the administrative elite. One must bear in mind that this elite is only one segment of the general societal elite, though an important one. Consequently, certain social groups (wealthier entrepreneurs in pre-1848 Prussia, aristocrats in the Third Republic) which enjoy generally high status and access to other elite roles may be almost excluded from the administrative elite. In Western Europe and Tsarist Russia, on the other hand, very few boys from lower classes (peasants, manual workers, frequently lower-middle-class elements) have entered administrative elites. Abundant data to substantiate this generalization could be advanced because, as noted earlier, stratification characteristics of European administrative elites have been a main focus of most previous studies. We shall consider some of this data in specific contexts, but the point is too generally accepted to need demonstration here.

For the present Soviet administrative elite, on the other hand, lower strata backgrounds are the rule rather than the exception. George Fischer's general elite sample indicates at least 47 per cent are of peasant origin, 28 per cent from worker families—a proportion which closely corresponds to an earlier, more limited examination of administrative elite backgrounds.[1] On the other hand, there is no doubt that Soviet children whose parents are better educated and have more prestigious positions have advantages comparable to those from similar Western families in entering professions. Alex Inkeles' and Raymond Bauer's study of the pre-World War II situation indicates that 65 per cent of the stratum they designate "professional-administrative"

---

[1] George Fischer, *The Soviet System and Modern Society* (New York, 1968), p. 67; Armstrong, *Soviet Bureaucratic Elite*, p. 19.

had sons in the same stratum; 17 per cent more had sons who were in semi-professional or white-collar jobs, and only 18 per cent had sons who were manual workers.[2] A 1965 Soviet survey of one representative province indicates that the proportion of specialists' children in the final grade of secondary school was 1.6 times as large as in the fourth grade of elementary school, whereas manual workers' children were only half as numerous, proportionately, in the secondary school grade.[3] It is possible that later generations of the Soviet administrative elite will reflect the advantages in access to skilled professions which advantaged families evidently provide their children. Such a trend would be compatible with the Progressive Equal Attrition Model which, as discussed in Chapter One, Soviet elite administrative recruitment approaches. In fact, this model is followed in the American Federal administration, where entrants from middle- and upper-class families predominate nearly as much as in contemporary Western Europe. Whether or not the USSR will move in the same direction is not as yet apparent, however.

For practical purposes we can consider all the administrative elites we examine, except the Soviet, as recruited from the aristocracy (we shall use the term interchangeably with "nobility") and the middle class ("bourgeoisie"). As noted above, in modern Europe there has been a high consensus on class definition and individual (familial) class identification. Because role definitions tend to accompany status definitions, European roles have also tended to be well defined and stable.

Noble and Bourgeois Role Definitions

Role stability, however, has a sharply different significance for the bourgeois and the noble. For the latter, the salient role is the noble role itself. It is, in fact, so salient that for nobles it tends to eliminate or subordinate other potential roles. Single role dominance is not unusual.[4] The situation becomes complicated, however, when a dominant class role like that of the noble is combined with an occupational role like elite administrator. Max Weber identified the tension between the aristocratic and the official roles, even in patrimonial bureaucracies, where the official based "his honor not upon his 'being' [like the noble] but on his 'function.' "[5]

---

[2] Alex Inkeles and Raymond A. Bauer, *The Soviet Citizen: Daily Life in a Totalitarian Society* (Cambridge, Mass., 1959), p. 81.

[3] David Lane, *Politics and Society in the USSR* (New York, 1971), p. 494.

[4] Brim, p. 139.

[5] Max Weber, *Economy and Society*, Vol. III (New York, 1968), 1,108.

For the noble, authority was ascriptive, i.e., he was inherently entitled to exercise it. A role in which authority was narrowly circumscribed was, therefore, objectionable. Consequently, the European nobility highly preferred military command roles. Often this preference is related to the feudal origins of the aristocracy as a conquering group deriving their status from military prowess. The same preference was evident, however, in Russia, where feudalism is very dubious as a historical category. Moreover, the Russian nobility comprised (by the late eighteenth century) very few families with more than a few generations of noble ancestry. Under Catherine II, for example, 80 per cent of the elected representatives of the nobility had military rank, in large part because hereditary nobles tried to avoid civil service positions.[6] Indeed, the nobles hoped to exclude men with civil *chin* altogether and to establish themselves as the "sole citizens of the realm," as they imagined their noble counterparts were in Spain and France.[7] As late as the 1840's the regime was obliged to take measures to prevent *all* noble boys entering the military, where discipline was regarded as less severe,[8] even though military models were used in civil service training schools. In Prussia, at the same period, about four times as many landless nobles were in career military service as in civil service.[9] Nobles were glad to send their sons to cadet schools, even though Frederick II had designed the institutions to uproot aristocratic particularism.[10] In France the nobility long preferred to accept into its ranks commoners who had shared the same military campaigns rather than civil officials of much higher status.[11] Even in England during the nineteenth century the number of boys going from major public schools to military careers increased from 7 to 12 per cent.[12]

In their formative period, Western European administrative elites were strictly auxiliary to the military.[13] The *commissarius* in France

---

[6] Paul Dukes, *Catherine the Great and the Russian Nobility* (Cambridge, England, 1967), pp. 23, 26, 75.

[7] Lentin (editor's introduction), pp. 25ff.

[8] Torke, p. 45.

[9] Fritz Martiny, *Die Adelsfrage in Preussen vor 1806 als politisches und soziales Problem: Erläutert am Beispiele des kurmärkischen Adels* (Stuttgart, 1938), pp. 64, 119.

[10] Otto Hintze, "Die Hohenzollern und der Adel," *Historische Zeitschrift*, cxii (1914), 12; Salomon Isaacsohn, *Das preussische Beamtentum*, Vol. iii (Berlin, 1884), 75.

[11] Marcel Reinhard, "Elite et Noblesse dans la Second Moitié du XVIIIᵉ Siècle," *Revue d'Histoire Moderne et Contemporaine*, iii (1956), 7.

[12] W. J. Reader, *Professional Men: The Rise of the Professional Classes in Nineteenth-Century England* (New York, 1966), pp. 212-14.

[13] Of the vast literature on this subject, see especially the seminal works, Gabriel Hanotaux, *Origines de l'Institution des Intendants des Provinces* (Paris, 1884), p. 5; and Otto Hintze, *Staat und Verfassung*, Vol. i, 2nd ed. (Göttingen, 1962), 242ff.

and Prussia (the prototype of the regular territorial official) was essentially the aide of the military commander. During the protracted period when semi-feudal lords made it impossible to exercise the king's authority without military support, the *commissarius* moved about with the army. As the armies themselves became permanent bodies with professional cadres, they depended more and more on the civilian auxiliary to draft manpower replacements and to raise money. It is not surprising that, as their relation became increasingly symbiotic, the military commander (usually a high noble) stressed his status superiority over the civilian *commissarius*.

The monarch's point of view was ambivalent. A major objective for the "rationalizing" monarch of the seventeenth and eighteenth centuries was attainment of universalistic authority by eliminating surviving feudalistic, particularistic claims. In order to obtain "absolute" authority, the monarch had to have officers, military and civil, dependent on him rather than on the aristocratic estate (*état* or *Stand*). The most direct method was to employ foreigners (more or less adventurers), a common practice in Russia and Prussia as late as the closing years of the eighteenth century. Another way was to appoint men with appropriate qualities of education and experience from lower domestic strata, in practice, the bourgeoisie. Frederick William I ruthlessly filled his high civil offices with bourgeois. Louis XIV was determined to separate status (*grandeur*) and power[14]—to break the connection between the authoritative role and the traditional noble authority status: "It was important that the public should know from the rank of those whom I chose to serve me that I had no intention of sharing my power with them."[15]

The inherent contradiction in this procedure was that it tended to weaken the monarch's support among a class which was still powerful. Recruitment is always a prime device for obtaining political support, but the importance of the nobility for the monarchy was heightened by the fact that (in Western Europe) both depended on the same feudal legitimizing symbols.[16] The king was, in principle, only the greatest of the nobles, the supreme military leader. It is not surprising that the French and Prussian kings were reluctant to displace great nobles from military command and traditional, honorific offices like the vestigial French *gouverneur*.

For a time the monarchs bypassed the honorific offices by filling new positions (e.g., the provincial intendancy in France or the *Steuerrat* in Prussia) with bourgeois or lesser nobles. It is not surprising, however,

---

[14] The phrase is Franklin Ford's, *Robe and Sword: The Regrouping of the French Aristocracy after Louis XIV* (Cambridge, Mass., 1953), p. 7.
[15] *Ibid.*   [16] Eisenstadt, p. 150.

that the monarchs eventually were led to make concessions to the no-bility on important civil offices. The aristocratic reaction of the late eighteenth century did not occur under weak kings like Louis XV and Louis XVI alone. Frederick II ("the Great") and Catherine II (also "the Great") required all the support they could obtain for their am-bitious territorial expansion. Consequently, they strongly desired a compromise with the nobility which would enlist its support. For Catherine it was comparatively easy to control the landed nobility, for Peter I's reformed *chin* structure had made service status supreme over hereditary status. The Russian provincial nobility provided poor material for positive tasks. But the fact that military like civil rank de-pended entirely on service made it easy for the Russian emperors to choose relatively competent military officers for seconding to civil tasks.

PRUSSIA—ACCOMMODATION OF ARISTOCRATIC AND ADMINISTRATORS' VALUES

The compromise between the monarchy and the nobility was facili-tated, in Prussia, by the aristocracy's somewhat increased appreciation of civil office. Just how far this appreciation went is disputed. As late as 1841 the Prussian king considered depriving nobles of their status if they did not serve in military or civil positions. Nobles found em-ployment by the hundreds in a significant, but low-level territorial post, the *Landrat*, which almost became a new particularistic office for the local nobility. Certainly nobles (many from a few great families) dominated the high offices which determined the status order and style of the administrative elite. During 1794-1806, three-fifths of the Prus-sian ministers and other high officials were of old noble families.[17] In 1820, although only one-fourth of the judges were nobles, 42 per cent of the higher administrative officials (including five out of six terri-torial chief administrators) were noble.[18] At the beginning of the take-off period (1842), three-fourths of the top ministerial central judicial officers were nobles, as were three-fifths of the chief territorial admin-istrators.[19] The latter (*Regierungspräsidenten*) were still over 50 per cent noble in 1916 and 13 per cent in 1925.[20]

[17] Bonin, pp. 143-47.
[18] John R. Gillis, *The Prussian Bureaucracy in Crisis, 1840-1860: Origins of an Administrative Ethos* (Stanford, 1971), p. 30.
[19] Reinhart Koselleck, *Preussen zwischen Reform und Revolution: Allge-meines Landrecht, Verwaltung und soziale Bewegung von 1791 bis 1848* (Stuttgart, 1967), p. 435.
[20] W. Kamm, "Minister und Beruf," *Allgemeines Statistisches Archiv*, XVIII (1928), 450; Wolfgang Runge, *Politik und Beamtentum im Parteienstaat: Die*

As will appear in Chapters Seven and Eight, these "service" nobles differed strongly from their rustic Prussian ancestors (or even some of their contemporary relatives) in education and culture. The desire to retain noble identity, however, was strong. Consequently, noble civil servants preferred offices which involved general exercise of authority—the closest civil surrogate of military command. As the phrase went, they accepted the replacement of *Tugend* (character or prowess) by *Dienst* (service). Gradually, in the late eighteenth century, even for noble office-holders, the concept of "servant of the state" replaced the feudal idea of "royal servant."[21] Increasing autonomy of the administrative elite was advantageous to all its members, but its attainment depended on solidarity of the aristocratic and middle-class members. As we shall see, this solidarity was largely attained by a new process of socialization. But it is important to understand that solidarity depended on accommodation of sharply differing concepts of the elite administrator's role. Just as the noble was constantly striving to define the administrative role as undifferentiated exercise of authority, with hereditary character counting more than specific qualifications, the bourgeois legitimized his claim to office by defining the role as a specialized, skilled activity. The bourgeois had to use superior education as a counter-legitimization to hereditary character, whereas the noble tended to be suspicious of "too much" learning.[22] Numerous epigrams (usually favorable to the aristocrat) reflect this dichotomy: "inheritance versus performance"; "noble according to the character of the noble, bourgeois according to the character of the vocation"; "middle-class people know only how to work, not how to govern."[23] Even Goethe wrote that "a commoner may acquire merit, by excessive efforts, he may even educate his mind, but his personal qualities are lost, let him struggle as he will."[24] The fundamental distinction between aristocratic and bourgeois class models was not confined to the admin-

---

Demokratisierung der politischen Beamten in Preussen zwischen 1918 und 1933 (Stuttgart, 1965), p. 171.

[21] See Otto Hintze's remarks in *Acta Borussica: Denksmäler der preussischen Staatsverwaltung im 18. Jahrhundert*, Vol. VI, Erster Hälfte. *Behördenorganisation und allgemeine Staatsverwaltung* (Berlin, 1901), p. 277.

[22] Georges Snyders, *La Pédagogie en France au XVIIe et XVIIIe Siècles* (Paris, 1965), pp. 397ff.

[23] Johanna Schultze, *Die Auseinandersetzung zwischen Adel und Bürgertum in den deutschen Zeitschriften der letzten drei Jahrzehnte des 18. Jahrhundert (1773-1806)* (Berlin, 1925), pp. 3, 133; Rosenberg, p. 181; Gustav Schmoller, "Der preussische Beamtenstand unter Friedrich Wilhelm I," *Preussische Jahrbücher*, XXVII (1870), 133.

[24] From *Wilhelm Meister*, quoted in Ernst Kohn-Bramstedt, *Aristocracy and the Middle Classes in Germany: Social Types in German Literature, 1830-1900* (London, 1937), p. 29.

istrative elite, nor, indeed, to Prussia. In eighteenth-century England, where professional administration was hardly relevant, Lord Chesterfield feared that Aristotle's "banausic man" would be the result of the loss of personal balance and freedom caused by middle-class professional specialization.[25] Conversely, as Howard Becker and James W. Carpenter pointed out, the overwhelmingly middle-class American society puts occupational identity above all else: the most significant question of a stranger is "What's your line?"[26]

Discussion of Prussian officialdom has often stressed its "unmodern" qualities, particularly its deference to aristocratic military styles. There is certainly an element of truth in this generalization, but the actual working out of the tension between bourgeois and noble role definitions was very complex. Three historic stages can be distinguished. In the eighteenth century, higher officials of bourgeois origin were ennobled. They then tended to adopt "ultra-cavalier" life styles by ostensibly suppressing bourgeois characteristics like concern for order, thrift, promptitude, and industry which irritated their new noble reference group.[27] But anyone even superficially familiar with nineteenth- and twentieth-century German officials knows that they (whether of noble or bourgeois origin) have not only possessed these qualities, but have taken great pride in them. These qualities eventually won out because noble officials also accommodated to bourgeois values.

In the second stage, noble officials accepted bourgeois educational requirements. These aristocratic concessions constitute, in fact, much of the content of their acceptance of "service" as a quality of nobility. This accommodation was achieved in the period between 1790 and 1830, the last preindustrial generation, as the administrative elite became an isolated stratum, recognized in 1794 as a corporate body.[28] This body resembled a distinct aristocratic class in many respects, as contemporaries had no trouble recognizing.[29] The official *Beruf* was regarded as a life achievement rather than a status dependent on audience expectations or actual achievements.[30] The main counter-role was the profit-seeker, defined as anyone whose achievement was measured

[25] Quoted in Robert Ulich, *The Education of Nations: A Comparison in Historical Perspective* (Cambridge, Mass., 1961), p. 99.

[26] Howard S. Becker and James W. Carpenter, "The Development of Identification with an Occupation," *American Journal of Sociology*, LXI (1956), 290.

[27] Rosenberg, pp. 148-49.

[28] John R. Gillis, "Aristocracy and Bureaucracy in Nineteenth Century Prussia," *Past and Present*, XLI (1968), 106-107, 124.

[29] Clemens Theodor Perthes, *Der Staatsdienst in Preussen: Ein Beitrag zum Deutschen Staatsrecht* (Hamburg, 1838), p. 48.

[30] Heinz Hartmann, *Authority and Organization in German Management* (Princeton, 1959), pp. 28-30.

by monetary rewards, particularly the emerging entrepreneurial role. According to their ideological legitimization, officials gave their lives for a cause, the private employee or businessman sold his.

The antimaterialistic ideology persisted into the third stage, despite very real concern for salary levels. To avoid "capitalistic considerations" the official would even have preferred, had it been feasible, to receive his remuneration in kind.[31] Even at the close of the Second Reich, an official suggesting that brief experience in private firms would be good for a young man entering the judiciary hastened to add that the latter would naturally be on a higher social plane than the private employees he dealt with.[32] Georg Michaelis, the last career official to become Chancellor of the Second Reich, wrote that an uncle whom circumstances obliged to work in a Bremen export-import house "showed that there was more of the official than the merchant in him . . . he never speculated" and in fact had no telephone![33] In some entrepreneurial circles (particularly during the Second Reich) there was a tendency to accept the derogatory administrative definition of the private business role. Given the Prussian administrative role definition, the sociologist Werner Sombart was doubtless right in regarding this role confusion as undermining the entrepreneurial spirit:

> And do we not encounter numerous entrepreneurs who strike us more as bureaucrats than merchants or businessmen? Correct in their business, meticulous in their orderliness, probably measured in their decisions, with a strong gift for the organizational without strong upward-mobility inclinations, they are exemplary administrative officials. Today they are lord mayors of a metropolis, tomorrow direct a great bank, today again they have a department in a ministry under their direction and tomorrow direct a syndicate. We leave aside the directors of state and municipal plants and semi-public enterprises which are constantly acquiring greater importance today.[34]

During the 1790-1830 stage, the distinctiveness of the administrative elite had been intensified by its strong tendency toward recruitment of officials' sons, as Table II shows. By the 1830's, as the attraction of official careers increased, closed recruitment declined. By obtaining

---

[31] Adolf Grabowsky, *Die Reform des deutschen Beamtentums* (Gotha, 1917), p. 4; Rosenberg, p. 94; Gillis, *Prussian Bureaucracy*, p. 198.

[32] Roland Behrend, "Der Unternehmer als Erzieher des Juristen," *Preussische Jahrbücher*, CLVII (1914), 249.

[33] Georg Michaelis, *Für Staat und Volk: Eine Lebensgeschichte* (Berlin, 1922), p. 9.

[34] Werner Sombart, *Der Bourgeois: Zur Geistesgeschichte des modernen Wirtschaftsmenschen* (Munich, 1913), p. 213.

higher educations, lower-middle-class men (sons of lower officials, teachers, and even some artisans and peasants) secured 25 to 30 per cent of the openings to the administrative elite. Eventually, entrance requirements were altered to avoid this kind of competition. Nobles had to be accepted, however. Between 1820 and 1852 they increased from 24 per cent to 32 per cent of the middle administrative elite categories.[35] By the 1860's, a carefully controlled recruitment process produced an administrative elite including the aristocracy and wealthier middle-class elements. Even in the third stage, officials' nostalgia for a closed administrative elite remained strong. The relatively small diminution of recruitment from official families (see Table II) was

TABLE II. ELITE ADMINISTRATORS WITH
ELITE ADMINISTRATOR FATHERS
(Per Cent)

Period	France	Great Britain	Prussia W. Germany	Russia
IA. Preindustrial (18th century)	44 ± 5	—	33 ± 10	20 ± 5
IB. Preindustrial (early 19th century)	23 ± 10	—	31 ± 10	40 ± 15
II. Take-Off	21 ± 10	—	26 ± 10	—
IIIA. Industrial Pre-World War I	—	4 ± 1	23 ± 5	—
IIIB. Industrial Post-World War I	25 ± 10	3 ± 2	22 ± 5	0
IV. Postindustrial	26 ± 5	14 ± 5	15 ± 10	—

viewed with alarm by writers who expressed their regrets for the days when family continuity in service was the pride and joy of Prussian officialdom.[36] Michaelis' conception of his own family is a paradigm of this attitude:

My father was descended from a family that one may call a family of officials. The available family tree shows that his father, Carl Friedrich Michaelis, was judge of the superior district court in Glogau, where he died in 1849. The latter's father was court and criminal affairs counselor in Glogau. The latter in turn was son of a Glogau merchant. But his brother, named Friedrich Gottlieb, was the pride of the family, for he had been named Finance Minister by Frederick the Great. The father of these brothers was a pharmacist

[35] Gillis, "Aristocracy," p. 114.

[36] Otto Most, "Zur Wirtschafts- und Sozialstatistik der höheren Beamten in Preussen," *Schmollers Jahrbuch*, xxxix (1915), 194; Heinrich Tisch, *Das Problem des sozialen Auf- und Abstieges im deutschen Volk dargestellt an hand einer Erhebung über die soziale Herkunft der Beamten in der Saarpfalz* (Dissertation, Heidelberg University, Philosophical Faculty) (Speyer, 1937), p. 43.

and counselor in Bernstein (Neumark). Other branches of the family tree show how influential was the example of a son who rose so high from a hitherto purely bourgeois and ecclesiastical family. From then on official, and also military officer careers, appear as more or less the normal thing in the Michaelis family.[37]

FIGURE 6. Elite Administrators with Elite Administrator Fathers

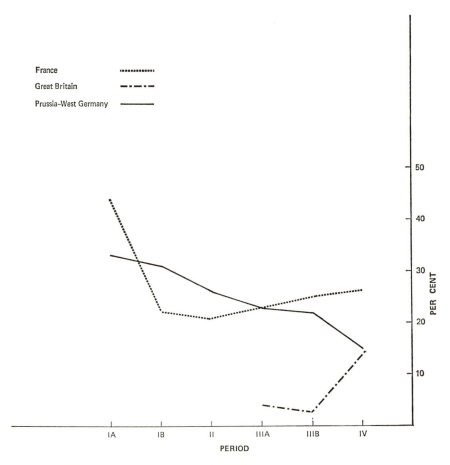

The Prussian administrative elite role, in summary, accommodated men of aristocratic and bourgeois origins by stressing its own distinctiveness as the guardian of a "state above classes." As an ideology this definition was effective, for it enabled higher officials to become assimilated into the aristocracy while retaining considerable independence and even a privileged position in recruitment. As we shall see, the ad-

[37] Michaelis, p. 8.

ministrators' claim to constitute a rationalized profession required further compromises with the aristocratic role model. If the administrators accepted the specialized occupational characteristics of the bourgeois, they were obliged to reject his entrepreneurial role. Consequently, the ideologies which legitimized the administrative elite well into the twentieth century really assimilated its role to traditional aristocratic roles as far as development was concerned, while posing the entrepreneur alone as a counter-role.

DOMINANCE OF BOURGEOIS VALUES IN THE FRENCH ADMINISTRATIVE ROLE

Because they needed nonparticularistic officials, French kings, like the Prussians, recruited middle-class elements. Gradually the higher French officials stabilized their position as the *noblesse de robe*, became a legally self-recruiting body (through purchase of office), and assimilated many elements of the noble life style. By the eighteenth century the *noblesse de robe* had an average of four generations in that status, not much less than the traditional nobility.[38] Nevertheless, there were crucial differences between the Prussian and French systems.

Part were due simply to difference in timing. The *noblesse de robe* evolved in a long process beginning at least in the fifteenth century, including several cycles of patrimonial regression. As a result, the distinctiveness of the *haute robe* from the traditional nobility was gradually but fully established. In the eighteenth century, assimilation of the two groups through intermarriage and *robe* estate purchase proceeded rapidly. Nevertheless, the *noblesse d'épée* (military nobility) rarely acquired civil office and *noblesse de robe* sons did not often go into military service. The *épée* retained a certain superior prestige but was divided among several status groups. The status superiority of the handful of dukes and princes was so great that by contrast the *robe* as well as the *épée* was recognized as a lesser aristocracy.[39] Since nearly all the chief officials were recruited from the *robe*, the civil nobility was closer to the seat of power. Moreover, most of these royal officials took great pride in being the sole representatives of central state interests, as contrasted both to their particularistic *parlement* cousins and the semi-feudal *épée* nobles.

[38] F. Ford, p. 132.
[39] L. Ducros, *La Société Française au Dix-Huitième Siècle* (Paris, 1922), pp. 51-52; Henri Carré, *La Noblesse de France et l'Opinion Publique au XVIIIe Siècle* (Paris, 1920), pp. 7, 37; Henri Brocher, *A la Cour de Louis XIV: Le Rang et l'Etiquette sous l'Ancien Régime* (Paris, 1934), pp. 19, 71.

While the eighteenth-century *robe* nobles had assimilated many elements of noble life style (dueling, hunting, use of the *de*), they consciously retained certain bourgeois characteristics, including habits of concentrated work, a certain sobriety of dress, and nominal educational qualifications.[40] The comment "Seriousness seems to have been a tradition of the Turgot family"[41] typifies a bourgeois style which (as we have seen) was not easily accepted in Prussia until a half-century later.

While the *robe* nobility was self-recruiting to a considerable degree (see Table II), over several generations it did offer a channel of mobility to the middle-class families who could afford the high entrance fees. In the opinion of the major authority for the period, the very fact that offices were venal promoted social mobility and increased support for the monarchical system.[42] The effort of the aristocratic reaction to choke off this movement, on the other hand, was a significant factor leading to the Revolution.

The Revolution was the culmination of a long process by which officials, instead of perceiving themselves as an isolated stratum, became the archetypal bourgeois. "We may ask ourselves if, in the last analysis, the image of the 'average Frenchman' has not been moulded by the myth of the public official which is so well known and so popularized in France."[43] Entrance to the administrative elite as the culmination of a family's social ascent was firmly established as a status goal. In the 1930's, fond parents contemplating their son commented, "he will enter the Polytechnique" as their *nouveaux riches* counterparts two hundred years earlier had murmured, "we shall buy him an office."[44] French writers have understandably emphasized the "plague of functionaries" which this bourgeois "vanity" produced.[45] From our point of view, however, it is important to stress that the official image was a thoroughly bourgeois one: stable employment, ultimately a pension, nonmobility, a small house, a mania for collecting.[46]

As Table II shows, actual self-recruitment of the French administrative elite was not much lower than in Prussia. But the elite's ideology

---

[40] F. Ford, p. 54.

[41] P. Foncin, *Essai sur le Ministère de Turgot* (Dissertation, University of Paris, Faculté des Lettres) (Paris, 1877), p. 3.

[42] G. Pages, "La Vénalité des Offices dans l'Ancienne France," *Revue Historique*, CLXIX (1932), 492; G. Pages, "Essai sur l'Evolution des Institutions Administratives en France du Commencement du XVIe Siècle à la Fin du XVIIe," *Revue d'Histoire Moderne*, VII (1932), 25-26.

[43] Henri Déroche, *Les Mythes Administratifs: Essai de Sociologie Phénoménologique* (Paris, 1966), p. 70.

[44] Charles Normand, *La Bourgeoisie Française au XVIIe Siècle: La Vie Publique —Les Idées et les Actions Politiques, 1604-1661* (Paris, 1908), p. 42.

[45] *Ibid.*, pp. 11-12, 42.   [46] Déroche, p. 71.

stressed open recruitment; concern for social mobility was qualified by the observation that it usually took three generations for a lower-class family to reach the top. Even that qualification represented a sharp distinction from Prussian concern for tracing official grandfathers and still more remote ancestors in the state service. French apologists for the administrative status quo have increasingly argued that higher administrators rarely even had fathers in like positions.[47] During the post-World War II period, only 26 per cent of a sample of officials gave "family and tradition" as a reason for their success, as compared to 38 per cent of bankers and industrialists and 53 per cent of members of certain literary professions.[48]

Ideological rejection of a closed official stratum also appears to be related to the timing of French administrative elite evolution. By the beginning of the take-off period, the French administrative elite was in some respects better established than the Prussian. The post-Napoleonic administrative elite contained many recruits from old *robe* families, as well as a high proportion of men from middle-class families attached to the elite administrative tradition.[49] The Revolution had ended competition from the old military aristocracy and the latter's revival under the Restoration was feeble. After the 1830 revolution the old nobility virtually withdrew from civil office.[50] However, its retreatist roles (particularly the military and the high clergy) continued to constitute counter-roles for defining the high administrator's role, which was therefore perceived as active if not necessarily development-oriented.

On the other hand, the general elite status of the French high administrator *between 1830 and 1850*, in contrast to the legally established position of his Prussian counterpart, was ambiguous. The commercial bourgeoisie which had triumphed in 1830 and the emerging entrepreneurs hesitated to direct their sons toward low-paid official careers by sending them even to a prestigious school like the Polytechnique.[51] The leading periodical commented that officials were the objects of

a sort of ostracism . . . it seems to some people that learned men who are capable, active, industrious, and often eminent yet who con-

[47] Pierre Lalumière, *L'Inspection des Finances* (Dissertation, University of Paris, Faculté de Droit) (Paris, 1959), p. 47.

[48] Alain Girard, *La Réussite Sociale en France* (Paris, 1961), p. 153.

[49] Pierre-Henry, p. 112; Nicholas J. Richardson, *The French Prefectoral Corps, 1814-1830* (Cambridge, England, 1966), pp. 199, 202.

[50] *Ibid.*, p. 204.

[51] A. Daumard, "Les Elèves de l'Ecole Polytechnique de 1815 à 1848," *Revue d'Histoire Moderne et Contemporaine*, v (1958), 229.

secrate their life to the service of the State for a salary which does not seem sufficient to the humblest industrialist are pariahs.[52]

The qualities of education and industry which the bourgeois administrator had had to conceal to avoid the noble's scorn in eighteenth-century Prussia were those which aroused the sympathy of the early nineteenth-century French businessman, while the dedicated service for low pay which made Prussian administration acceptable to the nobility brought the French service into disrepute. In some provincial areas, on the other hand, officials were isolated socially because they were despised by conservative Catholics. One should not, of course, make too much of these polar tendencies. As Adeline Daumard—whose works provide much information on the period—points out, French officials were isolated partly by preference, with about one-third of the various levels marrying daughters of their colleagues. When officials married outside their group, three-fifths secured dowries larger than their own property from their wives' merchant or liberal professional fathers.[53] Another writer assesses official status still more highly:

> State service [in the nineteenth century] greatly honored those who dedicated themselves to it. It conferred something that democratic evolution had caused to disappear, social rank. . . . Social rank [in provincial cities] did not depend on a man's wealth or even his personal value; it was assigned by the post the man occupied and the family milieu with which he was associated by birth or by marriage. Whoever benefited from social rank was admitted in what one then called "good society" or just "society" itself. The remainder of men did not, so to speak, count. But public office conferred social rank, and some offices the highest rank. This was the case, notably, with the magistrate and the officer. The social rank of the official, among other benefits it brought him, had a matrimonial value: the official married well, he was the son-in-law many families dreamed of, he had a right to what one called in those distant times an "heiress." And the public service profited greatly from all these things.[54]

These observations certainly indicate that the nineteenth-century French administrative elite was a privileged body. They equally point to its reference group as the upwardly mobile bourgeoisie rather than traditional elites. Among bourgeois, the liberal professions—because they had similar levels of education and "culture"—were the most salient reference group. "In the century in which we live, independ-

[52] Adeline Daumard, *La Bourgeoisie Parisienne de 1815 à 1848* (Paris, 1963), p. 26.
[53] *Ibid.*, pp. 331, 345.
[54] H. Truchy, "L'Elite et la Fonction Publique," *Revue Politique et Parlementaire*, 1927, No. 397, p. 340.

ence [of profession] is one of the first needs of life," a contemporary wrote.[55] But professionals (lawyers, physicians, and engineers) were, by definition, specialists. Next to their economic independence their personal attainments were most admired. In this sense, Charles Kindleberger's emphasis on the cult of prowess as contrasted to service appears entirely justified.[56] Like other Latin societies, French society retained an admiration for exceptional individual accomplishment, often emphasizing style and manner more than results. Still, the essentially bourgeois recognition (by an aristocratic pen) of the merit of specialized accomplishment appears in France at a date when the noble disdain for specialization still prevailed in Prussia and England:

> As the works of man receive their form from the molds through which they pass, man himself receives this form from the order of things in which he has lived, from his situation, from the offices he has filled; and it is remarkable that there is not one of the nine ministers who are the objects of our remarks in whom one does not find, at least in the first period of his administration, vestiges of what he was before his ministry.[57]

About the same time Napoleon I (to be sure, no aristocrat) demanded that members of his Council of State be trained as specialists in some branch of knowledge, though he was equally insistent that they be able to adapt rapidly to other fields.[58]

In sum, the reference group which defined the French elite administrator's role was the whole bourgeoisie, though not until late in the nineteenth or early in the twentieth century did the entrepreneurial segment dominate. This did not mean that the French elite administrator generally adopted a development role aspect, for the dominant bourgeois doctrine (laissez faire) made this difficult. Many bourgeois characteristics the French administrator did accept (or which he initiated), like the stress on security, had negative implications for development. On the other hand, the Frenchman, unlike the Prussian, did not define his role negatively by reference to an entrepreneurial counter-role, while accommodating to the aristocratic contempt for a role in material development. If nothing more, the French administrator retained more openness to doctrines calling for intervention in development.

[55] Daumard, *La Bourgeoisie*, p. 26.
[56] Charles P. Kindleberger, *Economic Growth in France and Britain, 1851-1950* (Cambridge, Mass., 1964), p. 93.
[57] Auget de Montyon, *Particularités et Observations sur les Ministres des Finances de France les plus Célèbres depuis 1660 jusqu'en 1791.* (Paris, 1812), p. 348.
[58] Charles Durand, *Etudes sur le Conseil d'Etat Napoléonien* (Paris, 1949), pp. 62, 299.

BRITAIN—ARISTOCRATIC VALUES WITHOUT A STRONG
NOBLE REFERENCE GROUP

For preindustrial England, aristocratic status depended on family ties. The only way for middle-class families to acquire such status was by purchasing estates. Proportionately even fewer of the families had feudal roots than on the Continent (a large majority of the peerage as well as the gentry dated no further back than the Tudors). Like travel ("the Grand Tour"), education was a desirable ornament, but it neither conferred noble status nor was essential to maintain it. Many nobles complacently accepted the common Continental appellation of Englishmen as "heretical boors."[59] Conversely, as with all aristocracies, certain kinds of activity were derogating: the gentleman could serve— if he did serve—only the Church or the Sovereign. Given the slight importance of military careers, patronage civil posts were significant. About 5 per cent of the gentry families secured them in the seventeenth century, as compared to 7 per cent of the Prussian nobility sample a century and a half later.[60] For reasons outlined in Chapter Two, however, by the mid-nineteenth century, administration had sunk so low in the eyes of the gentry that many preferred bank clerkships.[61]

Simultaneously with the decline of central patronage appeared a temporary ascendancy of distinguished middle-class families. For decades the surviving prestige of the aristocracy was a severe, in many cases a cruel, handicap for them. Chadwick, for example, was bluntly told (1841) he could not be a member of the Poor Law Commission he had designed: "I must frankly admit that your station in society was not such as would have made it fit that you should be appointed one of the commissioners."[62] Chadwick could look out for himself; men in more sensitive walks of life doubtless felt their handicap more severely. The British sociologist, Sheldon Rothblatt, interprets their reaction incisively:

Both dons and clergy regarded their past association with landed aristocracy as embarrassing and professionalization as replacement. But professional did not mean any particular training, but a genteel style of social and domestic life and "a particular social role that was

---

[59] Ian Weinberg, *The English Public Schools: The Sociology of Elite Education* (New York, 1967), p. 31.

[60] G. E. Aylmer, "Office Holding as a Factor in English History, 1625-42," *History*, XLIV (1959), pp. 234-36; Martiny, p. 119.

[61] Administrative Reform Association, *Official Paper No. 2: The Devising Heads and Executive Hands of the English Government; as Described by Privy-Councillors and Civil Servants Themselves* (London, 1855), pp. 15-16 (quoting Chadwick).

[62] Roberts, *Victorian Origins*, p. 146; cf. Kingsley, pp. 56-61.

not merely occupational but in fact profoundly moral; and it was at this point that dons began to exploit the status ambiguity of the designation professional and to emphasize the idea of professional behaviour, of compliance with a high ethical, altruistic standard as the predominant characteristic of a professional man."[63]

As a surrogate for the extended family ties of the eighteenth-century aristocracy, "as a social group, the elite ["upper stratum" in our usage] began to assume its modern character of an extended family of friends, rather than relatives, prone to exclusiveness and endogamy."[64] In fact, there was always a narrow but well-defined road to this stratum through the educational system. Mobility increase was considerable, as measured by the proportion of the administrative elite who had lower-middle-class or working-class fathers in 1950 as compared to 1888, or by the drop in the proportion of fathers who had held distinguished positions. But the difficulty of the road and the insecurity of the newcomer who finally reached the in-group took their toll, Roger K. Kelsall concludes after his searching investigation: men reached the elite with depleted energy and lack of the kind of courage which characterizes either real aristocrats or adventurers.[65] One-third of all Administrative Class officials questioned by the Fulton Committee tried to avoid disclosing their class origin, apparently because of family backgrounds lower than those of the people they deal with.[66] To us, this finding suggests that a high proportion of British civil servants feels personally insecure. They can neither adopt an aristocratic role implying unhesitant exercise of authority nor accept middle-class occupational specialization. The emphasis Kelsall finds on administration as a mysterious art requiring long experience and consisting of managing men tactfully and cautiously appears to reflect this ambiguity.[67]

A distinctive element of British experience has been the prevalence of aristocratic style and some aristocratic values in the absence of a really strong noble reference group. The military command aspect of the noble role, so prominent on the Continent, has been slight in England for centuries. The army was small and the navy hardly counted before the nineteenth century as an aristocratic field of activity. The actual contingent of peerage or even old gentry families in the new elite formed in the mid-nineteenth century was small compared to the noble part in the contemporary Prussian elite. When the new British

---

[63] Sheldon Rothblatt, *The Revolution of the Dons: Cambridge and Society in Victorian England* (London, 1968), p. 91.

[64] Weinberg, p. 51.   [65] Kelsall, pp. 162ff., 190-91.

[66] Great Britain, Committee under the Chairmanship of Lord Fulton. *The Civil Service.* Vol. II (2), 10 (London, 1968). Hereafter cited as Fulton Committee (with volume number).

[67] Kelsall, pp. 190-91.

elite adopted a reinterpreted gentry life style as a legitimizing ideology, military and feudal elements could be virtually neglected. Probably the element of career self-recruitment was important, too—adventurous and forceful (if not authoritarian) personalities found their outlet in colonial and military careers, while those of all social origins more concerned with status and security entered careers like the civil service and education.

The syndrome just analyzed suggests that the administrative elite would be reluctant to include any activist elements like development interventionism in its role definition. This tendency was enhanced by the attitude prescribed by the legitimizing ideology toward the entrepreneurial role. As Rothblatt points out: "This donnish conception of a professional man and of his responsibility towards authority resulted in an ideal of service that was sharply brought to bear against the Victorian businessman," and asks "Is it one of the ironies of history that the generation of the 1860's, employing a subtle donnish chemistry of ancient origin, had abolished the businessman and had at last triumphed over the philistines and the spirit of money-making?"[68]

Superficially, to answer this rhetorical question, the British elite administrator's perception of the entrepreneur's as a counter-role was identical to the Prussian administrator's. But there were basic differences. The Prussian administrative elite had a much stronger position in the general societal elite. The dominance of laissez-faire doctrines among British elites precluded the relatively weak administrative elite from assuming an interventionist role, whether for or against development.

Given the unstable and partially derivative class models of Tsarist Russia, we have not tried to establish what ideologies affected role identification there. As we have seen, until late in the nineteenth century, Russian society was not able effectively to absorb development doctrines of any kind. Later, it will become apparent that minimal progress in education and administrative organization were necessary to make the combination of these doctrinal and ideological elements meaningful.

In this preliminary examination of the relationship between doctrines and ideologies we have hypothesized broad limits for elite administrative role definition. Given the strength of the laissez-faire doctrine, the nineteenth-century elite administrator in any of the three societies was strongly inclined to perceive his role as noninterventionist. The Prussian and the French administrative elites which had been established in the preindustrial period were less likely to do this than the British, since their traditional legitimization had called for inter-

[68] Rothblatt, pp. 91, 271.

vention. The Prussian elite administrator's role definition was influenced by his need to accommodate the traditional antidevelopment values of his principal reference group, the nobility. Consequently, insofar as he was interventionist at all, the Prussian administrator's class model inclined him to antidevelopment positions. The French elite ad-

TABLE III. FATHERS' OCCUPATIONS OF ELITE
ADMINISTRATOR INDUCTEES
(Per Cent—Gross Approximations)

Period	Noble	Higher Official	Liberal Profession	Business and Manager	Teacher	Clergy	Lower Official	Shop-keeper and Clerk	Manual Worker
France									
Preindustrial	1	44[a]	7	18	0	0	30	0	0
Take-Off	8	20	20	16	—[b]	0	20	8	8
Industrial									
Post-World War I	6	21	10	20	—	0	20	15	8
Postindustrial	5	26	17	19	—	0	13	13	7
Great Britain									
Take-Off	8	8[c]	23	21	—	14	6	20	0
Industrial									
Pre-World War I	4	4	12	25	12	19	7	10	7
Industrial									
Post-World War I	4	3	12	25	10	10	7	14	15
Postindustrial	2	14	14	24	8	4	6	9	19
Prussia—West Germany									
Preindustrial	33	30	3	7	2	8	9	5	3
Take-Off	27	24	7	10	8	9	8	3	4
Industrial									
Pre-World War I	16	21	7	19	10	6	13	4	4
Industrial									
Post-World War I	5	23	8	23	—[b]	4	27	6	4
Postindustrial	—	14	22	12	—[b]	—	34	13	5
Russia									
Preindustrial	29[d]	29	—	5	—[b]	11	19	—	7

[a] Includes *noblesse de robe.*
[b] Teachers apparently included under lower officials.
[c] Not career officials.
[d] Nobles and higher officials indistinguishable.

ministrator confronted a strong anti-interventionist pressure, somewhat modified by the influence of doctrines like Saint-Simonism in his dominantly bourgeois reference group. Consequently, insofar as French administrative tradition inclined him to define his role as interventionist, the French elite administrator would be development interventionist.

We could turn directly to examination of the administrative elites "in action" (as in Chapter Thirteen) to see whether these hypotheses are valid. Given the limited evidence, this procedure would be unsatisfying. By a protracted examination of how ideological positions and doctrines differentially affected the socialization process, one may hope to provide more convincing evidence, as well as to indicate numerous other factors influencing an evolution which was much more complex than the scheme presented so far indicates.

CHAPTER FIVE

The Family and Socialization

Closed recruitment of an administrative elite significantly affects the relation of the administrator to the class structure of his society. Even when recruitment is from specific families, however, socialization by the family is only one aspect of segregated socialization for elite roles. The relative significance of familial socialization depends both on the family structure and the nature of the roles.

One must distinguish carefully between recruitment of sons for the elite administrative career and patrimonial transmission of specific offices. The latter practice is characteristic of preindustrial administrations; indeed, regression to patrimonial office-holding is a reliable indicator of cyclic aristocratic reaction. Obviously treatment of an administrative office as a family possession violates the principal of universalism, usually accepted as a criterion of "modernity." When patrimonial transmission of office is combined with hereditary local territorial attachments, the particularistic tendency is even more marked. Local magnates, combining traditional authority, economic power, and the legitimization conveyed by patrimonial office, become almost independent of the central authority. The danger for the latter is especially acute in Western Europe, with its surviving feudal characteristics. On the other hand, as indicated in Chapter Four, hereditary office transmission by purchase may offer avenues of social mobility, increasing regime support. We have endeavored to show elsewhere that a modified dose of patrimonial office-holding, where the family involved is not entrenched in a territory, may stimulate development interest.[1]

Generally speaking, however, the birth of the administrations we consider in this book coincides with elimination of patrimonial transmission. The case was clearest in Prussia. As the great historian Otto Hintze points out, before the eighteenth century hereditary possession of offices (generally avocations for prestigious men) was the rule.[2] By the time of Frederick II, only traces of venal office-holding remained. Frederick wanted to recruit officials' sons but not for the *specific* posts their fathers held.[3]

[1] Armstrong, "Old-Regime Governors," p. 20.
[2] *Acta Borussica*, VI, 18, 25 (Hintze's notes).
[3] Rosenberg, p. 81.

Recruitment of officials' sons has a significant bearing on a subject which we touched upon in the previous chapter—self-selection. If young men may choose alternative careers, and if they have a reasonably accurate perception of the demands of those careers, each career will tend to attract those men whose personalities are most adapted to the specific career demands. A retreatist administrative elite, for example, will tend to reinforce its characteristics by recruiting passive personalities or those which prize security highly. In patrimonial transmission, on the other hand, the most common rule is male primogeniture which, if strictly followed, obviously eliminates self-selection. While the evidence is mostly anecdotal, it appears that the stronger the vestiges of patrimonial recruitment for the administrative *career* the stronger the tendency toward primogeniture. Even after the Revolution a magistracy family like the Talabots expected the eldest son to enter that career, whereas his younger brothers were given considerable latitude in elite career choice.[4]

As the French educational historian, Georges Snyders, points out, the strength of primogeniture under the old regime had significant bearing on familial socialization. Eldest sons were reared strictly to make them accept the career and marriage arrangements the family considered essential. Younger sons had to be even more strictly socialized to be prepared to renounce marriage when family resources were limited.[5] Given the high mortality rates, sudden reversals of fortune forcing younger brothers to assume responsibilities incompatible with their previous socialization must have been frequent. Fiction (e.g., Thackeray's *Vanity Fair*) is full of these potentially romantic confrontations. A real-life example is an intendant of Languedoc who reluctantly entered the administrative career at the relatively advanced age of twenty-four only because his brother had died. In this instance, fate was kind to the administration, as Colbert shrewdly perceived after brief acquaintance with the novice administrator.[6] Unfortunately, anecdotal evidence is much more likely to provide us with examples of successes rather than the numerous failures which sudden reversals of fortune produced.

Traditionally, the European family was important in occupational training as well as recruitment. As late as the eighteenth century a noble father took his son on military campaigns to teach him the career

---

[4] Baron Alfred A. Ernouf, *Paulin Talabot: Sa Vie et Son Oeuvre* (Paris, 1886), pp. 2, 7; Michel Lhéritier, *L'Intendant Tourny (1695-1760)* (Paris, 1920), Vol. 1, 4ff.; Snyders, p. 255.

[5] *Ibid.*

[6] Florentin Astre, "Les Intendants de Languedoc," *Mémoires de l'Académie [Impériale] des Sciences, Inscriptions et Belles-Lettres de Toulouse*, 7th Series, Vol. III (1871), 35ff.

of arms. In quasi-technical fields like mining, parental instruction remained the principal training device well into the eighteenth century. In smaller-scale industries family training substituted for technical education far into the nineteenth century.[7] The practices just mentioned are distinct from entrepreneurial suspicion (discussed in later chapters) of elite types of education. In many cases (e.g., French Catholic textile families) an "impractical" secondary education was accepted while technical education specifically applicable to the family enterprise was rejected.[8]

Central administrations were, in a sense, pioneers in setting formal educational requirements. Even so, heavy reliance was placed on family socialization for specific careers. Colbert practiced a "fortunate nepotism" which enabled him to initiate his son and several other relatives in administrative practice.[9] Louis XIV apparently welcomed this practice, believing that the families of future ministers and intendants would socialize them enough to obviate the need for an administrative school. The king himself instructed the Dauphin on royal administration—on one occasion, at least, for several hours running.[10] One-half of a large sample of eighteenth-century provincial intendants came from families with at least one previous high administrator.[11] There is abundant evidence that specific instruction as well as general attitudes were imparted by these relatives. Similarly, Frederick William I gave considerable latitude to a few noble families in putting their relatives in high offices. Frederick II was careful to avoid succession to *specific* posts, but he believed that there was great advantage in having officials who had obtained "a good education and sentiments of honesty and as much as possible had been trained from their youth for the places where they were to be employed."[12]

Both administrators and observers expressed interest in parental in-

[7] Jean Lambert-Dansette, *Quelques Familles du Patronat Textile à Lille-Armentières (1789-1914): Essai sur les Origines et l'Evolution d'une Bourgeoisie* (Dissertation, University of Paris, Faculté de Droit) (Lille, 1954), pp. 527, 590; Jean-Paul Palewski, *Le Rôle du Chef d'Entreprise dans la Grande Industrie: Etude de Psychologie Economique* (Dissertation, University of Paris, Faculté de Droit) (Paris, 1924), p. 248; P. L. Payne, "The Emergence of the Large-scale Company in Great Britain, 1870-1914," *Economic History Review*, Series 2, xx (1967), 538; Horst Beau, *Das Leistungswissen des Frühindustriellen Unternehmertums in Rheinland und Westfalen* (Cologne, 1959), pp. 2off.

[8] Nicole Delefortrie-Soubeyroux, *Les Dirigéants de l'Industrie Française* (Paris, 1961), pp. 250-51.

[9] Yvonne Bezard, *Fonctionnaires Maritimes et Coloniaux sous Louis XIV: Les Bégon* (Paris, 1932), p. 7.

[10] Charles Godard, *Les Pouvoirs des Intendants sous Louis XIV, Particulièrement dans les Pays d'Elections de 1661 à 1715* (Dissertation, University of Paris, Faculté des Lettres) (Paris, 1901), p. 445.

[11] Gruder, pp. 34, 88-89, 117.

[12] Schmoller, "Das preussische Beamtenstand," p. 172; Rosenberg, pp. 82, 86.

struction for the specific duties of administration. They also recognized —occasionally explicitly—that the process of acquiring such knowledge was intimately bound up with more subtle attitudinal formation.[13] It is reasonably easy to establish some of the practical implications of the father-son relationship in career socialization. Possibly more penetrating examination of memoirs and biographies would yield, to scholars trained in psychological theory, insights into the effects varying types of this relationship had upon the sons' adult personalities. A brief look at a few theoretical propositions from recent social psychological literature indicates, however, the enormous difficulties involved in attempting this kind of application. One is the proposition that a father's low job autonomy leads to severe socialization of the son.[14] If this is generally true, one might expect that elite administrators whose fathers occupied similar elite positions would be better able to avoid the extreme pressures for achievement or withdrawal which have characterized upwardly mobile men whose fathers felt circumscribed in their activity. To apply the generalization meaningfully, however, one would have to be able to determine how important the father was, relatively, in socialization. As we shall see, even his role as a career instructor did not necessarily imply a close father-son relationship. Possibly a more plausible generalization is that a helpful but not restraining father image leads to ability to work in an established framework instead of insistence on "rugged individualism."[15] Perception of the father as a career guide might facilitate subsequent adjustment to the administrative organization. Conversely, the boy might become excessively dependent on the father image, with a resulting loss of initiative.

UPPER-CLASS PATTERNS OF FAMILIAL RELATIONS

The fact of the matter is that many predictions based on familial relations are indeterminate when applied to such complex careers as elite administration. The difficulty of applying such theoretical frameworks is enhanced by the fact that European elite family relations were usually quite different from the American context in which the theories were developed. It is true that the nuclear family was well established by the seventeenth century. In this sense, the societies we examine are modern, as compared to the traditional, extended-family type. The extended family was important—and remains so in French

---

[13] J. Schultze, p. 119.

[14] Alex Inkeles, "Society, Social Structure, and Child Socialization," in John A. Clausen (ed.), *Socialization and Society* (Boston, 1968), p. 110.

[15] William E. Henry, "The Business Executive: The Psycho-Dynamics of a Social Role," *American Journal of Sociology*, LIV (1949), 290.

and British upper-class milieus—for establishing the individual's place in social stratification. For example, many upper-class British families depend on grandparents' gifts to maintain the established pattern of sending their boys to public boarding schools. Frequently even rather remote relatives (*vide* Colbert) could be counted on for job placement. But this assistance became salient to the young man starting his career rather than to the small child. Even in seventeenth-century France, according to a recent study, the nuclear family was primarily thrown on its own resources for child-rearing.[16]

Where European elite families have differed most significantly from the American pattern is in the closeness of intergenerational relations. It is highly important to emphasize that parental career tutelage did not imply a close affective relationship. Indeed, such a relationship might have interfered with the strict training which was directed far more to perpetuation of long-term familial interests than to the son's individual welfare. For most European elites during all our periods, a low-affectivity family model has prevailed. As a recent British writer puts it, upper-class parents and children have been on visiting terms since Tudor days, with servants acting as foster parents.[17] After early childhood, the boarding school becomes the parent surrogate.

A psychological explanation for this institutional pattern is Freudian —the father's concern for limiting mother-son affection.[18] "In the stratum of society in which they moved it was considered unhealthy for a boy (it was usually a boy) to have too close a relationship with his mother."[19] Frequently, detachment from the mother is equated with inculcation of achievement motivation.

A less subtle explanation can also be advanced: the high demands which society made on an upper-class woman's time. In Old-Regime France as in twentieth-century England, so many duties (philanthropic, pseudo-philanthropic, and frankly "social") encumbered the mother of future elite officials that she had to leave most of their upbringing to others. Wet nurses were nearly universally employed for infant care. Frequently, eighteenth-century French parents preoccupied with Court life sent their sons to live with country relatives until they had reached the age for entering boarding school. However, the father was always in the background in adolescence to provide status definition and a reference figure for elite values. In England, as large domestic establishments (extended family, tutors, servants) became

[16] David Hunt, *Parents and Children in History: The Psychology of Family Life in Early Modern France* (New York, 1970), p. 90.

[17] S. G. Checkland, *The Rise of Industrial Society in England 1815-1885* (London, 1964), p. 291.

[18] Hunt, p. 175.

[19] Weinberg, p. 171, quoting a manuscript source.

impractical, parents were prepared to devote even less time to child-rearing than in the eighteenth century, with a resultant loosening of affective relations.[20]

Tsarist Russian upper-class patterns, at least in the late eighteenth and early nineteenth centuries, were not much different. Some writers see parallel tendencies in the USSR where most mothers have had to work and fathers were frequently absent, particularly in the generation after World War II. Surrogate socialization by formal educational institutions in the USSR is highly structured to convey the superordinate values which the family no longer instills. There are, however, notable differences between these situations and those common among upper classes in Europe. In contrast to the European pattern we are concerned with, socialization in the USSR is a mass rather than an elite phenomenon. The two patterns also are difficult to compare because not only are Soviet boys and girls unsegregated, but female figures (teachers and peer-group leaders) predominate heavily. The same is true, of course, of the United States—to the marginal degree to which structured socialization outside the family occurs at all.[21]

A pattern more directly relevant to our interest is the change in French bourgeois family relations in the early nineteenth century as the bourgeoisie replaced the old nobilities as the principal upper class. Even higher bourgeois families in Paris maintained stronger affectivity relations than aristocrats. After 1830, however, the higher bourgeoisie came under strong pressures to adopt *mondaine* behavior patterns to maintain class homogeneity. A rather striking indicator is the tendency to abandon intimate family social activity such as singing around the dinner table for postprandial separation of the sexes followed by formal piano recitals.[22] Fictional accounts corroborate this trend. The increasingly stylized social relations of the *Famille Boussardel* (Philippe Hériat) as it entered the great bourgeoisie of the mid-nineteenth century are in sharp contrast to the intimate, slipshod downwardly mobile Pasquiers depicted by Georges Duhamel. It is highly significant to note, as does a recent literary scholar, that Proust's Madame Verdurin, a classic example of the upwardly mobile bourgeoise, strove to secure celebrated professional musicians and made a show of respect for their talent. Aristocratic salons, on the other hand, continued to rely on conversation and card-playing; if they had music at all, it was by hired musicians.[23] In other words, in elaborating a distinctive style, the French

[20] *Ibid.*, p. 174; Snyders, p. 218.

[21] Bronfenbrenner, pp. 72-73, 80-98, 108-109.

[22] Edmond Goblot, *La Barrière et le Niveau: Etude Sociologique sur la Bourgeoisie Française Moderne* (Paris, 1967), pp. 96ff.

[23] Seth L. Wolitz, *The Proustian Community* (New York, 1971), p. 75.

upper-middle class competed with the aristocracy instead of imitating it. Boys reared in such families early acquired achievement models stressing personal, specialized distinction. Since elite administrators' families, whether or not the men were of higher bourgeois origin themselves, tended to adopt the life style of this class, the distinction between aristocrat and official was heightened.

SOCIAL ISOLATION OF PRUSSIAN ADMINISTRATORS' FAMILIES

Alone among nineteenth-century elite families we examine, the Prussian family insisted on raising its own children. Indeed, the increase of bourgeois elements meant that familial upbringing was more protracted than in the eighteenth-century elite when the Junker gentry sent its boys to cadet schools at the start of adolescence. "The spiritual unity" of the home and the school was an ideal with considerable practical significance; for example, fathers coached their sons in Latin. Boarding schools were virtually unknown. Within the family, forms of entertainment predominated—amateur music, family singing, theater parties—in which all could participate.[24]

The ability of the Prussian administrative elite to maintain its family-centered life style was due to several factors. The rustic provincial aristocratic life provided no *mondaine* model. Career patterns physically isolated *Beamten* families from cosmopolitan influences which might have drawn the mother from the home. Judges, for example, "stagnated" in careers which almost never took them to towns of over 20,000.[25] Administrative officials had broader experiences, but even their crucial career stage (*Regierungsrat*) was usually passed in smaller cities where officials set rather than emulated life styles. In the early nineteenth-century towns, the few nonservice nobles often did not possess the special education known as *Bildung* which was a prerequisite for upper-class social participation. Entrepreneurs and merchants (except a few patricians and, toward the end of the century, the very wealthy) kept to their own stratum for marriage and other social relations. The only large groups qualified by education to associate with the officials were deferential secondary school teachers and Protestant clergymen.[26]

[24] Fritz Blättner, *Das Gymnasium: Aufgaben der höheren Schule in Geschichte und Gegenwart* (Heidelberg, 1960), p. 165.

[25] Sellow, "Rang und Gehalt in Justiz und Verwaltung," *Preussische Jahrbücher*, LXXVIII (1894), 126.

[26] Kohn-Bramstedt, p. 257; Friedrich Zunkel, "Beamtenschaft und Unternehmertum beim Aufbau der Ruhrindustrie, 1849-1880," *Tradition*, IX (1964), 262; A. Ernst von Ernsthausen, *Erinnerungen eines preussischen Beamten* (Bielefeld, 1894), p. 83; cf. Johannes Ziekursch, *Beiträge zur Charakteristik der preussischen Ver-*

It appears that the isolation of official families persisted in the capital. Under Frederick II, Berlin was a small town; at the end of the Second Reich it rivaled Paris in size, but was far behind in prestige or cultural facilities. Though all higher officials could be received at the Prussian (Imperial) Court, middle-class women in their families could not. Even officials' wives of noble birth did not, it is said, frequent Court circles.[27] Frederick William I had established a strict separation of personal and official spheres which the administrative elite, in sharp contrast to its British and French counterparts, complacently continued.[28] For a while in mid-century young officials and intellectuals gathered in literary clubs like "Der Tunnel über der Spree." Generally, though, administrative elite relations with business circles (particularly financiers) were as slight as in the provinces.[29]

Prussian officials had more freedom in their personal life style in Berlin than in the provinces. In the preindustrial period several led dubious personal lives without injuring their careers. Baron C. A. von Hardenberg's scandalous divorce and dubious remarriage in another time or place (Berlin of the 1930's or London of the 1890's) might have been disastrous.[30] At provincial posts the official was expected to maintain a living standard—perhaps more material than moral—appropriate to his superior station. Pay rose steeply with age to enable the official to live prestigiously after he had acquired high rank. The low (sometimes nonexistent) salaries for men in their twenties and thirties kept out most without private means. For most of those who could maintain themselves through the arid years, postponement of marriage and drastic limitation (by nineteenth-century standards) of the number of children was hardly avoidable.[31] Confronted with an entrepreneurial counter-role emphasizing material achievement, the Prussian officials' reaction was social withdrawal. Any group with high status, especially if it is recruited semi-ascriptively, is likely to create a distinctive life style to avoid allowing material possessions to become the supreme class criterion.[32] The partially aristocratic model followed by

---

waltungsbeamten in Schlessien bis zum Untergange des friderizianischen Staates (Breslau, 1907), p. 94, for late eighteenth-century Silesia.

[27] Albrecht Wagner, *Der Richter: Geschichte, aktuelle Fragen, Reformprobleme* (Karlsruhe, 1959), p. 72; Rudolph von Delbrück, *Lebenserinnerungen, 1817-1867*, Vol. 1 (Leipzig, 1905), 113, 194.

[28] Schmoller, "Das preussische Beamtenstand," pp. 26off.

[29] Kohn-Bramstedt, p. 314.

[30] G. Ford, pp. iii, 277; cf. Friedrich and Paul Goldschmidt, *Das Leben des Staatsrath Kunth* (Berlin, 1881), p. 42, for a similar instance.

[31] Gillis, "Aristocracy," p. 121.

[32] Peter M. Blau and Otis D. Duncan, *The American Occupational Structure* (New York, 1967), p. 437.

the Prussian administrative elite undoubtedly led to the skewed salary scale, but the latter in turn had a feedback effect on heightening the quasi-aristocratic isolation of the official groups.

UPPER-CLASS HOMOGENEITY IN BRITAIN

In its openness to general upper-class social life, the British administrative elite was almost the polar case of the Prussian. According to a top administrator writing in the late 1930's, the differences between the elite administrator and other members of the higher professions (barristers, headmasters, publishers, Members of Parliament) with whom he associated were "slight and superficial against the fundamental likeness of belief and feeling. All through his career he is far more an Englishman of his age and class than he is a civil servant."[33] The elite administrator had, usually, two servants; he played golf and tennis; and, of course, he sent his children to public schools.[34] In style and interest this homogeneous upper-class world was different from the French upper-middle class, however. A Forsyte might collect paintings, but generally (as Galsworthy himself suggests) the nineteeth- and early twentieth-century British upper class was suspicious of the French emphasis on visual arts and beauty in dress and in the home.[35] As many observers have remarked, British upper-middle-class circles were less open than were the French to science as well as to the arts.

The reasons for this difference will appear later. Certainly the two elites were superficially similar in their metropolitan character. Most English elite administrators came from southeast English, if not London, families. More than any other elite we examine, their careers were exclusively metropolitan. Until World War I, at least, proximity of residence and the easy pace of work facilitated social intercourse. For decades after that, institutions like the London clubs made it easy for the administrators themselves to get together, although their families may have been more isolated. The main reasons why this metropolitan environment had such a low impact on socialization, however, lie elsewhere.

AMBIGUOUS SOCIAL POSITION OF FRENCH ADMINISTRATORS

The French administrators' careers introduced them to more varied milieus. Prefectural corps members normally spent their entire service

---

[33] Harold E. Dale, *The Higher Civil Service of Great Britain* (London, 1941), p. 109.

[34] *Ibid.*, p. 107.

[35] N. G. Annan, "The Intellectual Aristocracy," in J. H. Plumb (ed.), *Studies in Social History: A Tribute to G. M. Trevelyan* (London, 1955), p. 250.

in the provinces; members of other elite bodies spent some time there. At certain periods and places the social isolation of French officials' families in the provinces was as great as the Prussians'. In the 1830's a prefect in Royalist Maine-et-Loire, though friendly to Catholics himself, felt obliged to cease holding even official receptions in order to avoid incidents. The celebrated Baron E. G. Haussmann related how, when he was prefect in an outlying department during the same years, he had to face down an insolent provincial noble who omitted removing his hat in the prefectural office.[36] During the period between 1880 and 1910, provincial relations were equally strained. Conversely, conservative regimes required that the administrative elite maintain a prestigious style resembling the Prussians'. "The public character of the prefectural career and the involvement, to some degree total, of the personality" required in the 1870's that prefects be practicing Catholics and that their wives be good housekeepers.[37]

Declining relative salary levels for French officials led, as in Prussia, to a defensive reaction. Officials' life styles deemphasized material possessions while clinging to upper-middle-class status symbols like domestic servants. Though the data in Table IV relates directly only to

TABLE IV. FRENCH UPPER-MIDDLE-CLASS MATERIAL
STATUS SYMBOLS
(Per Cent in Each Group Possessing Each Item)[38]

Occupational Group	Real Property	Automobile	Servant	Telephone
Industrialists	84	82	67	87
Liberal Professions	57	56	46	75
Managerial Personnel	47	26	21	30
Higher Officials	33	25	25	34

the late 1940's, it is probably indicative of intraclass differences for the entire twentieth century. While officials were below all other upper-class occupational groups in material possessions (real estate, automobiles), they exceeded managers in the most socially prestigious categories (servants, telephones) despite the managers' higher incomes.

The general prestige of intellectual and artistic achievement among all higher bourgeois elements mitigated the administrative elite's inferior material position in the twentieth century as (see Chapter Four) in the Orléanist period. The eighteenth-century tradition that

[36] Eugène G. Haussmann, *Mémoires du Baron Haussmann*, 2nd ed., Vol. 1 (Paris, 1890), 121; de Barthélemy, *Souvenirs d'un Ancien Préfet, 1787-1848* (Paris, 1885), p. 160.

[37] Siwek-Pouydesseau, *Le Corps Préfectoral*, p. 29.

[38] Adapted from Marcel Bresard, "Mobilité Sociale et Dimension de la Famille," *Population* (Revue trimestrielle de l'Institut National d'Etudes Démographiques), v (1950), 563.

the *noblesse de robe* "represented at the same time the nobility, and arts and sciences" carried over to the post-Revolution administrative elite.[39] Physical proximity of most of these elements to Paris was also important. Under Louis XIV, elite administrators like others of the *haute robe* lived in the Marais district. In the first half of the nineteenth century they lived in the Luxembourg area (the old Tenth and Eleventh Arrondissements) along with nobles and the professional bourgeoisie, when *nouveaux riches* were moving to the Rue Saint Honoré and the Monceau area.[40] Attachment to prestigious but unostentatious Left Bank residence has been strong and persistent. Over a century later nearly half of a selected group of elite administrators had been born in four Parisian arrondissements, including three in the Luxembourg area.[41]

Any conclusions drawn from this sketch must be tentative, and largely negative. We cannot definitely ascertain the basic values which the elite administrator acquired through affect socialization in childhood. Probably he acquired considerable respect for authority, the established way of doing things, in all elite cultures. Possibly—though this is much less certain—families in some cultures (Prussian, English) stressed group adjustment more than others (French, Russian). It seems more certain that the interaction between family situation and class models reinforced the trends discussed in the preceding chapter. Doubtless children began to sense their position in the status hierarchy while still in the family milieu, but other societal mechanisms certainly were able to convey this sense adequately. Similarly, the openness of the French family to new currents of ideas may have stimulated its sons to innovative attitudes; but this stimulation was diffuse compared to specific socialization experiences encountered later. Despite the inherent difficulty of examining small-group culture at a distance, all of these questionable propositions could be more closely investigated, as David Hunt's recent book on the seventeenth-century French family shows, by intensive study of memoirs and belletristic literature. For the present, the firmest conclusion that one can reach is that the kind of European family in which most elite administrators grew up has been relatively less important as a socializing institution than the typical American middle-class family, which has been the basis for most theorizing.

[39] See Barber, p. 136.

[40] Daumard, p. 208. Of 177 known residences of *conseillers d'état* and *maîtres des requêtes* in 1773 and 1777 (there is considerable duplication of persons), 33 per cent still lived in the Marais, with another 25 per cent in the nearby Palais-Royal, and only 24 and 19 per cent respectively on the Left Bank and in the new Saint-Honoré area. Roland Mousnier, *et al., Le Conseil du Roi de Louis XII à la Révolution* (Paris, 1970), p. 35.

[41] Girard, p. 311 (derived from Lalumière, pp. 29ff.).

CHAPTER SIX

The Structured Adolescent
Peer Group

Two factors stand out in the adolescence of most European elite administrators: the critical role of the peer group and the care that societal elites devote to structuring the adolescent phase of socialization. There is little doubt that major segments of the elites have intuitively recognized that the period during which the child, emerging from the nuclear family, encounters peer relationships is critical for his subsequent role adaptation. For the first time the child necessarily orients himself more selectively by universalistic criteria of mutuality and impartiality.[1]

Some writers believe that the nuclear family (which, as we have seen, predominates throughout the periods we consider) entails difficulties for individuals who later enter large organizations.[2] Unstructured or adversely structured from the standpoint of elite organizational requirements, the plunge into unhierarchicized peer-group relations may increase these strains. Conversely, a structured peer-group socialization may establish a set of reference figures which will play a lasting part in adapting the individual to his occupational roles.[3] To quote Urie Bronfenbrenner, "If children have contact only with their own age-mates, there is no possibility for learning culturally established patterns of cooperation and mutual concern." Instead, the "quickly rising sadism of peer power" destroys civilized relationships.[4]

BOARDING SCHOOLS AS AN EARLY DEVICE FOR
RATIONALISM AND DISCIPLINE

As David Hunt points out, the sixteenth century in France was a period in which the central elites deliberately sought to make men more rational and self-disciplined.[5] A major focus of this emphasis was the curbing of mutinous youth by lengthening childhood sufficiently

[1] Talcott Parsons and Robert F. Bales, *Family, Socialization and Interaction Process* (Glencoe, Ill., 1955), p. 121.
[2] Robert C. Ziller, "Individuation and Socialization: A Theory of Assimilation in Large Organizations," *Human Relations*, XVII (1964), 344.
[3] See Inkeles, in Clausen, p. 92.
[4] Bronfenbrenner, pp. 117-18.
[5] Hunt, p. 36.

to permit extended socialization. Given the limited societal resources, the process of extending mass socialization had to be protracted and uncertain. The aristocracy clung to traditional extended family tutelage. Only the upper bourgeoisie could be transformed directly by enrolling its sons in boarding schools.

Similarly, a century later in Russia, educators in the central elite tried to make "new men" by removing boys from barbarous families to cadet corps and other boarding schools.[6] Unlike the French *collèges*, open to the entire upper class, Russian schools (one can scarcely distinguish between secondary and higher) were designed to prepare for specific branches of government service. The boys lived in a closed world of dormitory, chancery, or regiment. The best engineering school, the Transport Institute (which took boys at age fourteen) remained a closed institution until 1864, and the best *lycée* was narrowed in scope in 1848 by nominally restricting it to preparing youths for the Ministry of the Interior.[7] As more provincial schools were established, boarding became less important in these minor secondary institutions; but it did not disappear as the major elite preparatory mechanism in Russia until the Revolution. Despite rumors during the Khrushchev period and some subsequent experimentation with boarding schools for talented youth, day attendance has been virtually universal in Soviet secondary education.

Until late in the eighteenth century, French secondary education depended on utilizing seminaries which had been developed to educate the Catholic clergy. In the defensive stance assumed by the Church after the Council of Trent, isolation appeared to be the best method for carrying out this predominantly moral purpose. A major concern was contamination by the worldly attractions of Paris. The importance of the capital was so great that the major religious schools were in or near it. By the end of the seventeenth century, by far the largest Jesuit school was the Collège de Clermont on the Left Bank. The second most prestigious school, the Oratorian *collège* of Juilly, was an easy day's journey from Paris. When the Jesuit system was reconstructed in the mid-nineteenth century, the key unit, the Collège de l'Immaculée Conception, was also located in Paris. To avoid metropolitan distractions, all these *collèges* were designed as boarding schools. By the 1640's Clermont had ceased to be mainly a seminary;

[6] Marc Raeff, "Home, School and Service in the Life of the 18th Century Russian Nobleman," *Slavonic and East European Review*, XL (1962), 301.

[7] Raeff, *Origins*, p. 128; Ivan Ia. Seleznev, *Istoricheskii Ocherk Imperatorskago Byshago Tsarskosel'skago, Nyne Aleksandrovskago Litseia za Pervoe Ego Piatidesiatiletie s 1811 po 1861 God* (St. Petersburg, 1861), p. 423; N. I. Grech, *Zapiski o Moei Zhizni* (St. Petersburg, 1886), pp. 206ff.; Mikhail T. Iablochkov, *Istoriia Dvorianskago Sosloviia* (St. Petersburg, 1876), pp. 444ff.

a large majority of its boys went on to careers in general elite professions like administration, law, medicine, and the army.[8] Nevertheless, the ideal—though not, as we shall see, the practice—remained the isolated *interne* school.

It is significant that this ideal not only survived in nineteenth-century Catholic secondary education, but was strongly favored by post-Revolutionary secular elites. Although Enlightenment thinkers often criticized the boarding school, closed institutions like the Polytechnique were established as soon as the monarchy had been overthrown. It is certainly more than a coincidence that maximum prestige and influence of the Polytechnique as a "Republican seminary" was attained during its first half-century when military disciplinary control of the students' lives was strictest. On the eve of the Revolution, 44 per cent of French secondary school students were boarders. In 1909, 29 per cent of the public secondary schools (including disproportionately large ones) were *internes*. One-fourth of all state secondary school students were boarders as late as 1956.[9] Hippolyte Taine was certainly correct in pointing out that strict boarding schools were favored by both the Church and the state in France, whether or not his characterization of them as "barracks education" was warranted.[10]

Very probably the use of tutors and familial education were relatively more important in eighteenth- and early nineteenth-century England than among the French upper classes. Many English aristocratic families did patronize public boarding schools, but their reputation was not high until the 1830's. Successful middle-class families, on the other hand, avoided a public school education through which their sons might be "instructed to soar above the rank in which nature had placed them."[11] As late as the 1850's a strong argument was advanced (in relation to Civil Service reform) that family education was better than formal preparatory schooling.[12]

The basic change occurred in the generation between 1830 and 1860, i.e., those decades of social transition at the end of the take-off period.

[8] Gustave Dupont-Ferrier, *Du Collège de Clermont au Lycée Louis-le-Grand (1563-1920). La Vie Quotidienne d'un Collège Parisien pendant plus de Trois Cent Cinquante Ans*, Vol. 1 (Paris, 1921), 78.

[9] Paul Gerbod, *La Vie Quotidienne dans les Lycées et Collèges au XIXe Siècle* (Paris, 1968), pp. 102ff.; Stephen d'Irsay, *Histoire des Universités Françaises et Etrangères*, Vol. 11 (Paris, 1935), 130.

[10] Felix Ponteil, *Histoire de l'Enseignement en France: Les Grandes Etapes, 1789-1964* (Paris, 1966), p. 317.

[11] F. Musgrove, "Middle-Class Education and Employment in the Nineteenth Century," *Economic History Review*, XII (1959), 101.

[12] Argument by one Captain H. H. O'Brien, quoted by Edward Hughes, "Sir Charles Trevelyan and Civil Service Reform, 1853-1855," *English Historical Review*, LXIV (1949), 72.

According to some accounts, the rapid rise of the boarding school coincided with increasing pressure by a rapidly expanding upper-middle class for entrance to professional occupations. While those professions which were traditionally most acceptable were stationary in numbers, teaching and related activities offered new outlets.[13] Even if this explanation is true (it has been sharply contested), pressures for employment would not explain the distinctive direction which the secondary school system took. What seems much more important is the fact that the educators who transformed the old, slightly disreputable public school as well as the somnolent universities into major elite institutions were nearly all sons of business families, mostly Quaker or non-Conformist by religion.[14] Yet the new educational elite rejected both the local grammar schools traditionally attended by the middle class and the newer, innovative non-Conformist academies established early in the nineteenth century. Instead, these educators devoted themselves to restructuring locally endowed Established Church schools which had been the neglected preserve of the provincial landed gentry. These erstwhile particularistic institutions were to become the major integrating mechanism for a new upper class, the institutional expression of Thomas Arnold's "theology" of a new, embracing "establishment" uniting Anglican and non-Conformist.[15] In accomplishing this purpose, the headmasters and the Oxbridge dons elevated their own teaching professions from marginal clerical affiliates dependent on the aristocracy to the core segment of the new, integrated English elite.

RELIGIOUS DISCIPLINE VS. METROPOLITAN EXPERIENCE
IN FRANCE

In France schools were less salient as elite integrative mechanisms. Before the Revolution they were dominated by the *noblesse de robe* and less exalted middle-class elements. For example, three-fourths of the Clermont enrollment of Parisian boys was non-noble.[16] The noble contingent, however, was stronger among boarding students because the *épée* nobility was predominately provincial in residence. After the Revolution the nobility, reduced to a peripheral upper-class position, generally attended Catholic secondary schools. Doubtless this circum-

---

[13] Musgrove, "Middle-Class Education," pp. 101, 106.

[14] Annan, in Plumb, pp. 243ff.

[15] W.H.G. Armytage, *Four Hundred Years of English Education* (Cambridge, England, 1965), p. 107.

[16] Dupont-Ferrier, I, 67.

stance explains why, in the new Jesuit *collège* in Paris, only 37 per cent of the students were metropolitan.[17] The dominant higher bourgeois strata, on the other hand, generally sent their sons to state *lycées*; some, like Lycée Louis-le-Grand, the old Collège de Clermont, were actually secularized church foundations. For upper-middle-class boys, study in a great Parisian *lycée* was only a prolongation of their metropolitan experience. For a part of the lower bourgeoisie, on the other hand, attendance at Parisian schools did represent an urbanizing experience. For example, between 1794 and 1883, 85 per cent of the Polytechnique students were non-Parisians.[18]

Continuity of metropolitan experience would have been broken even by study in Parisian schools if these had really been isolated from the upper-class life of the city. In fact, the religious ideal of the isolated, "total" educational institution was eroded as early as the seventeenth century. In principle, *internes* were to set the tone of life at Clermont, but in fact the two thousand day students "whom the parents supervised too little or the teachers supervised badly were prone to lead, in the recesses between classes, the free life about Paris which our students lead today."[19] Inevitably, the *externes* drew the few hundred boarders with them in their urban adventures.

The students' taste for urbanity was not merely frivolous. Deliberately or not, upper classes made demands upon the schools which frustrated efforts to keep them cloistered. The public (including at times high Court personages) were welcomed at major school ceremonies and theatrical performances. Both Jesuit and Oratorian *collèges* established junior "academies" (in imitation of the Royal Academy) with competition in essays and rhetoric. The boys eagerly competed for the attention of the high personages who constituted their elite reference group. "The race of scholars attached more weight to the esteem of the Court and of the City than to the approbation of the regents of the *collège*."[20]

Clerical instructors at times expressed concern about the worldly ambitions these competitions inspired. In fact, however, the late eighteenth-century *abbé* was a member of the elite himself, on intimate social terms with the fathers of his charges. As will be discussed in the next chapter, this solidarity between instructors and the general elite was weakened in the nineteenth century. Enough contacts remained

---

[17] John W. Padberg (S.J.), *Colleges in Controversy: The Jesuit Schools in France from Revival to Suppression, 1815-1880* (Cambridge, Mass., 1969), p. 110.

[18] Pinet, *Histoire*, p. 488.

[19] Dupont-Ferrier, I, 236; Snyders, pp. 36-37.

[20] Dupont-Ferrier, I, 245, 286ff.; Barnard, p. 171.

between the select *professeurs* of the great Parisian *lycées* (particularly Louis-le-Grand and Henri IV) and the upper-middle class to allow the latter to act as the major reference group for students as well as instructors.

MORAL PURPOSE AND CLASS VALUES IN ENGLAND

Capital society was also the dominant reference group for late nineteenth-century English public schools. A. H. Halsey and M. A. Trow are on sure ground when they describe the reformed elite educational institutions as one of the means by which a "serious, if passing challenge to the central, metropolitan aristocratic culture of England by the provincial dissenting bourgeoisie" was rejected.[21] But the way in which these institutions played their part was quite different. Like the French eighteenth-century religious instructors, the headmasters and most of their staff were clergymen. Their objective was a moral education; the superiority of their own professional mission depended on this high purpose. Thomas Arnold's hierarchy of educational values rested on the "concept of the Christian gentleman, of reasonable cultural sensitivity, with a high moral code and a developed sense of social responsibility."[22]

Like the French clerics, Arnold and his emulators required that the schools be isolated so that they could do a thorough job of resocializing youths. The headmasters' concern was colored by a strong belief that "the honourable love of truth" which they identified with the upper-class way of life would suffer a "relapse" if middle-class boys went home to their tradesman families even for the holidays.[23] If the ideology which legitimized the new elite teaching profession was not entirely aristocratic, it definitely opposed the commercial side of bourgeois life. Much the same attitude persists in the headmasters' reasoning today:

> In very few cases do parents have the temperament, the knowledge and experience or the time to be ideal mothers and fathers. It is better for a boy to spend the school term in a house dedicated to meeting his needs than in a home where emotion may warp judgments, inexperience of the young may lead to mistakes, while pressure of business and social commitments may lead to neglect.[24]

[21] A. H. Halsey and M. A. Trow, *The British Academics* (Cambridge, Mass., 1971), p. 75.

[22] Checkland, *Rise*, p. 292.

[23] T. W. Bamford, *Rise of the Public Schools: A Study of Boys' Public Boarding Schools in England and Wales from 1837 to the Present Day* (London, 1967), p. 49.

[24] J.D.R. McConnell, *Eton—How It Works*, quoted in John Wakeford, *The*

Middle-class parents accepted these strictures as individuals because the public school was indispensable for certifying their family's social elevation. Whatever part Oedipal fears may have played in separating boys from home, upwardly mobile mothers have been as eager as their husbands to see their sons acquire the cultured accents which are daily testimonials to elite status.[25] As James Bryce wrote in 1868:

> When his [the manufacturer's] fortune is made, when his income begins to exceed a thousand or two per annum, he suddenly expands from the chrysalis into the butterfly, turns away from the class out of which he has risen. . . . The first step to this is to send his children away from home to a boarding school, nominally to get rid of the dialect, but really to get rid of their cousins . . . .[26]

EDUCATIONAL ELITE SCORN OF INDUSTRIALISM

From the standpoint of the elite as a whole, the leveling of boys' accents was not of use merely "to cure them of provincialism and give them ideas."[27] Although the eighteenth-century *collèges* did help boys from the Midi to lose their accents, provincial *lycées* have been quite effective in standardizing upper-middle-class French. After all, American and German elites appear to function adequately despite heterogeneity of intonation. The major value of the isolated boarding schools for the British upper class was to accommodate the basically urban life style of the predominantly middle-class boys to the "country" style of the aristocracy. Prior to the mid-nineteenth century the only way for the middle class to make this accommodation was to buy country houses and live as squires. This way was no longer entirely feasible for the enlarged upper-middle class. Though many successful Victorian middle-class families originated in provincial towns, they gravitated to London, acquired banking or commercial interests there, and (even if they did buy country houses) kept in touch with the city through their clubs.[28]

The elite educators, although often urban by family background, had always adopted semi-rural life styles, whether as curates, Oxbridge dons, or students. With a few exceptions the public schools they wished to transform were already in rural areas and initially dependent on gentry patronage. If the aristocracy was to maintain its prestige

---

Cloistered Elite: A Sociological Analysis of the English Public Boarding School (London, 1969), p. 37.

[25] Weinberg, p. 170.

[26] Quoted in F. Musgrove, *The Migratory Elite* (London, 1963), p. 24.

[27] *Ibid.*, p. 91.

[28] Annan, in Plumb, pp. 245, 249.

in relation to a middle class which had acquired most sources of power and wealth, it had to reinvigorate the mystique of "nostalgia for land."[29] Mobile middle-class families shared or affected to share this nostalgia, seeking refuge in natural beauty from the hideous urban surroundings. As indicated in Chapter Five, there was an alternative— the creation of urban visual beauty in dress, private interiors, and even city planning. For the late nineteenth-century English elite, however, this way led to a French affectation. Whatever the immediate causes, rural location became an essential for elite education. Thus, as Halsey and Trow point out, universities established in the nineteenth century were placed in expanding industrial towns close to their clientele; but those created after World War II have tended to be in old cathedral towns. As these authors incisively comment, the purpose is to avoid the provincialism which competing urban centers might foster by perpetuating elite institutions which are rural in atmosphere but cosmopolitan in elite attachments.[30]

Pastoral nostalgia is not, of course, an English peculiarity. It was an element of the French Enlightenment which influenced Jeffersonian insistence on maintaining an agrarian America as the "new garden of the world."[31] As in the physiocrats' doctrine, pastoralism is inevitably anti-industrial. What distinguishes nineteenth-century England is that pastoral arguments had to have an ideological basis. The history of railroad construction strongly suggests the presence of an ideological element. When the lines were started, landowners understandably experienced "both sober and hysterical anxiety about what would happen to farm livestock, game, and other wild life, the layout of farms, the drainage of the land, and the social stability of communities so recklessly laid open to influences they had never known."[32] In the 1820's, gamekeepers' attacks on surveyors for the Liverpool and Manchester Railway caused the directors to shift their route away from the lands of antagonistic gentry. After the passage (1845) of a more liberal condemnation act which compensated landlords for intangibles like access to their properties and the view from their manors as well as for the actual strip of land taken, aristocratic opposition to specific projects dissipated.[33] For the educational elites, the railroads may have brought no monetary rewards; but the good transportation they provided was essential if the out-of-the-way rural schools were to attract

29 Checkland, *Rise*, p. 284; cf. Bamford, pp. 4ff.

30 Halsey and Trow, p. 76.

31 Leo Marx, "The Impact of the Railroad on the American Imagination," in Mazlish, p. 210.

32 H. J. Dyos and D. H. Aldcroft, *British Transport: An Economic Survey from the Seventeenth Century to the Twentieth* (Leicester, 1969), p. 178.

33 *Ibid.; Early Victorian England, 1830-1865* (London, 1934), p. 250.

pupils from all over England. One might think that all of these circumstances would have made the educational elite indifferent to the railroads, if not actually favorable. The boys themselves were fascinated by the trains and their engineers, who had become a new type of folk hero. The public school masters, on the other hand, abhorred the railroads, ostensibly because they feared they would "contaminate" the boys.[34] Symbolically, long after railroad time was accepted as a rational standard in the 1850's, the Christ Church (Oxford) clock maintained the old local time.[35] Groups like landowners could be reconciled to the new technology, but the educators needed to oppose it to assert their own superiority.

In Russia, as in France, the pace-setting schools were in the capitals (St. Petersburg and Moscow). After a generation at Tsarskoe Selo (about as far from St. Petersburg as Juilly is from Paris), the outstanding Imperial school, renamed the Alexander Lycée, was moved to the capital itself. Unlike most French institutions, the Russian schools drew a large portion of their students from smaller cities, especially Germans (who had their own university in the little town of Dorpat) from the Baltic provinces. The closed, strictly disciplined schools tended, however, to eliminate specifically provincial traits. As its most famous pupil, Alexander Pushkin, wrote, the Imperial Lycée at "Tsarskoe Selo is the fatherland for us."[36]

PEER-GROUP DOMINANCE AND UNIVERSALISTIC VALUES

At first sight the most paradoxical feature of elite boarding schools is their strong emphasis on egalitarianism in the midst of the status-conscious European societies. For all schools recruitment was heavily biased toward upper-class families. In most societies selection bias for admission to the elite secondary school did not even require an ideological legitimization. Once students were admitted, however, they were treated with strict impartiality. If one reflects on the principles of adolescent socialization mentioned at the beginning of this chapter, the paradox disappears. Precisely because the boys were being prepared to accept universalistic values *in elite relationships*, they had to be socialized in the give-and-take of peer-group participation. At the same time, inculcating a strong sense of in-group identity prepared the boys for their status as members of an elite minority controlling the general society.

Even in Russia equality prevailed among boys in schools like the Tsarskoe Selo Lycée, although at times students were permitted to

---

34 Bamford, p. 60.   35 Dyos and Aldcroft, p. 199.
36 Raeff, *Origins*, p. 73.

bring their own serf-servants. In the French *collèges*, moral motives reinforced egalitarianism; the boys were to be accustomed to humility, hardship, and concern for others. At Clermont some concessions (private rooms and preceptors) were reluctantly made to students of high rank or wealth. In general, though, noble boys were treated like the others.[37] Bourgeois parents also exerted pressure (especially on the provincial Oratorian schools) for equal treatment of students. Until the 1830's boys from aristocratic English families generally attended Trinity College, while even those commoners who had been in the same public school went to Emmanuel. In the reformed universities, only Cambridge Trinity College remained aristocratic in student body. The other Cambridge colleges and the Oxford colleges had become socially homogeneous, though they tended for a time to regional recruitment, with boys from certain public schools seeking to remain together in the same college. From the moment of their transformation, the Arnold-type public schools themselves enforced universalistic standards among the boys, partly to avoid their escape from carefully structured achievement pressures to ascriptive family status.[38] In fact, a fundamental reason for in-group equality was the need (in what Ian Weinberg has classified as an "inmate" culture) to eliminate previous distinctions among the boys so that a new "total" structure could be imposed. The boy was to be resocialized by intense but flexible discipline combined with careful respect for his rights as a person.

In the French *collège* discipline was highly formalized. The Oratorians had a single religious preceptor supervise the student throughout his school career. In the Jesuit schools, one prefect directed ten to twenty pupils. Students were also used to watch over each other, for the aim was total surveillance to curb the dangerous and immoral tendencies of youth. "Eternal vigilance is annoying, but it is necessary."[39] In practice, discipline was usually mild because the educators disliked group and corporal punishment and because the institutions were unable to control nonboarders effectively. Nevertheless, the *surveillants* were outside the peer group both because of their religious state and their age. As a result the boys frequently banded together against them as antagonists.

The Republican schools continued the system of surveillance by older men. They were, of course, nonreligious, as had been the staff in some Old-Regime schools like the Ponts et Chaussées. Michel Crozier identifies the persistent pattern as follows:

[37] Dupont-Ferrier, I, 258; Snyders, p. 138; Barber, p. 138.
[38] Weinberg, p. 110; Rothblatt, p. 235; Musgrove, *Migratory Elite*, pp. 147-48; W. L. Guttsman (ed.), *The English Ruling Class* (London, 1969), p. 200.
[39] Quoted in Snyders, p. 39; cf. Dupont-Ferrier, I, 252; Hunt, pp. 35-36.

There is, on the one side, an intense rivalry between the children, who are led to compete fiercely against each other with the teacher acting as an impartial judge. On the other side, there is a very strong pattern of opposition between the teacher, who soars well above his pupils and delivers the truth in an unquestioned, uninterrupted way, and the "delinquent community" of the children, who can resist the strong pressure of the system only by resorting to an implicit negative solidarity and occasional anarchistic revolts, the famous *chahuts* ("uproars").[40]

All of these frictions were heightened when even a portion of the boys lived constantly together in the school:

In March 1883 the dean of the Lycée Louis-le-Grand expelled a student of the St. Cyr preparatory class. A few days later, when leaving the refectory, a certain number of students, instead of strolling as was the custom, gathered under a balcony. An instructor asked them to keep moving, but his order was greeted by whistles and songs began. . . . They hissed the name of the principal, then, breaking through a gate, attacked the dean's office and began to break the windows in the vestibule. Then they invaded the dormitory assigned to special mathematics students, sacked it, breaking the beds, emptying the mattresses, and smashing the wash stands. The rector was called on for help by the administration, and this high official decided to have a squadron of policemen intervene. . . . The rebel students did not surrender; heaping vulgar insults on the police, some armed themselves with iron bars and fragments of chamber pots. . . . The results were severe: twelve students excluded from all *lycées* in France, ninety-three expelled from the Lycée, sixteen permitted to reenter as non-boarding students, four readmitted after severe reprimands.[41]

Essentially the same system of surveillance was used in Russia; at Tsarskoe Selo servants were employed as monitors and informers in the dormitories.[42] Ultimately, even in elite schools, students banded together against the declining Tsarist authority (see Chapter Three).

THE MANIPULATED PEER GROUP

Unquestionably much of the originality of the public school lay in its adroit manipulation of the peer group. Much depended on careful recruitment. "The extent to which the school can rigorously select its

[40] Michel Crozier, *The Bureaucratic Phenomenon* (Chicago, 1964), p. 241.
[41] Gerbod, pp. 104-105.   [42] Seleznev, p. 154.

entrants has significance for the effectiveness both of the process of socialisation to behavioural conformity within it, and also of the social control techniques on the new boy."[43] For the "founders" like Arnold, the problem was more severe because the rising middle-class parents themselves were less socialized to the values of the school. The situation has also been aggravated by the fact that the boys (to a greater degree, probably, than in France) are often more cosmopolitan in background than the masters.

The secret of public school success has been to have the boys socialize each other. Acting as a group, they are far more effective in overcoming secrecy and resistance than even the best-trained adults. The key elements, recounted many times, are use of top-form boys as prefects with broad powers, including the disciplinary "fagging" assignment, over the younger boys. Shrewdly, the boy-prefect charge is set at five boys (compared to the fifteen to twenty assigned a French religious prefect), for the effective span of control among adolescent school boys is no larger than in other organizations. In recent years the public school prefect has suffered from overloading—his own academic preparation for the difficult university competition on top of his supervisory duties and athletic coaching. As a result, fears are expressed that he may deviate from the "well-rounded gentleman model."[44] Over the generations, however, the prefect system undoubtedly was "a good way to train an elite, which would have to rule in a growing democracy"—assuming that this phrase is not a contradiction in terms. More to our theme, the prefect system provided experience for nonspecialists in "a broad spectrum of administrative tasks."[45]

The public school counterpart to the prefect's authority has been the intense emphasis on teamwork. The rights of all the boys are respected, but the group comes first. The key principle has been that the boy should learn to avoid emotional concern except for things like sports which are inherently unimportant. As a result, in the future he can be counted on to serve established institutional goals without questioning their inherent significance. Obviously this value can be easily redirected to promote acceptance of elite consensus in committees.[46] The public school value pattern avoids the rigidity of the self-made man as well as the intense competitiveness for things that do matter (at least to the individual) common among French students. Moreover, the English ideal—until competitive examinations for university

[43] Wakeford, p. 91.

[44] Weinberg, pp. 24, 184; Bamford, pp. 79, 82.

[45] Weinberg, pp. 43, 49.

[46] Rupert Wilkinson, "Political Leadership and the Late Victorian Public School," *British Journal of Sociology*, XIII (1962), 322-23.

entrance required more stringent intellectual training—was tacit relegation of the intellect to a secondary place: at Harrow in the 1860's cricket alone occupied fifteen hours per week, as compared to less than twice that much time for all academic subjects.[47]

Emphasis on open-air sport was in line with the aristocratic tradition of race meets, hunts, and the like. The actual form of team sport, however, was an Oxbridge innovation. Thomas Arnold admired German gymnastics, but the most important influence seems to have been Charles Kingsley's gospel of "muscular Christianity," which spread down to the public schools in the 1870's.[48] Whatever their origin, the games the boys played were soon sharply distinguished from the masses': cricket and rugby have remained upper-class monopolies as contrasted to the popular soccer. The primacy of sports also reinforced the dominance on rural schools, with ample playing fields.

THE FIXATED PEER IDENTIFICATION GROUP

From the intense convergence of school, prefect system, and team spirit emerged a value pattern unique in large-scale industrial societies. It included the "old-boy" networks based on permanent trust if not deep affection among men who had spent their formative years together. Most secondary schools have been sources of lasting friendships—for example, the long amity of Haussmann, Ferdinand de Lesseps, and sons of the great Orléans family, formed at Lycée Henri IV, lasted through subsequent political vicissitudes.[49]

The unique public school phenomenon is what Weinberg calls the "remote control function." From our viewpoint, the phrase "fixated peer identification group" appears more precise if less elegant. Although an individual usually has several reference groups, he prizes one, his "identification group," as the "source of values" and perspectives.[50] The public school peer group was unquestionably the "identification group" for its adolescent members. But the intense resocialization it accomplished also gave it a prominent, commonly dominant, place in the rich "gallery of significant others" which an adult draws upon. As Brim points out, the figures in this gallery "may be strong enough to lead him to resist present environment even to the point of martyrdom," i.e., the earlier identification group has acquired perma-

---

[47] Reader, p. 105. Academic hours rarely exceeded 30 a week; Rugby in the same period had 22, *ibid.*

[48] W.H.G. Armytage, *The German Influence on English Education* (London, 1969), pp. 24, 27; Checkland, *Rise*, p. 291.

[49] Haussmann, I, ix, 26ff.

[50] Ralph E. Turner, "Role-Taking, Role Standpoint, and Reference-Group Behavior," *American Journal of Sociology*, XLI (1956), 327.

nent preponderance.[51] David Riesman has familiarized us with the related concept of the "inner-directed" man. Usually, however, the latter perpetuates the values learned from a father figure. The adolescent peer group, on the other hand, not only appears at a later stage of socialization, but has been more deliberately structured. Ordinarily, as subsequent chapters will show, the memory of the adolescent peer group was constantly reinforced by other institutions of British elite life. Here we may mention the formal "old-boy" associations which prevented "escape from its [the public school's] hold throughout their lives." Together they enrolled perhaps 1 per cent of adult British males —Eton alone has 12,000.[52] But the unique strength of the fixated identification group—demonstrated a thousand times by isolated colonial officers—is that it does not require the physical presence of the reference group. Instead, it "holds them by a bond invisible but unbreakable, at whatever distance duty may call them from the place it was forged."[53] The occasional deviant (like Galsworthy's hero in *A Flowering Wilderness*) was punished as much by himself as by others.

As Galsworthy implied, the public school ideal was especially adapted to an imperial mission which even in the 1920's had passed its zenith. To be sure, none of the educational reformers foresaw this mission, which was a late "graft" on the public school tradition. By the early twentieth century, however, headmasters stressed recruitment for the colonial service, which was a significant career outlet for their boys.[54] In their formative years, the real "mission" of the public schools was to train professional men. As Table V shows, even the military

TABLE V. THE PUBLIC SCHOOL AND THE
OCCUPATIONAL STRUCTURE[55]

Occupational Category	Father's Occupation (Rank Order: 1=Most Frequent)	Student's Preference	Actual Occupations of Boys Leaving Public School by Period (Approximate Ratios)		
			1820-1837	1846-1877	1884-1907
Business	1.4	2.9	.5	.4	.8
Professions	1.7	1.0	1.0	1.0	1.0
Agriculture	3.6	3.0	—	—	—
Armed Services	3.1	3.4	.2	.3	.3
All Civil Government	—	—	.3	.3	.4
N			c. 130	c. 500	c. 800

[51] Brim, in Clausen, p. 193.   [52] Weinberg, pp. 50, 57.
[53] Quoted from a headmaster's speech, *ibid.*, p. 97.
[54] Reader, p. 205; Robert Heussler, *Yesterday's Rulers: The Making of the British Colonial Service* (Syracuse, 1963), p. 85.
[55] Columns 1-2 based on a sample examined by Weinberg, pp. 149ff.; columns 3-5 based on data compiled from a sample of schools by Reader, pp. 212-14. The latter computation is very approximate, as Reader includes overlapping categories.

profession exceeded all government careers, including local, Home service, and colonial. Equally significant is the tendency of the public school to turn boys away from their fathers' usual occupation—business. "A forum for anti-trade and even anti-science snobbery, it instilled attitudes which were not generally sympathetic to risk-taking individualism and technological innovation" is one British sociologist's harsh judgment.[56] However, a distinction is in order. The kind of business which the public school socialized against was "getting and spending" in direct trade and the manipulative activity of the old entrepreneur. When corporate business itself became bureaucratized, it became a legitimate career prospect.[57]

The fragmentary data summarized in Table V suggests the increasing role of business as an actual occupational outlet for public school boys even during the nineteenth century. The more recent data (column 2) indicates that business competes strongly for students' career preferences, although not nearly as strongly as it would if the boys wanted to follow their fathers' occupations. This data may be compared to the figures in Table III, which indicate the high importance of British business families as sources of administrative elite recruitment, as compared to the Continent. Both types of data tend to support the inference that an extraordinary feature of British adolescent socialization has been replacement of values characteristic of the commercial bourgeoisie. In Prussia and France, on the contrary, the high level of self-recruitment of officials (see Tables II and III), together with the complex class relationships discussed in Chapter Four, has made this feature less salient.

Since public schools have tended to set the style for all British secondary schools, it is difficult, especially in utilizing aggregate data for recent decades, to decide which institutional categories to include when considering socialization effects. Day schools requiring high fees conform as closely to the public school model as their necessarily relaxed control over their pupils permits. Grammar schools are closer to the public-school type than other local schools depending wholly on tax support. The significance of the fee-paying school as a mark of upper-class status has to a considerable extent replaced that of the public school. In 1954, although only 67 per cent of persons with incomes over £1,000 had attended such schools, nearly all (95 per cent) sent their children to them. Conversely, only 7 per cent of British respondents indicated that they would make the financial sacrifice required to send their children to any type of fee-paying school, if they were offered places in one. As a matter of fact, only some 5 per cent of

[56] Wilkinson, p. 328.
[57] See Chapter Seven.

the children of the appropriate age level did enter such schools, although 10 per cent of all secondary school graduates came from them. As elite selection mechanisms, fee-paying schools were effective; they produced 60 per cent of Oxbridge entrants, six times the proportion of all secondary schools.[58]

FRATERNITIES AS A SURROGATE FOR THE STRUCTURED ADOLESCENT PEER GROUP

Lacking boarding schools, the Prussian elite could not experience the intense resocialization that the British, the Russian, and the French (apparently in that order) underwent. A recent historian of the *Gymnasium* has noted that socialization of bourgeois boys to aristocratic values (*Erziehung*), as contrasted to instruction (*Unterricht*), may be impossible outside of boarding schools.[59] In the eighteenth century, to be sure, the cadet academies tutored boys from provincial noble families in the social graces:

> The history of the *Ritterakademien* informs us that the young Cavaliers did not regard themselves as "students." No wonder, since indeed they were completely sure of themselves on the dance floor, in conversation, and in hunting; the theological or half-clerical teacher was taken aback by so much assurance.[60]

Probably a main source of weakness of the academies was just this inability of the low-status teacher corps to structure the socializing experience. The peer group appears to have been left to a considerable extent to its own resources: "not in learning but in life in common, in which one through conversation, games, dancing, and competition exercised and perfected himself in the qualities which were later expected of him."[61] At any rate, the noble academies never played a major role in preparation for civil administration, as contrasted to military careers. By mid-nineteenth century, suggestions that boarding schools be revived for boys destined to become officers were rejected because of the expense and because even faulty education by tutors at home was considered superior to boarding schools.[62]

There is no doubt that the nineteenth- and twentieth-century *Gymnasium* exerted a low socializing effect compared to boarding schools. In his suggestive comparison of fictional images, W. R. Hicks points out that the English boy, however vigorous and exceptional, adapts to

---

[58] Bamford, p. 47; Wakeford, pp. 27-29; Rothblatt, p. 272.
[59] Blättner, p. 334.   [60] *Ibid.*   [61] *Ibid.*, p. 307.
[62] Karl Demeter, *The German Officer-Corps in Society and State 1650-1945* (London, 1965), p. 287.

school pressures; in Germany, despite formally greater teacher authority, he conquers or escapes because the peer group is weaker. Very likely weak, unstructured adolescent peer-group socialization allowed greater scope for parental authority—which may be the real source of the myth of the authoritarian German father.

Structurally, the effect of peer-group pressures had to be lower not only because of the daily "escape" to the ascriptive family milieu, but because of the small size of the school peer group itself. Middle-class fathers with higher education as well as nobles regarded secondary school study in their home towns as advantageous both financially and pedagogically. Since, as we have seen, such men dominated each provincial town, they were able to obtain a regular secondary school (*Gymnasium*) even if it meant that middle-class families had to send their children to a type of school which they disliked.

As Table VI shows, graduating classes were extremely small in both France and Prussia—too small, Prussian commentators readily recognized, for efficiency. However, as we saw earlier, most provincial French *lycées* were not very relevant for elite education. British, Russian, and French *elite* secondary schools tended to be considerably larger. In the eighteenth century, the Collège de Clermont numbered

TABLE VI. CONTINENTAL SECONDARY SCHOOLS[63]

Period	Number of Schools			Annual Number of Graduates		Annual Number of Graduates per School		
	France	Prussia	Russia	France	Prussia	France	Prussia	Russia
Preindustrial	500	90	84	2,000	600	4	7	c. 15
Industrial (Pre-World War I)	590	230	196	8,000	4,000	14	17	c. 20

[63] The French figures are from Gerbod, pp. 12, 96-97, 136. "Early nineteenth century" in this case refers to 1809 when there were about 500 state and private secondary schools enrolling 50,500 students. The number of male graduates is estimated at 2,000 on the basis of the fact that there were about 3,000 twenty years later when the number of state enrollees was only 30 per cent greater, although private schools had increased considerably. Figures for 1914 are more precise. German data for the early nineteenth century is from Friedrich Paulsen, *Geschichte des gelehrten Unterrichts auf den deutschen Schulen und Universitäten vom Ausgang des Mittelalters bis zur Gegenwart*, Vol. II (Leipzig, 1897), 287 (91 recognized *Gymnasien* in Prussia in 1818); at which time there were about 600 graduates (Blättner, pp. 144-45), as contrasted to 3,972 in 1884. There were, however, over 5,300 graduates by 1900; consequently the French and Prussian figures should not be taken as indexes of societal educational attainment. Joh. Conrad, *Das Universitätsstudium in Deutschland während der letzten 50 Jahre: Statistische Untersuchungen unter besonderer Berücksichtigung Preussens* (Jena, 1884), p. 223, gives the number of 232 Prussian *Gymnasien* for about 1884. Russian figures are from V. R. Leikina-Svirskaia, *Intelligentsiia v Rossii vo Vtoroi Polovine XIX Veka* (Moscow, 1971), pp. 52-53; totals for boys' *gimnazii* and their students for 1860 and 1899. Annual graduates are for selected major *gimnazii* in St. Petersburg, Moscow, and a few provincial centers.

about 200 boys in each upper grade, though Juilly had far fewer. A century later Louis-le-Grand graduated as many as 70, and Lycée Henri IV half as many. Similarly, Eton had on the order of 30 boys in each upper form.[64] The Prussian elite, particularly boys destined for the elite administration, were, on the contrary, likely to be educated in the small *Gymnasien* of the provincial towns where their fathers were serving.

Apart from the weakness of peer-group influences—or simply absence of competitive stimulation in classes—the Prussian boy lacked exposure to cosmopolitan influences. As was discussed in Chapter Five, the relatively isolated *Beamte* family, however well-educated, was not urbane; consequently, it could not supply a very wide range of social experiences. Even when he went to the university, the Prussian youth very likely lived in a small town, for centuries earlier distrust of bourgeois and popular influences had led to location of most German universities in little places like Göttingen, Heidelberg, and Halle.[65] At the university level, however, some integrating experience was indispensable for men who were to assume elite roles. Increasingly in the second half of the nineteenth century formation of an interlocking elite composed of the officials, the nobility, and the upper-middle class required (as Joseph Ben-David and Randall Collins suggest) an upper-class socializing mechanism.[66] Since the small-town *Gymnasium* was necessarily promiscuous, to acquire elite socialization upper-class students had to be segregated at the university level.

National integration of the provincial upper-class students was also required. In the eighteenth century Prussian youths were legally restricted to Prussian universities, but by the late nineteenth century wealthier ones moved freely to non-Prussian institutions like Heidelberg, or to Göttingen, acquired by Prussia as late as 1866. At the same time, as Ben-David and Randall point out, it was important to respect the nominal unity of the university student body and to preserve the general competitive atmosphere by requiring upper-class youths to compete with students from the lower-middle strata.[67]

The solution to this complex socialization requirement was what one may call a "delayed adolescent peer-group" experience. Some of this experience was acquired in military service, which inculcated

[64] Gerbod, p. 98; Weinberg, p. 57; Dupont-Ferrier, I, 129.

[65] Franz Eulenburg, "Die Frequenz der deutschen Universitäten von ihrer Gründung bis zur Gegenwart," *Abhandlungen der philologisch-historischen Klasse der Königlich-sächsischen Gesellschaft der Wissenschaften*, XXIV (1906), 79.

[66] Joseph Ben-David and Randall Collins, "A Comparative Study of Academic Freedom and Student Politics," in Reinhard Bendix (ed.), *State and Society: A Reader in Comparative Political Sociology* (Boston, 1968), p. 419.

[67] Cf. *ibid.*, p. 420.

absolute loyalty and obedience, but also fostered upper-class solidarity among reserve officers. By 1900, 70 per cent of the elite administrators had had such service, many in aristocratic regiments.[68] The most important mechanism, however, was an adaptation of the originally "subversive" student fraternities. The *Korporationen*, formed in the eighteenth century, were accepted as part of the status quo earlier than the *Bursenschaften*, which the Prussian authorities still suspected in the 1860's. Eventually, however, both types of fraternities (in contrast to looser, *Wandervogel* youth groups not specifically associated with the universities) became prime instruments for segregating upper-class students.

The fraternity was particularly suitable because, like the early public school, it already embodied much of the semi-aristocratic model which constituted the basis for class coalescence. This observation is not entirely novel. Max Weber noted that remnants of "knightly style" included both British social clubs and German fraternities.[69] In the heat of World War I another German writer went so far as to accuse Rhodes scholars of importing into the German universities, via the fraternities, "foreign and inimical" habits of social privilege, dilettantism, and emphasis on sports:

> They recruit from the same strata as English [clubs], the upper stratum of rulers, land-owning nobles, large industry, higher officials, and army, or from circles which eagerly strive for social attachment to these groups. Just like the English student associations, they are based on worldly education and concern for lasting contacts which draw their members throughout their lives into a ring of fraternity brothers which will watch over them and also assist them in social and career concerns as the Freemasonic lodges do for their German middle-class lodge brothers.[70]

The original fraternities developed in the same milieu as the Rosicrucians, with the same pseudo-feudal and obscurantist pretensions. In contrast to France, the nobility dominated German university life in the critical century and a half between the impoverishment of the burghers in the Thirty Years' War and the Napoleonic Wars.[71] In the seventeenth century German aristocrats had adopted French customs like formal dueling with the rapier.[72] By the end of the eighteenth cen-

---

[68] Gillis, *Prussian Bureaucracy*, p. 204.

[69] Weber, *Economy*, III, 999.

[70] Richard Schmidt, "Die akademische Vorbildung des deutschen Beamtentums," in Grabowsky, p. 68.

[71] Eulenburg, p. 79.

[72] Max Bauer, *Sittengeschichte des deutschen Studententums* (Dresden, n.d.), pp. 60-61.

tury the bourgeois element in the student body was much stronger. In a development which included a reaction against French influences, an accommodation with the noble model, and an aping of Masonic rituals, archaic "medieval" styles were revived by the fraternities.

Stylized duels with the "German" saber became the major criterion for distinguishing elite fraternities from lower-middle-class student organizations. After the *Bursenschaften* agreed to "give satisfaction" for ritual insults, they were accepted on a par with the *Korporationen*.[73] As a rule, absolute rulers formally forbade duels, partly because they were costly in time and lost manpower, but also because they strengthened aristocratic solidarity. When the Russian war minister D. A. Miliutin proposed (in the 1860's) courts of honor and duels as devices to raise morale, they were attacked as "democratic" precisely because they would have promoted equality among military officers, and with it solidarity against the autocratic Tsar.[74]

Among nineteenth-century German upper-class youths, however, dueling had become the supreme symbol of equality for the in-group and exclusion of all others. As long as he accepted the quasi-aristocratic group standards, the wealthy bourgeois fraternity youth was treated as an equal. The fraternities were major forces for socializing students to accept aristocratic contempt for "too much" learning. Instead the Prussian "all-around man" was required to devote most of his early university years to drinking sessions and the ceremonial duels. Neither practice was really more dangerous than the rugby field, but their deliberately archaic quality tended to divorce the student even more, perhaps, from contemporary technological and economic developments.

The effect of the fraternities on overcoming provincialism is far more ambiguous than that of the great French or British boarding schools. After 1849 the *Korporationen* successfully formed associations linking individual university fraternities, but the *Bursenschaften* had more difficulties with their cartels. Essentially the associations were loose leagues of independent clubs rather than national organizations. Some organizations stressed particular localities in recruiting; generally university students tended to associate with men from the same part of Germany. As a curious example, one may cite a cram file marked "only for Rhenish or Westphalian blood."[75] But the "old gen-

[73] Georg Heer, *Geschichte der deutschen Bursenschaft*, Vol. IV. *Die Bursenschaft in der Zeit der Vorbereitung des Zweiten Reiches, im Zweiten Reich und im Weltkrieg von 1859 bis 1919* (Heidelberg, 1939), p. 29.

[74] Hans Peter Stein, "Der Offizier des russischen Heeres im Leitabschnitt zwischen Reform und Revolution (1861-1905)," *Forschungen zur Osteuropäischen Geschichte*, XIII (1967), 433.

[75] Eugen Richter, "Die Vorbildung der höheren Verwaltungsbeamten in Preussen,"

tlemen" in government and business who constituted the force for continuity in the fraternity system had no difficulty singling out novices from "acceptable" fraternities for favor. The dueling scar was as ineradicable as the public-school accent.

ARCHAISM AS A MECHANISM FOR ACCOMMODATING ARISTOCRATIC VALUES

All European elites, except the Soviet, have perceived the need for segregated intensive socialization at the adolescent stage. Probably Marion J. Levy is right in generalizing that such strong socialization is required to eliminate particularism and provide universalist culture in any semi-traditional feudal society (he cites Japan) which recruits its bureaucracy from a specific upper class.[76] In the nineteenth and early twentieth centuries Europe had long ceased to have a traditional social order, but upper-class recruitment was still dominant. In fact, in Great Britain and Prussia the peculiar difficulties of amalgamating new and older upper-class segments required stronger adolescent socializing institutions than had hitherto existed.

In this perspective, as in others we have noted, France appears more "modern." An elite secondary school system dominated by semi-bourgeois elements had already evolved during the preindustrial period. General acceptance of bourgeois values during the early nineteenth century greatly reduced the pressures for segregating adolescents so that they could be resocialized to aristocratic values. As a result, the adolescent peer group was less stable, less under general elite control than in the other two countries or in Russia until near the end of the nineteenth century. Even in Russia, as Marc Raeff writes, the shifting of adolescent allegiances to the boarding school peer group and its prolongation in impersonal service organizations constituted (in the early nineteenth century) a "pedagogical orientation [which] formed in the nobility a self-image and social ethic much more like those of the Western bourgeoisie than of the feudal aristocracy."[77] On the other hand, there was no need for Russian, still less French, adolescent peer groups to adopt the archaic anti-industrial symbols which accommodation with the aristocratic class model produced in England and Prussia. A very recent Soviet work points out that Russia proper (the former Baltic German Dorpat University was an exception) has never

Preussische Jahrbücher, XVII (1866), 13; cf. Michaelis, p. 42; Adolf Wermuth, *Ein Beamtenleben: Erinnerungen* (Berlin, 1922), p. 32.

[76] Marion J. Levy, Jr., *Modernization and the Structure of Societies: A Setting for International Affairs*, Vol. 1 (Princeton, 1966), 116ff.

[77] Raeff, *Origins*, pp. 129, 140.

had "university towns" like those of England, Germany, and the United States, isolated from the main metropolitan centers.[78] The closed Russian institutions, however, were no more conducive to adolescent acquaintance with currents of ideas in the broader society than were the English boarding schools or the Prussian provincial milieu. Because of the dominance of day pupils and the established salience of outside elite reference groups, French adolescents in the great metropolitan schools were much more open to ideas and values prevailing in the upper-middle-class circles.

[78] B. S. Khorev, *Problemy Gorodov: Ekonomiko-Geograficheskoe Issledovanie Gorodskogo Rasseleniia v SSSR* (Moscow, 1971), p. 163.

CHAPTER SEVEN

The Classics Barrier

O NE major aspect of the secondary school has been to serve as the structural focus of the adolescent resocializing process. From the point of view of the European upper class, an equally important aspect has been as a screening device to stabilize class status. For the old aristocracies, of course, no institutional mechanism was necessary; the quality of nobility, acquired at birth, was self-sufficient. The bourgeoisie, on the other hand, ostensibly depended on achievement criteria. Strict adherence to these criteria is by definition opposed to hereditary transmission of status; yet, as we have noted at many points, the higher bourgeois family tried successfully to transmit its status to its children. Inheritance of material possessions alone was not sufficient, since the adult status increasingly was related to occupation. Under the universalistic principles which the middle classes themselves had fostered, however, occupations had to be recruited by universalistic criteria, generally educational. What these criteria were, however, depended not only—as many writers have assumed—on the interests of the middle class in general, but on those segments particularly involved in the educational process.

As the figures in Chapter Ten indicate, whatever the formal educational requirements for entrance to the administrative elite career prior to 1945, the actual level at which a large majority of a male cohort ceased to be eligible in any European society (except the Soviet) was at secondary school completion age. The cutoff point for eligibility to the administrative elite generally reflected the conditions governing admission to other societal elites. As a French newspaper noted in 1845, "A new nobility is being formed . . . quietly, the nobility of the baccalaureat, the feudality of lights."[1] Few who did not complete secondary education were admitted; a large majority of those who did finish secondary education eventually acquired elite occupational roles. In contrast to the United States, and still more to the USSR, during the take-off and industrial periods an overwhelming majority of Western European secondary school graduates went on to complete higher education as well. This generalization also applies to the last generations of pre-Revolutionary Russia. With certain exceptions (mainly Russian), secondary school education was identical for future

---

[1] Quoted in Daumard, p. 272.

administrators and for those who entered other elite occupations. A close examination of how the secondary school acted as a selection mechanism is, therefore, essential to our theme.

One approach, of course, was explicit limitation of secondary school entrants to those whose parents already had upper-class status. To some extent, this approach has been followed by the English public schools, which even interview parents of prospective students. At present, quite a few students from lower-class families are admitted. Even in the nineteenth century formal exclusion of such elements was impossible because terms of endowment of the old public schools stipulated that local boys be instructed. Under the universalistic legal principles governing French and German state education, admission could not be denied on class grounds. With a few exceptions, only in Russia did entrance requirements formally favor noble boys.

In practice, however, few lower-class boys entered the European secondary schools. A high proportion of entrants from lower segments of the middle class dropped out. The reasons why this happened will be explored in detail below, but the general causes are evident. The nature of the curriculum made it virtually impossible for a boy to enter much after the beginning of adolescence (the usual formula has been "eleven plus"). Consequently, the decision was wholly his parents'. The course of study was long: six to eight years, not counting higher education and frequent unpaid training periods for careers like higher administration. While it is hard to reach meaningful estimates of the financial burdens of elite education, Table VII suggests, with surprising uniformity for widely dispersed situations, how heavy costs might be.

TABLE VII. COSTS OF ELITE EDUCATION[2]

Situation	Approximate Date	Cost per Student per Annum	Cost as Proportion of Minimal Upper-Class Income
Parisian *collège*	1750	700 livres	one-half
German Law Faculty	1830	225 thalers	one-half
German Law Faculty	1910	2,000-3,000 RM	one-third
Oxford	1835	£ 200-250	two-fifths
Eton	1960	£ 600	one-third

[2] It should be evident that the data is highly approximate, especially estimates of costs as a proportion of "minimal elite income." It is equally obvious that merely citing monetary costs (even if they could be related to real values) would be virtually meaningless. The French *collège* cost is based on Adrien Delahante, *Une Famille de Finance au XVIIIe Siècle: Mémoires, Correspondance et Papiers de Famille Réunis et Mis en Ordre*, Vol. 1 (Paris, 1880), 104, who explicitly notes that the cost for two boys in the Collège des Grassins during seven years equaled their

It would be misleading, however, to suggest that the ratio of cost of education to income was always the most significant factor. As Table VII shows, seeing that their sons obtained elite educations has been a staggering burden for administrative elites. Complaints have been numerous, from the mid-nineteenth-century Prussian officials to the upper-middle-class Englishman today, that a father cannot assure his son the same standard of education that he himself was given. Yet these groups do manage to bear the burden, partly by accepting relatively low material living standards. Indeed, as we saw in Chapter Four, a key to the attitudes of the administrative elite has been its determination (especially in Prussia) to avoid letting wealth be the prime criterion for status. The marginal advantages that administrative elite families (and associated upper-class segments) do have are their comprehension of the significance of educational screening mechanisms and their strong motivation to utilize them. It is hardly surprising that these strata possess these advantages, for they played a crucial part in establishing or perpetuating the secondary education requirements.

RELIGIOUS DISCIPLINE AND CLASSICS CURRICULUM

The essence of the screening mechanisms can be identified in one word: classics. Like boarding schools, study of the classics was not invented to fit the requirements of the new elites.

> The creators of the Victorian Public School did not consciously devise an education for a governing class; they continued and adapted what had originally been the universal type of education, and because their schools were better than anything else available they attracted those who were or wished to become gentlemen.[3]

Latin was the staple of European education well beyond the Middle Ages. It played an essential part in international communication—ecclesiastical, diplomatic, and even commercial—until the seventeenth

---

parents' household outlays for the same period. Koselleck, p. 483n, provides the 1830 German figure and the information that it equaled half a *Landrat*'s annual salary. Lysbeth W. Muncy, "The Junkers and the Prussian Administration from 1918 to 1939," *Review of Politics*, IX (1947), 489ff., provides the second German figure. Guttsman, *English Ruling Class*, p. 217, provides the Oxford cost estimate; it was generally estimated that a man with £1,000 a year at that time was reasonably well off, and one with £500 might be considered near the minimal elite level. The Eton figure is from the *New York Times*, May 1, 1963, and is compared to starting Administrative Class salaries of £500 (1950's) rising to £4,500. Cf. Wakeford, p. 30, for a slightly higher estimate.

[3] Martin L. Clarke, *Classical Education in Britain, 1500-1900* (Cambridge, England, 1959), p. 170.

century. In England for a century more the general attitude of the aristocracy was one of indifference toward curriculum content; whatever had been taught traditionally was good enough. As Lord Chesterfield told his son: "Classical knowledge is absolutely necessary for everybody, because everybody has agreed to think and to call it so."[4] His typically pragmatic viewpoint was very little removed from his mid-twentieth-century successor in the peerage, C. P. Snow. When asked why he was sending his son to Eton (after opposing privileged secondary schools), Lord Snow replied: "It seems to me that if you are living in a fairly prosperous home it is a mistake to educate your child differently from the majority of people you know socially."[5] A late eighteenth-century Englishman explained the situation more cynically: "The advantages of a classical education are two-fold—it enables us to look down with contempt on those who have not shared its advantages, and also fits us for places of emolument, not only in this world, but in that which is to come."[6] Nevertheless, by the end of the eighteenth century, Latin was declining in England. Many schools emulated Eton's emphasis on Latin versification, but Oxford and Cambridge (the only universities in England) were instructing more in English and assigning greater weight to subjects like mathematics.[7] The public school curriculum was not particularly important as long as it was preparing boys for military, legal, and clerical careers, the traditional occupations of the aristocracy.

The declining hold of Latin on eighteenth-century European aristocracies is better demonstrated in Prussia and Russia. Frederick II encouraged logic, rhetoric, a little Latin and no Greek in his *Ritterakademien*. Apart from the *Galantoria* (riding, fencing, dancing) subjects, noble academies emphasized the subject dearest to Frederick—French. The dominant reference groups for all eighteenth-century German education were the princely Courts which adopted French styles rather than the vegetating middle-class Latin schools in the towns. But where Latin was stressed it was taught as a living language, even in Lutheran schools.[8] For Prussia, a measure of Latin was also important for strictly pragmatic reasons after half of the kingdom came to consist of recently acquired Polish and Silesian territories. There, much upper-class education had been provided, as in France, by Jesuit schools which stressed Latin both for ecclesiastical reasons and because it was convenient for the ethnically mixed population. "For

---

[4] Armytage, *Four Hundred Years*, p. 66.
[5] *New York Times*, February 14, 1965.
[6] Armytage, *Four Hundred Years*, p. 66.
[7] Clarke, pp. 48, 67.
[8] Paulsen, II, 75, 311; Blättner, pp. 50, 108, 307.

jurists, in contrast [to the Protestant clergy] Greek was definitely dispensable, but Latin was indispensable not only because of Roman law, but because of the new Polish territories, where nearly all the educated strata speak Latin," the Prussian educational minister believed in 1798.[9]

Adoption of Latin in Russian schools under Catherine II confirms the view that the language retained considerable instrumental value. Russians needed it to share in Western European culture. Although Russians had no Latin ecclesiastical background of their own, even the mid-eighteenth-century Orthodox seminaries were called "Slavic-Greek-Latin Academies." A generation later their most famous product, Michael Speransky, taught the traditional Latin school subject of rhetoric at the Alexander Nevsky Seminary.[10] Under Catherine, it is said, an official could obtain advancement on the basis of a good knowledge of Latin and Russian.[11]

For Catherine herself and for the higher nobility, however, French was far more important. It was the main vehicle for European upper-class arts—literary, moralistic, theatrical.[12] The Jesuits, sheltered in Russia and Prussia after their condemnation by Pope Clement XIV, stressed Latin rhetoric. Their schools (which, it is said with slight exaggeration, trained a whole St. Petersburg elite generation) were preferred because they provided a French education without the danger of Revolutionary contamination.[13] Despite fears of revolution, the evident progress of science and technology in France did undermine the prestige of a classical education still more. During Alexander I's "Enlightenment" period, French was increasingly regarded as the vehicle for science, mathematics, and technology as well as the fine arts.[14] It was the language of instruction of the new Transport Institute and vied with Latin in the curriculum of the Imperial Lycée.

The situation in France itself was more complex. As a Romance-language, Roman Catholic country, France has naturally been on more intimate terms with Latin than the other countries we study. The educational dominance of the Jesuits, with their strong ultramontane centralizing interests, heightened the importance of Latin. But these were far from being the only reasons why Latin persisted, not merely as an important subject, but as the language of instruction. According to

[9] Paulsen, II, 96, 100ff.   [10] Vucinich, I, 107; cf. Dukes, p. 27.
[11] Adrian Moiseevich Gribovsky, *Vospominaniia i Dnevniki* (n.p., n.d.), p. 31.
[12] Vucinich, I, 128.
[13] Eduard Winter, "Die Jesuiten in Russland (1772 bis 1820)," in Willi Göber and Friedrich Herneck (eds.), *Forschen und Wirken: Festschrift zur 150. Jahr-Feier (Humboldt University, Berlin)*, Vol. III (Berlin, 1960), 181-82; Raeff, *Etat*, p. 300.
[14] Vucinich, I, 192.

Georges Snyders, Jesuit educators believed, perhaps subconsciously, that Latin instruction would further their aim of isolating their vulnerable pupils by setting a barrier between their thoughts and words and those of the profane city so close at hand.[15] In the seventeenth and early eighteenth centuries, Latin instruction and boarding school surveillance were meant to serve the same predominantly moral objective.

Like other educational elites, however, the Jesuits were not entirely masters in their own schoolhouse. In establishing educational standards they were obliged to consider the interests of social groups whose children they instructed. Moreover, cultivated Jesuits shared much of the outlook of other upper-class societal groups. This factor was important in eroding efforts to maintain boarding schools as "total" institutions. The situation was more ambiguous as far as the classics were concerned. The works of the great Greek and Roman poets and rhetoricians had been tolerated—despite obvious deviations from Christian morality—ever since the early centuries of the Church. After the Renaissance the pagan classics were so universally acclaimed that the alternative Greek and Latin literature—the patristic writings—was hardly conceivable as the basis for education. Neither teachers nor the public would have tolerated such a drastic change in curriculum. Moreover, the religious teachers argued, the classics were sufficiently remote from the experience of the student that suitable passages could be safely abstracted for moral instruction. A minority did contend that the pagan elements introduced during the Renaissance were the source of the "sickness in modern society."[16] Similarly, a century later Prussian Catholics attacked "the established school monarchy or school religion" based on the "heathen classics."[17] In spite of such criticism, however, Latin, if not Greek, remained a staple of Catholic secondary instruction in both France and Prussia.[18]

Apart from Jansenist institutions which gradually disappeared, the Oratorian schools were the leaders in vernacular instruction. Latin was taught out of French grammars, French was the language of instruction in the first four years, and French history and composition were stressed. In military academies operated by the Oratorians, French was the sole language of instruction, for the military nobility in France as elsewhere was uneasy in Latin. Oratorian Juilly also stressed the same aristocratic skills as Frederick II's noble academies (fencing, riding, and dancing).[19] Earlier, under Louis XIV, the regime

[15] Snyders, p. 67.　　　　　[16] Padberg, p. 172.
[17] Paulsen, ii, 348; Conrad, p. 103.
[18] Padberg, pp. 110, 180.
[19] Barnard, pp. 158ff., 166-67; Gruder, p. 19; Ponteil, pp. 42-43.

encouraged recent French history as a kind of official propaganda vehicle to glorify the monarch as contrasted to antique heroes.[20]

Along with the progress of the French language appeared more concern for physics and science (earlier discounted as too temporal). Some provincial *collèges* even set up one-month courses in mechanics and sciences. "Many cultivated adults attended these courses, which had no scientific value, but did have the merit of popularizing a new discipline."[21] A more fundamental trend, suggested by Table VIII, was the complete subordination of Latin to French in the cultivated society of the day. Whatever they had used in the *collège*, adult educated Frenchmen obviously read their own language. It is significant, too, that the predominance of the vernacular was established in French publishing around the turn of the sixteenth century. Germany remained at least a century behind.

TABLE VIII. LANGUAGE OF PUBLICATION OF BOOKS
APPEARING IN FRANCE AND GERMANY[22]

Country and Period	N^a (Annual Average)	Latin	French (Per Cent)	German	Other
France, 1598-1616	146	25	73	0	2
Germany, 1701-1710	1,213	41	1	58	0
France, 1699-1701	238	8	92	0	0
Germany, 1791-1800	3,529	6	5	89	0

[a] The reader should note that absolute numbers of publications, as explained in n. 22, are wholly incomparable.

The Revolutionary era definitely subordinated the classical languages to French, despite the fondness of Republican and Imperial orators for classic analogies. As inscriptions on his monuments indicate, Napoleon I believed that French rather than the customary Latin should be the national ceremonial language. Instruction was almost wholly in French in the new national prestige institutions, with mathematics and science taking the place of rhetoric.

[20] Henri-Jean Martin, *Livre, Pouvoirs et Société à Paris au XVIIe Siècle (1598-1701)*, Vol. II (Geneva, 1969), 841.

[21] Irsay, II, 115.

[22] French figures from H.-J. Martin, I, 76, 87, based on surviving deposits of books published in France in the Bibliothèque Nationale. The German figures (Paulsen, II, 690) include *all* books listed in catalogues of the Frankfurt fairs. Obviously the latter numbers will be larger than the total of books published in Germany in the period; the French figures are almost certainly smaller. There is no reason to think, however, that the vernacular:Latin ratios were affected by these factors either from country to country or over time.

CLASS INTERESTS AND THE REVIVED CLASSICS EMPHASIS

Given the decline of the classics in preindustrial Europe, one might have anticipated their rapid relegation to a position of tertiary significance in the secondary curriculum. Instead, a remarkable revival occurred on the eve of industrialization and even during its progress. The mere fact that this occurred suggests that ideological factors were involved. The form and circumstances of the classical revival in secondary education differed enormously in each of the countries. As a result, the legitimizing arguments were varied and complicated. Advanced, as the arguments were, by leading educators of the day and generally accepted by intellectuals, it is not surprising that their ideological content has often escaped detection. By confronting arguments for classic predominance which appear plausible enough within the framework of a single system with contradictory reasoning from another system, the comparative method discloses the ideological nature of the trend.

The Russian case is simple but interesting. It would be a misuse of terms to call the official emphasis on classic instruction there an ideology, for the regime was entirely forthright in arguing that classics emphasis was a prophylactic against revolutionary infection. During Alexander I's last years, the Russian regime became less enthusiastic about adopting Western European "progress"; the Decembrist uprising (1825) accelerated this trend. A special target was the model elite school, the Tsarskoe Selo Lycée. Resentful over their expulsion seven years earlier, Jesuit writers pointed out that several Lycée graduates were among the conspirators, as contrasted (so it was alleged) to none from Jesuit schools. Educators at the Imperial Lycée, of course, rebutted these charges, but they were definitely on the defensive.[23] Nevertheless, for several decades regime opinion (through a process of reasoning which is not altogether clear) feared the classics as purveyors of radical French ideas like Saint-Simonism.[24] In 1848 the classic content of secondary education was even diluted in favor of the "neutral" natural sciences. At many points, too, extreme military deficiencies compelled educational stress on technology, regardless of other considerations. By 1871 the strictly reactionary education minister, D. A. Tolstoi, however, took an intransigently proclassics stand:

Some subjects influence the development of all sides of the human mind, ennobling it and making it more sublime. The study of clas-

---

[23] The documents are reproduced in Seleznev, pp. 53-55 and Appendix, pp. 10-12.
[24] Vucinich, I, 368. Leikina-Svirskaia, p. 35, however, expresses the Soviet position that the main purpose of the classics curriculum was to favor the privileged class rather than to provide indoctrination.

sical languages and literature belongs to this category. Other subjects lead only to a one-sided development of young people. Since these subjects exercise no influence on moral and aesthetic education, they attract the exclusive and premature attention of young people either to political and social problems, as in the case of jurisprudence, or to the material world, as in the case of the natural sciences. In the study of ancient languages—and sometimes in the study of mathematics—all the knowledge imparted to the students is under constant and nearly errorless control, which discourages the formation of independent opinions. In all other subjects, particularly in the natural sciences, the student's interpretation of acquired knowledge is beyond the teacher's control. For this reason, these subjects may engender personal opinions and differing views.[25]

Explicit utilization of classics for their tranquilizing effect is one thing. A sudden infatuation with classic authors at a point in history when strong group interests appear to be at stake requires more subtle scrutiny. The intense German enthusiasm for Greek which produced the educational formula known as *Bildung* was definitely a group phenomenon, not a regime imposition. In a single generation (beginning in the late 1780's and essentially completed by the end of the Napoleonic wars), both the noble academies and the old Latin schools were replaced by a *Gymnasium* education built around the Greek classics.[26]

A strong factor favoring this trend was nationalism. Under Frederick II the aristocracy (with his ardent support) had become Frenchified. The reaction against French influence developed slowly in the late eighteenth century, then intensified after Napoleon's aggression. In Protestant Prussia the reaction was directed against the whole sphere of Latin European cultural and theological dominance. Instead of the placid use of Latin which had persisted for two centuries after the Reformation, writers contended that "the discovery and simultaneous advancement of Greek is the accomplishment of the Germanic peoples who freed Greek for its own sake from the Latin which was still surviving." It was even argued that the Greek and German tongues were fundamentally closer than the other European languages.[27]

Bildung, however, was much more than a nationalist reaction. There is little doubt that the new education was a distinctly bourgeois product:

[25] Reprinted with permission of the publishers from *Science in Russian Culture* (Vol. II, 1861-1917), by Alexander Vucinich (Stanford: Stanford University Press, 1970), p. 60.
[26] See Paulsen, II, 312, and Blättner, p. 122.
[27] *Ibid.*, pp. 109, 124.

Not ignorance of French, but rather ignorance of Greek, they [young bourgeois intellectuals] asserted, excluded one from higher and freer education. In fact, introduction of Greek as the obligatory subject in the schools was carried out at the same time that the bourgeoisie entered society. . . . In the 19th century, the dukes and princes also had to decide to learn Greek in order not to fall behind in education. There, as far as I can determine, are the essential factors which led to the surprising change in the nature of education and the constitution of the schools.[28]

Insofar as it rejected the noble stress on instruction in *Galantoria*, on social graces, on "knowing" for the sake of play, *Bildung* was antiaristocratic. It was also antiabsolutist, in that it proclaimed the creation of a "new man," glorifying individual reason. The Prussian regime did, in fact, fear that the new trend was dangerously liberal as well as impractical.[29] For many years administrators, the military, and landlords were nominally exempt from the Greek requirement. Nevertheless, Wilhelm von Humboldt's immense prestige among the top administrative reformers, combined with the group pressure discussed below, secured formal requirement of Greek as the basic subject for *Gymnasium* graduation (1812). Only government insistence maintained an important place for Latin in the curriculum. In 1834 university admission was made wholly contingent on *Gymnasium* graduation; the following year military officers were also required to have completed the *Gymnasium* sixth form.[30]

As frequently happens in such a cultural development, the final formal triumphs of the Greek *Gymnasium* occurred after the zenith of its popularity. Some signs of returning emphasis on Latin appeared in the 1830's, and that language predominated in the *Gymnasium* by the 1860's.[31] Much earlier, however, a Greek-classic education had become essential for upper-class society. According to Friedrich Paulsen, by the beginning of the nineteenth century the dividing line for marriage and social intercourse was no longer between noble and bourgeois, but between those with *Bildung* and property and those without either.[32]

It is certainly not an accident that this development coincided with the ascendancy of the administrative elite as an autonomous, self-perpetuating stratum. It is true that the older generation of administrators themselves lacked complete Greek educations, but they universally saw that their sons made up for this omission. As was shown in Chapter Four, the emergence of an autonomous administrative elite depended on a tacit compromise whereby top administrators of noble origin set the style and bourgeois officials secured the acceptance of

---

[28] Paulsen, II, 311-12. [29] *Ibid.*, II, 545.
[30] Blättner, pp. 122, 126, 135; Kohn-Bramstedt, p. 156.
[31] Blättner, p. 141. [32] Paulsen, II, 388-89.

educational attainments as an achievement requirement. *Bildung* (i.e., the new secondary education) was only a part of the educational achievement criterion, which depended more heavily (as will appear later) on the legal requirement.

On the whole, however, *Bildung* fitted the needs of the initial phase of noble-bourgeois accommodation. As Humboldt himself wrote in 1793, "Greek literature is and must remain a subject of study for the few."[33] The cost of *Gymnasium* education, as indicated earlier, restricted it to families who had both the minimal means and a very strong conviction of its virtues.

These circumstances may explain why the new secondary education was acceptable, even useful, to dominant elements in the elite. It would be hard to argue, however, that the special form this education assumed was indispensable. As we have seen, some upper-class administrators regarded *Bildung* as rather dubious. As with any other enthusiasm, personal convictions—particularly Humboldt's—were important. But the special position of the pedagogues is inescapably significant. Until the emergence of the Greek *Gymnasium*, Prussian middle-class education had been largely in the hands of the Lutheran clergy, which had a very low social status compared even to eighteenth-century Anglican curates. Even if they were not ordained, until the beginning of the nineteenth century secondary school teachers were identified with the clergy, for they normally studied in the same theological faculties.[34] At the same time, the rationalist tendencies of the Enlightenment were undermining the traditional faith of clergymen's sons, who constituted about 20 per cent of the Prussian university student bodies. Creation of the "new man" through concentration on Hellenic antiquity provided a secular creed to replace the older religion. Traditional Protestants as well as Catholics recognized that *Bildung* inculcated skeptical attitudes. As a surrogate for French Enlightenment ideas, the new rationalist creed had the immense advantages of satisfying national sentiments on the one hand and avoiding a head-on clash with conservative regime interests on the other. At the same time, insistence that the "crown of human education" could be attained only by intense study of the original Greek classics made the pedagogues indispensable.[35]

The first generation of educational humanists in the *Gymnasien* insisted that they were generalists, not just linguists. Each teacher had, in principle, to be prepared to teach all subjects, for they constituted not practical specialties but a moral entity. As in both the *collège* and the public school the basic legitimization of the *Gymnasium* education was moral formation of youth. By asserting this value, the Prussian educa-

[33] Blättner, p. 114.   [34] *Ibid.*, p. 145.
[35] Conrad, p. 103; cf. Paulsen, II, 348.

tional reformers, like the English, simultaneously legitimized their own role as a central segment of the elite, far above the older clerical generation.

Nevertheless, a homogeneous elite of the British type did not develop in Prussia during the first third of the nineteenth century. The great Prussian reform in secondary and higher education occurred a half-century *before* the British; since Prussian industrialization was a half-century *later*, the impact of the two developments was quite different. The educational elite (if that term does not exaggerate its importance) always remained definitely subordinate to the administrative elite. The inflated claims of Greek education—and with them the putative dominance of the pedagogues—diminished rapidly during the middle of the nineteenth century. Instead, the *Gymnasium* teacher retreated to the honorable, but decidedly secondary status of a specialist in mathematics, in history, or, usually, in classic languages.[36]

Popularly known by then as a "philologist" (i.e., a scientist in the German sense of the term), the *Gymnasium* teacher could be moderately satisfied with his status advance.[37] In background as well as in professional identification his ties to the clergy had been attenuated. Data on the fathers of students in the philosophical faculty (where *Gymnasium* teachers prepared) at Halle University (1850-54) indicates only 15 per cent were pastors. The proportion decreased somewhat (to 9 per cent) in 1887-91. Conversely, the same data indicates that teaching ultimately became a significant channel of upward mobility for clergymen's sons: 4 and 22 per cent respectively of all pastors' sons at Halle University in those periods studied in the philosophical faculty.[38]

As Table IX shows, the declining emphasis on Greek in the *Gymnasium* curriculum did not mean a corresponding advance for science and German. Latin actually increased in significance throughout the rest of the nineteenth century. More important, the philological approach of the *Gymnasium* set the style for all secondary education. Instead of moral elevation, rigorous but fragmented training in modern as well as classic languages was the major emphasis of all secondary schools during the latter part of the nineteenth century and beyond. From its beginnings the *Gymnasium* education presupposed that its students came from educated family atmospheres; an "intellectual crisis" would have occurred if many sons of merchants and industrialists had entered. *Bildung* reinforced family ties for the educated milieus led by the administrative elite and it justified exclusion of the "uneducated" from their circle. "Realistic" subjects were scorned as being for "merchants," although some in fact resembled the practical

[36] Blättner, pp. 148, 187.   [37] *Ibid.*, pp. 145-46.
[38] Conrad, pp. 51-52.

aspects of the old noble academies. Indignantly rebuffed when they sought to obtain a secondary education without Greek for their sons, the rising Rhenish entrepreneurial stratum of the mid-nineteenth cen-

TABLE IX. CURRICULUM DISTRIBUTION IN ELITE
SECONDARY SCHOOLS
(Per Cent of Major Subjects)[39]

Period	Latin	Greek	Total Classics	Literature, Native and Foreign Languages	History	Religion and Philosophy	Total Humanities	Total Science	Mathematics	Natural Sciences
France (Classics Specialization)										
Take-Off	—	—	37	25	15	5	82	18	—	—
Industrial Pre-World War I	—	—	47	21	14	6	88	12	—	—
Postindustrial	(16	10)	26	31	15	6	78	22	12	10
Germany (Classics Specialization)										
Take-Off	(34	16)	50	14	10	8	82	18	12	6
Industrial Pre-World War I	(27	14)	41	20	10	8	79	21	14	7
Industrial Post-World War I	(22	15)	37	20	13	8	78	22	14	8
Postindustrial	(23	7)	30	20	15	7	72	27	14	13
France (Science Specialization)										
Postindustrial	(0	0)	0	47	15	2	64	36	20	16
Germany (Science Specialization)										
Postindustrial	(0	0)	0	36	19	9	64	36	18	18
Great Britain (Public School)										
Industrial (1860)	—	—	77	9	—	—	86	14	14	0
Russia										
Preindustrial	(11	—)	11	48	11	4	74	26	5	21
Take-Off	—	—	—	—	—	—	80	20	—	—
Industrial (1964)	—	—	—	14	21	—	35	65	21	44

[39] Curriculum distribution is approximate, particularly for "literature, native and foreign languages," "history," and "natural sciences," where subject assignment is somewhat arbitrary. Sources for France, Take-Off (up to change in 1880 discussed in text) and Industrial (1890), Antoine Prost, *Histoire de l'Enseignement en France, 1800-1967* (Paris, 1968), p. 251; Postindustrial (1960's), George A. Male, *Education in France* (Washington, 1963), p. 93. Dates for German data (all from Blättner, pp. 237, 293): 1856, 1901, 1925, 1956 (Schleswig-Holstein). Cf. Poignant, p. 47, for very similar figures for 1968. British data for Rugby, in Reader, p. 104. Russian Preindustrial based on first and last years of Tsarskoe Selo Lycée curriculum (less military subjects), Seleznev, pp. 59-60; Take-Off from Vucinich, II, 40; Industrial (Soviet), from Lane, p. 495.

tury avoided the state secondary schools and thus remained excluded from the upper class.[40]

As a study of the backgrounds of a sample of nineteenth-century Prussian entrepreneurs shows (summarized in Table X), the propor-

TABLE X. INCREASE IN ELITE EDUCATION FOR BUSINESSMEN[41]

Period Britain	Period Prussia	Great Britain Public Schools		Great Britain Secondary Education and Above		Prussia (Rhineland-Westphalia) Secondary Education and Above	
		Per Cent of All Businessmen	Per Cent of Initial Period	Per Cent of All Businessmen	Per Cent of Initial Period	Per Cent of All Businessmen	Per Cent of Initial Period
1900-1914	1810-1830	7	100	63	100	28	100
1915-1919		10	140	68	108		
1920-1924	1831-1850	16	230	71	113	41	150
1925-1929		21	300	80	127		
1930-1934		22	315	84	133		
1935-1939		23	340	88	140		
1940-1947	1851-1870	29	415	93	148	69	245
	1871-1890					80	345

tion of men with secondary and higher education did increase markedly. Similarly, by 1964, 95 per cent of a sample of German managers had at least completed secondary schools, whereas only 52 per cent of their fathers (of varied occupations) had done so.[42] The philological approach has continued to serve, on the other hand, as an effective barrier to the use of the secondary school as a mobility channel for the lower classes. As a recent educational historian points out, in West Germany Latin is still nearly always the ground for secondary school

[40] Blättner, pp. 124, 159, 286; Helene Nathan, *Preussens Verfassung und Verwaltung im Urteile rheinischer Achtundvierziger* (Bonn, 1912), pp. 8ff.; Friedrich Zunkel, *Der Rheinisch-Westfälische Unternehmer, 1834-1879: Beitrag zur Geschichte des deutschen Bürgertums im 19. Jahrhundert* (Cologne, 1962), p. 106.

[41] British data adapted from *Management Succession: The Recruitment, Selection, Training and Promotion of Managers* (London, 1956), pp. 14-15, 91 (Total N = approximately 2,500), derived from personnel records and interviews of managers of larger companies. Periods are based on years of birth of managers; we have added twenty in each case to approximate period of secondary school completion. The same procedure was followed with data in Beau, pp. 66-67. The latter data is derived from entrepreneurial biographies; N (by periods indicated) = 109, 72, 89, 130.

[42] Zapf, p. 142.

failure. Though the wealthier groups have long adjusted to the secondary school requirement, as recently as 1960 only 7 per cent of the graduates were of manual worker and peasant origin, as contrasted to 64 per cent in the population of the Federal Republic.[43] It is impossible to know how many lower-class and lower-middle-class families have not failed because, perceiving classics as superfluous, they avoided the secondary school system altogether.

As early as the 1890's, the great educational historian Friedrich Paulsen sharply analyzed the ideological nature of this emphasis:

> At the beginning of the century they [classical languages] were significant in requiring the noble to attend the *Gymnasium*, and thereby accept equality. Now, by lengthening the course and making the entrance to the *Gymnasium* more difficult, they have the effect of keeping the lower elements out. Naturally, that is more the result of an instinctive inclination than of a conscious calculation. Nevertheless, it is an important consideration in leading many quarters to maintain instruction in the ancient languages. . . . We are still far from the goal of this movement, which, as in England, allows only sons of the "propertied and educated" to attend the university; but we in Germany are nonetheless rather remote from the state of affairs that still prevailed at the beginning of the century, when no one was excluded from the university purely through lack of means. And in society a strong feeling is manifest that this is a good development. . . . Among members of the learned professions, among officials, physicians, teachers, and even pharmacists and dentists, everywhere one encounters this opinion. The influx of sons of propertyless and uneducated parents lowers the honor of the Estate, therefore it is in the Estate's interest to increase the educational prerequisites so that no more can enter.[44]

CLASSICS AS LEGITIMIZATION OF BRITISH EDUCATIONAL ELITE ASCENDANCY

Paulsen's comparison of German and English development is valid insofar as it stresses the secondary school as a screening device. As institutional devices for helping to bring about a coalescence of middle-class and aristocratic elements, however, the two educational systems differed markedly. The key difference was the relative importance of the educational elites themselves. The *Gymnasium* teacher wanted to be the central elite element accommodating noble and upper bour-

[43] Walter Tröger, *Elitenbildung: Überlegungen zur Schulreform in einer demokratischen Gesellschaft* (Munich, 1968), pp. 301, 348, 352.
[44] Paulsen, II, 681-82.

geois values. Except briefly and imperfectly (between 1790 and 1840 to set outside limits) he was unable to assume that role. Even during that period, teachers were definitely inferior in status to the administrators. Afterwards they were only a marginal element in the expanded bourgeois-aristocratic coalition suggested in Paulsen's analysis. In Great Britain, as noted previously, the transformation of the public school and the universities was the central factor in the "theology" by which the upper-middle class and the gentry reached an accommodation. R. L. Archer's analysis of a half-century ago is still impressive:

> Probably the reason why English education was aristocratic was that the English Church was aristocratic, which in its turn was because Henry VIII and Elizabeth had secured that the bishops should be virtually state-appointed officials. What the State was, the Church became; what the Church was, the universities became; and what the universities were, education became.[45]

One does not need to pursue the historical analysis as far back as Archer does to demonstrate that the role of clergymen in the transformation of the English educational system was far more important than in Prussia. The Oxbridge fellows as well as the headmasters were ordained. In both countries the establishment of education as a high-status profession was accompanied by a considerable decline in the relative position of the clergy, however. As late as 1843 the proportion of Cambridge graduates (based on the records of two colleges) taking orders was 28 per cent, probably similar to the Prussian university share a decade earlier (at that time over one-half of the Halle students studied theology, but many did not become pastors). By the end of the century, Halle theological students were less than a fifth of the total, while only 7.5 per cent of Cambridge graduates entered the ministry.[46] In effect, secular guardians of youth had taken over. It is not surprising that while effectively supplanting the clergy, both groups of pedagogues stressed their moral mission. The English made the transition with much less friction, however, for they maintained the stance of allies rather than rivals of the Church.

As in Prussia and in France, their utility for moral education was a key factor in arguments for stressing the classics in the English public school. The Anglican Church saw classics, together with rural isolation and sports, as hardy defenses against new doctrines like utilitarianism and economic liberalism. Over three-fourths of the public school curriculum and two-thirds of the masters were devoted to classics instruc-

---

[45] R. L. Archer, *Secondary Education in the Nineteenth Century* (Cambridge, England, 1921), p. 104.
[46] Conrad, pp. 51-52; Musgrove, *Migratory Elite*, p. 173.

tion. Through meticulous attention to grammar, classics study was an excellent school for application to detail. Selected classics were used to teach Christian responsibility, showing how to adjust to a crisis but avoiding too much intellectual curiosity.[47] Although several great headmasters preferred Greek to Latin, there was no sense of defensiveness toward Latin Europe. Instead, both antique cultures could be drawn upon for civic training. Rome presented a model for future empire-builders, Athens for a property-owning democracy. Through these examples boys could be prepared for considering contemporary British problems without the need for recourse to dangerous Continental theorists.[48]

Like the Prussians, English educators insisted on subordinating practical subjects to their goal of molding human character. Matthew Arnold (a key figure between 1851 and 1888 as H. M. Inspector of Schools as well as a literary lion) caustically criticized Cornell University as founded "on a miscalculation of what culture truly is, . . . calculated to produce miners, or engineers, or architects, not sweetness and light."[49] There were, however, basic differences between the Prussian and the English approach to the classics. Men like the Arnolds were true scholars, interested in the subject matter and historical background of the classics they expounded. But Thomas Arnold feared that the division of labor in German scholarship led to an overly skeptical attitude toward the religious basis of the morality he cherished; it tended to be a "continental apology for anarchic free-thinking" or at least a diversion from civic life. Basic to the scorn for the philological approach was the fear that it would turn the boys and their schoolmasters alike into specialists.[50] As we have seen, this is precisely what happened as the Prussian secondary school teacher retreated to a marginal elite role in the mid-nineteenth century. Even a generation later, British educators were not obliged to assume so limited a role. Consequently they continued to treat classics (like sports) as a subject for carefully coached gentlemanly amateurism: "a sort of game which required detachment rather than involvement. To be involved was to be self-interested."[51]

Precisely because the aristocratic style was so pronounced, early English public school education was, in principle at least, less open than Prussian to the lower classes. Costs of boarding school were much higher than in Prussia, where the secondary schools were free. Some

[47] Wilkinson, p. 325; Bamford, p. 62; Weinberg, pp. 35-36.
[48] *Ibid.*, p. 43; Clarke, p. 170.
[49] Armytage, *Rise of the Technocrats*, p. 203.
[50] Rothblatt, p. 201; cf. Armytage, *German Influence*, pp. 33, 41; Clarke, p. 117; Archer, p. 145.
[51] Weinberg, p. 42.

public schools confronted a legal problem in this respect, for the terms of their endowments required them to admit local boys free or at a low fee. Here the classics ideology was especially useful. By dropping the lower forms, public schools made certain that pupils who had not prepared under tutors or in preparatory schools were insufficiently equipped with Latin to enter.[52]

The initial reaction of active businessmen and entrepreneurs as well as the working classes was to reject the public school as an impractical waste of time. Most Manchester manufacturers of the 1850's sent their sons to private academies or to local grammar schools until age fourteen or fifteen. At that point the boys went to work, for public school until the age of eighteen (much less Oxbridge B.A.'s) would make them "unsettled for commercial pursuits" and even cause them to see their parents as "vulgar and beneath [their] dignity."[53] Those parents who did want higher education for their sons soon found the public school indispensable, however. After the 1830's the "reformed" Oxbridge examinations demanded more extensive classical reading and composition than other schools could supply. This factor appears to have been a principal reason for the demise of the non-Conformist schools. By 1868 only a trickle of boys went from the old grammar schools to the universities.[54] To be sure, newer types of day schools developed in the late nineteenth century but (partly on the advice of H. M. Inspectors of Schools) they based their instruction in classics as in sports on the public school model.

As Table X indicates, there is a fairly close correspondence between the degree to which businessmen in Great Britain and the western Prussian industrial regions ultimately accepted the types of schooling prescribed by their societal elites. What is especially interesting is that this trend reverses our normal expectation for asynchronous comparison: i.e., the British development occurs nearly a century later, although British industrialization was completed at least a generation earlier than the Prussian. Apparently the elite schooling established in Prussia well in advance of industrialization was only very gradually able to establish itself among the groups most involved in the industrialization process. In England a new elite education, developed at least partly as a reaction against industrialization and the elites who accomplished it, was able to triumph somewhat more quickly. In addition, significant concessions were made to the German entrepreneurial elite—to a minor extent in the curriculum of the *Realgymnasium* and

[52] Bamford, pp. 200ff.

[53] J.P.C. Roach, "Victorian Universities and the National Intelligentsia," *Victorian Studies*, III (1959-60), 138, 145; *Early Victorian England*, p. 244.

[54] Rothblatt, p. 45; A. E. Musson and Eric Robinson, *Science and Technology in the Industrial Revolution* (Toronto, 1969), pp. 91, 115.

similar institutions, to a much greater degree in the separate *Technische Hochschule* discussed in Chapter Nine. In England, on the contrary (to mention just one facet of an issue that will be discussed at length later), Matthew Arnold sharply opposed John Bright's efforts to promote technical education.[55] The German philological method, however remote from the natural sciences, probably also maintained a measure of respect for the scientific method, as contrasted to the purely literary English approach.[56] It seems fair to conclude that the weight of the homogeneous British elite formed *after* industrialization was simply too strong for the entrepreneurs to be able to resist the aristocratic bias of the new education. In Prussia a more fragmented elite retained vestiges of other educational options which arose during the course of industrialization.

CLASSICS AS LEGITIMIZATION OF A MARGINAL FRENCH EDUCATIONAL ELITE

Consideration of the French secondary school system strengthens these conclusions. As noted earlier in this chapter, the Revolution and its Napoleonic aftermath appeared to have reduced the classics, already on the decline, to a relatively minor aspect of the curriculum of the state schools. Between 1815 and 1880 emphases varied (conservative regimes generally favored Latin), but generally elite education was bifurcated:

> General culture was the special *formation* of the juridical and political cadres of society alone; technical and economic cadres most frequently escaped humanities and rhetoric. This perhaps explains why business circles enjoyed less respect despite their wealth.[57]

About 1880, however, a subtle change occurred. During the next decade the part of Latin and Greek in the curriculum increased somewhat (see Table IX). More important, in France as in Prussia and England, the method of the classics invaded the general literary education. Both classics teachers and their students, it is said, treated the modern language sections (in the same building, rather than in separate schools as in Prussia) contemptuously. To raise their prestige, modern section teachers accepted a considerable element of Latin and taught other literary subjects on the classics model. Even in post-World War I science sections, where Latin itself was not required, the French language in particular was taught on the model of Latin.[58]

[55] Armytage, *Rise of the Technocrats*, p. 203.
[56] Archer, p. 145.   [57] Prost, p. 58.
[58] *Ibid.*, pp. 253, 256; cf. Ponteil, p. 266.

As Antoine Prost has written, the argument that Latin was irreplaceable for training the mind in logic and rigorous reasoning had to be accepted on faith if one did not wish to be branded as uncultured: "Throughout our period [1880-1930] the notions of *humanities and of the elite are congruent.*"[59] One is immediately struck by the fact that "our period" corresponds not to conservative political predominance, but to the height of Third Republic "radicalism." At the beginning of the period, to be sure, there was considerable conservative support for the classics. In a typical expression of the alliance which then existed between the Church and the upper classes, Monsignor F.A.P. Dupanloup—far from the most conservative prelate—exclaimed, "Despite all your efforts the directing classes will remain the directing classes, because they know Latin."[60] The classics were, indeed, the fundamental means by which the upper bourgeoisie set an educational requirement for the elite. But it would hardly have been possible for conservative groups to impose their standards on the state schools for so long against the will of the instructors, who constituted an indispensable apparatus of the Left parties. Indeed, leftist politicians have so often been former *lycée* instructors that a certain direct continuity of interest is apparent.

In contrast to the Prussian and British educational elites, the French *professeurs de lycée* were not, of course, clergymen's sons. Nor were secondary teachers a self-perpetuating group; only 5 per cent (1900-1914) were sons of secondary school instructors. Fourteen per cent were sons of lower-status primary school teachers, and at least three-fifths of the total were from other lower-middle-class, working-class, or peasant families.[61] In other words, the secondary educational profession, instead of constituting a slight lateral advance from the clergy and related professions, was a major upward mobility channel. Knowledge of Latin and Greek was the visible certification of upward mobility, cherished all the more because in many provinces the social status of the *professeur* was ambiguous. Frequent transfer—in contrast to the customary lifelong tenure in a Prussian town or a public school—reduced the instructor's chance to establish a social position. Lacking proper family connections (since he came from a lower stratum), it would have been hard for him to acquire such a position at best. Like the higher administrator, the instructor was scorned as a laicist, liberal, or worse. The one type of social circle which did accept him was composed of Masonic, freethinking, politically leftist business and professional men.

As long as knowledge of the classics was accepted as qualitatively

[59] Prost, pp. 331-32.

[60] Quoted in *ibid.*, p. 332.

[61] *Ibid.*, p. 363.

different from all other culture, however, the *professeur* commanded a measure of deference. Without the Latin seal, as Edmond Goblot points out, many a bright, self-educated man who left school before the *lycée* would be recognized as superior intellectually to its graduates.[62] "The good *professeur* is not distinguished by his method but by his qualities," and his students, too, were not philological specialists, as in Prussia, but boys who learned a style rather than a science. The resemblance of this style to the noble model of the "whole man" is striking. Indeed, French education stressed, as a leading educational official, Ferdinand Buisson, said in the 1880's, aptitudes which "make the man" rather than those which "make the worker" who can transform nature.[63] As will appear in subsequent chapters, the decades of the Third Republic were also those when other societal trends turned French elites closer to the British and Prussian accommodation to aristocratic models.

Clarification of the apparent paradox of such a trend during the most bourgeois period of French political life is, no doubt, very complex. But merely establishing the close link between the search for status of the secondary educational elite and the resurgence of quasi-aristocratic educational models is extremely significant. The inertia of tradition is far stronger in Western Europe—perhaps in Russia and America as well—than many interpretations concede. As long as group status is crucial, any elite may turn to ideologies utilizing symbols drawn from earlier prestige patterns.

Because they are intellectuals—indeed the largest, most stable, and frequently the most influential body of intellectuals—educators are especially adroit at producing these ideological combinations. Usually the educational elite is so marginal to the general elite structure that it cannot make an ideological pattern prevail unless it is at least adaptable to the needs of more powerful groups. Thus (as we shall see) the minor resurgence of classics under the Third Republic did not prevent the persistence there of a stronger pattern of scientific and technological education than elsewhere in Western Europe. Similarly, the Greek enthusiasm of the Prussian educators had to be modified after a generation to conform to the more limited requirements for educational exclusiveness of the coalescing upper class. Only rarely does an educational elite attain such lasting influence as did the British.

Although this analysis has diverted us from our main theme, it has been indispensable. At several points we have noted the reinforcing effect (for example, in isolating students from contemporary ideas) of classic curricula upon the organizational aspects of the secondary school discussed in Chapter Six. Analysis of curriculum emphasis is

[62] Goblot, p. 84.   [63] Quoted in Prost, p. 340.

essential to understand the barriers which make secondary school completion the narrow gate to elite careers in general. Finally, the symbiotic relation between educational elite and administrative elite which our analysis has suggested is extremely significant. For France, the relationship was too complex to discuss at this point. In Russia and Prussia, the administrative elite was nearly always dominant, but the educational elite had a significant auxiliary influence on defining the administrative elite role. In Britain, the situation was reversed—a factor which goes a long way to explain the peculiar position of the Administrative Class.

An elaborate summary of the effects of adolescent socialization would be out of place at this point. A few salient characteristics should be recalled, however. Although the range of curriculum variance was great—from the domination of science in Soviet secondary schools to its reduced position in the Third Republic *lycée*—French and the Russian secondary schools, training at least a portion of the administrative elite, have provided more scientific subjects than the secondary schools where British and German elite administrators have usually studied. For French youths destined for administrative elite careers, the school has tended to reinforce the effects of their metropolitan family backgrounds open to currents of new ideas. For Russians, the reinforcing effect was less (since a greater proportion of families were provincial), and the closed Tsarist secondary institutions were less accessible to social ideas. Prussian *Gymnasien*, on the other hand, reinforced the provincial quality of the younger boys' upbringing, while English public schools tended to provide an artificial rural experience for boys from urban backgrounds. Conversely, the English schools strongly inculcated universalistic values. For adolescents who later became elite administrators the structured peer group was important for socializing to universalist values *within* the egalitarian group. In the USSR this adolescent peer group, consisting at least of all secondary school graduates, has constituted a considerable fraction of the cohort; for other societies the privileged in-group has been a very small minority of the age group. In these terms, the Old-Regime French and the English secondary school socialization to universalist values was strong, whereas the small, isolated Prussian *Gymnasium* had a relatively slight socializing effect. The university fraternities were a weak substitute integrative mechanism. Tsarist adolescent socialization had great ethnic and social background differences to overcome, but had a considerable integrative influence. In the nineteenth and twentieth centuries, the great Parisian *lycées* continued to inculcate universalist values for their select student bodies, although they could not overcome the deep disintegrative trends in the upper classes.

CHAPTER EIGHT

Higher Education as Ideology

I F SECONDARY education has been the barrier to be surmounted for entering the general elite, the university has been the gateway to the administrative elite in particular. As in the case of the French textile families, many European upper strata have considered secondary education adequate formal preparation for private elite roles. With limited exceptions—mainly Russia and Britain until the late nineteenth century—higher education has been required for administration. Consequently, the crucial importance of the secondary educational stage has been its monopoly on preparation for the university. Once over the hurdle of the appropriate secondary school, a majority of European youths do complete some type of higher education. A smaller proportion, as the graphs in Chapter Eleven show, completes the particular type of formal higher training required for entrance to the administrative elite. The natural conclusion would be that the secondary school certifies eligibility for general elite roles while the higher institution provides separate training for particular elite roles. In some measure, of course, this is true. One of the most significant characteristics of the formal entrance requirements for the administrative elite, however, is that they do not really prescribe (as Max Weber assumed in his model of bureaucracy) specialized training necessary, in an instrumental sense, for the occupation.

OXBRIDGE AS PROLONGED GENERAL EDUCATION

This proposition can be demonstrated without difficulty in the case of the British. In effect, Oxford and Cambridge have always been prolongations of the literary and classical education of the secondary schools. As noted earlier, this does not mean that Oxbridge played an auxiliary part in the great educational transformation of the nineteenth century. On the whole, the reform of the universities preceded the reconstruction of the public schools. The headmasters were Oxbridge graduates and drew much of their inspiration from mentors and fellow students who remained in the university colleges. What is notable is that boys who went up to Oxford or Cambridge were doing what eighteenth-century Continental youths did by prolonging their secondary school studies. The Faculté des Arts of Paris, for example, consisted of a number of residential *collèges*. Frequently students left them at about the age of seventeen to enter one of the specialized faculties, but youths stayed in the same *collège* for another two years of philosophy. Others prolonged their studies in the same manner in *collèges* (like Juilly) remote from any university. In Germany, too, the philosophical faculty before the early nineteenth-century philological revolution was at once a preparatory school for the specialized faculties and a terminal general educational institution.[1] The only real difference between the Continental and the English prolongation of general education was that English boys moved from small schools to the two university centers for continued studies.

Whereas most Continental universities had three specialized faculties, by the nineteenth century Oxbridge had none. Given the classics ideology and rural nostalgia of the nineteenth-century educational transformation, it was out of the question for the old universities to acquire such facilities. Although the medical faculties long present at small German universities did struggle on, by mid-nineteenth century medical advances demanded urban locations. There was no such physical necessity for maintaining English legal schooling in London, but the established position of the Inns of Court would have made it difficult, at best, to remove the main center of instruction. As the Oxbridge dons perceived their role, it was to train gentlemen; if these gentlemen wished professional training, they could go elsewhere later.[2]

If, therefore, the old universities were to retain preeminence in upper-class education, the principle that what really counted was a prolonged "all-round" literary education had to be established. There was no difficulty with the Anglican ministry (which had always prepared in the general colleges), nor with the education profession itself. Obviously some special preparation was needed for men who would concentrate on law, as will be discussed later. Given their established position, physicians also had to be accepted as professionals; other manipulative occupations, as we shall see, were simply not accepted as upper class.

THE AMATEUR ADMINISTRATOR AS LEGITIMIZATION OF THE OXBRIDGE CURRICULUM

It was neither necessary nor desirable to dismiss government administration so summarily. Although in the 1830's the age of the colonial service and expanding home government was still a generation away,

---

[1] Louis Liard, *L'Enseignement Supérieur en France 1789-1889*, Vol. 1 (Paris, 1888), 11; Barnard, p. 167.

[2] Halsey and Trow, p. 47.

the Indian civil service was already important. Through personal experience as well as observation, the educational reformers used India as a major reference point (more important than Continental developments) in approaching the problem of relating a professional civil service to the transformed universities. The Indian experience was an object lesson in the course professional training might take if the universities did not broaden their concern. First at Fort William in Calcutta (1800), then at Haileybury College in England (1809), the East India Company set up its preparatory institutions. Finding "crass ignorance and gross apathy about Indian subjects at the Universities,"[3] the Company provided its own training in Persian, Hindi, Bengali, and (at Haileybury) a sensible assortment of courses on general and Indian law, classics, mathematics, and history (which Thomas Malthus taught). The "gentlemen" students were carefully selected but their preparation was instrumental rather than aristocratic—games were not allowed to become "the business of life."[4]

There is no evidence that the obvious utility in Indian service of an intensive language program influenced the British educational emphasis on classics, although one might suspect that alumni of Haileybury like Charles Trevelyan retained a lasting bias in favor of linguistic study. Another aspect of the Indian experience did have a significant feedback to England. As discussed in Chapter Twelve, the "all-round" capacities of the district officer, working without European technical staff, reinforced the aristocratic belief in amateurism. "Sovereign contempt for professional mysteries" in the legal field, where district officers adjudicated according to "the manners and usages of the people rather than by any abstract theories drawn from other countries" was a significant aspect of this attitude.[5]

The 1855 reform of entrance requirements for the Indian civil service deliberately did away with Haileybury College. The reform was a kind of rehearsal for home civil service reform; both were sponsored by the same group of educators. The principles of the successful Indian reform were: 1) a competitive entrance examination with few required subjects, and those (e.g., composition) very general; 2) a wide range of optional subjects in the main portion of the examination, each requiring thorough knowledge; 3) options corresponding to the Oxbridge curriculum, thereby ensuring predominance of its students (in

[3] Frederick C. Danvers, et al., Memorials of Old Haileybury College (London, 1894), p. 33.
[4] Ibid., p. 13; Philip Mason, The Men Who Ruled India, Vol. 1 (London, 1953), 28off.; L.S.S. O'Malley, The Indian Civil Service, 1601-1930 (London, 1965), p. 236; Sir Edward Blunt, The I.C.S.: The Indian Civil Service (London, 1937), pp. 34-35.
[5] Mason, I, 308; O'Malley, p. 37.

fact 40 per cent of 462 successful candidates in the first decade were from the two English universities and 17 per cent more from Queen's College, Dublin); 4) a service dominated by gentlemen generalists, for "open competition did not involve attracting the ill-bred and ill-balanced middle class into the Indian service."[6]

Ironically, fear (shared by Queen Victoria and influential officials) that a really competitive examination would admit undesirable elements frustrated reform of the home civil service. "It was left to Gladstone, a few heads of colleges, and a cluster of professors to suggest that the new method would not entail a lowering of social standards," but would strengthen the service's ties to "the new educational elite of the public schools and the universities."[7] The celebrated 1854 Northcote-Trevelyan "reform" in fact did little more than establish a minimal degree of literacy for clerkships. Public school and university graduates apparently showed less interest in the home service after 1854 than before.[8]

The principles of the India reform were finally made effective in the home service by an 1870 Order in Council which Gladstone (then prime minister) issued on his own initiative. Entrance to an upper division of "clerks" was by a difficult competitive examination. Six years later acceptance of the Playfair Commission recommendations made it difficult for lower clerks to enter the upper division. The division into Administrative and Executive Classes did not take final shape until after World War I, but one can consider the elite administrative career, following competitive entry at an early age, to have been established in the 1870's.

The direct evidence that this career was designed for the upper strata of British society relates primarily to the pre-World War I period. For example, in 1875 a War Office official bluntly rejected the suggestion that lower division clerks might be promoted on the basis of meritorious performance: "No, not without examination. I think he should pass such an examination as would give him educationally the status of a gentleman."[9] After that period concern for egalitarian social principles precluded frank expression of this aim.

Roger Kelsall identifies one pressure for change in the increased number of upper-middle-class families which individually lacked the kind of political influence the gentry had possessed, yet could qualify

[6] Robert Moses, *The Civil Service of Great Britain* (New York, 1914), p. 61.
[7] Briggs, p. 443; Hughes, "Sir Charles Trevelyan," p. 71; Hughes, "Civil Service Reform," p. 76.
[8] See data in Bamford, p. 210.
[9] Great Britain, House of Commons, *Parliamentary Papers, 1875. Reports from Commissioners*, xxiii, 9, Civil Service Inquiry [Playfair], p. 43.

their sons for government careers by giving them elite educations. In purely quantitative terms, however, the new upper division civil service provided only a trickle of jobs compared to the large numbers of upper-middle-class youths entering professions. Fritz Morstein-Marx, in an early work, suggested that (following the 1869 election) concern for "socialist" working-class penetration of the civil service was a major factor.[10] Yet there are enough evidences of hesitancy to provide support for Oliver MacDonagh's argument that reformers like Lord Macaulay did not want to establish completely exclusive class recruitment. As Sir Charles Trevelyan later wrote: "these early [1854] supporters of it [reform] *might be counted upon the fingers*, and if the matter had been put to the vote in London society, or the clubs, or even in Parliament itself *by secret voting*, the new system would have been rejected by an overwhelming majority."[11] Under the circumstances, much of the force of the reformers'—even Gladstone's—arguments that the measures would increase upper-class entry may have been designed to secure the minimal requisite political support.

This is not to say that these arguments were inaccurate, for the reformers correctly believed that their administrative entrance requirements were a significant step toward consolidating the new upper class. But there seems little doubt that the goal which interested them most was enhancement of the prestige of the educational system with which they were more directly associated. Gladstone, the dominant political figure, still took an intense interest in the affairs of his old university, Cambridge, even in such matters as faculty appointments.[12] Although the new administrative elite actually provided relatively few openings for university men, dons saw it as an alternative for what they perhaps incorrectly perceived as diminishing private professional opportunities. More important, access to an administrative elite would provide a new reference group for both dons and undergraduates, more prestigious than the Anglican clergy whose upwardly mobile sons still provided nearly one-third of the undergraduates.[13] In effect, virtual restriction of the administrative elite to Oxbridge graduates would certify the central place of the universities in the societal elite.

In suggesting this ideological core of the civil service reforms, one need not question the sincerity of the reformers. As a matter of fact, Trevelyan and Macaulay at least appear to have believed implicitly in

[10] Kelsall, p. 3; Morstein-Marx, "Berufsbeamtentum," p. 475.

[11] Quoted from a personal letter to the author, Dorman B. Eaton, in his *Civil Service in Great Britain: A History of Abuses and Reforms and Their Bearing upon American Politics* (New York, 1880), p. 430.

[12] Rothblatt, p. 177.

[13] *Ibid.*, p. 260.

certain psychological propositions which in the mid-nineteenth century, as today, looked very dubious. We have suggested that the real effect of early selection is to perpetuate family advantage, as well as to minimize costs of socializing to values which the system emphasizes. Macaulay believed, however. "that men, who distinguish themselves in their youth above their contemporaries, almost always keep to the end of their lives the start which they have gained."[14] Consequently, he believed a competitive examination was a virtually infallible way of distinguishing inherent talent. Basically uncommitted to the values which Macaulay's argument unconsciously concealed, Chadwick had no difficulty in finding a counter-argument, even in 1854:

> Many an awkward-looking fellow of no great attainments is found to distance his more elegant and university-educated competitors in the long run, because he has steadiness and self-command; it is found that whatever he can do, he can be trusted to do; he is punctual, regular, industrious, and pains-taking; acquires soon a knowledge of official details and a power of carrying them out; knows all that is going on, and can always be referred to with reliance. In time, he cannot be done without, and will and must be promoted. Had it been a question of acquired knowledge, he would have stood no chance with a university examiner, because he has not a smattering of the calculus, and does not make Latin verses. He understands accounts, however, which are of much greater importance, though the examiner himself in all probability, neither knows nor values them. He is not above hard work, or below it, or afraid of it.[15]

The suspicion that the interests of the universities have remained central is substantiated by developments since the reforms. In the nineteenth century, the links between the headmasters and the Oxbridge faculty were so close that it is difficult to distinguish the interests of the two groups in monopolizing administrative elite opportunities. Since then, the share of the public schools in competitive entrance to that elite has slowly declined to one-third or one-fourth. The public school model has indeed permeated other educational institutions, particularly the Oxbridge colleges, which have increasingly served as surrogates for the "domestic" quasi-total experience of the boarding school.[16] From the point of view of interests involved, however, the weight has shifted drastically toward the universities which, as Table

---

[14] Quoted in George O. Trevelyan, *The Life and Letters of Lord Macaulay*, Vol. 1 (London, 1876), 343.
[15] Quoted in Moses, p. 77.   [16] Weinberg, p. 142.

XI indicates (and careful regression analysis of many factors substantiates), have maintained their overwhelming preponderance of competitive administrative elite entrants.[17]

The dominance of the interests of the universities is also suggested by recent trends in employment of Oxbridge graduates. Although only a few dozen a year of the best graduates could expect to enter the administrative elite before World War II, it was a prized goal when other employment considered suitable was either unattractive or (like law and medicine) dependent on private means and contacts. As Ian Weinberg points out, the public school master was an unattractive career goal for the Oxbridge graduate who could not coach athletics

TABLE XI. EDUCATIONAL BACKGROUND OF BRITISH
ADMINISTRATIVE ELITE
(*Open Competition Entrants*)[18]

Period of Entrance	Public Schools (Per Cent)	Oxbridge (Per Cent)
1899-1908	42	82
1906-1910	—	82
1925-1936	62	90
1948-1956	25	72
1956-1960	29	80
1961-1965	37	80

and was not attracted by the prospect of devoting all his time to adolescent boys.[19] Such a graduate tended to be shy, introvertive, and inclined to anonymous, passive roles rather than to those demanding responsibility and open competition.[20] Careers like writing and social work provided limited opportunities. The great expansion of university teaching after World War II, however, has opened up the pros-

[17] J. F. Pickering, "Recruitment to the Administrative Class, 1960-64: Part II," *Public Administration*, XLV (1967), 173; cf. Rosemary G. Stewart and Paul Duncan-Jones, "Educational Background and Career History of British Managers, with Some American Comparisons," *Explorations in Entrepreneurial History*, IX, No. 2 (1956), 61-71, for a comparable analysis of Oxbridge graduates in private management.

[18] 1899-1908 data for men entering by open competition examination (N = 253) (Dale, pp. 55ff.). Probably the data understates the proportion of competition entrants from public schools. Data for all other periods for all university open competition entrants. 1906-1910 (N = 473) includes entrants to Indian and Eastern services as well as home service (Cohen, p. 173). All other data based on Fulton Committee, III (1), 75 and IV, 322. N's for all latter periods over 300, except 1948-1956, N = 177.

[19] Weinberg, p. 115.

[20] Anthony Sampson, *Anatomy of Britain* (London, 1962), p. 454.

pect of careers in institutions modeled on the Oxbridge colleges where such men have felt most comfortable. " 'But it's not industry which is jeopardising our recruitment so much as the universities' one of the [Civil Service] commissioners said, 'it's the academic types who tend to try for the civil service, and those are now finding the idea of an academic career more attractive, especially as the new universities make more jobs.' "[21]

Apparently the Oxbridge faculty encourages this trend. While recent entrants to the Administrative Class ranked their academic mentors as the greatest source of *information* for their career choice, only 17 per cent indicated that *encouragement* by the university instructors had been a reason for their making that choice.[22] The Fulton Committee reviewing British administration problems appeared to view this development with some concern. One wonders whether in fact it is not a trend which will profit all concerned. In either case, the dons appear consistent in their basic position. For a century the administrative elite provided a prestige goal for their charges, demonstrating that commitment to the educational elite's values provided the surest avenue to the societal elite. As a "retreatist" administrative elite became somewhat less prestigious and its methods of recruitment more subject to universalistic challenges, the universities have turned to alternative channels to legitimize their role.

This conclusion is, however, jumping ahead of our analysis. For the mid-nineteenth-century reformers the effect of university dominance of competition for high military and civil administrative posts was evident: they were worth a hundred thousand fellowships.[23] No doubt Trevelyan intended this as hyperbole; but the estimate is so disproportionate to the actual employment opportunities provided by administration that he must have meant to emphasize the effect on student achievement motivation. Here was a clear recognition of what we call today "feedback." It is all the more curious therefore—unless we assume ideological factors were at work—that the reformers, their supporters, and generations of defenders of the examination system overlooked the potential feedback of examination content on university *curricula*. Even an acute analyst like John Stuart Mill failed to note this obvious connection.[24] Instead, they have argued that in order to

[21] *Ibid.*, p. 226.
[22] Fulton Committee, III (2), 85, 399.
[23] Personal letter quoted in Eaton, pp. 430ff.; cf. "The Northcote-Trevelyan Report," pp. 9ff.
[24] H.R.G. Greaves, *The Civil Service in the Changing State: A Survey of Civil Service Reform and the Implications of a Planned Economy on Public Administration in England* (London, 1947), p. 35.

get the best undergraduates, entrants must be examined on the subjects best taught at Oxbridge.

Proceeding on this basis, the examinations proposed in the 1850's, those actually established in the 1870's, and the requirements still prevalent in the 1960's have in effect selected those applicants who are best in any subject taught at Oxbridge. As early as 1895 this meant 38 subject options. Like the arguments used to defend early selection, the examination content has been justified by educational psychological reasoning which was open to question even in the 1850's. Macaulay made the basic assumption that intensive learning in one subject is transferable to another.[25] As his argument for the Indian civil service examination put it, "We believe that men who have been engaged, up to 21 or 22, in studies which have no immediate connection with the business of any profession, and of which the effect is merely to open, to invigorate, to enrich the mind, will generally be found in the business of every profession superior to men who had, at 18 or 19, devoted themselves to the special studies of their calling."[26] Again, Macaulay failed to convince Chadwick, who, in the same passage quoted above, commented: "No merchant or banker would require his clerk to undergo an initiatory examination in the Antigone of Sophocles or in De-Morgan's Differential and Integral Calculus . . . yet the qualifications he requires are quite as high as those of a Government clerk. . . ."[27] The argument failed also with Rowland Hill, another non-Conformist associate of Bentham. He pointed out that under Macaulay's proposed examination requirement George Stephenson could not have become an engineer, and urged that specialized practical knowledge be required in the Post Office, which Hill was successfully reorganizing.[28]

Over a century later a top civil servant, Sir Maurice Dean, repeated the essence of Macaulay's argument that a specialized examination

> would limit most undesirably the free choice of school and university subjects. The right to make a free choice is more valuable than the benefit to be derived from the study of public administration. After all, the main purpose of university training is to acquire mental muscles; I sometimes think that the subject doesn't matter provided it is sufficiently difficult.[29]

[25] Kingsley, p. 97.
[26] Quoted in Frederick F. Ridley, *Specialists and Generalists: A Comparative Study of the Professional Civil Servant at Home and Abroad* (London, 1968), p. 200.
[27] Quoted in Moses, p. 77.
[28] George B. Hill, *The Life of Sir Rowland Hill*, Vol. II (London, 1880), 250; Howard Robinson, *The British Post Office: A History* (Princeton, 1948), p. 259.
[29] Sir Maurice Dean, "The Public Servant and the Study of Public Administration," *Public Administration*, XL (1962), 23.

While ostensibly rejecting the obsolete "cult of the generalist," the Fulton Committee recommendations similarly urged that a method of entry (Method II) be retained to attract the best graduates and avoid early specialization for "a rigorous and disciplined habit of mind . . . can be imparted by 'irrelevant' as well as 'relevant' studies."[30]

In the short run, feedback effects of examination content (as is the case with most social feedback effects) would not have altered the qualifications of the most talented graduates. Very likely, concern for the short run impressed the "pragmatic" British mind. In the longer run as well, however, the examinations actually prescribed enabled dons to maintain their prestige by teaching just what they preferred to teach. Their ability to concentrate on their favorite subjects was heightened by another explicit, but dubious, psychological assumption of the reformers: that intense preparation in a few subjects is superior to a broad course distribution.

The basic argument for concentration at the university level was that a young man—in contrast to a boy—could become intellectually proficient only by deep mastery of one or a very few challenging subjects. As noted above, this mastery of detail was assumed to be directly transferable to professional activity like administration. There is no doubt that this assumption was, in a sense, contrary to the aristocratic model. The reformers did not, in fact, expect administrative elite entrants to be a cross section of the elite aspirants produced by the public schools, but to consist of the more intellectually talented among them. Although a majority of Oxbridge students has come from fee-paying schools, in recent years (as in the 1850's) only one-fifth to one-third of Oxbridge enrollment has come from boarding schools. In the 1850's a minority of public boarding school students went to any university. Public school boys from families of aristocratic lineage have tended, on the whole, to prefer politics or the military to the administrative elite.[31] The administrative elite was designed to be essentially middle class in its emphasis on achievement by industrious employment of talent in endeavors which the educators certified as worthy.

An indicator of the interests behind the insistence on concentrated study of a university subject is provided by the curiously persistent horror of "cramming." While no educational or administrative system favors last-minute *ad hoc* preparation, most regard such cramming as inevitable when difficult examinations are taken for high career stakes. Intensive short courses at Georgetown University to prepare for the United States Foreign Service examination or at the Ecole Libre des

[30] Fulton Committee, I, II, 30.
[31] Bamford, p. 47; Rothblatt, p. 22; Dale, p. 69.

Sciences Politiques for the French service were widely patronized during the interwar period without obviously deleterious results. A notorious *Referendarfabrik* in Potsdam in the mid-nineteenth century aroused some indignation but more amusement.[32] In England, it is reported that cramming began as soon as the Indian civil service competition made it worthwhile. Nevertheless, beginning at least with the MacDonnell Commission (1914) most reviews of administrative elite qualifications have expressed the fear that any requirements not part of the regular university programs would result in candidates' gaining unfair advantage by acquiring a stock of information which would be forgotten as soon as the examinations were passed.[33] Clearly this reasoning strengthened the conclusion that only those subjects which the Oxbridge faculties offered by the usual four-year tutorial method were valid objects of learning. It also represented a concession to the aristocratic model of learning as an amateur, leisurely activity pursued for its own sake rather than for some self-interest.

The nature of the subjects actually offered at the universities also represented some concession to the aristocratic ideal of the "whole man." They ranged from Oriental languages and archaeology to English literature and history, but the classics and the classics approach remained, as in secondary schools throughout Europe, the core of the offerings. Northcote had urged that Cherokee be an examination subject if it were taught, but one can be fairly sure that if it had been taught its grammar would have looked like Latin.

Macaulay had been good in literary subjects, not in mathematics, science, or athletics; he had entered the bar, but did not take the profession seriously, as compared to his literary and political interests. Gladstone shared much of this background and interest. Both—and others of their group—saw literary emphasis, and particularly the classics, as a barrier to the infiltration of atheism and other dangerous Continental ideas: "Comteism, St. Simonianism, Fourierism are absurd enough."[34]

Table XII indicates the continuing dominance of literary subjects among administrative elite entrants. Somewhat naïvely, a strong apologist for the Administrative Class expressed alarm during the interwar period over the drastic decline in mathematics entrants. Actually a large majority of the "mathematics and science" concentrations prior to World War I was provided by students who had pursued the Cambridge specialty, pure mathematics. As Everett Hagen has pointed out,

[32] Richter, p. 12.
[33] Bamford, p. 241; Archer, p. 221.
[34] G. O. Trevelyan, II, 457; cf. Ridley, p. 11; Checkland, *Rise*, p. 91; Rothblatt, p. 177.

TABLE XII. UNIVERSITY SUBJECT CONCENTRATION OF
BRITISH ADMINISTRATIVE ELITE[35]

Period of Entrance	Highly Successful Administrators (Per Cent)				Open Competition Entrants (Per Cent)		
	Classics	Other Literature	History	Total Literary	Total Literary	Social Sciences	Mathematics Science
Late 19th Century	35	9	4	48	—	—	—
Early 20th Century	30	19	8	57	80	—	14
Interwar	20	10	14	44	75	7	13
1948-1956	—	—	—	—	66	20	3
1957-1963	—	—	—	—	70	13	3

a highly abstract subject like pure mathematics, in contrast to techno-logical subjects, is acceptable to a traditional elite.[36] Nevertheless, pure mathematics has had increasing application in industrial societies. Graduates in this field have had far wider opportunities than those in literary subjects; consequently, their desire to compete for administrative class entrance has greatly diminished. What is at work is a variant of Gresham's law: if all subjects have equal weight as entrance requirements, those with least relevance for other careers will tend to predominate in the administrative competition.

Was, then, as Lord Robert Cecil testily remarked in 1856, the whole development of a British administrative elite "neither more nor less, from beginning to end, [than] a schoolmasters' scheme"?[37] Social de-

---

[35] Data on "highly successful administrators" is taken from John S. Harris and Thomas V. Garcia, "The Permanent Secretaries: Britain's Top Administrators," *Public Administration Review*, xxvi (1966), 34, with periods (in which their subjects became Permanent Secretaries) adjusted to estimated period of service entrance by subtracting twenty. It should be noted (as explained in Chapter Eleven) that a sizeable minority of top officials had been promoted from positions which did not require university study at all. As the data indicates, virtually all "open competition entrants" have university educations. Scattered data on the early 1900's is drawn from Dean, p. 24, and Cohen, p. 173. Data for the interwar period from Dean, p. 24, and H. Finer, *The British Civil Service* (London, 1937), pp. 92-93. Post-World War II data from Great Britain, *Parliamentary Papers, 1964-65. Sixth Report from the Estimates Committee. Together with the Minutes of the Evidence Taken before Sub-Committee E and Appendices.* Recruitment to the Civil Service (London, 1965), pp. 30ff. For open competition entrants, "literary" subjects include classics, modern languages, literature; "social sciences" include "PPE" (philosophy, politics, and economics), as well as specialization in law, political science, and economics separately.

[36] Everett E. Hagen, *On the Theory of Social Change: How Economic Growth Begins* (Homewood, Ill., 1962), pp. 36ff.

[37] Hughes, "Civil Service Reform," p. 62.

velopments are rarely that simple. As noted at many points in this analysis the reform movement was closely linked to the integration of upper-middle- and aristocratic class elements as well as to the peculiar interests of the educational elite. What we have suggested is that, in this instance, the ideology was shaped predominantly by the latter.

Legal Education as a Mechanism for Value Accommodation in Prussia

When one analyzes the Prussian experience, an even more complex layering of latent motivation and ideological legitimization comes into sight. Superficially the Prussian bureaucrat was the specially trained antipode of the British amateur; indeed, Weber derived his model of rationalized bureaucracy largely from the Prussian case. As far as entrance requirements were concerned, the key element was legal training.

The value of systematic legal codes as devices for national integration is beyond dispute. Indeed, lawyers were as common in higher administration in England as on the Continent from Tudor times through the eighteenth century. Their eclipse dates in part to the decline of central patronage (see Chapter Two). A major watershed, however, was the rigid division of the legal profession into a larger body of solicitors, trained mainly as apprentices, and an elite of barristers. The latter were nominally trained at the Inns of Court, but actually did not need any institutional instruction beyond the Oxbridge B.A. Instead, they learned by reading and practice—during a long period of little or no income which required personal wealth and contacts for successful completion. By the end of the nineteenth century, legally trained civil servants were rapidly disappearing in the administrative elite.

> At one time [prior to 1910] it had been virtually a rule that Home Office juniors should take their law examinations and should be called to the Bar, but the steadily growing pressure of work had already made that a practical impossibility for my generation.[38]

Similarly, in the mid-nineteenth century the Inland Revenue Board Solicitor's Office had hired university graduates with the expectation that they would acquire legal knowledge by apprenticeship.[39] By the 1930's, law experts like other experts were staff specialists outside the administrative elite body.

Continental observers have, of course, been familiar with the British

[38] Sir Harold Scott, *Your Obedient Servant* (London, 1959), p. 30.
[39] Moses, p. 119.

development. They explain it as a peculiarity of common-law societies, arguing that in Roman-law countries expert legal knowledge is indispensable for all higher administrators:

> The main reason (still widely misunderstood) which long ago required a legally educated specialized body of officials in Europe arises, however, from the difference in the legal structure. It is astounding that representatives of the American military authority constantly try to get around the fact that the so-called common-wisdom law (case-law) was replaced in Germany, at least as early as the 17th century, by abstract, norm-oriented written law. One may complain about this if he likes; but once the common law is replaced by a scientifically conceptualized legal system like the Roman law, application of this law necessarily requires legally educated officials.[40]

It is, the author continues, precisely because the substance of the Roman law is limited to a few thousand paragraphs (as contrasted to the libraries of law books necessary for case law) that the official can utilize it. One might think that this would be a strong argument for *minimal* legal training for officials (as presently practiced in France) rather than the actual German system of protracted legal experience. Ernst Kern's argument is also somewhat weakened by consideration of the strength of legal training in the United States—a common-law country like England. For example, over one-fifth of Federal program managers have studied law and a sizeable proportion of American corporate managers (more important, to be sure, in the less dynamic firms) have law degrees.[41] Even more telling is the fact that for nearly two centuries a notable, though minority, element of French top administrators has functioned (in a system where Roman law has deeper roots than in Germany) with no formal legal education at all. These considerations suggest that the customary German arguments for intensive legal training are, to say the least, not self-evident. To discover their ideological content one must, as in the English case, pursue the tedious but illuminating process of tracing their origins.

Until the late eighteenth century, Prussia (like Russia for decades longer) was essentially a garrison state preoccupied with the minimal societal organization needed for defense and national integration in an extraordinarily exposed geographic position. Frederick William I was

[40] Ernst Kern, "Berufsbeamtentum und Politik," *Archiv des Öffentlichen Rechts*, Neue Folge, xxxviii (1951), 108.

[41] Mabel Newcomer, *The Big Business Executive: The Factors That Made Him, 1900-1950* (New York, 1955), pp. 82, 87; John J. Corson and R. Shale Paul, *Men Near the Top: Filling Key Posts in the Federal Service* (Baltimore, 1966), pp. 165ff.

mainly concerned with constituting a body of officials who would act unreservedly as instruments of his integrative purposes. His "police state" (to use the Prussian historians' term) was erected, however, on a substructure of semi-feudal, particularistic institutions sometimes called the "old" or "German-Medieval *Rechtsstaat*." Farther west in Germany these institutions were primarily served by legally trained officials drawn both from the urban patriciate and the nobility. In Prussia, however, urbanization was still so low that Frederick William was able to replace the old "jurists" and "civilian" nobles (except in certain strictly judicial posts) by his own instruments, mainly commoners chosen for their demonstrated ability and complete dependence on the Crown.[42]

As a result, the Prussian administrative service in its formative period was almost unique in Germany in not requiring legal entrance examinations. Instead (as discussed in Chapter Nine) Frederick William I commanded chairs of cameralistics in the principal Prussian universities to train officials in practical tasks.

As we have seen, Frederick II felt compelled to reach a compromise with aristocratic interests. Like Russian nobles, the *Junkers* tended to scorn judicial service, for they thought of judges as low-status clerks, comparable to the legal stewards they employed on their estates. In contrast to the Russians, however, the Prussian nobles and the bourgeoisie had the example of their western German cousins immediately at hand. Legal training did not derogate from German noble status; consequently, the Prussian aristocracy could accede to its requirement in return for bourgeois' officials acceptance of fundamental aristocratic models. Frederick himself seems to have miscalculated the effect of a precise legal administration. Impressed as he was by Enlightenment ideas, Frederick believed (contrary to his father's wiser view) that precise laws would restrain bureaucratic discretion in favor of royal power. In 1771 the first higher administrative examinations were instituted. They were anything but egalitarian; nobles were wholly exempted for a time and others were deterred, unless wealthy or favored by special exemptions, by high examination fees. But by limiting the sovereign's range of recruitment, the regulation was a small step toward an autonomous administrative elite.[43]

While Frederick lived, the new legal code did not notably restrict the sovereign. Under his weaker successors, shaken by the catastrophic

[42] Heffter, p. 23; Ernst von Meier, *Französische Einflüsse auf die Staats- und Rechtsentwicklung Preussens im XIX. Jahrhundert*, Vol. II (Leipzig, 1908), 88; Schmoller, "Der preussische Beamtenstand," pp. 154-58; Hintze, *Staat*, p. 249; Rosenberg, pp. 62-64; Demeter, p. 274.

[43] Otto Hintze, "Preussische Reformbestrebungen vor 1806," *Historische Zeitschrift*, LXXVI (1896), 443; Brunschwig, pp. 149ff.; Rosenberg, pp. 176, 180.

defeats of the Napoleonic wars, the new concept of the *Rechtsstaat* merged with other reform ideas to serve as a legitimization of official autonomy. As servants of the state, officials were to be accountable to no one as long as they acted within their legally defined sphere, although the definitions were formally established by the monarch. Despite its fundamentally bourgeois character, high noble officials (Karl von Beyme as well as Humboldt) fostered the *Rechtsstaat* ideology. A key institution was the new University of Berlin, which translated the exaltation of Hellenic studies into a general glorification of pure knowledge based on research.

The empirical conglomeration of subjects called cameralism could not meet the Berlin standards, especially since its principal seat, Halle University, had been ceded to Saxony. The intricate, highly developed discipline of law was acceptable. Stimulated by the new educational spirit, the law faculties had endeavored to make their subject even more theoretical and "scientific." Even under Frederick II students had been more strongly attracted to law lectures than to required courses in cameralism. Moreover, the law faculty could rely on the legitimacy of German tradition, a strong argument when acceptance of rational French models (which the Prussian rulers, like Alexander I of Russia, probably preferred) was close to treason.[44]

Reforming officials had serious reservations about the increasing dominance of legal considerations. Even Hardenberg, called the "first dictator of the bureaucracy," said that cameralists as well as jurists were required.

> Every position in the State, without exception, is to be open not to this or that caste, but to the service and the skill and competence from all strata. Each shall be the object of general emulation and in none, be he ever so small or humble, shall the idea of advancement be deadened.[45]

During the generation following the reforms (approximately 1807-40) the idea of the *Rechtsstaat* served as the principal legitimization

[44] Eckart Kehr, "Zur Genesis der preussischen Bürokratie und des Rechtsstaates," in Hans-Ulrich Wehler (ed.), *Moderne deutsche Sozialgeschichte* (Cologne, 1966), pp. 44-51; C. J. Friedrich, "The Continental Tradition of Training Administrators in Law and Jurisprudence," *Journal of Modern History*, XI (1939), 131ff.; Irsay, II, 186, 194-96; Joseph Ben-David and Awraham Zloczower, "Universities and Academic Systems in Modern Societies," *Archives Européenes de Sociologie*, III (1962), 57.

[45] Georg Winter (ed.), *Die Reorganisation des preussischen Staates unter Stein und Hardenberg. Erster Teil: Allgemeine Verwaltungs- und Behördenreform.* Vol. I. *Vom Beginn des Kampfes gegen die Kabinettsregierung bis zum Wiedereintritt des Ministers vom Stein* (Leipzig, 1931), p. 34.

of the semi-autonomous *Beamtenstand*. During this period (as discussed in more detail in Chapter Ten) legal training defined the elite administrator, although it was by no means sufficient ground for attaining that status. The end of this period is marked by three developments which are hardly coincidental: 1) beginning of the take-off for industrialization; 2) decline in vigor and self-confidence in the administration; 3) end of the self-recruitment of the official stratum. Under sharper economic pressure than in the eighteenth century (the proportion living off their estates declined from one-half in 1820 to one-fourth in 1850 and one-sixth in 1880), the nobles turned to legal preparation for the higher administration. Between 1820 and 1870 their proportion increased from 7 to 15 per cent among a relatively stable number of law students.[46]

The influx of noble students was both a cause and an effect of the position of the law faculties as the most prestigious in the Prussian universities. Since the Middle Ages law had had the reputation of being the most aristocratic branch of study. Up to 1600, most Germans studied law abroad, especially in Italy (82 per cent of the German students at Padua during the period 1546-1630 were in law).[47] The expenses of travel and, in the early centuries, purchase of manuscripts restricted the subject to wealthy patricians and nobles. Later, the prospect of an unpaid apprentice stage (often abbreviated for nobles) following upon costly university studies drove poorer youths to fields like theology and teaching where they could expect to begin earning immediately after graduation. The rising total costs of entrance to the administration in the middle of the nineteenth century tended to exclude both the sons of higher officials and men of lower-class origin. From 28 per cent in the 1850's, the former declined to 16 per cent in the 1870's, in a Halle University law student body which had increased 15 per cent. Sons of peasants and artisans declined from 11 to 8 per cent.[48] Both nobles and the wealthy bourgeois' sons took their places.

As Table XIII shows, high-status recruitment remained a characteristic of the law faculties to the end of the Weimar period. There are many indications that it prevails under the German Federal Republic as well. Law study was also attractive to noble students—and to those who emulated them—because it remained closer than other major subjects to the aristocratic style. Theology was out of the question, medicine was a severe discipline requiring close contact with the lower

[46] Gillis, "Aristocracy," pp. 113-14; Gillis, *Prussian Bureaucracy*, pp. 31, 205; Conrad, p. 106.

[47] Eulenburg, pp. 120, 126; Stoelzel, pp. 61ff.

[48] Gillis, *Prussian Bureaucracy*, pp. 200, 202-203.

orders, and philosophy was the creature of fundamentally bourgeois stress on philological specialization. In non-Prussian Germany, where 28 per cent of Prussian law students went by 1880, not only was law a traditional noble field of study, but it conferred the prestige of science

TABLE XIII. SOCIAL ORIGINS OF GERMAN STUDENTS
IN HIGHER EDUCATION, 1931[49]
(Social Class, Per Cent)

Subject	Upper	Middle	Lower
All Subjects	36.6	56.7	5.9
Law and State Science	46.8	49.1	3.5
Economics	42.3	51.2	5.7
Construction Engineering	31.1	62.5	5.2

without much of the pain.[50] Once admitted, students did not need to compete strenuously, for on completing law school a large majority (70 per cent between 1906 and 1913) passed the initial examination for official posts.[51] It is worth noting that this situation exactly reverses the American conditions examined by Robert Merton, where law students competed intensely to obtain class standings that would ensure successful starts in a competitive profession, while medical students, once admitted, were deliberately shielded from competitive pressures.[52]

As the highest status subject of study, law in Germany was a field where the upper-class student could relax, and he did. Fraternity membership was especially strong among law students, with the attendant distractions excused (as sports were in the public school) because they "developed character." Poor attendance at law lectures was notorious. From Friedrich von Motz (an outstanding early nineteenth-century finance minister) to Georg Michaelis, Prussian officials who made their mark later in life confess that they spent their time on fraternity activities and other diversions instead of law study, and that their professors did not regard them highly.[53]

The relation of the examinations to the instructional staff was cru-

[49] Adapted from Svend Riemer, "Sozialer Aufstieg und Klassenschichtung," Archiv für Sozialwissenschaft und Sozialpolitik, LXVII (1932), 558.
[50] Conrad, pp. 43-44.
[51] Prussia, Königliches Preussisches Statistisches Landesamt. Statistisches Jahrbuch, Zwölfter Jahrgang (Berlin, 1915), p. 481.
[52] Merton, et al., Student-Physician, pp. 150, 209.
[53] Erwin Nasse, "Die Universitätsstudien der preussischen Verwaltungsbeamten," in Die Vorbildung zum höheren Verwaltungsdienste in den deutschen Staaten, Österreich und Frankreich (Leipzig, 1887), p. 161; Krueger, in Grabowsky, p. 84; Herman von Petersdorff, Friedrich von Motz: Eine Biographie, Vol. 1 (Berlin, 1913), 12; Ernsthausen, p. 33; Michaelis, p. 42.

cial. The eighteenth-century monarchs had hoped to compel the law professors (insofar as they were not replaced by cameralists) to pursue useful rather than theoretical lines of instruction by having officials conduct the examinations.[54] In other words, the Prussian kings perceived what British administrative reformers apparently could not conceive a century later: he who sets the examinations for the most prestigious careers shapes the educational process, for ambitious students will seek out those instructors and subjects which are most helpful for preparation.

Unfortunately—as far as the Prussian sovereigns' goals were concerned—they understood the feedback effect but completely miscalculated its direction. Instead of compelling academics to be more practical, the examinations permitted officials to select according to their own criteria. High judicial officials who were delegated to examine aspirants for apprenticeship administration had little regard for academic standards. As will appear (in Chapter Ten), later admission to a permanent elite administrative career depended on somewhat different criteria than those used in the examination taken at the close of university studies. Even for the subsequent "great examination," however, aspirants "shopped around" for superior courts which had a reputation of being easy. Obviously this process put a premium on the "insider's" knowledge; there is also no doubt that upper-class candidates were often favored.[55] Equally important was the fact that while some law professors were included in the examination boards the dominant judges nearly always excluded economics professors. The reasoning was precisely the same as Sir Maurice Dean's: a specialized examination would limit the student's "academic freedom" to choose courses. In practice, students ignored regulations (like one of 1879) providing for inclusion of economics and "financial science," preferring to concentrate on the legal subjects which they knew they would face on the examinations. Quasi-aristocratic, antispecialist values were also reflected in the argument that ability to handle people was more important for the aspiring official than examinations. Even critics who have recognized that the administrator's dynamic role is essentially different from the judge's static one contend that legal preparation is good intellectually (again, the argument that there is a carry-over from one subject to another) and *prevents* too early specialization.[56]

The position of the law professor in the argumentation for requiring

[54] Ben-David and Zloczower, p. 57.

[55] Gillis, *Prussian Bureaucracy*, p. 45; Ernsthausen, p. 81; Georges Blondel, *De l'Enseignement du Droit dans les Universités Allemandes* (Paris, 1885), pp. 46, 52-57; Richter, pp. 1, 11, 12.

[56] Nasse in *Vorbildung*, p. 168; Geib, pp. 335ff.

extensive legal training for all higher administrators has been significantly different from that of the Oxbridge dons' position on Administrative Class requirements. Under the Second Reich nearly all law professors were unhappy with student performance and professionally dissatisfied with control of examinations by outside agencies. Conversely, many successful administrators were highly critical of the abstract quality of law lectures. Professors in other fields (particularly economics and sociology) sharply criticized both sides of the legal qualifying procedure. In contrast to the general British consensus (between the 1870's and the 1920's) on the virtues of the administrative elite selection process, waves of sharp criticism have assailed Prussian and German requirements from at least the 1840's to the present. A great legalist like Otto Gierke deplored the neglect of economics and "state science" while purely technical legal procedures like interrogation occupied places in the curriculum.[57]

On the balance, under the Second Reich the law faculties accepted the prestige which the *Juristenmonopol* brought them, but certain officials were at least as enthusiastic defenders of the whole preparatory system:

> In our view there can be no more difference of opinion concerning the value of a thorough legal preparation, combining practical and theoretical elements, for the future administrative official than there can be over the requirement that all study classical languages in the *Gymnasium*, regardless of whether they intend to enter the philological career or some other.[58]

From time to time high Prussian officials did experiment with devices to secure better practical training for their recruits. Higher officials of the newer Imperial agencies (mainly because of seconded military and naval officers) were only 80 per cent legal in training as compared to 90 per cent or more in the Prussian service proper.[59] Under Weimar, on the other hand, elite administrators and law professors banded together defensively against Social Democratic attacks on the *Juristenmonopol*. As a result all experimentation with other career training was shelved.

[57] Otto Gierke, "Die juristische Studienordnung," *Jahrbuch für Gesetzgebung, Verwaltung und Volkswissenschaft*, I (1877), 3, 8, 15; cf. Perthes, p. 61; and particularly the collective works cited above: *Vorbildung* (1886), Grabowsky (1917), and K. Pintschovius, *Volkswirte als Führer oder als Fachbeamte? Eine Sozialwissenschaftliche Untersuchung* (Munich, 1930), which serve as convenient summaries of a variety of viewpoints.

[58] O. Fischer, "Die Vorbildung für den hoheren Verwaltungsdienst im Königreiche Sachsen," in *Vorbildung*, p. 15.

[59] Kamm, pp. 443, 445, 450.

LAW AND THE EVOLVING CLASS BALANCE IN FRANCE

In the evolution of legal requirements for administration, as in other aspects of national integration, France was far ahead of Prussia (although not of western Germany). Effective reincorporation in the French monarchy between the thirteenth and fifteenth centuries of the southern areas where Roman-law practice had never completely died out made it possible to use law as a significant instrument for integration in a way that was impossible in Germany. Despite the periodical aristocratic reaction and the venal transmission of legal offices, Roman law played a substantial part in the spread of universalistic norms. The length of the national integration process and the relative security (by the seventeenth century) of the French state softened somewhat the pressures for arbitrary central action. Thus Colbert's "meddling despotic police" was somewhat milder than Frederick William I's "police state"; and the counter-ideology, a *bonne police* (mere maintenance of order) was correspondingly weaker than nostalgia for the old *Rechtsstaat*.[60]

Law was an essential aspect of the quasi-bourgeois style of the *noblesse de robe*. Like the classics, law taught one how to organize arguments, citing the historical precedents which constituted legitimizing symbols in the general rhetorical culture.[61] Conversely, no amount of legal training in itself even nominally qualified one for high office, which had to be purchased or obtained by special favor. Privileged young men in law faculties knew, therefore, that they were meeting a largely formal requirement. As a result, eighteenth-century French legal study was even weaker than in Germany, arousing complaints that "men of little standing, brought up in the sloth of the schools of Paris, go on to issuing judgments in the Palace [of Justice]."[62]

In a sense, the Revolution itself was the work of lawyers who had little standing—i.e., *avocats* excluded from the judicial and administrative posts of the *noblesse de robe*. Jean Anouilh's striking time-dimensional juxtaposition of "Poor Bitos," the rancorous prosecutor of the Liberation, and his spiritual predecessor, the bloodthirsty lawyer Robespierre, dramatically portrays a continuity in French history. Law study was interrupted by the Revolution, but it resumed in private institutions as early as 1805. "The new dynasties born of the Revolution and the Directoire were predominantly barristers, attorneys and judges."[63] There appears to have been little distinction among regimes:

[60] Pages, "Essai," p. 18.   [61] F. Ford, pp. 188ff.
[62] Comte de Boulainville, *Etat de la France*, Vol. 1 (London, 1727), xiii.
[63] J. M. and Brian Chapman, *The Life and Times of Baron Haussmann: Paris in the Second Empire* (London, 1957), p. 9; cf. Joseph Aynard, *La Bourgeoisie*

certainly law was prestigious under the Restoration, but it continued to be the major higher preparation for high administration and politics under the July Monarchy, the Second Empire, and the Third Republic. Conservatives favored law as a traditional class symbol, while distrusting its rationalistic tendencies; radicals recognized its value for mobility.

Throughout the three generations between the Revolution and the Republican triumph in the late 1870's, however, law remained only one of two major avenues to the elite administration. Usually law predominated, but at brief intervals of revolutionary upheaval the more technological orientation represented by the military engineering and artillery corps and the Polytechnique were in the ascendancy. Like the recrudescence of the classics, law became more important during the "radical" years of the Third Republic. There is some connection between the two phenomena. Intensive Latin was justified as required by future students of Roman law. The Ecole Normale followed by a *lycée* instructorship was one significant channel of upward mobility. As under the Old Regime, however, law remained the *best* resource of the young man "who has more talent than legitimacy."[64]

The increase in law training among prefects (the corps with the greatest number of upwardly mobile members) illustrates the point. Under the republican Gambetta 70 per cent were legally trained; from 1876 to 1918, 94 per cent; and during the interwar period 91 per cent. Though lawyers remained a majority both among Vichy prefects and those installed by the Fourth Republic, the near monopoly of the Third Republic was not regained.[65] In the meantime, however, as in Prussia, law had become less available as a channel for mobility. Lengthening the term from three to four years raised a further barrier (as it did in Prussia) to poor youths. It is true that degrees (*licenses*) showed a steady increase from 900 per year in the 1850's to 2,500 per year in the 1930's, with a corresponding decrease in the enormous wastage of students dropping out before completion. It appears, however, that this increase was due mainly to a recognition by wealthier bourgeois elements that legal training was very important for their sons. The most highly educated lawyers have increasingly been associated with industry and commerce (40 per cent in 1964) as contrasted to private practice (34 per cent) and government (24 per cent).[66]

Française: Essai de Psychologie Sociale (Paris, 1934), p. 160; Eschmann, pp. 137, 153, 202ff.

[64] Vicomte G. Avenel, *Les Revenus d'un Intellectuel de 1200 à 1913: Les Riches depuis Sept Cent Ans* (Paris, 1922), p. 261.

[65] Siwek-Pouydesseau, *Le Corps Préfectoral*, pp. 31, 34.

[66] *Le Figaro*, March 3, 1964.

Certainly the relative increase in legally trained Financial Inspectors, the corps closest to the *grande bourgeoisie*, points in the same direction. By the time of the Fourth Republic the proportion of working-class youths in the law faculties was lower than in most other branches of higher education.[67]

Institutionally, the center from which legal doctrines and legal styles radiated during the Third Republic was the Council of State. In 1872 its broadened competence led the law schools to base their administrative law instruction primarily on rulings of the Council. As one French analyst aptly puts it, this led to an overconcern with the pathological (contentious) aspects of administrative activity as contrasted to what were, at least potentially, dynamic institutions and organizations. Part of this formalistic trend was due to professors' complete monopoly of instruction in the law faculties, as contrasted to the cooperation between academics and practitioners in other elite higher educational institutions. Another factor was the increasing tendency of members of the elite technical corps to withdraw to routine activity or private enterprise. What these factors add up to is the trite but important observation that the Third Republic, at least as compared to its predecessors and the Fifth Republic, was a "stalemate society." The kind of administrative elite training required in Great Britain served definite interests of the educational elite; the Prussian legal variety was fostered by the administrative elite itself. Under the Third Republic, on the other hand, no clear pattern of group interests, and hence no persistent—much less consistent—ideology legitimizing training requirements appears. In legal training as in other areas, the situation was confused and varying because the society itself was not moving in a discernible direction. Certainly this observation should caution one against attributing dominant importance to patterns of administrative elite preparation or, in fact, to the administrative elite itself.

CONVERGENT EFFECTS OF LEGAL AND LITERARY STYLES

Some effects of the types of elite administrative training dominant in Britain, Prussia, the German Federal Republic, and Third Republic France on elite administrative role definition have been suggested. We shall be in a better position to assess the overall impact of emphasis on legal procedures and styles after examining (in Chapter Ten) the significant differences in postinduction socialization in Prussia and France. Enough evidence has been adduced already, however, to suggest how constricted was the rationalizing effect of supposedly special-

[67] T. Feyzioglu, "The Reforms of the French Higher Civil Service since 1945," *Public Administration*, xxxiii (1955), 184; cf. Lalumière, pp. 13, 25.

ized entrance requirements. As Weber's rather neglected predecessor, Gustav Schmoller, pointed out as long ago as 1870, the more examinations were required in the Prussian service, the greater the success of sons of the favored official stratum.[68]

Shmuel Eisenstadt's proposition that imperial bureaucracies are more inclined to traditional, legalistic attitudes than are the monarchs appears to be substantiated by the old-regime history of both France and Prussia.[69] The dynamic effect of legal prescriptions on overcoming particularist attitudes during national integration can be succeeded by stagnation when judicial methods are used to administer a more complex societal system. As early as the 1840's, expert critics of German trends warned of the unhappy effects of mixing judicial and administrative methods.[70] Newspapers generally sympathetic to the governmental system of the German Federal Republic echo these criticisms over a century later: the *Juristenmonopol* leads Bonn administrators to accept rigid legal restrictions complacently instead of seeking ways for governmental initiative or planning.[71]

A more precise, though indirect, effect of legal dominance of formal preparation is exclusion of alternative subjects which might positively affect role definition in economic development. We shall examine some of these alternatives in detail in the next chapter, but their minimization by legal preemption of the curriculum needs to be emphasized here. Law tends to become an end in itself; all the substance of administrative activity is regarded (as a German law professor advocated in 1868) as auxiliary.[72] The same abstraction from reality has been apparent in France in periods of legal ascendancy. In 1885 a French professor of law, Georges Blondel, published a scathing critique of German legal and administrative training. Its objectivity was attested by numerous German reviewers; indeed, Blondel is almost equally critical of his own colleagues. His detailed comparison of curricula in the Paris and Berlin law faculties shows that several branches (Roman law, civil procedure, penal law) of a specialized nature received heavier attention in the Prussian faculty.[73] Both curricula were overwhelmingly

[68] Schmoller, "Der preussische Beamtenstand," p. 171.
[69] Eisenstadt, p. 164.
[70] R. Mohl, "Ueber die wissenschaftliche Bildung der Beamten in den Ministerien des Innern, mit besonderer Anwendung auf Württemberg," *Zeitschrift für die gesamte Staatswissenschaft*, II (1845), 149.
[71] Roman Schnier, "Haben wir die richtigen Beamten?" *Die Zeit*, December 16, 1966; Emmerich Francis, "Beamte—Spezialisten für das Allgemeine," *Frankfurter Allgemeine Zeitung*, March 15, 1966; Jörg Eckart, "Hierarchie von vorgestern," *Die Zeit*, October 1, 1965; "Volkswirte im zweiten Glied," *Der Volkswirt*, May 4, 1962.
[72] Schäffle, "Zur Frage der Prüfungsansprüche an die Candidaten des höheren Staatsdienstes," *Zeitschrift für die gesamte Staatswissenschaft*, XXIV (1868), 608-609.
[73] Blondel, p. 76.

theoretical and abstract, with the Prussian giving somewhat more attention to administrative law. On the other hand, Paris alone taught political science. With the increasing indispensability of the supplementary studies of the Ecole Libre des Sciences Politiques, at least a precedent for more policy-oriented approaches was established. Conversely, German law studies have continued to maintain a virtual monopoly of administrative preparation. Nevil Johnson has recently summed up the current situation:

> A legalist approach to administrative activity is a dominant characteristic of the German tradition of government, and there is so far little sign of fundamental change in this respect. Indeed, political and constitutional changes since 1945 have strengthened this tradition rather than weakened it.[74]

At first sight, the British Administrative Class competition is a real "liberty hall" compared to the rigid German specifications. In practice, legal dominance of German elite administrative requirements has had almost exactly the same effect on excluding other kinds of career preparations as has the nominally unlimited range of subjects for the British administrative entrance. In both cases a relatively unchanging field of study, deriving its inspiration from preindustrial periods, has prevailed. Like most stable bureaucracies of the past (the Chinese Mandarins or the Byzantine literati come to mind), the German and the British have prepared their aspirants by mastery of intricate, often graceful patterns of words and categories which bear little direct relation to societal patterns. One would be tempted to conclude that these superficially different but convergent styles are inevitable for a stable administrative elite—if the alternatives were not so clearly posed by contemporary experience.

[74] Nevil Johnson, "Western Germany," in Ridley, p. 147.

CHAPTER NINE

Alternatives in Higher Education

I F LAW IS (almost) the world's oldest profession, engineering is nearly the newest. In contrast to the professions taught in the four traditional university faculties by a regular body of "scientific" instructors legally qualified to certify their successors, engineering depended on "this formation, at once familial and practical, [which] is a characterisitic trait of the old technical administrations."[1] Long after the eighteenth-century Prussian civil administration had abolished patrimonial transmission of ordinary offices, mining officials were allowed to transmit their posts to their sons, for there was no other way to ensure the supply of highly trained personnel. Even after formal training was instituted in France, succession of provincial chief engineers was tolerated. Dynasties of district engineers were common even under Napoleon I.[2]

MILITARY NECESSITY AND ENGINEERING TRAINING

The crucial element in the transition to formal, rationalized preparation for engineering was military necessity. A French corps of fortification engineers was organized in the sixteenth century. The first formal training institution was the Royal Academy of Architects (1671), with aristocratic overtones in its fine arts and architecture activities, but also providing advice on fortifications, mines, and bridges. A generation later the Ecole Royale de Génie was founded as a military engineers' school at Mézières. Impressed by Sébastien Vauban, the great military engineer, Louis XIV received engineers and personally went over their plans. All these contacts helped Colbert establish the corps of Ponts et Chaussées as the first permanent body of civil engineers. It was not, however, until 1744 that the Ecole des Ponts et Chaussées was established at Paris.[3]

Both military and civil engineering schools had no difficulty surviv-

[1] Petot, p. 129.

[2] Rosenberg, p. 79; Manfred Janowski, "Prussian Policy and the Development of the Ruhr Mining Region, 1766-1865" (Dissertation, University of Wisconsin, Madison, 1968), pp. 25ff.; Pierre Clément, *Lettres, Instructions et Mémoires de Colbert*, Vol. IV (Paris, 1867), 444n; Petot, pp. 18, 186.

[3] Frederick B. Artz, *The Development of Technical Education in France, 1500-1850* (Cambridge, Mass., 1966), pp. 30, 32, 47; Jacques Guttin, *Vauban et le Corps des Ingénieurs Militaires* (Dissertation, University of Paris, Faculté de Droit, 1947), pp. 37-38; Aubry, p. 11; King, p. 92; Petot, p. 73.

ing the Revolution which (as the foundation of the Polytechnique indicates) was at least verbally enthusiastic about scientific and technical progress. Continuity was maintained by Gaspard Monge's movement from the directorship of Mézières to the Polytechnique, and by an influx of students from Old-Regime engineering families. Later, as Ben-David writes, there was a "re-emergence and reinforcement under Napoleon and the Restoration of the same constellation of social forces which furthered the growth of science during the last decades of the *ancien régime*."[4]

Before exploring the aspects of these forces which affected technological administration, it is important to note that the French innovations retained their appeal to Europe despite their takeover by "usurpers." Soon after foundation of the Polytechnique, European ambassadors vied to secure places in its student body for their protégés. Pursuing the active Russian interest in borrowing French advances (for example, a French engineer became commander of the Kiev district engineering forces in 1770, although he could scarcely speak Russian), Alexander I secured four Ponts de Chaussées graduates to form the instructional nucleus of the Transport Institute. Possibly political second thoughts led him to choose as director of the new Transport Corps a Spanish nobleman (Augustin de Béthencourt). Under the Restoration, Russian dependence on French engineering was maintained by securing, in rotation, the services of French engineers in the Transport Corps.[5]

It is an indication of the relative status of engineers in Russia and Germany that a leading instructor of the first real technical institute in Germany was a former member of the St. Petersburg Academy of Sciences (to be sure, he was of German origin). The new Freiberg Mining Academy in Saxony was well in advance of anything of its kind in Prussia. The first German civil engineering school was also founded in a small state (at Karlsruhe in Baden).[6]

OVERCOMING ARISTOCRATIC ANTIPATHY TO
MATERIAL MANIPULATION

The fundamental barrier to professionalization of engineering (as Everett Hagen has pointed out) was the antipathy of aristocratic

[4] Joseph Ben-David, "The Rise and Decline of France as a Scientific Centre," *Minerva*, VIII (1970), 161.

[5] Pinet, *Histoire*, p. ix; Petot, p. 470; Cameron, *France*, p. 56; Stephen P. Timoshenko, "The Development of Engineering Education in Russia," *Russian Review*, XV (1956), 174-78; M. Krutikov, "Nachalo Zheleznodorozhnogo Stroitel'stva v Rossii (iz Zapisok P. P. Mel'nikova)," *Krasny Arkhiv*, CIC (1940), 140n.

[6] Artz, *Development*, p. 76; Walter Hoffmann, *Bergakademie Freiberg* (Frankfurt, 1959), pp. 35, 48.

strata to an occupational role centering on manipulation of materials. As discussed in Chapter Four, command of men was the central feature of the aristocratic role; literary attainments (in the broadest sense) represented an increasingly acceptable compromise with bourgeois standards. Material manipulation, on the other hand, was "dirty work" associated with the lower classes.[7] Even in twentieth-century United States more students in fields like engineering have persistently come from manual worker families than have law students (24 per cent compared to 18 per cent in 1910; 31 per cent versus 19 per cent in 1940).[8]

Part of the genius, or good fortune, of the originators of formal civil engineering training in France was to recognize this status difficulty. The association of engineering with military prowess was an important remedy. At first, however, chiefly nobles or wealthy bourgeois "living nobly" were admitted to Mézières for fear that later in their careers others could not move among the aristocratic alumni of the Ecole Militaire. By the time the Ponts et Chaussées school was founded, however, few aristocratic recruits were available. Instead, students were drawn from the lower ranks of the Ponts et Chaussées corps and from sons of men at that level. It is a striking indication of the importance attached to resocializing these men that they were kept eight years in the school, often until the age of thirty-three.[9] J. R. Perronet, its director, left no doubt about the objective:

Each of us must contain within himself the germ which produces the scholar and the man of the world. Our most essential characteristic is education, for, ordinarily, attitudes depend on it. Further, this lack [of education] cannot be concealed; it appears in every action, it intrudes at each instant, it attracts disdain. The public, occasionally unjust, extends this disdain to all those who are destined to fill the same posts. We have more than one example of the consequences, which cannot be remedied as long as one does not remove the cause.

The lack of good birth, although a prejudice, nearly always means neglected education. We may put it more strongly: the inconveniences which it entails are infinitely consequential. Men who would be able to do honor to a corps sometimes fear compromising themselves, judging a body by the part which discredits it.[10]

[7] Hagen, pp. 76ff.

[8] Joseph R. Gusfield, "Equalitarianism and Bureaucratic Recruitment," *Administrative Science Quarterly*, II (1957-58), 535.

[9] Aubry, p. 11.

[10] Quoted in E.J.M. Vignon, *Etudes Historiques sur l'Administration des Voies Publiques en France aux Dix-Septième et Dix-Huitième Siècles*, Vol. II (Paris, 1862), 283.

Not only did Perronet see that the students were given a minimal education in social and cultural graces, he demanded that after graduating to technical posts they live in "good society" and obtain his permission to marry. The strength of his conviction that only careful preparation and prudence would establish the new profession is shown by his own refusal to become head of the Corps after the brilliant *intendant des finances*, D. C. Trudaine, and his less capable son had held that post. Instead, Perronet insisted on the appointment of an *intendant* whose prestige (as a lawyer and member of the *noblesse de robe*) would assure adequate representation of the Corps among the administrative elite.[11]

The fact of the matter is that it was impossible for a technical administrator (as such) to acquire elite status in eighteenth-century Europe. Some of the differences between social stratification in Russia and Western Europe are indicated by the fact that very early in the nineteenth century, under a regime which was nominally more conservative than Louis XVI's, Russian technical officials became an integral part of the administrative elite. While Alexander I still reigned, his brother Nicholas founded (1819) the Chief Engineering School for military engineers. Numbers of the predominantly middle-class graduates of this school, the Transport Institute, and the Mining School founded in the eighteenth century were able to advance rapidly in *chin*. Many attained hereditary nobility and a few reached the top levels of the civil and military administration. As Emperor, Nicholas I appears to have continued to favor engineer administrators despite the fact that engineer and artillery officers (like their counterparts in contemporary France) were more revolutionary than line officers.[12]

The peak of influence of technically educated officials came under Alexander II during the reforms of the 1860's. While education minister Tolstoi was insisting on classics emphasis in most secondary schools, war minister Miliutin increased the mathematics and technological component of the military *gimnaziia* curriculum and reduced insistence on rigid hierarchy and discipline. Even General Staff officers were brought into contact with technical training by sharing the first two years of their course with geodetic survey officers. During the same period, special privileges of free discussion were accorded to the

[11] M. de Dartein, "La Vie et les Travaux de Jean Rodolphe Perronet, Premier Ingénieur des Ponts et Chaussées, Créateur de l'Ecole des Ponts et Chaussées," *Annales des Ponts et Chaussées*, xxiv, 8e série (1906), 70ff.; Petot, pp. 157ff., 171.
[12] John Shelton Curtiss, *The Russian Army under Nicholas I, 1825-1855* (Durham, 1965), p. 146; Vucinich, I, 172; Walter M. Pintner, *Russian Economic Policy under Nicholas I* (Ithaca, 1967), pp. 48, 95; Stein, p. 380.

St. Petersburg Technological Institute (a generation later a seedbed of Marxism) and Moscow technical institutes.[13]

Military considerations played a predominant part in the rapid rise in prestige of Russian engineers, but other factors were also important. The economic backwardness of the country called for utilizing every expedient. The autocracy was more able to resort to instrumental means than were regimes in strictly stratified Western European societies. Economic backwardness itself kept upper strata from commanding resources sufficient to establish an educational system which could be used as an ideological device for channeling social mobility. One indicator of the unresponsiveness of the educational system to upper-class manipulation was the bitter feeling of nobles of older lineage toward the closed educational institutions preparing recruits for specific branches of government service. Particularly during the period of general European aristocratic reaction in the third quarter of the eighteenth century, nobles complained in vain that these schools and subsequent service transfers disrupted family ties.[14] Another indicator of the inability of the Russian upper strata to manipulate education is the marginal importance of legal training in administrative elite preparation. As Marc Raeff writes, the autocracy was uncurbed because there was no bureaucracy to create a *Rechtsstaat*.[15] It seems paradoxical that the regime itself sought time and again to develop such a legally oriented body of administrators. Eighteenth-century training sections attached to the State Senate and other central bodies were supposed to provide a basic legal education for adolescents. As soon as a family acquired nobility, it tried to avoid sending its sons there, preferring the military academies. Failure of the Senate *iunker* schools prevented Speransky from requiring legal training on the German model for administrative entrance. Even Baltic Germans commonly left their own law faculty at Dorpat without finishing because degrees were not required for service entrance.[16]

When science became suspect during the extreme conservativism of 1819-53, law was favored in the universities, which had twice as many law as science students in the late 1820's. Apparently hereditary nobles regarded legal studies more favorably. By that time, however, the elite technical schools with their military prestige already offered an alter-

---

[13] *Ibid.*, pp. 367, 371, 401; Armytage, *Rise of the Technocrats*, p. 195.

[14] Lentin, pp. 12ff.

[15] Raeff, "Russian Autocracy," p. 90.

[16] James T. Flynn, "The Universities, the Gentry and the Russian Imperial Services, 1815-1825," *Canadian Slavic Studies*, II (1968), 490ff.; Torke, p. 170; Iablochkov, pp. 483ff.; Dmitrii Kobeko, *Imperatorskii Tsarskosel'skii Litsei: Nastavniki i Pitomtsy, 1811-1843* (St. Petersburg, 1911), p. 7.

native. By 1914 there were 12,947 students in engineering and related technical subjects (to be sure, there were only 7,880 engineers altogether with *completed* higher education), half again as many as the law students.[17]

AUTONOMOUS ENGINEERING TRAINING IN PRUSSIA

There is no doubt that the military needs of Prussia were at least as pressing as those of France and Russia. Artillery and engineering positions provided the best opportunities for bourgeois to become officers during the eighteenth century. Both technical corps remained low in status well into the middle of the nineteenth century, however.[18] As a result military engineering could reflect little prestige on the civil branch. Just as engineering was becoming established after the Napoleonic wars, Greek and law influences at their apogee in the administration led to exclusion (see Chapter Ten) of specialists from decision-making.

The solid Prussian elementary education (which, let us emphasize, was favored by the same group around Wilhelm von Humboldt which considered Greek alone adequate for the select few) provided a foundation for advanced technical training. By the mid-nineteenth century the *Technische Hochschule* constituted a significant higher educational pattern distinct from the universities. Engineers complained that the legally trained administrators set technical certification at a low level corresponding to the inferior status of specialists in the administration. Nevertheless, engineer critics admitted, segregation of their preparation from the philologically and legally dominated universities was helpful. In the *Technische Hochschule* a distinctive professional role developed, inciting engineers "to utilize their own potential for accomplishments to the optimum degree, to obtain scope for engineering operations, to open up for direct action their Promethean creative potential."[19]

[17] Vucinich, I, 226; S. A. Fediukin, *Privlechenie Burzhuaznoi Technicheskoi Intelligentsii k Sotsialisticheskomu Stroitel'stvu v SSSR* (Moscow, 1960), p. 7; L. K. Erman, "Sostav Intelligentsii v Rossii v Kontse XIX i Nachale XX v.," *Istoriia SSSR*, 1963, No. 1, p. 172. Erman indicates 852 law students in *detached* law schools for 1907 and 854 for 1914. Leikina-Svirskaia, p. 58, indicates 7,182 in the university law faculties in 1899. For 1900, 8,000 would seem a reasonable estimate, with possibly a slight increase by 1914, but as Leikina-Svirskaia's earlier figures show, law enrollment was subject to sharp fluctuation.

[18] Demeter, p. 18; Görlitz, p. 107.

[19] Helmut Klages and Gerd Hortleder, "Gesellschaftsbild und soziales Selbstverständnis des Ingenieurs," *Schmollers Jahrbuch*, LXXXV (1965), 671; A. Riedler, "Zur Frage der Ingenieur-Erziehung," *Volkswirtschaftliche Zeitfragen*, XVI (1895), 23-26; Wigard Siebel, "Soziale Funktion und soziale Stellung des Ingenieurs," *Jahrbücher für Sozialwissenschaft*, XIII (1962), 73.

In his isolation from the general elite, the early Prussian engineer naturally turned to industrial entrepreneurs as the prime reference group. Friedrich Krupp (with his crucial role in Prussian military success) did much to raise the status of engineers by his speeches as well as his example.[20] The scarcity of theoretically trained engineers gave them a strong economic position and a certain social prestige, although at first they were only sub-directors. Beginning about 1900, functional division of corporation executive boards offered engineers more access to top private management. After World War I they already tended to predominate.[21] As Table XIV shows, in the Federal Republic scientists and engineers are the largest highly educated management group.

TABLE XIV. FIELDS OF CONCENTRATION OF BUSINESS
EXECUTIVES WITH HIGHER EDUCATIONS *(1950's)*[22]
(Per Cent)

Country	All Technical and Science	Engineering Only	Law	Economics, Business
France	55	(51)	9	10
German Federal Republic	36-57	(45)	19-21	17-21
Great Britain	42	(20)	9	35
Soviet Union	100	(100)	—	—
United States	46	—	15	31

Suggestions that engineers had a significant role to play in system-wide coordination of the economy were made even before Walther Rathenau. Except in war crises, however, German engineers never had the opportunity to assume major administrative roles. As soon as situations stabilized, the *Juristenmonopol* reasserted its commanding position. The German Federal Republic, like Prussia prior to 1933, is unique among the societies we study in its sharp bifurcation of preparation patterns between governmental administrative elites and pri-

[20] Conrad Matschoss, "Vom Ingenieur, seinem Werden und seiner Arbeit in Deutschland," *Beiträge zur Geschichte der Technik und Industrie*, xx (1930), 4ff.

[21] Fritz Croner, *Die Angestellten in der modernen Gesellschaft: Eine Sozialhistorische und Soziologische Studie* (Frankfurt, 1954), p. 84; Hartmann, pp. 163-65.

[22] Data for France adapted from Delefortrie-Soubeyroux, p. 58, industrial directors (c. 1950, N=over 2,000). West German lower-range data from Hartmann, pp. 164-65, leading members of industrial firm boards of directors (c. 1958, N=c. 2,000), and Zapf, p. 139, managers (1964, N=200). British data from G. H. Copeman, *Leaders of British Industry: A Study of the Careers of More than a Thousand Public Company Directors* (London, 1955), pp. 119, 142 (c. 1954, N=c. 1,650). Soviet data from Jerry Hough, *The Soviet Prefects: The Local Party Organs in Industrial Decision-Making* (Cambridge, Mass., 1969), p. 47, all Ministers in industrial and construction areas appointed in 1940's and 1950's (N=53). United States data from *Fortune* survey (c. 1950, as cited in Copeman, p. 142).

vate managerial elites. Increasingly the *Technische Hochschulen* assert their equality with the older legal elite preparation by providing their students with broad managerial training modeled on American schools of business.[23] As compared to the pre-World War I period, the relative status of the German elites, if not reversed, is drastically altered.

STATUS DISADVANTAGE OF ENGINEERING IN ENGLAND

In England (we deliberately exclude Scotland), the situation of the engineering profession has been much more ambiguous than in Germany. The archetypal industrial revolution, as Chadwick implied in arguing that proposed civil service requirements would have excluded men like George Stephenson, depended to a considerable extent on engineers' accomplishments: "Quite rightly the mid-Victorians chose engineers as their folk heroes."[24] British engineers were sought as much as the French for practical construction tasks throughout the early nineteenth-century world—for example, to design the Havre-Paris railroad and the first railroad bridge across the Dnieper River at Kiev. All the while, however, civil engineering remained essentially an apprenticed craft. It is said that the noted canal-builder, Thomas Telford, a founder of the Institution of Civil Engineering in the 1820's, did not know the elements of geometry. In contrast to France, the rationalizing intellectual followers of Bentham tended (like contemporary *New* England merchants and industrialists) to regard technical advances as the products of "mechanics," and science as unrelated to practical application. Qualifying examinations were not legally established for civil engineers until 1898.[25]

A crucial factor in the slow professionalization of engineering was the reluctance of the British military establishment to incorporate engineer officers. Partly this was due to limited requirements for ground warfare, but even in applying technology to shipbuilding (as contrasted to seamanship) the French were so far ahead that British captains preferred to command prizes. In the Peninsular campaign, Wellington relied (sometimes at considerable cost) on the bayonet rather than the sapper. His preference arose partly from the poor provision of engineer troops but apparently typify the persistently preindustrial attitude of British army officers.[26] As late as the mid-nine-

---

[23] Hartmann, pp. 194ff.   [24] Briggs, p. 395.

[25] Polyani, pp. 119-20; Olinthus J. Vignoles, *Life of Charles Blacker Vignoles* (London, 1889), pp. 121, 340; John B. Rae, "The Engineer as Business Man in American Industry: A Preliminary Analysis," *Explorations in Entrepreneurial History*, VII (1954), 96ff.; Reader, p. 71.

[26] Whitworth Porter, *History of the Corps of Royal Engineers* (London, 1889), pp. 310-11.

teenth century, engineer or artillery service was regarded as dubious for gentlemen precisely because commissions in those branches, unlike the line, were not purchased.[27]

After the Napoleonic wars a School of Military Engineering (Chatham) was founded, but not until 1863 was entrance there or at the older artillery-engineering school at Woolwich wholly competitive.[28] Trained engineers retired from the military were important in railroad and other private activities. In general, however, civil engineering was left to its own resources to pass on acquired skills. The business community (like the German engineers) suspected that continued reliance on eclectic methods was better than attachment to the traditional universities; businessmen did not welcome the establishment (1875) of a chair in engineering at Cambridge. The Royal College of Chemistry was supported between 1850 and 1875 by private employers who feared a fully public institution would leak their "secrets." Part of the difficulties of the Royal School of Mines (1862) arose from fears that institutionalization of the mining craft would be equivalent to "Germanism." Actually, it would take more than a century for England to have any institution approaching the great *Technische Hochschulen* in broad technological training capacity.[29]

Right into the post-World War II period the status of the British engineer has remained low. Science has been regarded as "fit for a gentleman" (perhaps a rather odd one), but engineering has not, partly because of its low educational status. Most engineers are trained, as in Germany, in special schools; but only one-half receive higher degrees. As late as 1959 only 40 of 630 new members of the Institute of Marine Engineers were university graduates. Of a sample of business executives with university degrees, only 17 per cent were engineers (as compared to 25 per cent in science). On the other hand, British management in the twentieth century has steadily increased its proportion of Oxbridge and public school alumni.[30] This trend stands in sharp contrast not only to the German trend analyzed above, but to American experience. United States corporation heads with technical degrees increased from 7 per cent in 1900 to 33 per cent in 1964, with a still larger proportion of younger executives in this category.[31]

The British trend has been, in fact, for the managerial elite (at least in larger corporations) to become more like the Administrative Class.

[27] Reader, p. 74.   [28] *Ibid.*, p. 97; Porter, pp. 310-11.

[29] Reader, pp. 131, 140-41; Armytage, *German Influence*, p. 75.

[30] Copeman, pp. 119, 142; Kenneth Prandy, *Professional Employees: A Study of Scientists and Engineers* (London, 1965), pp. 19ff.; Robert Millar, *The New Classes* (London, 1966), pp. 70-73.

[31] Jay M. Gould, *The Technical Elite* (New York, 1966), p. 82; Newcomer, p. 87.

It is possible that recent developments like the Fulton Committee report will accelerate this trend by providing the administrative elite with an engineering minority comparable to the corporations'. Up to the 1970's, however, all convergence was accomplished by corporate movement toward the civil service model. Although C. P. Snow pressed for more scientists and engineers as "future directed" compared to the "short-term" views he saw predominating in the Administrative Class, exactly three men trained in science were recruited to that class in the decade (1948-57) he served as a Civil Service Commissioner.[32]

By the middle of the nineteenth century, engineer training was well established in France and Russia as a route to elite administrative posts. In Britain and Prussia it had developed in an isolated way which, given the intense ideological commitment to other preparation, precluded acceptance of engineers in the administrative elites. French development after the Napoleonic period indicates technology's potential for altering the elite structure, but also the formidable difficulties of accomplishing this through substitution of engineering training for traditional elite socialization mechanisms.

As discussed in Chapter Three, soon after its foundation the Polytechnique became a center for propagating radical social doctrines as well as rationalizing techniques. Without the Polytechnique, Saint-Simonism probably would have remained a minor intellectual curiosity like Owen's or Blanqui's ideas. Early in the 1790's (in one of the first systematic "elite studies") the Polytechnique directorate refuted charges of being anti-Revolutionary by showing that 116 of 274 students were sons of artisans and peasants, as contrasted to 39 rich bourgeois and two nobles.[33] By 1815 the Polytechnique's reputation was so high that the Restoration tolerated it in spite of the students' vigorous anticlericalism. The school was a main force in the 1830 revolution, and its graduates were intellectually dominant among the 1848 revolutionary leaders.

In the late nineteenth century, after the final triumph of the bourgeoisie, the political complexion of the Polytechnique, the Ecole des Ponts et Chaussées, and the Ecole des Mines altered gradually but drastically. The Polytechnique remained a channel of mobility for the lower bourgeoisie, but increasingly industrialists saw it as a means for securing excellent training and valuable contacts for their sons. There is no reason to doubt a Soviet historian's contention that a parallel development occurred in the Russian elite engineering schools of the late

[32] Weinberg, p. 143; Sir James Dunnett, "The Civil Service Administrator and the Expert," *Public Administration*, xxxix (1961), 227.
[33] Pinet, *Histoire*, p. 132.

nineteenth century. Their students became more heavily noble and wealthy bourgeois in origin and many became directors and managers of private companies on graduating.[34] Still imbued with the Saint-Simonian idea of a semi-private administration paralleling and intersecting the governmental one, French engineers did not regard close association with the wealthy bourgeoisie as a renunciation of their roles in planning the economy and transforming nature. This role perception was clearest during the dynamic periods of the July Monarchy and the Second Empire, but a residue persisted under the Third Republic. As Table XV indicates, private managers were somewhat more likely to have engineering and scientific backgrounds in the middle years of the Third Republic than later, though the Polytechnique con-

TABLE XV. HIGHER EDUCATIONAL BACKGROUNDS
OF FRENCH MANAGERS[35]
(Per Cent)

Period of Education	All Engineering and Science	Polytechnique	Law and Ecole des Sciences Politiques
1900-1909	54	21	19
1910-1929	59	22	16
1930-1949	44	22	25

tingent remained constant. On the governmental side, during the decades of legal dominance elite engineer graduates dominated the technical corps, which still performed major administrative tasks. In addition, limited numbers of Polytechnique graduates were assured entrance to the Financial Inspector corps and even—despite the legal nature of its activity—the Council of State.

ROLE CONFLICT AMONG ENGINEER ADMINISTRATORS

As Amitai Etzioni has commented, "when people with strong professional orientations take over managerial roles, a conflict between the organizational goal and the professional orientations usually occurs."[36] The impact of engineering preparation on an administrator's role definition can hardly fail to instill an element of eagerness to participate in industrial development. Not only is the engineering profession closely related to industrialization, but professional status depends on the importance attached to this process. The very strength of this iden-

[34] Fediukin, *Privlechenie*, p. 7.
[35] Adapted from Delefortrie-Soubeyroux, p. 101. The sample (N=487, 1,273, 364, by periods) is of industrial directors active about 1950. We have added twenty to periods of birth to indicate approximate period of completion of education.
[36] Amitai Etzioni, *Modern Organizations* (Englewood Cliffs, N. J., 1964), p. 79.

tification has posed role problems when the engineer ceases to be a staff aide and assumes direction of major resource allocation activities.

Just as criticism of static legalism is endemic in Prussian administrative history, concern for excessive outlays by engineers repeatedly appears in French sources. Despite Vauban's reputation and royal favor, Colbert preferred a private contract to his aid in building the great Languedoc canal.[37] A sympathetic observer two generations later expressed a similar concern:

> All that one had to fear [about the Ponts et Chaussées corps] was that in the course of perfecting it one did not make it too expensive by multiplying subaltern personnel. The love of command insinuates itself so readily in the human heart that it would not be surprising if the chief engineers were too submissive to this flattering voice, demanding more sub-inspectors and sub-engineers than the service would require if they worked more themselves and did not waste their time in social contacts.[38]

A century later French engineers, when assigned a project, tried to build it so well that it became a monument to their professional skill.[39] Isaac Péreire wrote:

> Whatever the talent of our engineers, talent which we are the first to recognize, we must say that they are far from being dominated by the spirit of prudence and economic calculation which animates [private] companies. They are generally indifferent to money matters. They need to be guided, reined in by a calculating administration motivated by private interest. The tendency of the engineers to take pleasure in the construction of fine works without concerning themselves with the importance of the costs is indeed the principal source of the difficulties with which the companies have had to contend from the beginning and still must combat daily.[40]

Similarly, mid-nineteenth-century Russian critics of French projects in their country stressed the exorbitant costs. On the other hand, thirty years later Sergei Witte found the Russian Transport Corps itself quite unable to relate projects to costs. A half-century after Witte, "gigantomania" (like the insistence on huge dams and expensive hydroelectric installations when coal-generated electricity would have been

[37] Clément, IV, c.
[38] Charles Duclos, *Essais sur les Ponts et Chaussées* (Amsterdam, 1759), p. 114.
[39] Arthur L. Dunham, "How the First French Railways were Planned," *Journal of Economic History*, I (1941), 2, 18-20.
[40] Isaac Péreire, *La Question des Chemins de Fer* (Paris, 1879), p. 45.

cheaper) was a besetting weakness of the dominantly engineer-trained Soviet administrative elite. Overriding concern for meeting material planned targets has consistently led Soviet industrial managers to pay little attention to quality as well as cost reduction except in crucial military fields. The continued French emphasis on quality, on the other hand, may (according to Andrew Shonfield) have more beneficial application in mid-twentieth-century technology where high quality with minimal regard for cost is critical.[41] It is hard not to defer to an economist on this kind of a question. When the layman considers the magnificent technology of French color television (shared, significantly, with the USSR) and its impractical expense, he is bound to have his doubts, however.

A much broader question, which can only be suggested here, is the ability of the engineer administrator to take into account the *social* costs of his projects. It is hardly accidental that the trend toward segregating an elite of highly trained engineers from routine specialists appeared in those societies (France and Russia) where engineering became established as an elite administrative preparation. Confidence in being an elite by training was almost indispensable if the new professionals were to make their way among elite administrators still somewhat attached to aristocratic models. A concomitant of this confidence, as the French sociologist Nora Mitrani wrote, was the tendency to adopt abstract rationalization to the neglect of human values. The "rational" administrator believes he can carry over his ability in engineering situations (where, at least in principle, he can know all the factors) to "human engineering" or "economic humanism." Moreover, she continues, the psychoanalytic compensation mechanism for his excessive rationality is naïve mysticism, religiosity, conventional morality, and devotion to charismatic leaders. The suppressed human values reappear as infrahuman or superhuman. In any event they are extremely unhealthy as guides to broad social planning. While he notes that Party primacy is still unquestioned, Jeremy Azrael sees a similar trend among Soviet managers:

> Like Lopatkin, many of them are fascinated by the notion that their technical expertise implies special political rights—rights that attach to them as members of a self-perpetuating elite ("upper-story men" in Dudintsev's phrase) who are predestined to rule the world in accord with the dictates of a scientific rationality. This rationality, in

---

[41] Shonfield, p. 79; A. I. Chuprov, *Rechi i Stat'i*, Vol. III (Moscow, 1909), 147; N. A. Kislinsky (ed.), *Nasha Zheleznodorozhnaia Politika po Dokumentam Arkhiva Komiteta Ministrov: Istoricheskii Ocherk*, Vol. I (St. Petersburg, 1902), 100ff.

turn, implies comprehensive economic planning and all-embracing social control.[42]

Such "technocracy" is almost the mirror image of the traditional "all-rounder" model: the literary or legally trained administrator, influenced by aristocratic models of character and command, assumes that he can direct without special knowledge; the technocrat assumes that his specialized knowledge provides a key to every situation. As Herman Finer once wrote (criticizing simplistic American and German approaches): "they know more than all about it, but do not know what it is all about."[43]

A Soviet "Technocracy"?

It is not surprising that the engineering approach to administration has been most common in France, the United States, and the USSR, somewhat weaker in Germany and Tsarist Russia, and nearly absent in Great Britain. One is tempted to seek a happy mean among these societal models. In societal analysis, however, it is not necessarily the middle way but the complex way, or *ways*, which lead to a more satisfactory synthesis.

As Michel Crozier has pointed out, it was French high administrators' relentless search for the "one best way" which led (in the 1930's) to abandoning the "world of means" to engineers.[44] A generation earlier, Henri Fayol, himself an engineer by training and experience, typified this trend. It is true that Fayol rejected the overemphasis of technical accomplishments in the great French technical schools: "the chiefs of industry and engineers need to know words and how to write; they don't need mathematics."[45] Nevertheless, his proposed Center of Administrative Studies (for government and private management) would evidently have derived much of its framework from Rathenau's proposals and Taylorism.

The American influence of Frederick Taylor and his epigones like Elton Mayo lie outside our immediate concern. It is undoubtedly significant, as Warren G. Bennis has pointed out, though, that Taylor's management theory was first presented to the American Society of Mechanical Engineers (1895). In effect, the theory tends to "confirm

[42] Jeremy R. Azrael, *Managerial Power and Soviet Politics* (Cambridge, Mass., 1966), p. 156; Nora Mitrani, "Ambiguïté de la Technocratie," *Cahiers Internationaux de Sociologie*, xxx (1961), 105-108, 110ff.

[43] H. Finer, p. 89.

[44] Michel Crozier, "Pour une Analyse Sociologique de la Planification Française," *Revue Française de Sociologie*, vi (1965), 150.

[45] Palewski, *Le Rôle*, pp. 497-500; Marcel Torti, "Les Mathématiques à l'Ecole National d'Administration," *Promotions* (1957), No. 42, pp. 27-29.

a stereotype of the engineer."[46] The persistent impact of Taylorism in the Soviet Union is remarkable. As early as 1918 Lenin approved the League for Scientific Organization of Work (NOT) and the League for Time. Primarily the organizations used Taylor's ideas to stimulate a rural, semi-traditional labor force to industrial standards of promptness and assembly-line diligence. There was, however, a strong effect on the direction of managerial role perception as well. While some of the early Bolshevik industrial directors distrusted Taylorism because of its capitalist origins, like Alexander I a century earlier most believed Russia had to borrow any advanced techniques available. A leading interpreter of Taylorism, P. M. Kerzhentsev, wrote that "our Taylorists (they are found especially among engineers)" tended to be reasonably critical about applying Western European and American methods.[47]

The simplicity of Taylorism and the complete assurance of success in production which it offered appealed to Soviet engineers. Quite possibly Taylor's influence as well as Rathenau's, Fayol's, and Saint-Simon's led the Soviet leadership to consider engineering and related technical training sufficient for the administrative elite. As late as 1959 the Academy of Sciences of the USSR formally reported that:

> no special provision is made for the training of professional administrators; a sufficient grounding in the necessary administrative sciences is acquired in the relevant subject-fields, in general higher educational establishments. The fullest and most specialized teaching of administrative sciences is, of course, provided in the Schools of Law and Economics, since there is a fairly large demand for lawyers and economists in the administration of government departments.[48]

As the last lines suggest, in the USSR as in Great Britain, lawyers and economists have been considered to be staff specialists. In fact, most are employed in the less prestigious government agencies, with few in Party careers. As George Fischer's recent study shows, "a man with a degree in engineering or agronomy is believed by these [Soviet] writers to have many of the skills needed to do good economic work" in the

[46] Warren G. Bennis, "Leadership Theory and Administrative Behavior: The Problem of Authority," *Administrative Science Quarterly*, IV (1959), 263-66; Marian V. Sears, "The American Businessman at the Turn of the Century," *Business History Review*, XXX (1956), 406.

[47] P. M. Kerzhentsev, *Printsipy Organizatsii* (Moscow, 1968), p. 7; cf. A. N. Shcherban', *Nauchnaia Organizatsiia Truda i Upravleniia* (Moscow, 1965), p. 163.

[48] "The Teaching of Administrative Sciences in the Higher Educational Establishments of the Union of Soviet Socialist Republics," Report of the Academy of Sciences of the USSR, *International Review of Administrative Sciences*, 1959, No. 4, p. 453.

practical sense.[49] A famous French administrator told us that Soviet plant managers whom he visited became noticeably warmer when they discovered that he was an engineer, not an economist by background. As early as 1936 when only 29 per cent (230 of 796) of the directors of the largest Soviet industrial enterprises had higher educations at all, 182 had completed higher technical schools as compared to 32 from economics departments.[50] As the small sample reported in Table XIV indicates, the ratio of engineers at the top of the Soviet economic administration has increased since then.

Early Soviet emphasis on engineering approaches was inspired by the dynamic Leninist development interventionist doctrine; this emphasis made a great deal of sense for resource mobilization. The persistent engineering emphasis appears to be a concomitant of the unduly prolonged Russian effort to industrialize. The 1930's, in particular, were a time of tardy effort to complete basic industrial development which had been interrupted by World War I and the Revolution. In a sense, Soviet experience in the first Five Year Plans reversed the Marxist prediction that the "administration of things" will be most important after the attainment of material abundance under full communism. This is not to say—we have treated the question at length elsewhere—that the 1930's was a period in which people were not administered with a heavy hand. However, given the ruthless social control by other agencies, a certain portion of the administrative apparatus (chiefly industrial ministries and enterprises) could virtually disregard human factors. With a very tight supply of capital and expertise, masses of labor and raw materials were poured into a limited range of vital production objectives. Certainly there is a sense in which getting on with construction tasks is more important psychologically and cheaper in the long run than nice calculations of minimal costs in labor and materials. However, the "campaign" methods rationally used in this early period affect role perceptions in a way which constitutes a heavy mortgage on the future, when scarce resources have to be allocated for complex economic purposes. As we shall see in Chapter Eleven, a measure of awareness of this problem is now evident in the USSR, along with increasing attention to mid-career training in more sophisticated managerial techniques. In the Soviet brand of "technocracy" both the production objectives and the persons of the "technocrats" were utterly at the mercy of political manipulation. A detailed comparison with transitory "revolutionary" regimes in Western Europe lies outside the scope of this study. It is worth noting in passing,

[49] Fischer, p. 37.
[50] A. F. Kharvin, "Captains of Soviet Industry," *Voprosy Istorii*, No. 5 (May 1966), condensed trans. in *Current Digest of the Soviet Press*, XVIII, No. 28, p. 3.

though, that Rathenau under the High Command, Speer under Hitler, the "X" (Polytechnique) group under Vichy, and (in a far milder and more complex way) the French planners under DeGaulle likewise relied on and were dominated by strong political authority. It is, indeed, questionable whether "technocracy" can ever be more than a synonym for a special kind of elite administration underwritten by a distinct, potent political authority.

PREMATURE ATTEMPTS TO EMPHASIZE ECONOMICS

The reader may have noticed hints in the preceding pages that economics offered an alternative to technical as well as literary preparation for higher administrative careers. In Chapter Three the great obstacle to adequate development interventionist doctrines was identified as imperfection of economic theory and its statistical apparatus. Now we must see how this inadequacy, as it was gradually overcome, affected administrative elite preparation.

In the eighteenth century, cameralism not only was favored by the Prussian kings but held its own in smaller centers like Mainz. There was even an interchange between practice and pedagogy, for various cameralist professors had been active administrators. Frederick William I's maxim was that "Men make good stewards [Wirte] who themselves have been stewards and officials and have held high charges; who know how to handle a pen and an account book, and who are vigilant and healthy people."[51] As early as Peter I, a primitive case-study system was used in Russian closed training institutions to accustom the boys to practical administrative problems.[52] A practical economic component was included in the Tsarskoe Selo Lycée curriculum, despite the Imperial comptroller V. V. Camphausen's grumbling that philosophy and political economy would lead to revolutionary unrest, for "if I wanted to punish one of my provinces I would have it governed by a scholar."[53] Cameralism died hard in Germany, despite competition from legal "science" and Hardenberg's decision to relax requirements for cameralism on the administrative examinations. There were even proposals to transplant cameralism to France by men dissatisfied with the legal emphasis of administrative training.

Much the most striking nineteenth-century effort to develop an integrated alternative to legal or technological preparation for administrators was the Ecole Nationale d'Administration of 1848. Here was

51 Schmoller, "Der preussische Beamtenstand," p. 168.
52 Raeff, "Etat," p. 299; Seleznev, pp. 320ff.
53 Torke, p. 164.

the "republican seminary" which the Polytechnique was too narrowly technological to be.[54] In fact, the revolution brought to ephemeral power a team of Polytechnicians; the commission it delegated to found the E.N.A. contained several engineers. Nevertheless, the new school was eclectic rather than technical. Alongside mathematics and science, Greek, Latin, and rhetoric could be offered on the entrance examination, for the objective was to combine youths from the *lycée* and the technical school. Throughout, however, emphasis was on "how" rather than on "what" the candidate knew. The curriculum provided a combination of legal and literary subjects (French, general science and culture, international, private, and criminal law) and a collection of subjects resembling cameralism (agriculture, mining, public works, administrative history, comparative administration, financial and commercial economics). A significant precedent was a two-year "novitiate" (the critic was not far wrong in referring to the "seminary") of practical experience for each candidate before he took the final examination. All this was to prepare one hundred young men per year to fill one-third of the higher administrative vacancies.[55]

Before 1849 was over, the swing away from radical republicanism closed the E.N.A., but not before it had attracted admiration from Germans critical of their own legal monopoly. A French leftist critic three generations later laid the demise of the first E.N.A. to the "reaction" of landed capital against its catering to industrialists.[56] A more likely explanation (apart from the political fortunes of its founders) is that the E.N.A. was simply ahead of its time. Individual courses might (we cannot be certain) have been useful to acquaint the student with practical subjects like mining. What the program lacked was a central theoretical principle (the "science of organization" the school sought was never really developed) to integrate the instruction as a guide for administrative policy. Without such a principle the eclectic curriculum, like cameralism, could not compete with the prestigious law faculties. The "replacement" for the E.N.A. was the provision of more chairs in the Paris law faculty. Even more significant, of 210 E.N.A. students traced a generation later two-thirds were in careers related to law, one-fourth were in business, and only one-twelfth engineers.[57]

What distinguishes the French experience from that of other Euro-

[54] Conseil d'Etat, p. 473.

[55] Charles Tranchant, *Notice Sommaire sur l'Ecole Nationale d'Administration de 1848 et sur les Projets Ultérieurs d'Institutions Analogues* (Nancy, 1884), pp. 9-18.

[56] Augustin Hamon, *Les Maîtres de la France*, Vol. II (Paris, 1937), 217.

[57] "Une Enquête sur l'Ecole Nationale d'Administration," *L'Etat Moderne*, XI (1938), 327; Tranchant, pp. 6off.

pean societies was the continued search for a more satisfactory elite administrative preparation. There seems little doubt that the tension between the two established preparatory routes to administrative careers, partially corresponding to divisions within the administrative elite itself, fostered this quest. The continued search probably reflects deeper societal tensions as well.

The next major innovation was the foundation in 1871 of the Ecole Libre des Sciences Politiques (commonly known as the "Sci Pol"). Its organizers (Taine, Albert Sorel, Ernest Rénan, and Emile Boutmy) were neither lawyers nor technical experts, but men of letters. They admired the tutorial system of "Anglo-Saxon" universities, as contrasted to the formal lectures customary in France.[58] In practice, innovations at the Sci Pol appear to have reflected the *collège* tradition more than the English model. A bitter leftist critique in the 1930's accused the school of "Jesuit methods": full occupation of the student's time to keep him out of trouble, screening of reading materials, and discrete guidance of students to approved courses.[59] Our own observation of the new Sci Pol (1952) does bear out the charge that students were steered away from instructors critical of regime policy (at that time French colonialism). On the other hand, the old Sci Pol was extraordinarily *mondaine*, i.e., open to upper-class society. Like all of the great nineteenth-century French schools, it was located on the Left Bank, but the Sci Pol was not a boarding school. Since it was essentially a final stage of higher education (for some students it was little more than a cram course) rather than a complete preparatory program, its socialization impact was low. The Sci Pol offered young aspirants to administrative careers an excellent if brief opportunity to get acquainted with the workings of metropolitan life after the rigidities of the *lycée* and law faculty and before the pressures of official duties.

The departure in formal curriculum from the law faculty program was considerable. Sci Pol study included economics (taught from a laissez-faire position), administrative law and organization, "financial science," fiscal legislation, and public accounting. On the whole, the curriculum represented a compromise between that of the law faculty and a pragmatic economic orientation. Four-fifths of the instructors were from the various University of Paris faculties or governmental positions, leaving only a scattering from private business.[60] On the other hand, the Sci Pol received private business subsidies from the start.

Much the strongest criticism directed against the Sci Pol, especially

[58] Conseil d'Etat, p. 473; Lalumière, pp. 27-28; Feyzioglu, p. 74.
[59] A. Hamon, II, 222.   [60] Feyzioglu, p. 81.

in the interwar period, was the class bias of its recruitment, which was much stronger than that of the government institutions. At least in the last years of the Sci Pol tuition was not high, but the lack of scholarships (until 1938) kept out the less wealthy. It is estimated that 85 per cent of the students were from the higher bourgeoisie, nearly all Parisian.[61] Since during the 1899-1936 period virtually all entrants to the great administrative corps (except the prefectural and the technical services) spent at least a short time at the Sci Pol, it did look like an instrument of upper-class monopoly.

E.N.A.—TRIUMPH OF ECONOMICS-CENTERED TRAINING

By 1938 dissatisfaction with the Sci Pol as well as with administrative fragmentation had led to a detailed project for a new Ecole Nationale d'Administration; the school was actually founded in 1945. It is highly questionable whether the objection of class bias has really been met. Entrance is by grueling competitive written examination. Not only is there no tuition but students are paid small salaries. In order to have a serious chance in the open competition, though, candidates must have spent at least three years in previous higher education; nearly three-fourths of the first E.N.A. classes had completed university studies, mostly in law.[62] Many take advanced work at the Sci Pol (now a state school renamed the Institute of Political Studies) as well. These higher educational stages (and, of course, the mandatory *lycée* preparation) are now free; but supporting a young man through them poses a heavy burden for a family with a moderate income. One-third of the E.N.A. openings are reserved for lower-ranking officials, but many successful candidates are men with higher education who have chosen this route because the competition is less severe. Much more important, 87 per cent (1953-63) of the top E.N.A. students who obtain *Grands Corps* assignments have entered the school through the open competition.[63] In effect, therefore, some nine-tenths of recent entrants to *Grands Corps* (nontechnical branches of the administrative elite as we define it in Chapter Ten) have been young men (there are a few women now) with family backgrounds and wealth sufficient to see them through a long and arduous preparation for the E.N.A. Consequently, it is not very meaningful that a smaller proportion of *all* E.N.A. students (60 to 65 per cent) are from the higher bourgeoisie, as compared to prewar Sci Pol enrollment. It is

[61] Kessler, p. 154.
[62] *Ibid.*; Thomas Bottomore, "La Mobilité Sociale dans la Haute Administration Française," *Cahiers Internationaux de Sociologie*, XIII (1952), 172.
[63] Kesler, p. 255.

possible that the upper classes are more strongly represented in the administrative elite now than before World War II, when neither entrance nor lateral transfer was monopolized by a single preparatory institution.[64]

The E.N.A. has nominally met the second need perceived in the interwar period—a unified experience for the majority of the administrative elite recruits. Whether in practice this means a unified administration will be discussed later. In its early years the E.N.A. program was differentiated in accordance with the administrative branches which students intended to enter. Aside from the diplomatic section (which lies outside our concern) curriculum differences were not very great. For example, Ministry of Interior officials complained that only one-eighth of the instruction in the general administration section (where their candidates prepared) was focused on public law and administrative questions peculiar to the Ministry.[65] The remaining sections were for economic and financial administration and for social administration—neither designed for a specific ministry. Even in the early years, former students urged more, not fewer, courses in common.[66]

The core of E.N.A. instruction is economics. In contrast to the old Sci Pol, however, it is Keynesianism, not laissez-faire economics. At last—so its enthusiasts think—the integrating doctrine which cameralism and the old E.N.A. lacked has been found. There are, let us recall, two elements in any development interventionist doctrine: 1) a psychological stimulus to active role definition; 2) a theoretical and statistical apparatus for effective macro-economic intervention. Certainly Keynes' theory appears to provide the first element for the younger elite administrators who have passed through the E.N.A. The anti-Malthusian aspects of the theory provide the rationale for the "mystique of expansion" which has replaced the long period of stalemate society.[67] The fact that Michel Debré, who struggled from 1938 on to establish the E.N.A., led the way in applying Keynesian theory as a Financial Inspector and then as DeGaulle's first premier undoubtedly has heightened confidence in the practical import of the economic doctrine. Being the least doctrinaire of development doctrines, Keynesian-

[64] Cf. Fulton Committee, v (2), 670; Bernard Gournay, "Un Groupe Dirigéant de la Société Française: Les Grands Fonctionnaires," *Revue Française de Science Politique*, xiv (1964), 224.

[65] Association du Corps Préfectoral et des Administrateurs Civils du Ministère de l'Intérieur. *Du Récrutement et des Débouchés des Cadres Supérieurs du Ministère de l'Intérieur*. Rapport présenté au nom de la Commission du Statut par M. R. Bonnaud Delamare, Préfet de l'Aisne (n.p., n.d.), p. 7.

[66] Thomas Bottomore, "Les Hauts Fonctionnaires Français," *Promotions* (1955), No. 33, pp. 56-57; Feyzioglu, pp. 71-72.

[67] Kesler, pp. 244, 263.

ism is acceptable to the basically bourgeois outlook of the administrators. Following Keynes, they can maintain flexible, intimate relations with private management consonant with the established practices of common socialization and frequent interchange of roles.

These practices are favored by the second basic element of the instructional program, the *stage*. The nearest English equivalent to this term is "work-study," which conveys a misleading impression of an arrangement designed to help impecunious students. In France the *stage* is an old tradition reaching back to Ponts et Chaussées training assignments under the Old Regime. Early Polytechnicians visited industries, performed manual work, and were given long vacations to keep them in touch with practical affairs.[68] For some decades the great advanced technical schools have also used the *stage* system. Formal study is interspersed with work assignments integrated in the overall study program and directly relevant to the students' career objectives. At the E.N.A. the director of *stages* is, perhaps, the single most important staff member. He not only assigns students but carefully follows their progress on the job and after return to formal study. During the second year, assignment to a prefecture is critical for relating the student to the kind of field administration which (as discussed in Chapter Twelve) has played such an important part in French administrative evolution. The student's final class standing (which determines his ability to choose his career line) depends to a considerable degree on the prefect's evaluation. The student, on the other hand, is also required to submit a critical evaluation of the prefecture. In his third year the student has a briefer *stage* in private enterprise designed to make future contact with the private sector smoother.

In the course of his study in the E.N.A.'s rather unimpressive Left-Bank quarters as well as during the *stages*, the aspiring administrator encounters a world far removed from the formalities of traditional French secondary and higher education. Formal instruction by the case method is based, usually, on actual files of administrative agencies rather than on model cases. Most crucial is the fact that 80 to 85 per cent of the instructional staff has consisted of active members of the *Grands Corps* or the next highest level of administration (*administrateurs civils*).[69] These men are carefully selected by the school's council not only for their expert knowledge of administration but for their ability to inspire—i.e., to socialize—students to the values of the elite

[68] Pinet, *Histoire*, p. xvii; cf. Brian Chapman, *The Profession of Government: The Public Service in Europe* (London, 1959), p. 91.

[69] André Bertrand and Marceau Long, "L'Enseignement Supérieur des Sciences Administratives en France," *International Review of Administrative Science*, xxvi (1960), 14, 19.

administration. Increasingly instructors have been alumni of the E.N.A. itself, only a decade removed in age and experience from the students they guide. The ambitious student is set a model sufficiently close in age to make the rewards of emulation seem proximate and calculable.

There is a reverse side to this model which is not so openly avowed. By limiting academic instructors to about one-tenth, the E.N.A. effectively interrupts the relation of its students to educational elites. Politically, this removes a leftist influence from an administrative body which has been consistently, though slightly, right of center, and facilitates rapprochement with private-sector managerial elites. Limitation of academics also reduces the impact of educational ideologies which, as we have seen, have distorted general elite socialization in France and administrative elite socialization in Prussia and Britain.

The mere fact that the E.N.A. must interrupt its students' pattern of socialization is a weakness, for the effectiveness of early adult occupational socialization resides mainly in reinforcing patterns developed at earlier ages. Prior socialization of the upper-middle-class young men who constitute the majority of E.N.A. enrollees has not, to be sure, been dominated by leftist academic elements. There is much more variety of instructors' attitudes in the law faculties and the great Parisian *lycées*, to say nothing of the Catholic *collèges*, than this summary description implies. No doubt, too, youths are selective in their teacher-models. Familial and peer-group influences have generally inculcated values which E.N.A. socialization can recombine to establish career objectives like zeal for accomplishing great tasks and a sense of the superiority of state interests.

The extreme dominance of earlier literary education does, however, appear to pose certain problems. Understandably, the E.N.A. alumnus is proud of the traditions of French education:

> In a world where, apart from the Latin countries, the directing classes have little by little unlearned the niceties of life, where the Dniepropetrovsk factory director and the chief counsel of Standard Oil lead the same enervating, annihilating life, they [E.N.A. students] undertake to cherish a tradition which has done honor to Europe.[70]

Humanism, however, does appear to contribute to a certain tendency of E.N.A. graduates to delight in discussion, participate eagerly and brilliantly in planning and preparation, but shrink from execution. As we shall see, this tendency is not confined to France. It appears in-

---

[70] A. Gourdon, "Les Grands Commis et le Mythe de l'Intérêt Général," *Promotions* (1955), No. 35, p. 54.

creasingly to affect administrative elites which are highly selected and equipped with socially prized intellectual skills. Among the widely differing administrative corps in France, this kind of E.N.A. "retreatist" tendency is more readily visible. The difficulty an E.N.A. product has in adapting to abrasive human relations appears earliest, it is said, in the politicized atmosphere of the prefecture.[71] The problem is also related to direct management (as contrasted to economic and financial planning) in nationalized industry.

Because it does include other elements which may act as reference groups, the French administrative elite may overcome retreatist tendencies among E.N.A. graduates by compelling emulation of managerial and political role models. Conversely, E.N.A. alumni may redefine their roles to include only policy and planning activities. The school has now provided administrative entrants for a full quarter-century. Our time perspective of centuries cautions us against making final judgments of the effectiveness of a pattern which has persisted even that long, however.

The E.N.A. may have contributed to another defect of French economic management. As was noted in the case of the technical education, division between a small layer of elite officials and a larger layer of indifferently trained and inadequately socialized specialists is a perennial French problem. By focusing (as Michel Crozier does in *The Bureaucratic Phenomenon*, though not in other works) on the latter layer, one derives a quite different estimate of the dynamism and effectiveness of the French system than if one concentrates on the elite. Which element predominates depends on a multitude of circumstances. At present, raising the level of the mass of middle-level managerial and administrative personnel is as important as improving the elite. For example, during 1962 and 1963 one-third of the competitive examinations for administrative positions just below those reserved for E.N.A. graduates produced too few candidates to fill vacancies. Only one-fourth provided serious competition. Indeed, the E.N.A. itself had fewer than one-half as many candidates per vacancy in 1963 as in 1946.[72]

If the attractions of private careers were matched by an upgrading of managerial capacities in the private sector, the trend to fewer administrative applicants might be welcomed. In fact, only 5 to 10 per cent of those entering junior managerial posts (about 1967) received postentrance training in business management. Preentry training was virtually unavailable. There has been a halting effort—also sponsored

[71] Kesler, p. 262.
[72] "La Crise de la Fonction Supérieure," *Le Monde*, March 11-12, 1964.

by Debré—"to develop knowledge of the methods of administration and direction of enterprises and to facilitate training personnel for responsible posts." It is significant that its promoters insist that their intention is to "animate" existing training institutions to adopt Harvard Business School methods rather than to create a new, elite "E.N.A. for the private sector."[73] The existing E.N.A. is, without a doubt, the most significant innovation in elite administrative preparation which Europe has seen in many decades. Consequently, it deserves the closest attention; but its ultimate contribution remains uncertain.

[73] "La Fondation Nationale pour l'Enseignement de la Gestion des Entreprises Va Etre Mise en Place," *Le Monde*, February 14, 1968.

CHAPTER TEN

Induction to Higher Administration

No MATTER how heterogeneous their recruits' backgrounds, no matter how late induction occurs, all social groups perform a certain measure of socialization. When recruits anticipate long-term involvement with the group and perceive it as salient to their interests, socialization to the group norms is considerable. Although the phenomenon may be equally significant among politicians, corporation board members, and bishops, political scientists have probably dealt with this type of late socialization more than other social scientists. Investigation of prestigious legislative bodies like the United States Senate has demonstrated that, although a limited range of deviance is permitted, pressure on new members to internalize minimal group norms is intense. These observations do not contradict social psychological emphasis on the primacy of infantile and adolescent socialization. They do, however, indicate the importance of closely scrutinizing the socializing environment within elite administrative organizations.

One should not assume that there is a sharp distinction between pre-service and in-service socialization. Probably a good many U. S. Senators, elected in a party landslide, have experienced little or no anticipatory socialization to their new roles. Future European elite administrators (even, as we shall see, in the USSR) almost invariably become aware of their career prospects at least a few years in advance. In fact, as was examined in the preceding two chapters, the higher educational experience of most young men who eventually enter the administrative elites is structured to create this awareness. The Oxbridge experience is least structured, for at graduation a young man is just as well equipped to continue toward any other elite profession as to enter the Administrative Class. Nevertheless, material resources and personal inclinations have tended to sort out fairly early those undergraduates destined for the higher civil service. In nineteenth-century Prussia such a high proportion of law faculty graduates entered the administration that studying law was almost tantamount to opting for government service, although the choice between judiciary and elite administration remained open. In present-day France the E.N.A. formally as well as practically is the general induction stage for the administrative elite. Only its special nature as a successor to earlier nonservice schools led us to treat the E.N.A. as a preservice institution.

Avoidance of a sharp delimitation between preservice and in-service socialization is a major method by which most European administrative elites have maximized the utility of selective recruitment and preservice socialization in reducing the cost of socializing inductees. The less the inductee perceives a break in the continuity of his value structure, the less he is apt to resist subtle pressures to recombine these values for organizational ends. Whether society in general profits from this economizing of elite administrative resources is open to question; there is little doubt that the administrative elite finds the pattern attractive.

The Judiciary as Induction Mechanism

The peculiar development of Prussian induction mechanisms indicates how these considerations are complicated by the mix of historical circumstances affecting preservice socialization. Isolation of the official *Stand* during the early nineteenth century was a significant factor in its position as a quasi-autonomous social stratum. Group isolation directly affected familial socialization; officials' interests indirectly contributed to the prevalence of small local secondary schools. Both factors delayed socialization of youths to universalistic values, whether in terms of upper-class solidarity or national integration. The university experience, with its fraternity attachments, was only a moderately effective surrogate for the adolescent adaptation to a national upper-class peer group which French, British, and even Russian boys experienced. On the other hand, because they so often came from official families, or at least families (e.g., *Gymnasium* teachers') which respected the official model, Prussian administrative elite entrants already had a highly favorable and at least minimally accurate perception of the elite administrator's role.

If we shared the assumptions of functional analysis, we might be inclined to hypothesize that in-service socialization would compensate for these emphases by stressing general elite integrative values more than the peculiar solidarity of the administrative elite. Our fundamental conflict model, on the other hand, suggests that the identity of the administrative elite as a distinct societal interest would lead it to reinforce group solidarity more intensively, utilizing ideological arguments as legitimization.

One of the most persistent elements of this ideology has been the insistence on a highly distinctive induction stage. Although the historical nomenclature is complicated, for convenience young men at all stages before the "great" or second examination will be referred to as *Referendare*. There have been four peculiar aspects of the *Referendar* induction as compared to most French inductees and the British assistant principal. One is that the decisive and more difficult examination came several years after active service had begun. It is true that in "normal" periods about the same proportion (one-sixth to one-third) failed the first as the second examination.[1] When pressures for appointments were severe (as in the 1850's) the final examination became the main elimination mechanism.[2] As a result, entrants knew that they stood a considerable chance of being dropped after investing at least three years, often many more. The second peculiarity of the Prussian system was the unpaid nature of this service. Even in the West German Federal service a *Referendar*'s salary may be as little as 30 per cent of the next higher grade.[3] In the eighteenth and nineteenth centuries, at least, these two factors virtually precluded any but the wealthy from starting on the administrative career route, or even entering the law faculty.

The other two peculiarities of the Prussian system are more complicated. The Prussian elite administration was distinguished by its use of the judiciary as its induction agency. Only the pre-Revolutionary French administrative elite (because of its origin in the *noblesse de robe*) also used courts as a training stage. In Germany, in contrast to France, socialization to judicial norms has grown in importance. The current West German requirement is very predominantly legal, as compared for example to the Prussian requirement of 1879. At that time judiciary trainees spent two years in various courts plus one year in prosecutors' and private law offices. Administrative inductees also spent two years in the courts and two more in administrative assignments. Thus, three generations ago, the *Referendar* spent one-half of his probationary period directly preparing for his future career. The *Referendar* in the Federal Republic spends less than 30 per cent of his 3½-year induction in administrative training. The West German states require from 19 to 27 months in the regular courts and prosecutors' offices, 3 to 5 months in private law offices, and up to 15 months in labor and administrative courts.[4] Despite many fluctuations, the long-term trend toward increased judicial training is unmistakable. Until 1817 legal study was not an absolute requirement, and even for a time after that court service was not. At least partially separated induction for *Gerichtsreferendare* (judicial trainees) and *Regierungsreferendare* (administrative aspirants) continued until 1869. For a decade after that every inductee had to pursue judicial training alone, ostensibly because the administrative branch was oversupplied with candi-

---

[1] Prussia, Königliches Preussisches Statistisches Landesamt, p. 481.
[2] Gillis, *Prussian Bureaucracy*, p. 45.
[3] Wagner, p. 142.   [4] *Ibid.*, p. 139; Blondel, p. 52.

dates. During the following quarter-century (as described above) half of the novice administrator's training was distinct. From 1904 until the collapse of the Second Reich only *Gerichtsreferendare* were admitted. By 1917 half of the top officials and three-quarters at the intermediate level had begun service as judges. The same long judicial induction was generally maintained under the Weimar Republic, partly to provide a formal barrier against Social Democratic candidates. In the early years of the Nazi regime, before the regular administration was severely disrupted, however, the Ministry of the Interior required only six months' court service as compared to two and one-half years' administrative training. As noted above, since World War II very heavy judicial emphasis has prevailed.[5]

The fourth peculiarity of the Prussian system was the virtually complete discretion of the administrative elite in selecting its recruits. The two examinations were *qualifying*, not competitive. Whether a candidate could start an administrative career ordinarily depended on the decision of the principal territorial officer, the *Regierungspräsident*. Under these circumstances much depended on when the latter approved a candidate. During periods when candidates were approved immediately after their university studies or after only two years in the judiciary, anticipatory socialization to administrative norms was probable. If the *Regierungspräsident*'s approval was delayed until induction was completed, only very ambitious or very well-connected young men could resist absorbing judicial norms along with the vast majority of his peers in the induction process (frequently 90 per cent were destined for judgeships).

Young men persisted, nevertheless, to seek administrative careers which were regarded as "incomparably finer" than judgeships. Even when an extra year of unpaid *Regierungsreferendar* apprenticeship was required, the higher pay levels generally attained in the administration made the sacrifice worthwhile in a strictly financial sense. But the main considerations were family tradition and status. Nobles who set the administrative style looked down on judicial activity even when they accepted the legal preparatory requirement. During the formative period of the autonomous administration (1700-1806), 44 per cent of the candidates for higher administrative positions were noble, as compared to 12 per cent for the judiciary. In the later years of the Second Reich the proportion of nobles among entrants to the

---

[5] Lotz, in Grabowsky, pp. 39-41; Geib, pp. 320ff.; Bosse, in *Vorbildung*, p. 151; "Enquête sur le Recrutement et le Perfectionnement des Agents du Cadre Administratif Supérieur," *Revue Internationale des Sciences Administratives*, x (1937), 447, 451.

administrative service had sunk to 23 per cent, but it was still much larger than in the judiciary. Even at the end of the Weimar period, law students expressed a two to one preference for the scarcer administrative posts.[6]

If the judiciary's prestige was so much lower than the administrative elite's, one may well ask why the latter permitted its recruits to receive so heavy a socialization to judicial norms. Even during the periods when most recruits were selected in advance (there were always some late optants for the administrative career), they spent a considerable time in the courts after their university legal education. They spent additional months preparing to be examined by judges and law professors. As suggested in Chapter Eight, the answer is the administrative elite's need to justify its autonomy by emphasizing the *Rechtsstaat* principle. In a symbolic change following the Prussian defeat by Napoleon, the principal territorial administrative organs became *Regierungen*, a title formerly borne by the superior provincial courts. The new *Regierungen* acquired a limited civil jurisdiction—enough to legitimize their claim to being quasi-judicial tribunals. Much later some Federal Republic officials came close to asserting that, like judges, they were not accountable for their official acts.[7]

Closely related to the administrators' group interest in asserting autonomy was the interest in asserting that administration was a specialty requiring long legal preparation, even though real legal practitioners (judges) were treated with a certain condescension. As we saw, the accommodation between noble and bourgeois administrators rested on general acceptance of this peculiar specialized occupational requirement. Very quickly the requirement for prolonged legal experience also became a device for excluding the increasing number of specialists in construction, accounting, forestry, medicine, religion, and even education. In the territorial governing bodies these officials were permitted to report and to vote on their special subjects. In 1825, however, they were deprived of the right to vote when other questions arose and were discouraged from entering the discussion on such subjects. The justification for this discrimination among officials was partly based on the familiar argument that generalists alone could understand all questions, and partly on the ground that legal training was required to pass on questions affecting private rights.[8]

[6] Sellow, pp. 121, 129; Wilhelm Tietjens, "Der akademische Nachwuchs der Beamtenschaft als gesellschaftliches Problem," *Der Beamte*, III (1931), 190; Brunschwig, p. 156.

[7] See Kern, and the critique by Otto Kuster, *Archiv des Öffentlichen Rechts*, Neue Folge, XXVIII (1952), 364-66.

[8] Koselleck, pp. 246-47, 281.

The dominance of legally trained officials is just as strong in the Federal Republic:

> It means, therefore, that whilst officials in professional careers (in the British sense of "professional") are not in any formal sense subordinate to their colleagues trained in law (who to the German way of thinking are just another species of professional), they do in fact in many areas of administration have only limited influences on the determination of major issues. To put it another way, their policy making role is often marginal. . . . It follows from what has just been said that the promotion prospects of non-legal specialists are not on the whole as good as those of the lawyer-administrator. Admittedly this is a generalization for which no statistical evidence is available.[9]

One of the most difficult problems in dealing with present-day West German administration is, as Johnson remarks, the lack of statistical information. Our tortuous efforts at constructing Federal Republic career patterns (see the Appendix) reflect the lack of comprehensive published statistics. An American can sympathize with the difficulty of maintaining data on administrators divided among units of a federal system. There is, fortunately, another way to get at evidence on the persistent domination of legal norms and styles. As we have noted on several previous occasions, receptivity by one system (social, educational, or administrative) of readily available ideas generated in another is a good test of congruence between the two systems. A striking practical application of this test is provided by the history of the Speyer Higher School for Administrative Sciences. Established in 1947 with the assistance of French occupation authorities, the Speyer school was designed as a German version of the Ecole Nationale d'Administration. Originally limited to the state of Rhine-Palatinate, Speyer soon became a training option for *Referendare* from the other states and the Federal service. Instead of providing three years' integrated experience like the E.N.A., however, Speyer training was limited to three or four months after the *Referendar* had already spent two years in the courts. Instead of the crucial *stages* to socialize the students to the activities of general territorial administration and acquaint him with the private sector, Speyer provides brief excursions to government offices. Instead of an instructional staff of young, active administrators on detached service, most teaching has been conducted by academics.

Although less legalistic than the law faculty approach, the curriculum is dominated by law subjects. Four of the eight professors (in 1967) were in that field, in addition to all of the part-time faculty. Only one of four seminars was on a legal topic; a historian, an economist, a

[9] Johnson, in Ridley, p. 147.

sociologist, and (until his untimely death) the renowned German-American comparative administration expert, Fritz Morstein-Marx, taught the others. The colloquia and lectures were mainly on law themes, however. In sum, while it has been a useful interlude for the *Referendare* (some 500 per year, perhaps half of those not destined for purely judicial careers) who attend, Speyer has tended to adjust to the legalism which pervades German administration today as in the past.[10]

Speyer reinforces earlier socialization experiences of its students in another way. It is the epitome of the isolated, slightly archaic side of the official's background. Extremely difficult to reach by rail, distant (by German standards) from major cities even by highway, Speyer is a delightful cathedral town virtually untouched by war devastation. One gets the impression of Bonn carried to an extreme. Both towns present a marked contrast to *parvenu* nineteenth-century Berlin, though even Berlin, as we noted earlier, could not compete with Paris and London as a cosmopolitan center. Bismarck's personal efforts to arrange closer contact among officials stationed in Berlin by devices like "get-acquainted" breakfasts and the general practice of rotating promising men to Berlin ministries early in their careers were meant to overcome the disadvantages of provincial backgrounds.[11] In West Germany geographic mobility is also a sign of higher official status, but the mobility necessarily is mainly among the states. Thus the higher an official's class origin, the more likely he is to make his career in a state other than his home state: only 32 per cent of a sample of upper-middle-class officials were stationed in their home states, as compared to 48 per cent from the lower-middle class and 53 per cent from the upper-lower class.[12] Nearly identical educations and induction systems do permit a degree of career mobility and mutual understanding which has accomplished many of the national integrative aims of the earlier socialization system. On the other hand, isolation from metropolitan social currents and from the major industrial forces of the society persists.

INDUCTION AS ABSORPTION IN THE SOCIETAL ELITE

There is a curious resemblance between the ways in which the German administrative elite clings to quaintly provincial symbols and the

[10] See Hochschule für Verwaltungswissenschaften Speyer, *Personal- und Vorlesungsverzeichnis: Wintersemester 1966-1967*; "Was lernen die Regierungsräte?" *Die Zeit*, March 5, 1965.

[11] Wermuth, pp. 34, 50; Kurt Wiedenfeld, *Zwischen Wirtschaft und Staat: Aus dem Lebenserinnerungen* (Berlin, 1960), pp. 2ff.

[12] Zapf, p. 83.

British Administrative Class creates a bucolic enclave in one of the world's greatest metropolises. Unlike the Prussians, British elite administrators have frequently been metropolitan in family origin. More than any other administrative elite we examine, their careers are spent in the national capital. Yet preinduction socialization has been mainly acquired in rural surroundings, accompanied by implicit if not outright disparagement of urban, industrial values.

At first sight, Whitehall, the setting of the Administrative Class's activity, is emphatically metropolitan. The general milieu in which higher officials move acts as a counter to this setting, however. The dignified, comfortable official quarters appear deliberately designed to emphasize traditional, leisurely procedures as contrasted to urgency and mechanization. The rhythm of the year (before World War II) was adjusted to an aristocratic pattern: six weeks' vacation in summer to permit a long country retreat; three more weeks when Parliament was not in session. Most work was, indeed, accomplished during a ten weeks' stretch when Parliament was out and Whitehall in action.[13]

Within a few years after the segregation of upper-divisional clerks, they developed a corporate spirit—marked by sports teams, musical groups, etc.—resembling Oxbridge and the public schools.[14] Today service clubs and Cabinet canteens act as surrogates for Oxbridge college dining rooms. One prominent civil servant publicly regretted the lack of commons and chapels to provide a spirit of corporate equality.[15] On the other hand, the general setting of the administrator's London life is structured to avoid overidentification with the administration as compared to the general elite. Although their position has deteriorated since World War II, the great clubs (especially the Reform and the Union) were crucial, virtually unique mechanisms for general elite contact. "There could be further magnifying and merging in later life in the privacy of the clubs where the loyalties and ethos of school could be renewed."[16] Their location on Pall Mall and Carlton House Terrace, a short walk—through the Horse Guards' Parade past the green expanse of St. James' Park—from the Whitehall Ministries enhanced the atmosphere of spacious seclusion.

The elite administrator—as one writer in the 1930's expressed it—had an upper-class, not an upper-middle-class life style and standard of living, at least away from home. Few had fathers who had "dreamed" of aspiring to it.[17] Even in private situations the elite ad-

---

[13] Dale, p. 32.

[14] Paul-Marie Gaudemet, *Le Civil Service Britannique: Essai sur la Régime de la Fonction Publique en Grande Bretagne* (Paris, 1952), p. 24.

[15] Edward Bridges, *Portrait of a Profession: The Civil Service Tradition* (Cambridge, England, 1950), p. 21; cf. Sampson, p. 225.

[16] Checkland, *Rise*, p. 293.   [17] Dale, p. 51.

ministrator was usually comfortable because of the general upper-class depreciation of material display. Juniors could not, of course, enjoy all these amenities; but as gentlemen, corporate equals, they participated, occasionally in person, vicariously at all times. For the recruit it was an attractive and nearly certain (if he was reasonably capable) prospect.

What stands out in this initial confrontation of the recruit with his new career was the continuity, the lack of traumatic new experiences, the sense of security and assurance for the future. Bucolic style, aristocratic attitudes, corporate loyalty combined with easy intercourse with the general elite—all reinforced preservice socialization patterns instead of interrupting them, as did the E.N.A. and even the *Referendar* stage. For administrative recruits from lower-middle-class backgrounds, adjustment to the service was no doubt difficult, although their Oxbridge college experience had provided an introduction. As Weinberg writes, the latter had to acquire the "subtleties of social interaction" while their public school colleagues were concentrating on technical details like those of the administrative service.[18] As we noted in Chapter Eight, lower-class administrators apparently never completely get over a certain feeling of insecurity.

ORAL EXAMINATION AS A SCREENING DEVICE

The induction stage was relatively undramatic because recruits were very carefully selected. The written examination introduced in the 1870's effectively excluded nearly everyone except Oxbridge honors graduates. Shortly after World War I some observers thought that the examination might be losing its effectiveness as a device for screening out unsatisfactory elements. Despite the fear expressed by some higher civil servants that critics would see it as an obvious device for class bias, the supplementary oral examination instituted by the Leathes Committee (1917) was retained to detect (it was said) alertness, nervousness, good manners, and ability to deal with the public.[19] As Herman Finer wrote at the time, the oral examination introduced a marginal differentiation favoring men with pleasant manners and proper accents.[20] After World War II a minor portion of the Method I examination remained oral. This does not seem to have lowered non-Oxbridge candidates' overall standing, though the prospect of an oral encounter may have deterred some.[21] Method II was made predominately oral; it consists of elements such as team projects and protracted individual presentations.

18 Weinberg, pp. 22-23.   19 Kelsall, p. 65.   20 H. Finer, pp. 103-104.
21 Fulton Committee, III (2), 17; Pickering, p. 186.

Follow-up studies of successful candidates indicate that Method II entrants are more successful in service than Method I entrants.[22] Perhaps perception of this prospect has led an increasing number of examinees to opt for Method II. As Table XVI indicates, Method II has not only become the method preferred by a large majority of candidates, but the proportion of non-Oxbridge graduates choosing the Method II competition has increased somewhat. As a result Oxbridge graduates have declined as a proportion of all successful Method II candidates. On the other hand, Oxbridge candidates using Method II quickly became a majority of *all* successful candidates, and have retained that position. What this data implies is that a method which assures Oxbridge preponderance has rapidly become the main method of Administrative Class entry. Acceptance of the Fulton Committee recommendations means that this method will be retained.

The Fulton Committee rejected the Treasury's (i.e., the administrative elite's) suggestion for "starred entrants" after the Administrative Class is officially abolished, on the ground that singling out entrants in this manner would perpetuate a division of the civil service into upper and lower classes.[23] To an outside observer, it appears that retention of Method II will accomplish very much the same thing by singling out a special group of entrants for the attention of their superiors. Whether Method II entrants are really superior in ability, or whether they simply possess qualities more attractive to the administrative elite, it will be surprising if they do not remain a distinct elite among the many thousand inductees envisaged by the new system.

While Method I will require specialized subjects relevant to the administrative career, Method II will, as during the past half-century, admit any university subjects. In other words, the preferred route to the top will still be fully available to men with literary educations. Consequently, one cannot avoid suspecting that the new system will also perpetuate the attitude that teaching administration is "committing the crime of learning from books something one just *does*. It is rather like venturing into matrimony only after a course of Havelock Ellis which, for a healthy nature, should not be strictly necessary."[24]

After the care devoted to his recruitment and socialization, the young man entering the service as assistant principal before World War II was assumed to have a healthy nature. What it led to in matri-

[22] *Ibid.*, p. 185; Fulton Committee, III (2), 117.

[23] Fulton Committee, I, 164.

[24] Charles H. Sisson, *The Spirit of British Administration and Some European Comparisons* (London, 1959), p. 28, quoted in Geoffrey Kingdon Fry, *Statesmen in Disguise: The Changing Role of the Administrative Class of the British Home Civil Service, 1853-1966* (London, 1969), p. 121.

TABLE XVI. ENTRANCE TO BRITISH ADMINISTRATIVE ELITE [25]
(University Graduates in Open Competition)

Period	Annual Number by Method				Method II as Per Cent of Total		Oxbridge Graduates as Per Cent of Method II		Successful Oxbridge Graduates Opting for Method II as Per Cent of All Successful Candidates
	Candidates		Successful						
	I	II	I	II	Candidates	Successful	Candidates	Successful	
1948-1956	187	303	35	23	62	40	58	86	34
1957-1963	133	370	24	42	74	63	67	88	55
1964-1965	134	416	28	78	76	73	56	76	56
1966-1967	260	674	18	113	72	86	45	64	55

[25] Recalculated from data in Fulton Committee, III (1), 87.

mony was a private matter between him and his bride; what it led to in administration was nearly as private between him and his departmental superiors. Most simply told the neophyte to get on with the job. This was not quite as simple as it seemed, for the new man obviously could not supervise experienced Executive Class subordinates, nor would it have been seemly to place him under the orders of those whom he would eventually command.[26] As a rule the inductee spent his time reading files and composing minutes on them, with the hope that in doing so he would learn the affairs of the department. Since his only practical recourse in case of difficulty was asking questions of other junior administrators, the new assistant principal was impressed with the necessity of group loyalty. This process also reinforced the habits of thoroughness, accuracy, attention to detail, discretion, and loyalty which school sports and classics had already instilled. Before World War II only 5 of 21 departments had more systematic induction. The Ministry of Health, for example, had a brief initiation period; the Labour Ministry (apparently unique among British departments) required a six-month tour of duty away from London.[27]

A very early elite administrator wrote that "business is seldom really and usefully transacted otherwise than in writing."[28] Since then, the administration has continued to stress minutes, even resisting (like Michaelis' Prussian uncle) innovations such as the telephone. As late as the post-World War II period, the Treasury lacked accounting and economics expertise. A generation earlier, Finer had argued that since the Civil Service took in only raw material "it imposes on the Service itself the duty of establishing post-entry training."[29] Harold Laski feared an "inbred" staff college, but hoped the universities would teach public administration.[30] Lack of field experience for recruits was a recurring theme of criticism.

After World War II, various experiments in early in-service training culminated in the Centre for Administrative Studies (Regent Park, London). The Centre provided for about the same amount of formal in-service training as Speyer: a three-week course after the inductee had served six months covered a long list of topics like "administration in Scotland" and "administrative tribunals" in ninety-minute sessions.

[26] Charles K. Munro, *The Fountains in Trafalgar Square: Some Reflections on the Civil Service* (London, 1952), p. 34.

[27] Fry, p. 111; H. Finer, p. 97; Dale, p. 90.

[28] Sir Henry Taylor, quoted in Sisson, p. 320.

[29] H. Finer, p. 71; Munro, p. 28; Samuel H. Beer, *Treasury Control: The Coordination of Financial and Economic Policy in Great Britain* (Oxford, 1956), p. 58; Sir Thomas L. Heath, *The Treasury* (London, 1927), p. 148.

[30] Harold J. Laski, "The Education of the Civil Servant," *Public Administration*, XXI (1943), 19.

Two years later the assistant principal was given a twenty-week course at the Centre, focusing on economics, management, statistics, and data processing. Some reports indicate that Oxbridge literary B.A.'s did very well. Anyone who has watched selected graduate students with considerable social science background grappling with these subjects during their entire first year is entitled to be skeptical.

If the Fulton Committee recommendations are fully implemented, a staff college like the E.N.A. will train large numbers of inductees for all services. Many top administrators undoubtedly desire recruits prepared to utilize the tools of cost-benefit analysis and quantitative economics (there is less emphasis on other social sciences and technology) in planning and policy recommendations.[31] Yet there is a persistent concern that careers should be launched at an early age, that assistant principals should not be delayed from "getting on with the job" by more training on top of the four-year B.A. This attitude is, of course, a reflection of the "all-rounder," generalist preference: "The British bureaucratic tradition discounts, and administrative practice largely disregards, specialized qualifications" now as in the past.[32] This tendency closely parallels the Prussian, still more the West German, emphasis on legal implementation. Today the West German administrative elite has moved far from the central position in the societal elite once occupied by the Prussian service. British elite administrators, for reasons discussed earlier, never had such a decisive position; but since World War II they appear to be less influential than ever. For both services, emphasis on administration for administration's sake may represent the defensive side of a basically retreatist stance. It is only a decade since an outstanding civil servant, Arthur Salter, feared that with top officials chosen for " 'general administrative ability,' administration as such, as distinct from the practical purposes it should serve, might become a fetish."[33]

THE CORPS AS CAREER FOCUS

Examining in-service socialization in the Prussian and the British systems has been relatively simple because novices have been inducted by a single process for relatively undifferentiated service. The French recruit, on the contrary, has ordinarily been inducted into a particular

[31] Georges Langrod, *Les Problèmes de Formation dans la Fonction Publique en Grande Bretagne*, Extract of No. 2 of *State Sociale* (Turin, 1963), p. 153; Fry, pp. 123ff.

[32] Michael J. Brennan, *Technocratic Politics and the Functionalist Theory of European Integration* (Ithaca, 1969), p. 28.

[33] Arthur Salter, *Slave of the Lamp: A Public Servant's Notebook* (London, 1967), p. 17.

branch of the service; hence one must examine a range of distinct processes. These corps should not be confused with simple division of an administrative service by departments. As we saw, departments have a great deal to do with the British entrant's first years, and of course his career prospects (examined in Chapter Eleven) are strongly affected by departmentalization. Without the intense preservice socialization to common values which British novices have experienced, American administrators are much more affected by departmental divisions. According to one recent study, 56 per cent of Federal higher officials (i.e., what European administrations would consider upper-middle level) have spent their entire career in one Cabinet-level department. A great many have spent their careers in a single bureau, often one related to their professional specialization.[34]

The corps attachments which divided the French service from the Napoleonic period until 1945, and remain highly significant today, are of a different order. In the first place, the small number of corps prevents the fragmentation which reduces most American or British departments, as such, to relative impotence on general policy questions. In a pluralist society, the more numerous the units into which the administration is divided the greater the likelihood of each becoming attached to its clientele's special interests. The relatively large scope of activities of each corps offers some protection against its becoming the prisoner of a single pressure group. It is customary to speak of five *Grands Corps*, plus two great technical corps. Since the diplomatic corps lies outside the scope of this study, and the Accounts Court (Cour des Comptes) is not really on a par with the others, one need consider only five bodies: the Financial Inspectorate, the Council of State, the prefectural corps, the Ponts et Chaussées corps, and the Mining corps. The close relationship of the two technical corps makes it possible to consider them as one, leaving only four major divisions in the administrative elite.

These corps are distinguished from ordinary departments by the fact that legally and in practice they are corporate bodies as well as branches of government. As a result, membership opens up varied, immensely significant career opportunities apart from the formal tasks of the parent corps. Like a tightly organized elite profession, the corps as an institution advances the careers of its members and the members reflect credit on the corps. As a result socialization to the values and style of individual corps is intense and highly specific. A recent French analyst, Marie Kessler, emphasizes this aspect:

[34] David T. Stanley, *The Higher Civil Service: An Evaluation of Federal Personnel Practices* (Washington, 1964), p. 33; Bendix, *Higher Civil Servants*, p. 63.

Another concept can complete and even supplement that of "organization:" the concept of "corps," which up to now has not been analyzed theoretically, yet which is frequently exemplified by the French administration. . . . One may summarily list the basic characteristics common to all the corps as the common traditions and privileges uniting a peer group. It appears that one may approximately define a corps as a collectivity whose unity and coherence depend on a diffuse constraint exercised by traditions and solidarity, which result in turn from carrying out the same function or belonging to the same institution. Generally corps benefit from privileges which distinguish them from the social environment and give rise to feelings of self-satisfaction.[35]

It is essential to understand that the corps phenomenon has always coexisted in France with a considerable measure of homogeneity within the administration and among societal elites in general. We have seen some of the bases for this homogeneity in the common secondary education. The degree of elite homogeneity has followed a great concave curve from an apex in the eighteenth century to a low point in the late nineteenth century, then (so it seems) to a new apex in the postindustrial period. Certainly the administrative elite, at least, has become more unified through the activity of the E.N.A. and similar institutions. The phenomenon of the Jean Moulin Club (founded during the political crisis of 1958) appears to point in the same direction for the general elite; it is significant that at that time one-third of its members were high officials.[36]

Under the Old Regime there was, strictly speaking, a single administrative elite. Nearly all were members of the *noblesse de robe;* they had been educated in the *collèges* and the law faculties. The core consisted of the officials associated with the Conseil du Roi. The system of royal councils was very complicated; for our summary purposes it will suffice to consider the Privy Council of State for Finances and Direction, usually called the Council of State. The Council of State was a corps rather than a mere administrative agency. Junior members (*maîtres des requêtes*) learned affairs of state under the watchful eyes of great administrators like Colbert or Jean Orry, or indeed Louis XIV himself. Unlike the Prussian service a century later, Colbert and his successors were convinced that the spirit of the royal administration was essentially different from the spirit of the judiciary. It was good

[35] Kessler, p. 16.
[36] *Ibid.,* p. 209; Jean Meynaud, *La Technocratie: Mythe ou Réalité* (Paris, 1964), p. 146.

that the young *maître* had experienced the latter, but further socialization was essential to imbue him with the values of the king's service. Logical thinking, clear, carefully compiled reports, and the spirit of command were the essentials. Only after an induction period varying from months to many years could the *maître des requêtes* prudently be dispatched to the territorial service as *intendant de province*. Many *maîtres* were retained in the Council itself, frequently acting as *intendants des finances* in charge of various departments (e.g., Ponts et Chaussées). Ultimately many *intendants de province* returned to the mother institution as *conseillers d'état*, the Council's highest grade.[37]

Napoleon I reorganized and simplified the Council of State. Although no longer the sole elite corps, it was designed to be his principal advisory body. As we have seen (Chapter Four), he wanted experts in many subjects besides law who could rise above their specialized roles. In the short run, officers from the judiciary, the administration, and above all the military filled the posts, together with Revolutionary figures.[38] In the long run, Napoleon wanted to make the Council a socializing agency for recruits who would eventually be seconded to high posts throughout his empire. Consequently, he added a lower stage (*auditeur*) to the two of the Old-Regime institution. Partly because of the brevity of the First Empire, a minority (27 per cent) of the *maîtres des requêtes* were men who had been trained as *auditeurs* and only a scattering of *conseillers d'état* had been *maîtres*.

The foremost authority on the post-Revolutionary Council of State contends that it did not provide a regular career until 1872.[39] During the following half-century, the proportion of vacancies in the higher ranks filled by promotion (nearly always on the basis of seniority) gradually increased until young men entering as *auditeur*s knew that there was a reasonable prospect of rising to the top of the corps. Until 1880, like Prussian inductees, the *auditeur* was unpaid and faced a second examination during the probational period. As the proportion of higher posts filled by the Council itself increased, the *auditeur*'s treatment became less severe. The entrance examination, administered by a jury of Council members, remained a severe test of legal knowledge; but it included an oral portion in which "resemblances in attitudes between members and candidates played a part."[40]

[37] Gruder, pp. 52ff., 93; J. Necker, "De l'Administration des Finances de la France," quoted in Pavel Ardashev, "Materialy dlia Istorii Provintsial'noi Administratsii vo Frantsii v Posledniuiu Poru Starago Poriadka," *Uchenyia Zapiski Imperatorskago Iurevskago Universiteta*, XII (1904), No. 1, 471ff.; Lhéritier, I, 50; Mousnier, pp. 24-25, 34-39.

[38] Durand, *Etudes*, pp. 60, 266, 306, 329.   [39] Kessler, p. 40.

[40] *Ibid.*, p. 150; Walter R. Sharp, *The French Civil Service: Bureaucracy in Transition* (New York, 1931), p. 149; Freedeman, pp. 28-29.

Auditeurs were treated as colleagues in an elite body. Cases before the Council were assigned to members of any rank; all entered the discussion, although (unless they were *rapporteurs*) members lower than *conseiller* could not vote on general matters.[41] The permanent head (vice-president) ceased to have a dominant position after World War I. The Old Regime had established the tradition of a "familiar, courteous" tone in relations with subordinates as "among enlightened men."[42] With a few exceptions this custom was maintained in the Council, with intellectual ability and forensic skill counting for more than age or rank. A strong sense of corps solidarity has been reflected in opposition to high-level appointment of outsiders (particularly prefects and Ministerial Cabinet directors who, before World War II were often rewarded for political services by being made *conseillers*).

A high proportion of Council career members are Parisian by origin and education. Their corps careers rarely take them out of the capital. Very recently a tour of inspection of lower tribunals has been instituted; new entrants from the E.N.A. have, of course, served at least a year in the provinces.[43] The Palais Royal headquarters itself possesses what a French student of administration designates a "sacral atmosphere."[44] It is close to the administrative and artistic center of the metropolis, although (especially in the nineteenth and early twentieth centuries) this urban area was hardly in touch with modern technological or industrial development.[45]

The principal task of the Council of State is to regulate relations among state agencies and between them and the general public. It does this on the basis of the uniquely refined body of French administrative law. As indicated earlier, by the late nineteenth century the significance of this regulatory activity was so great that it became the central subject for preparing most elite administrators. While other corps have moved to less formal fields of activity, the Council has necessarily remained the "incarnation of legality."[46] Even in this respect, according to the most thorough study of the Council, it lacks a doctrine which would inspire a consistent line of decision-making by members on detached service. Under the Third Republic it tended to favor laissez faire and some corporatist tendencies, but has more consistently promoted centralization and state direction.

A relatively small, although increasing proportion of Council mem-

[41] Kessler, p. 179; Freedeman, pp. 66ff.

[42] Pavel Ardashev, *Les Intendants de Province sous Louis XVI* (Paris, 1909), p. 408.

[43] Conseil d'Etat, p. 119.   [44] Déroche, p. 49.

[45] See Wolitz, p. 30, on the varying impact of technology and industry on *fin de siècle* Paris society.

[46] Kessler, p. 216.

bers are on detached service to full-time assignments in other government agencies: 3 to 7 per cent between the wars, less than 10 per cent in 1946, 21 per cent in 1964. Most of those who do temporarily leave Council activity assume analogous functions of interpretation, regulation, and adjustment of state activities to human relations in agencies like the Social Security Administration and the Ministries of Justice, Education, and Cultural Affairs. Those few who enter private employment are in demand in financial institutions as a guarantee of their probity. Fewer than one-fourth (i.e., fewer than 5 per cent of the total Council membership at a given moment) are in state economic management or planning agencies like the Ministry of Transport. This distribution is partly due to tradition but is probably more a matter of self-selection.[47]

Council of State members lack experience in economic activity and tend to distrust it.[48] These attitudes confirm our earlier conclusion that a body of administrators who are primarily legalist in their extended training and activity will rarely produce men who will take the initiative in development intervention. It is important to note, however, that the presence of a corps like the Council of State in an administration with a heavy technological component has an entirely different significance from the *domination* of the administrative elite by men with legal outlooks. With the reduced but tangible influence it has enjoyed in the last thirty years, the Council has served as a balance wheel to ensure consideration of the human factor in French administrative operation.

Nevertheless, the relative prestige of the Council of State and the Financial Inspectorate serves as a useful indicator of French administrative activity in the economic sphere. The Inspectorate has been the slight but steady career preference of top E.N.A. graduates. While Third Republic ministers preferred to select Council *maîtres* as their staff directors (if they did not choose ex-prefects or other political figures), in recent years about as many Financial Inspectors have been chosen for these prestigious posts. In terms of rotation to crucial administrative posts outside the corps, the Inspectorate, as discussed below, is far ahead of the Council.

In a sense this attainment is the culmination of a subdued competition which has lasted nearly three centuries. Strictly speaking, there was no royal financial administration under the Old Regime. The basic centralized tax system was the Ferme Générale, nominally a speculative private business. In practice, the Ferme was in many respects a public administration. Although the forty directors (*fermiers*) pur-

47 *Ibid.*, pp. 253, 268, 280.
48 *Ibid.*, p. 222.

chased their offices, they were expected to have legal training like other elite administrators; in addition many received thorough training in accounting and other business practices before entering upon their duties. Some were ineffective administrators, but until about 1770 most appear to have worked assiduously under the direction of the principal royal minister, the Contrôleur Général.[49] Just three years before the Revolution, the financial administration was reorganized on a centralized basis. The present Inspectorate was formally instituted in 1828. After the Revolution the financial manipulative aspects of the Ferme devolved for a time on private banks; but for several decades the principal central banks have been directed by elite administrators, usually Financial Inspectors. In this respect as in the details of their socialization, the Financial Inspectors are the real successors of the Ferme apparatus.

The Louvre headquarters of the Inspectorate, like the Palais Royal (a hundred yards distant) conveys a "sacral atmosphere." The famous Ministry of Finance library provides a central meeting place for Inspectors comparable to the Council library. In contrast to the Council, however, the Inspectorate has followed a centuries-old induction practice which interrupts the metropolitan habits of its novices. The inspection tour (tournée) was a major aspect of the work of young aspirants to the Ferme. "The tourneur was often the most crucial figure in the Company management," for it was vital to avoid dissipation of revenues.[50] Like the eighteenth-century inspection team, Financial Inspectors seek to keep the subordinate officials "on their toes" (en haleine) by unannounced descents on provincial offices. Recent recruits are thrown on their own resources in delicate contacts with older, more experienced subordinates whose records must be inspected meticulously. A junior member has rarely been dismissed for inadequate reports, but (before World War II) they were considered by the jury which conducted his second examination; the results might affect his promotion chances for years.[51] His only recourses for advice, support, or even social contact are other team members (junior and senior) who generally stay at the same provincial hotels.[52] Protracted

[49] George T. Matthews, *The Royal General Farms in Eighteenth-Century France* (New York, 1958), pp. 47-48, 58; Delahante, I, 203ff., II, 11ff.; Pierre Roux, *Les Fermes d'Impôts sous l'Ancien Régime* (Dissertation, University of Paris, Faculté de Droit) (Paris, 1916), pp. 193, 253; H. Thirion, *La Vie Privée des Financiers au XVIIIe Siècle* (Paris, 1895), pp. 20, 143.

[50] Matthews, p. 199; Delahante, II, 39; cf. Roux, p. 193.

[51] De Peyster, "L'Inspection Générale des Finances en France," *Revue Internationale des Sciences Administratives* (1939), No. 4, p. 679; J. de Fouchier, "Le Rôle de l'Inspection Générale des Finances dans l'Administration Française," *Revue Politique et Parlementaire*, No. 537, August 10, 1939, p. 274.

[52] Lalumière, pp. 112ff.

work under intense strain in the isolated team milieu rapidly instills strong feelings of solidarity among young men who, in the ordinary course of French education, have become highly individualistic. One can hardly expect that basic values will be altered at their advanced age (about twenty-four before World War II; now, with E.N.A. training intervening probably about twenty-five). What seems to occur is that the basic school and family loyalties are redirected to intense loyalty to the corps, combined with considerable sense of superiority toward other officials even when they are of the same educational and social background.

Along with corps solidarity goes considerably more hierarchical subordination than in the Council. Seniority plays a relatively small role in promotion through the six Financial Inspector ranks. Many leave the corps around age forty when they perceive their chances for further advancement are small, as contrasted to the usual practice in the Council of remaining to retirement at seventy. Although the entrance examination (before the E.N.A.) was not as crucial as the Council's, the jury of active Inspectors had as many candidates (seven to ten) for each opening and was equally careful to select young men who appeared adaptable to its values.[53]

A generation ago it was hard to define these values:

> The Inspectorate is also an intellectual method which successive generations have passed on and which now takes many forms. For example, one cannot but be impressed by the extreme reluctance of Financial Inspectors to employ new economics terminology. Only rarely do they agree to use it. They desire to preserve in their words and compositions a style accessible to the average man, to the "honest" man in the 18th century sense.[54]

Clearly what is described above is a *style* rather than a methodology such as careful collection and manipulation of statistics according to economic theoretical principles or a doctrine such as economic interventionism. In the early 1940's the Inspectorate discovered in Keynesianism both method and doctrine. That it did this earlier than the other corps is no doubt due both to economics training and involvement with financial matters of great import. Recruits to the Inspectorate included a higher proportion of graduates from schools like the Polytechnique than did Council *auditeurs*, and of course fewer with law degrees. Overwhelming majorities of both groups of inductees had passed through the old Sci Pol. One would have to have information (probably unobtainable) on course distribution to be sure Inspec-

[53] *Ibid.*, pp. 13ff., 21.   [54] *Ibid.*, p. 23.

torate entrants were better prepared in economics, but the weight of the examination suggests that they were. It included relatively small elements of law and mathematics, but much on laissez-faire economics, finance, and administration.[55]

At the same time, Inspectorate doctrine remains fundamentally favorable to a mixed economy. This attitude has been fostered by an extraordinary degree of *pantouflage* (movement to private employment) by men with great family wealth who have entered the service primarily for experience in managing large affairs, and by men who simply find private salaries irresistibly attractive. The favorite Inspectorate method of operation—financial manipulation—also is adapted to a mixed economy now as it was in the eighteenth century. Today the immense economic leverage of the public sector facilitates skillful use of budgetary variance, loans to expanding firms, and tax credits. Consequently, it is understandable that about half of the Inspectors not engaged in the narrowly regulatory activity of the institution itself are in the Ministry of Finance or in great nationalized financial institutions like the Banque de France or the Crédit Lyonnais. The proportion on such detached service has steadily risen. In the post-industrial period it has approached one-half; even before World War II, the proportion on detached service (one-third of all Inspectors) greatly exceeded that of the Council of State.

Only one-tenth (i.e., one-twentieth of all Inspectors at a given moment) are actually engaged in industrial direction.[56] In the final analysis, the "vocation" of the Inspectorate, like the Ferme before it, is handling money. As a result, the Inspectorate fits very well the tendency of E.N.A. graduates to engage in planning and policy-making rather than commanding men. As we shall see (Chapter Twelve), the prefectural corps is rather more strongly oriented to directing in this sense. As far as management of nationalized enterprises is concerned, however, the great technical corps have remained most important. Though the Mines corps and the Ponts et Chaussées corps are rivals to some extent, their common basic education at the Polytechnique makes them far closer to each other than to the *Grands Corps*, especially since the latter have been recruited from the E.N.A. The Mines corps is dominant in the railroad system; although the head (1953) was a member of the Council of State, 111 of 159 top managers were Polytechnicians. Similarly, the Electricité de France director was from the Accounts Court, but 87 top managers were Polytechnicians, as compared to 9 Sci Pol graduates. Only the Road Transport Division (engaged mainly in regulatory activity) in the Ministry of Transport

[55] *Ibid.*, p. 21.   [56] *Ibid.*, pp. 87, 128.

was, recently, directed by a Financial Inspector; most other divisions were under members of the Ponts et Chaussées corps.[57]

Two features of technical corps socialization appear to equip their members for managerial roles. One is the strict hierarchical principle which accustoms them to commanding at an early age. The second is the provincial isolation of the early and middle stages of the engineers' careers. Their experience almost reverses the British elite administrators': after years of training in metropolitan schools, technical corps members must adjust to carrying out weighty tasks in an isolated, provincial setting. Both these characteristics probably contribute to the engineer-administrator's belief that he can solve any problem by expert manipulation of materials and relatively simple direction of the human component. As discussed in Chapter Nine, these attitudes have contributed to "technocracy."

Corporate solidarity is high in the technical corps. In part this appears to be based on a long struggle to escape the domination of legally trained administrators. As indicated in Chapter Nine, an engineer was unacceptable as director of the pre-Revolutionary Ponts et Chaussées corps. Napoleon I, despite his admiration of technology, put a financier in charge, with a directing council composed of men with classical educations. Well into the mid-nineteenth century similar supervision aroused complaints of overcentralization and interference.[58] Even today one hears expressions of resentment of the "talkers" (lawyers, philosophers) who, technical corps members think, dominate other corps. As we shall see, the mistrust is reciprocated.

The division of the French administrative elite into four divergent and highly self-conscious groups—prefects, Financial Inspectors, Council of State and related Accounts Court members, and engineers —may produce severe tension leading to deadlock. During the Third Republic such tension was one factor contributing to the stalemate society. On the other hand, even during that period corps division kept open alternative routes to the top administration excluded by the legal-literary pattern which won out in Britain and Prussia. The ascendancy of the E.N.A. alters the situation. Is it likely that such fundamentally different patterns of socialization as those the Council of State and the Financial Inspectorate have produced can be perpetuated among men so far along in age, training, and sense of adherence to a common elite as the E.N.A. graduates? The record is not

[57] Delefortrie-Soubeyroux, pp. 156-58, 165, 173; Ridley, p. 107; Charles Brindillac, "Les Hauts Fonctionnaires," *Esprit*, XXI (1953), 864.

[58] Petot, pp. 412, 420. This directing council is not to be confused with the "general council" of engineers. Cf. M. J. Cordier, *Mémoires sur les Travaux Publics*, Vol. I (Paris, 1841), 31ff.

clear, but it appears that a certain measure of self-selection has led young men to the corps whose pattern they fit best. The prefectural corps, as suggested earlier, may be an exception. For the past quarter-century the combination of residual differences among E.N.A. graduates and sharper differences between them, older prefectural corps members, and elite engineers appears to have produced a beneficent rather than an obstructive tension.

ATTENUATED CORPS ATTACHMENTS IN RUSSIA

In France the corps have operated in an administrative system which approaches what we have designated the Maximum Ascriptive Model. Everything else being equal, the earlier young men are inducted into a corps, the easier it is to socialize them to the intense attachments needed if corporate identity is to be maintained among members carrying out diverse assignments. This factor seems to imply that the closed training institutions of Tsarist Russia would produce maximum corps attachments. In fact, the corps phenomenon was greatly attenuated by conflicting aspects of the administrative structure.

Upon completing the special training institutions (e.g., the Senate *iunker* schools), young men were transferred in a rapid, haphazard way to various central departments and even provincial posts. As we shall see in Chapter Eleven, the prospects of a regular career (a major factor in promoting organizational solidarity) were drastically jeopardized by seconding of military officers to top civil posts. Most important of all was the fact that the Tsarist system, unlike the Western European systems, inducted vastly more numerous recruits than could hope to attain top positions. The overall ratio of beginners to top openings in the *chin* system was approximately forty to one.

The observations just made represent what can be designated the "conventional wisdom" of the historiography of Tsarist Russia. Even this body of opinion recognizes that the great technical corps (Transport and Mines) were exceptions. Together the Transport Institute and the Mines Institute graduated (in the second half of the nineteenth century) about one hundred engineers per year. Men in these corps perhaps did not enjoy quite as clear career prospects as their French counterparts. The best graduates entered service four ranks higher than the minimum as compared to the five-rank advance other elite schools could provide. Examination of a few biographies suggests that elite engineers had to wait longer for top-rank administrative posts than nonspecialists of comparable education. Nevertheless, they dominated major managerial tasks. Until Sergei Witte and his specially recruited aides with economics and accounting backgrounds displaced them in the late 1880's, the engineers controlled much of the railroad construction and management of private as well as nationalized railroads.[59] The Transport engineers' duties were predominately provincial, but (like the French technical corps) their training was metropolitan and they retained a center for corps solidarity in the directing council in St. Petersburg.

What has received less attention is the development of an attenuated type of corps attachment around non-technical institutions during the mid-nineteenth century. We have barely scratched the surface of this complex phenomenon, although data exists for extensive investigations. The basic factor permitting such attachment was the privilege given honor graduates of certain schools to enter the *chin* system at advanced levels. The Imperial Legal Institute and the Imperial Tsarskoe Selo Lycée were most privileged. Honor graduates started in the ninth rank (thus avoiding the five lower) and nearly all graduates gained at least two ranks. The Imperial Page Corps and the Nezhin Juridical Lycée were almost as important. Together (in the second half of the nineteenth century) the four institutes graduated 85 students per year, an overwhelming majority of whom entered the civil service.[60] Our data for the Tsarskoe Selo Lycée presented in Table XVII indicates that very nearly half of the total graduates ultimately attained the top four *chins* of the civil service scale. This means that their chances were twenty times as great, on the average, as the typical "higher" civil service entrant (there were numerous employees below the *chin* system). Data on the Lycée's successor (the Alexander Lycée) is incomplete, but it suggests (see Table XVIII) that, on the eve of the 1860's reform period and the industrial take-off, its young alumni, too, advanced far more rapidly than was typical for civil servants. If the Tsarskoe Selo-Alexander Lycée pattern holds approximately for other elite institution graduates, it would appear that as many as one-third of the top civil posts (in the middle of the nineteenth century) may have been filled by their graduates. The fact that only one-fourth of the members of the Governing Council had studied at universities as late as 1897, compared to one-fifth who had studied at the Imperial Legal Institute alone, tends to support the conclusion that, as in France, there was a distinct path via elite schools to top office.[61]

The statistical analysis suggests that in the mid-nineteenth century there was an elite among the enormous mass of *chin* officials. The evi-

[59] Leikina-Svirskaia, pp. 69, 121; Von Laue, *Sergei Witte*, pp. 48, 72.
[60] Torke, pp. 88-89; Iablochkov, p. 602; Leikina-Svirskaia, pp. 69, 75ff., 79-80.
[61] *Ibid.*, p. 81.

dence that this resulted in corps attachments is more fragmentary. Certainly the elite schools, with their intensive *interne* socialization produced strong, lasting "old boy" attachments, as attested by personal accounts and the schools' elaborate efforts to keep in touch with alumni. The significance of career patterns is not so clear. Since most elite institutions were attached to specific ministries, career induction was specialized. The Imperial Legal Institute and the Nezhin Juridical Lycée prepared for the Ministry of Justice, the Alexander Lycée for the Ministry of the Interior. In the earlier part of the nineteenth century, however, the Tsarskoe Selo Lycée had not been so specialized. Of Tsarskoe Selo graduates whose high-level assignments can be

TABLE XVII. TSARSKOE SELO LYCEE GRADUATES'
FINAL RANKS[62]

Rank	N	Per Cent of Total Graduates
1st *Chin*	1	.4
2nd *Chin*	23	10
3rd *Chin*	38	16
4th *Chin*	49	21
Unspecified First Four *Chins*	3	1.3
Total Attaining First Four *Chins*	114	49

traced, the largest group (26 per cent) was in legal regulatory agencies like the Senate, with 14 per cent each in offices related to the Ministry of the Interior, and in financial agencies. Twenty-seven per cent were in diplomatic or Imperial Court assignments which lie outside our scope. Even more fragmentary evidence suggests that earlier career assignments had been still more diverse. Thus there is little indication of a really distinctive career pattern for Tsarskoe Selo graduates, as compared to that of the technical corps. On the other hand, the Tsarskoe Selo Lycée graduates did concentrate on activity in the great

TABLE XVIII. ALEXANDER LYCEE GRADUATES'
RANKS ATTAINED, 1844-1859

Rank	N	Per Cent of Total Graduates
5th *Chin*	22	8
6th *Chin*	29	10
7th *Chin*	59	21
8th *Chin*	58	21
9th *Chin*	22	8

[62] Tables XVII and XVIII compiled from data in Seleznev (Appendix) and Kobeko, pp. 477, 505ff.

central regulatory agencies, as contrasted either to managerial assignments or provincial administrative posts. It appears, although the evidence is scanty, that similar broad patterns prevailed later in the nineteenth century, with officials inducted into the Ministry of the Interior, for example, later transferring to other central regulatory agencies.

These three branches, which we can identify as putative corps divisions, reappear in the Soviet administrative elite. Again, a basic distinction is between the central (Moscow) agencies and the territorial posts. At the province (*oblast*) level frequent interchange between state and Communist Party posts (in line direction as contrasted to staff activities like indoctrination) produces a distinctive career with elements of solidarity resembling a corps.[63] This solidarity has been a major political factor since Joseph Stalin's death, although the political success of the territorial apparatus has tended to reduce its cohesion by enabling members to move to top positions in other aspects of the elite administration. In the 1940's and early 1950's, at least, the central Party apparatus constituted another distinct career pattern, reminiscent in certain respects of the St. Petersburg regulatory agencies.

Finally, there has been the economic managerial apparatus, including both the central agencies (Ministries and State Planning Commission) and the enterprise managers in the provinces. Between 1939 and 1957 the latter were virtually insulated from the ordinary administrative pressures of the Party-state apparatus in the provinces. As we indicated earlier, the predominantly engineer-trained managerial apparatus was thereby enabled to concentrate on material manipulation, with human resources placed at its disposal by the social control agencies. At that time—and for several years afterward—elite administrators with technical education and experience were a small minority in both the central Party apparatus and the territorial apparatus. Thus the strong sense of solidarity between the "self-made" elite administrators of the territorial apparatus, in particular, served to reinforce the quasi-corps distinction vis-à-vis the economic management.

Between 1957 and 1964, in a complicated maneuver which has more to do with Soviet politics than with administration, Nikita Khrushchev disrupted the central managerial administration.[64] By the time it was reconstituted after his removal, the proportion of Party officials (territorial and central) with engineer training had risen considerably.

[63] Armstrong, *Soviet Bureaucratic Elite*, pp. 54ff.; cf. T. H. Rigby, *The Selection of Leading Personnel in the Soviet State and Communist Party* (Dissertation, University of London, 1954), pp. 181ff.
[64] See John A. Armstrong, "Party Bifurcation and Elite Interests," *Soviet Studies*, XVII (1966), 419ff.

Today it is a question whether the distinctions between the three types of officials outlined above are sufficient to produce lasting group solidarities of the corps type. Certainly Soviet doctrine discourages such tendencies. The most that can be said at present is that Russian experience, as in the general adaptation of technological training to elite administrative preparation, has more closely resembled the French corps pattern than have the other European administrations.

CHAPTER ELEVEN

Career Patterns and Prospects

M<small>UCH</small> of the preceding discussion has assumed that men entering the elite administration have not consciously chosen to accept its values. As indicated in Chapter One, we do make the assumption that basic values are learned in childhood and adolescence without conscious awareness of their significance. Socialization for the administrative elite occurs partly through processes by which these values are recombined without the individual member's conscious effort. We even assume that groups like elite administrators advance arguments (ideologies) which are the products of their interest positions ("false consciousness") rather than the result of conscious calculation. We have, however, no intention of advancing a determinist interpretation by assuming that *all* aspects or even the "fundamental" aspects of the social process are explicable by analyzing "automatic" processes. We have noted at various points how individuals in key positions have influenced developments. We also assume that within limited contexts most elite administrators rationally calculate their own interests. Surely one would anticipate that a critical context for such rational calculation would be estimation of their "life chances" or (within the specific context which concerns us) their "career prospects."

As a rule socialization becomes less effective with advancing age. Rational calculation of career prospects need not diminish for older men, however. Very little discussion has been devoted to "ambition theory," as Joseph Schlesinger terms politicians' calculation of their chances of obtaining high office.[1] It would appear, however, that men who have progressed a considerable distance in their careers (i.e., are in their thirties) are better equipped to perceive possibilities of advancement and to calculate their own chances rationally than very young men. Consequently, the former may well have stronger motivations to conform outwardly to prevalent group values which will assist their advancement than the young man who gives less thought to the future.

For our purposes, the utility of this interpretation requires three assumptions. The first is that socialization is significantly affected, even among adults, by external conformity to group values. Such feedback

[1] Joseph A. Schlesinger, *Ambition and Politics: Political Careers in the United States* (Chicago, 1966), pp. 9, 14.

produces, no doubt, much less intense socialization than the less direct, more unconscious processes experienced at earlier ages. Upwardly mobile men are notorious for their ability to make apparently drastic allegiance shifts. Nevertheless (as Gunnar Myrdal contends) even mature adults' lip service to a set of values has some socialization effect, because of the "strain to consistency" among proclaimed values.[2] For our purposes it is sufficient to assume that this "strain" has even a minimal effect.

The second assumption is that a considerable proportion of administrators are motivated by ambition to reach top posts; the third is that personal efforts arising from ambition constitute a major factor in career success. If promotion were entirely by seniority or purely by hazard, perception of career prospects would not be very meaningful. Schlesinger does, in fact, assume that ambition is intense among the politicians he studies, and that their striving plays a crucial part in their attainment of high office. But are these assumptions warranted in administrative elites like those in Western Europe where ascriptive influences are strong and seniority is often a major factor in promotion?

A given group of inductees to these administrations may contain a high proportion of men with low motivation. As was discussed in Chapter Eight, this would appear to be a strong possibility for the Administrative Class. Nevertheless, Brian Chapman (a severe critic of the postindustrial administrative elite in Great Britain) appears to be right in contending that a considerable measure of ambition is required to reach top posts.[3] To put the matter another way, at least a sufficient number of men to fill the top posts are ambitious; and ambition is a significant if not dominant factor in their attaining these posts. Consequently, how these men perceive the chances of advancement in the elite administrative structure is very important.

VARIATIONS IN CAREER PROSPECTS

The grosser variations in career prospects indicated in Figures 7-10 indicate some of the most important differences from period to period and among national administrations. The latter differences tend to be more significant than those between periods of the same administration. This finding confirms our general observations concerning the continuity of European administrative systems. We should emphasize that we are concerned at this point exclusively with prospects for ad-

---

[2] Gunnar Myrdal, *An American Dilemma: The Negro Problem and Modern Democracy* (New York, 1944), pp. 1,028ff.

[3] Chapman, *Profession*, pp. 281-82.

vancement for Western Europeans pursuing regular administrative careers, i.e., those who enter at early ages by meeting stringent educational requirements. Consequently, the relevant higher openings to which they can aspire exclude the portion filled by lateral entrants. We have already noted that the general nature of the graphs in Figures 7-9 (for the three Western European systems) tend to conform to the Maximum Ascriptive Model advanced in Chapter One. Since this model assumes that selection for the administrative elite has occurred at an early age, the right-hand portion of the curve will approximate a vertical line. In fact, the empirically derived graphs for France, Great Britain, and Prussia do consist of nearly vertical lines between points a_3 and a_1 (i.e., the in-service portion). The simplicity of these curves is enhanced by the use of a logarithmic scale which minimizes small differences. In fact, the ratios of annual inductees (a_3) to top positions (a_1) vary from 3:1 (France, preindustrial period) to 17:1 (Prussia, take-off period).

Two major conclusions can be drawn from examining the evidence summarized in Figures 7-9. First, in no Western European administration was ascent to top positions *assured*. Ambitious members of the administrative elite at the intermediate as well as the induction stage could perceive the utility of efforts to excel in whatever way appeared conducive to favorable consideration by superiors. Second, the chances for attaining promotion were sufficiently high to make the prospect a "good gamble" for ambitious men. A rational calculation would take into account the fact that a certain portion of one's peers at any stage would not actually compete for top posts because of lack of ambition, physical incapacity, or departure for other occupations. Hence, the actual career prospects of the determined official have been somewhat better than our calculations indicate. Conversely, in administrations (particularly the French) where prospects appear to have been very high, variations in promotion patterns among corps (as discussed in the preceding chapter) increased promotion chances to over 50 per cent in certain bodies (e.g., the Council of State) least prone to development interventionist roles, while decreasing promotion chances to a level approximating the other Western European administrations in the more dynamic corps.

Did administrators actually perceive their chances to be roughly equivalent to those we have calculated? Scattered but impressive evidence indicates that they did. Numerous biographies and memoirs more or less explicitly present copy-book models for successful advancement. Occasionally an "insider" lays out a quantitative calculation of the chances for career success. For example, Harold E. Dale indicated the career steps a successful Administrative Class official

FIGURE 7. Career Prospects, Great Britain

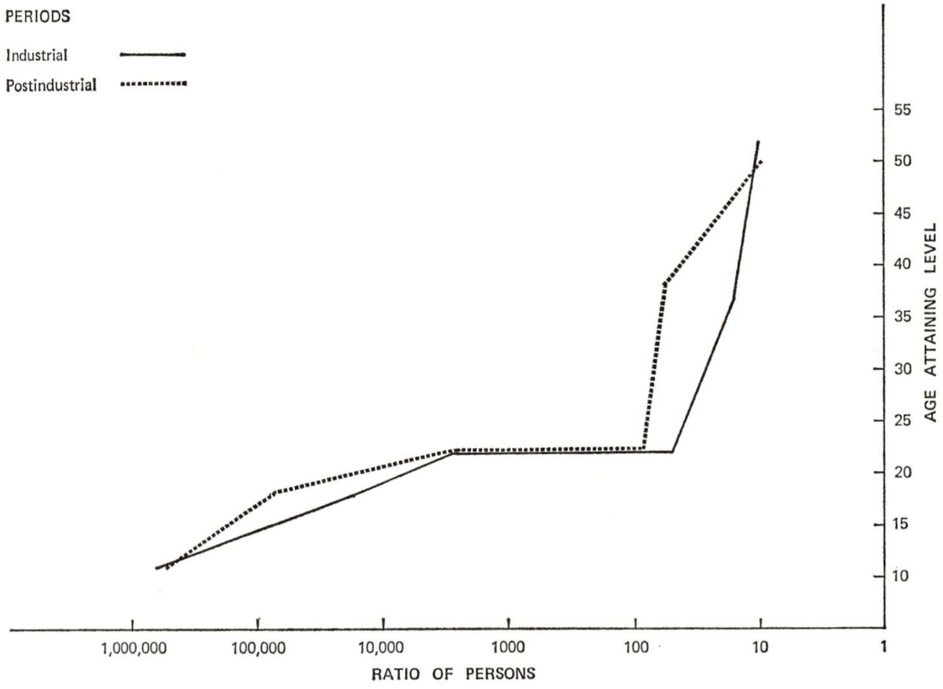

PERIODS

Industrial ▬▬▬▬

Postindustrial ▪▪▪▪▪▪▪▪▪▪

AGE ATTAINING LEVEL

RATIO OF PERSONS

FIGURE 8. Career Prospects, France

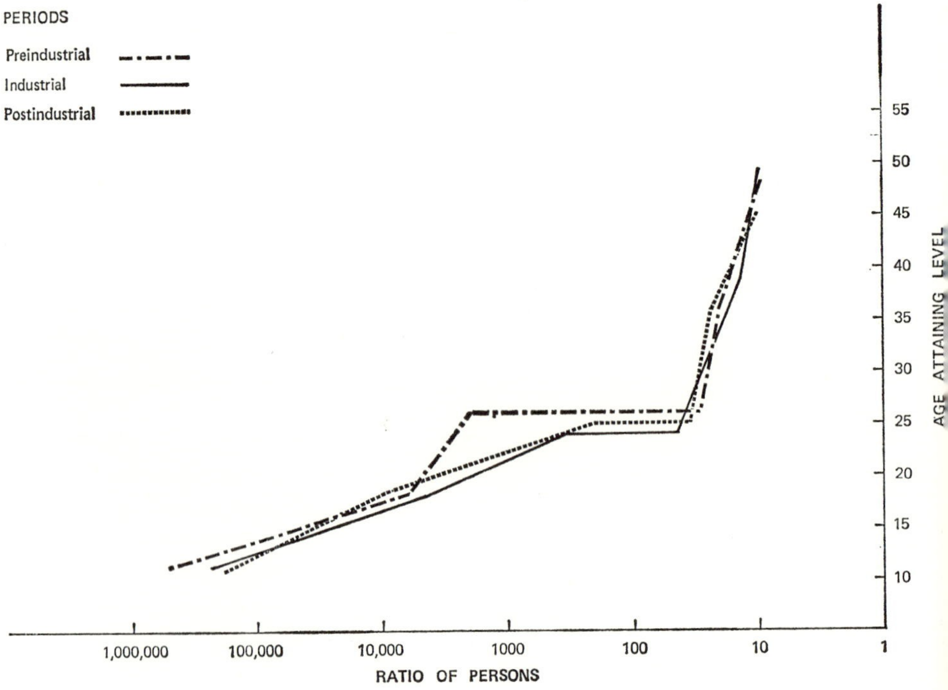

PERIODS

Preindustrial ▬ ▪ ▬ ▪ ▬ ▪

Industrial ▬▬▬▬

Postindustrial ▪▪▪▪▪▪▪▪▪▪

AGE ATTAINING LEVEL

RATIO OF PERSONS

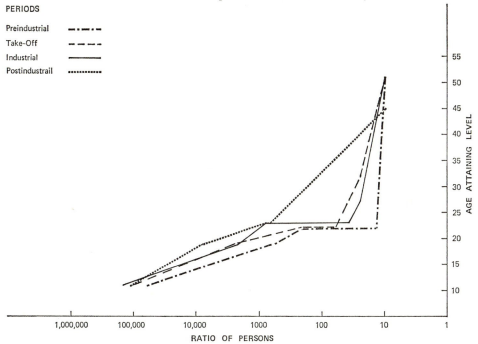

FIGURE 9. Career Prospects, Prussia—West Germany

AGE ATTAINING LEVEL

RATIO OF PERSONS

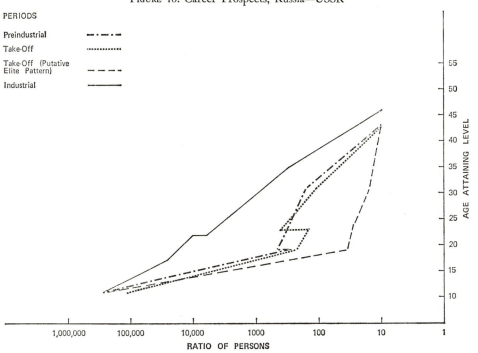

FIGURE 10. Career Prospects, Russia—USSR

AGE ATTAINING LEVEL

RATIO OF PERSONS

should have taken at specific ages during the interwar period.[4] Pierre Lalumière presented a similar model for the Financial Inspectorate in the postindustrial period.[5] We have encountered only one survey which tries to get at junior elite administrators' perceptions of their career chances directly. The Fulton Committee (1968) found that four-fifths of a very small sample of Administrative Class entrants (30 expressing definite opinions) thought they had good chances of reaching top posts.[6]

RELATIVE INFLUENCE OF DEPARTMENTAL ROLE MODELS

However accurately or inaccurately administrators perceive their gross chances of attaining high posts, they are undoubtedly also influenced by more subtle differences in career prospects. As was briefly discussed in the preceding chapter, what matters most to ambitious *Grands Corps* members is not speed of promotion in rank, but the prestige and the challenge of assignments outside the Corps. For example, a junior member of the Council of State with a taste for large-scale regulatory activity may be much more concerned with becoming Director of Social Security than attaining the prerequisite grade of *conseiller d'état*. A novice Financial Inspector may be influenced to define his role as development interventionist by the calculation that within two decades he will head a bureau like the Budget Directorate which has great potential for altering economic trends.

It is obvious that these considerations apply in some degree to more unified administrative elites. It would be interesting to trace in detail probability patterns for movement to different types of posts for the Prussian and British administrations. Very likely such monographic research would require archival records, although the published biographies would provide a start. Not only is the endeavor beyond the scope of this study; we have some doubt that it would add significantly to the reliability of our conclusions concerning development interventionist role perceptions. The major reason is that the actual range of administrative posts open to the junior elite administrator in Prussia and Great Britain has been relatively small. Essentially, posts in the interior and the finance ministries and in newer agencies concerned explicitly with planning and management in the nationalized economic sector are relevant (see Chapter One) to our consideration. As discussed in Chapter Twelve, the cross-cutting effect of territorial administration reduces significance of variations among the agencies just mentioned. For example, prefects consider it something of a disgrace

---

[4] Dale, pp. 5ff.   [5] Lalumière, p. 174.
[6] Fulton Committee, III (2), 15.

to hold even a high post in the Paris offices of the Ministry of the Interior which supervises the prefectural system.[7] In Prussia, on the other hand, young men who served as *Referendare* in the *Bezirks-regierungen* (also under the Ministry of the Interior) regarded transfer to the Berlin headquarters as the "Guards assignment" of the whole Prussian administrative service.[8] In West Germany the Federal and state ministries of the interior also include a key segment of the administrative positions.[9] Without any field service of Administrative Class officials at all, the British equivalent (the Home Office) is relatively unimportant.

Because their elite posts are centralized, finance ministries have had a more consistently important position over time and among national administrative systems. In periods when development interventionist influences were significant in the Prussian administration (see Chapter Thirteen), the Ministry of Finance played a key part. The French Finance Ministry has been the major *point d'appui* of the Financial Inspectorate. The Tsarist (but not the Soviet) Finance Ministry had extensive supervisory powers over (at various times) railroads and most other state economic activities. The British Treasury has occupied a still more salient position in relation to the administrative elite.

For the first forty years of its existence the British administrative elite was fragmented. Informal interdepartmental associations (and some formal ones, like the magazine, *The Civilian*) began to tie the upper-division clerks together. Indeed, service integration was one argument presented to the Playfair Commission for a distinct administrative elite. Without it, a witness asserted, "the Public Service would suffer for want of that sort of freemasonry which exists between people who have had a certain degree of education." Another witness urged recruiting men who "have the *esprit de corps* of our public schools and our Universities."[10]

Doubtless informal contacts among men of similar backgrounds facilitated the first major interdepartmental activity, the series of measures related to the Liberal Government's Labour Exchanges and National Insurance Program (1905). In order to plan necessary legislation and to implement it, promising young administrators were detached to the Treasury. The impact of World War I maintained the momentum of cooperation across departmental lines, although sharp interdepartmental conflicts persisted into the 1920's. In 1919 the Permanent Secretary of the Treasury was formally made head of the entire Civil Service. Soon he gained the authority (in the name of the

---

[7] Association du Corps Préfectoral, p. 11.
[8] Wermuth, p. 34.　　　　　　　　　　[9] Zapf, pp. 8off.
[10] Quoted in Fry, p. 45.

Prime Minister) to review "all suitable candidates for the Civil Service as a whole" when appointments were made to top posts.[11] Two forceful Permanent Secretaries (Warren Fisher and Edward Bridges) used the post during the interwar and immediate postwar period to unify the Administrative Class. The prestige of the Treasury has also been slightly enhanced by its direction of in-service training; but, as we have seen, this is not a major factor in Administrative Class careers. More significant has been the practice, starting in the 1930's, of transferring the most promising assistant principals and principals to the Treasury, regardless of the department they started in.

Treasury ascendancy has had a crucial impact on administrative elite role definition in two ways. Despite the Treasury's potential economic leverage, until at least the 1960's its officials perceived themselves as regulators rather than financial manipulators. In the 1930's Fisher had indeed utilized the Treasury's financial powers, but (apparently because he took a neo-Malthusian position on economic growth) he reduced foreign policy and defense expenditures to a dangerous degree. Other departments also resented what they regarded as Treasury utilization of budgetary allocation powers to get its way in interdepartmental committees.[12] After World War II, just as postindustrial problems became pressing, a reaction against this centralized power won out. According to one commentator, "Civil Service democracy" required compromise in interdepartmental committees rather than Treasury initiative.[13] Samuel Beer commented in 1956: "Although the positive State has arrived, Treasury control remains essentially negative. It must if the initiative is to remain with departments."[14]

The "negative" or at least passive role perceptions of men in the top posts to which he aspired undoubtedly influenced the ambitious junior in the 1940's and 1950's to adapt his own role definitions. As a prominent civil servant described it:

> More important, in my view, than the attitudes of Governments was the attitude of the top ranks of the Civil Service itself, and especially those in the Treasury. . . . In the first place, the Treasury itself was purely regulatory. . . . It itself did nothing "constructive" directly, and the result in my experience was that it never fully understood

[11] Henry Legge-Bourke, *Master of the Offices: An Essay and Correspondence on the Central Control of His Majesty's Civil Service* (London, 1950), p. 9; Salter, pp. 13-17; Fry, pp. 14ff., 48-49.

[12] Legge-Bourke, pp. 5, 21ff.; cf. Walker, pp. 10, 12; Munro, pp. 26-31; Fry, pp. 58ff.; Bridges, p. 11.

[13] Professor Austin Robinson, quoted in Beer, p. 76.

[14] *Ibid.*, p. 109.

the nature of constructive activities. . . . Members of the Administrative Class were not expected to have the qualities of push-and-go or the organising abilities necessary to drive any constructive undertaking through to success, and if they possessed them, it did not tell particularly in their favour.[15]

The special emphasis of the Treasury on the "all-rounder," its lack even of a large subordinate staff of economists, accountants, and the like, also strengthened general Administrative Class biases against specialists.[16] Indeed, the process of producing a homogeneous Administrative Class in place of separate departmental upper divisions was a factor in reducing what little specialization might have been maintained —given the socialization discussed earlier—in the British administrative elite.

The results were particularly disturbing in departments like the Ministry of Transport, which necessarily dealt primarily with specialized technical problems. Not until 1963 was a recommendation made that the chief engineers of the Ministry should be at the level of its deputy secretary for highways on the grounds that the morale of the Ministry's engineers was undermined by their feeling that they were being kept in the background and that most important decisions were taken by the Administrative Class administrators. Even then, apparently, status parity for engineers was confined to subdivisions like the Bridges Engineering Group, while sections concerned with policy-making, financial policy, and Parliamentary questions continued to be preserves of the Administrative Class.[17]

TRANSFER RATES AND AGE LEVELS

The degree to which junior members of an administrative elite will be influenced by specific departmental role models will evidently depend on the frequency of transfer. If an official spends a very long portion of his career in a single post, or a series of closely related posts in the same department, his socialization will tend to be compartmentalized. As noted above, the Treasury sought to avoid such departmentalization by controlling high-level appointments. As early as 1936 somewhat fewer than half (8 of 18) of the permanent secretaries had spent most of their careers in the department they ultimately headed. This proportion (36 of 84) was maintained during the postwar years.[18]

[15] Munro, pp. 26-27.
[16] Fry, pp. 58-59.
[17] D. E. Regan, "The Expert and the Administrator: Recent Changes at the Ministry of Transport," *Public Administration*, XLIV (1966), 150, 163-64.
[18] Fulton Committee, IV, 598-99.

In 1942 only 46 of 103 directors had spent their entire careers in the agencies they headed.[19]

The induction stage of the Administrative Class, like the *Referendar* stage and the E.N.A., provides for much more rapid transfer. During their three-year terms, assistant principals have held three or more posts (not counting formal training periods). What arouses more criticism is that these brief assignments continue to be the practice for principals, who are transferred every six to eight months instead of the two years envisaged in 1944.[20]

Disruptive personnel practices were a source of complaint under the Tsarist regime and are common in the USSR. Frequent wholesale replacement of Soviet middle-level personnel (for example, Party district secretaries) is primarily a screening device. During the period of crisis at the end of World War II, half of the district Party secretaries were dismissed in the Ukraine, Belorussia, and even an area like Kazakhstan, remote from the front. In the late 1950's, over half were demoted within three years of appointment (in the Russian Republic).[21] Today there is some realization that too frequent transfers can be wasteful.[22]

At higher levels the USSR has maintained key officials in some posts for periods even longer than Western norms. One recent sample of plant directors averaged about seven years.[23] This figure is identical to that of British permanent secretaries (1900-63, N=186).[24] Similarly, the seven permanent heads of the French Council of State (1898-1939) averaged six years in office.[25] On the other hand, Home Office assistant secretaries (1960's) averaged three-year terms, and Board of Trade presidents and vice-presidents during the early nineteenth century averaged two.[26] In France, directors in the Ministry of Finance (1950's) have averaged three to four years in office.[27] The terms of directors in all Ministries studied by Siwek-Pouydesseau came to virtually the same average: 4.1 years for 1944-58 and 3.4 for 1958-66.[28] In preindustrial France the *contrôleurs généraux* averaged 4.6 years.[29]

[19] Legge-Bourke, p. 7.

[20] Fry, pp. 118-19; Fulton Committee, II, 21.

[21] John A. Armstrong, *The Politics of Totalitarianism* (New York, 1961), pp. 175, 332.

[22] *Pravda* editorial, "Organizers of Production," November 10, 1969, condensed trans. in *Current Digest of the Soviet Press*, XXI, No. 45, p. 27.

[23] Estimated from data in Hough, p. 61.

[24] Recomputed from Harris and Garcia, p. 38.

[25] Calculated from biographical data in Conseil d'Etat, pp. 337ff.

[26] Fulton Committee, IV, 585; Prouty, p. 109.

[27] Lalumière, p. 141.

[28] Jeanne Siwek-Pouydesseau, *Le Personnel de Direction des Ministères: Cabinets Ministériels et Directeurs d'Administrations Centrales* (Paris, 1969), p. 73.

[29] Montyon, p. 340; cf. Petot, p. 17; Ardashev, *Les Intendants*, p. 80.

Slightly more representative data for top territorial officials presented in Table XXI (Chapter Twelve) indicates a range of variance in a single post of two and one-half to seven years, apart from some longer terms apparently due to patrimonial regression. This considerable range in average term length does not appear to vary significantly from country to country.

Somewhat similar negative conclusions on intersystem variance result from an examination of age levels in administrative elites. Induction for those entering a regular elite career service falls in the early or middle twenties; only the peculiar closed institutions of the early Tsarist regime enlisted adolescent boys for specific administrative agencies. Figures 7-9 indicate that men move to the middle level of administration between their late twenties and middle thirties, but this is partly an artifact of our specification of "middle-level" posts. We have specified those formal positions which appear approximately equivalent in prestige and responsibilities, but given the considerable variance in intermediate steps one should not attach undue significance to this selection.

Top positions are much more carefully defined in formal organizational structures, and their empirical significance has been more frequently analyzed. Consequently, we are on surer ground in specifying entrance to this level of the administrative elite. More difficulty arises in estimating age levels. Where aggregate data for the ages of top officials has been assembled, it is usually reported as a median or an arithmetic mean for all holding office at the time of the study rather than as the age of entrance to high office. As explained in more detail in the Appendix, we have frequently found it possible to transform average (or median) age in office to entrance age by subtracting a figure equal to one-half the average time such office is held, but the statistical results must be recognized as estimates.

We arrive at a range of forty-three to fifty-two as the average age at which top administrative elite posts were acquired in the administrative systems we examined (taking the administration during one period in each country as one system). While this range is considerable, it limits inferences concerning variation in physical capacities of the administrators. No elite was so old *on assuming office* as to lead one to expect that many of its members would be incapacitated. Dispersion rates—which we were unable to calculate precisely for administrative systems—were sufficiently great that some considerable *portion* of each group of elite administrators *may* have been too old for maximum effectiveness. Specific bodies of officials (generally small in number, like the vice-presidents of the Council of State) have assumed office at very advanced ages. Some elite administrators—like the group just mentioned—have remained in office to such advanced ages that they constituted gerontocracies. On the whole, however, either because of attractive pension plans, political upheaval, or assumption of purely honorific posts, retirement age for all periods and systems we have studied appears to average close to sixty. It seems, therefore, that a relatively smaller proportion of European elite administrators holds office at advanced ages than is the case with management (see Table XIX).

The average age spread for our administrative systems is rather lower than that of most U. S. Federal administrators' ages (forty to fifty-nine, with an average of forty-nine) on assumption of the relatively low career posts which they finally attain.[30] Data for top managers in industry is available only for ages at the time they were studied, as presented in Table XIX. If one assumes that the average manager has held his post about five years, it is clear that a large majority came into office at approximately the same age as our administrators. In view, however, of the differences between even the German and the British samples, the data must be interpreted cautiously.

TABLE XIX. AGE LEVELS OF TOP MANAGERS, ABOUT 1950[31]
(Per Cent)

Age Level	France	Great Britain Sample		West Germany Sample		Soviet Union	United States
		1st	2nd	1st	2nd		
Under 40	15	12	9	2	30	5	1
40-49	⎰ 61 ⎱	43	30	12	30	20	22
50-59		35	31	52	28	66	46
Over 59	24	10	31	33	11	9	31
Average		50	55	—	—	52	—

From the point of view of effect on socialization to elite values, variance in the minimal age level for attainment of high office is more significant than gerontocracy, except insofar as the latter blocks promotion avenues. If inductees perceived strong chances of attaining high office by, let us say, age thirty-five, their receptivity to socialization pressures might be reduced—i.e., they might retain more "personal

---

[30] Stanley, p. 36.

[31] French data recalculated from Delefortrie-Soubeyroux, p. 101 (N=2,947); includes managers of state industrial enterprises. American data from Stewart and Duncan, p. 65, summarizing data from studies by Abbeglen and Warner. West German column 1 from Zapf, p. 139 (N=257); column 2 from *Die Führungskräfte der Wirtschaft: Eine Untersuchung für* Die Welt *durchgeführt vom EMNID Institut für Industrielle Market- und Werbeforschung* (n.p., n.d.), p. 36. Soviet data from Hough, p. 77. British data from *Management Succession*, p. 7, summarizing (column 1) Acton Society study, and (column 2) Copeman study.

initiative." In fact, few considerable bodies of elite officials have attained top office before the lower limit of forty-three which we indicated above. Revolutionary elites (which lie outside our scope) are commonly younger. Even at the end of the Napoleonic period, the median age of all prefects in office was under forty.[32] On the other hand, Napoleon I's *conseillers d'état* averaged on appointment between forty and fifty, i.e., they were within our "standard" range.[33] In the USSR, the Great Purge of 1936-38 carried away the Revolutionary generation, bringing to high office an administrative elite with an average age level of thirty-five to forty.[34] Perpetuation of this group in office has led, however, to a steadily increasing age level, which now exceeds those of Western European administrators.

Twenty years ago Harvey C. Lehman concluded, after a systematic study of American and British political leaders, that there was a tendency for age levels on attainment of high office to rise between the eighteenth century and the mid-twentieth century.[35] Our data does not support this conclusion. Some specific groups (notably the *intendants de province*) were young; because character is vastly more important to the aristocrat than achievement, the young noble is inherently fit to command. Innumerable instances of the practical effect of this viewpoint can be found in administrative elites of the preindustrial period. On the other hand, the same point of view leads to respect for older nobles, regardless of their capacities. Their prolonged occupancy of offices frequently results in delay in promotion for younger men who would otherwise be considered entirely qualified. What one finds, therefore, is a much wider range of dispersion in early administrative elites, but an average age very similar to later elites.

There is a sense in which the generally negative results of our investigation of rate of turnover as well as age of appointment are "disappointing." Any advance in understanding factors affecting elite administrators' socialization requires close scrutiny of potentially significant factors, however. We have discussed these two in some detail because it has often been hypothesized that variance in age levels and turnover are significant indicators of systemic differences. While it is admittedly fragmentary and approximate, the data we adduce tends to reject such hypotheses insofar as general administrative elites are concerned. Given the large number of variables we must consider, we have no regrets that some factors appear to be invariant.

[32] Richardson, p. 197.   [33] Durand, *Etudes*, p. 319.
[34] Armstrong, *Soviet Bureaucratic Elite*, pp. 21ff.; cf. David Granick, *Management of the Industrial Firm in the USSR: A Study in Soviet Economic Planning* (New York, 1954), p. 42.
[35] Harvey C. Lehman, *Age and Achievement* (Princeton, 1953), pp. 269ff.

PROBLEMS OF LATERAL ENTRY

We have noted elite administrators' strong resentment against outsiders at several points in our consideration of the nineteenth- and early twentieth-century French *Grands Corps*. Frequently this resentment seems to be more intense than reduction of promotion prospects by outside appointments warranted. The *maîtres des requêtes* of the Council of State had (after 1923) very good prospects for promotion, but apparently still resented appointment of prefects as *conseillers*. E.N.A. graduates whose grades entitle them to make a career in elite corps like the Council resent lateral transfer to top posts of fellow students who ranked lower.[36] What seems to be at work is a strong attachment to the concept of a defined career pattern. Anyone who reaches the top of the career ladder without having gone through the initiation stages is regarded as a threat, even if the material injury to career officials' chances is negligible.

The Prussian service was most successful, through the *Juristenmonopol*, in excluding lateral transfers. As we have seen, insistence on the lengthy judicial experience was used to keep out Social Democratic nominees. This requirement also effectively excluded high status military officers, except in special agencies like the Imperial offices of the Second Reich. The available evidence suggests that the administrative elite of the Federal Republic is equally successful in maintaining its exclusiveness.

The British case is more complicated. The literary educational requirements do not in themselves preclude upper-middle- or upper-class men from entering at any point in their lives. The "all-rounder" emphasis would appear to favor such lateral entry. The 1918-22 period did bring about what one civil servant called "this irruption of the barbarians," special postwar entrants who by 1939 comprised two-fifths of the top 80 officials.[37] Although these men frequently shared the general upper-class background of Administrative Class career officers, the service took steps to prevent recurrence of this type of lateral entry. On the other hand, the administrative elite has always made provision for considerable promotion from the lower levels of the civil service. In practice this means Executive Class officials who usually are lower-middle class by origin and nearly always lack higher education. Between 1890 and 1911 almost one-fourth of the upper-divisional appointments came from this source, or from specialist classes. In the interwar period the proportion of promoted men increased somewhat. By 1929, 14 per cent of assistant principals and principals and 20 per

---

[36] Kessler, pp. 156, 163.   [37] Dale, p. 60.

cent of assistant secretaries were promoted from lower grades; 9 per cent more had been transferred in. Between 1938 and 1953 virtually one-half of all appointments to the Administrative Class were by promotion rather than competition.[38]

What, therefore, the British administrative elite has been in the last fifty years, at least, is a fairly equal compound of elite career service administrators and men of varying backgrounds promoted for ability. The compromise is, however, somewhat more apparent than real. While direct entrants from outside the administration in the periods following the World Wars have apparently had approximately equal chances to reach top posts, promoted men rarely do. It is very unusual for a promoted official to obtain the early sign of distinction, appointment as a minister's private secretary. Most men from lower grades are appointed as principals when they are considerably older than their competitive entrance colleagues. If promoted men reach the intermediate level (assistant secretary) at all, they are at an age (forty-five or higher) when successful men among the competition entrants are already entering top posts. Similarly, men promoted directly to assistant secretary (about one-twelfth of the total in recent years) have usually gone as far as they will in the service.[39]

Lateral transfer serves both to subdue outside criticism of the Administrative Class and to provide some prospect of advancement for talented and ambitious men in the Executive Class who otherwise might become embittered. Having achieved such a highly unusual promotion (obviously only an extremely small proportion of the large Executive Class can possibly enter the small Administrative Class), promotees are apt to be deferential toward the style and values of the elite administration. Several observers also see them as excessively cautious, even more disinclined to initiative than their competition-entry colleagues.[40]

No special socialization mechanism is provided for lateral entrants. There is a three-month course open to Administrative Class officials who have completed ten to twenty years service, and who are consequently in their late thirties or early forties. Conducted at the Administrative Staff College in Henley, the courses stress case studies of administrative problems by student teams. A large majority of the one hundred to two hundred men who have taken these courses each year have been non-Civil Service, including many private managers. This factor provides administrators a brief opportunity to become acquainted with other elites at a crucial point before attaining top posts.

[38] Kelsall, pp. 40, 48, 53, 56; Fry, p. 166.
[39] Harris and Garcia, pp. 33ff.   [40] Greaves, p. 66.

Supervisors are reported to be adverse to letting their best subordinates attend for such a protracted time, however.[41]

During the take-off period, outside appointments were so frequent in most French elite administrations that it was difficult to speak of a career service. By the industrial period (i.e., the Third Republic) a measure of stabilization had occurred, but even in the early years of this century half of the *conseillers d'état* and at least a similar proportion of prefects were appointed without previous experience in their branch of service. In the 1930's up to one-third of the directing engineers of the Ponts et Chaussées and Mines corps were men promoted from lower ranks who had not attended the elite corps schools.[42] For the technical corps, promotion prospects have probably remained similar to those of the interwar period. As we have seen, however, prospects of lateral transfer in the *Grands Corps* have been vastly diminished by the near monopoly of E.N.A. graduates.

LATERAL ENTRY AND THE PROGRESSIVE EQUAL
ATTRITION MODEL

Lateral entry obviously has an entirely different significance for administrations where early selection for an administrative elite does not take place. The American Federal service inducts large numbers of university-trained specialists. Average entrance age for those who eventually attain fairly high posts is twenty-eight—only a few years higher than for recent Western European career inductees.[43] In order to attain the relatively small number of higher level administrative positions, the American recruits must adapt while in service to the values of generalist administration. In other words, anticipatory socialization must make them more like the elite administrators we have been discussing.

Many entrants do not perceive this necessity, however, for government employment "attracts the specialist because of the opportunity to work on a large scale."[44] After a time, persons who entered with this conception find that their specialized accomplishments are limited by the size of the organization and their own exclusion from its commanding posts. As a result, there is a high degree of frustration at lower levels of the administration. Even those who do perceive the need to adjust to generalist administrative values are uneasy in anticipatory socialization for what is, for them, a new and unclearly defined role. Consequently they tend to fall back on their secure professional role

[41] See Chapman, *Profession*, p. 126, on this general tendency in contemporary European administrations.
[42] Sharp, p. 188.   [43] Stanley, p. 25.
[44] Bendix, *Higher Civil Servants*, p. 49.

by restricting their ambition to middle-level administrative posts intimately related to the professional specialization they possessed when they entered the service.[45]

This tendency is, of course, reinforced by the fact that true top-level posts (comparable to those in European administrations) are generally reserved for discretionary political appointment. Many political appointees are selected because of their presumed skill as lawyers or in other professions. As a result they bring their own professional role conception to the higher ranks of the service. Lloyd Warner and his associates saw lateral entry to high posts as helping the service in "escaping the routinizing influence of white-collar bureaucracy."[46] In the absence of provisions for systematic in-service socialization (at any level), however, role conflict appears to be intensified by this practice.

No matter how ambitious an American career civil servant is, and no matter how strong his socialization to specifically administrative values, he has to face the prospect of direct subordination to outsiders when he has proceeded to the top of his truncated career ladder. Apart from the organizational friction and high level of frustration which this situation entails, it results in great wastage of potential administrative talent. Since professionals frequently have higher social status as well as larger salaries than "Federal bureaucrats," even those men who have adjusted to the generalist administrative role may find complete reversion to their professional roles attractive. Many leave administrative activity in their late forties, just at the age when European elite administrators and American industrial managers are making their maximum contribution in top positions. A study made during the 1940's found that one-quarter of the higher level administrators had left for a wide variety of nonadministrative posts. Some of these were in Federal agencies, but nearly all were in the civil servant's original profession. Only 3 or 4 per cent entered business; the expression "I don't feel any satisfaction in dealing with things" appears typical. In their way, these men are nearly as remote from entrepreneurial values as German or British administrators.[47]

Lateral Entry and the Russian Variant of Progressive Equal Attrition

A review of aspects of the U. S. Federal administration has seemed worthwhile at this point because the American situation superficially

[45] William Lloyd Warner, et al., *The American Federal Executive: A Study of the Social and Personal Characteristics of the Civilian and Military Leaders of the United States Federal Government* (New Haven, 1963), p. 195.

[46] *Ibid.*, p. 155.

[47] *Ibid.*, p. 224; Stanley, p. 28; Bendix, *Higher Civil Servants*, p. 66.

resembles the one which has prevailed in Russia for two centuries. As was discussed in Chapter Ten, the middle of the nineteenth century saw the tentative development of elite career patterns. Even for civil servants during that period, as Table XX indicates, competition from outsiders for top-level posts (the first four *chins*) was severe. Instead of coming from business or political occupations, however, the Russian outsiders transferred laterally from the military. Except during Alexander I's reign, military predominance among the important gubernatorial corps was continuous. Military officers were a distinct minority in the ministries (particularly if one excludes, as Table XX does *not*,

TABLE XX. TSARIST ELITE ADMINISTRATORS WITH CIVIL AND MILITARY RANK[48]

Period	N	Governors		N'	All Administrators with Service in Central Ministries after Attaining Top Four Chins	
		Military Chin *Only*	Civil Chin		Military Chin *Only*	Civil Chin
		(Per Cent)			(Per Cent)	
1762-1800	98	68	.32	53	41	59
1801-1825	69	36	64	59	32	68
1826-1855	88	60	40	158	35	65
1856-1881	55	69	31	109	32	68
Total	310	60	40	379	35	65

technical corps officers who always had military *chin* although their duties were similar to those of the great French technical corps). Even in the ministries, however, the potential occupancy of desirable posts by outsiders combined with the generally low prospects of attaining top rank to dampen ambition. Military styles, common in civilian socialization and reinforced by the prestige of the military officers seconded to high posts, heightened the rigidity of the system. Together with the excessive emphasis on seniority this was undoubtedly responsible for the adherence to bureaucratic routine which writers like Gogol and countless foreign observers deplored.

Even compared to the Tsarist system, the ratio of Soviet administrative inductees to available top posts is enormous—we estimate it as 1,200 to one. The ratio is scarcely very meaningful, however, since (at least in past decades) there have been no specific educational requirements for reaching top positions. As recently as 1938 a majority in middle-level Party and state positions did not even have regular secondary educations.[49] Of a large sample of high administrators (1958-62) at

[48] John A. Armstrong, "Tsarist and Soviet Elite Administrators," *Slavic Review*, XXXI (1972), 15.

[49] Armstrong, *Soviet Bureaucratic Elite*, p. 32.

least 38 per cent had no higher education when they entered administrative service.[50]

On the other hand, the vast majority of persons entering lower ranks of the administration have no aspiration to reach the top. The regime's monopoly on published information probably precludes a majority of young people from even perceiving the values required of men in high posts. Many who do perceive these values reject them as too harsh or demanding. This appears to be true especially of young men from well-educated families, who much prefer high status careers in specialized fields to getting involved in the "dirty work" of the Party bosses or even in industrial management. There is a considerable amount of evidence that Party officials themselves do not encourage their sons to take official posts. This phenomenon may be due partly to a desire to avoid nepotism. The fact that many sons obtain excellent specialized educations and assume prized positions on graduation leads one to suspect, however, that their administrative elite fathers have used their influence to steer their sons to alternative privileged careers.

Under these circumstances Soviet selection of top administrators differs considerably not only from the elite career pattern prevalent in Western Europe, but from the American mass-induction pattern. There are two major sources of recruits. One is the full-time Party apparatus itself. Nominally this body numbers about 150,000, but expert observers believe that in fact this number should be tripled to take into account primary Party organization secretaries whose non-Party jobs are more or less sinecures.[51] Out of this group, approximately 15,000 reach intermediate-level posts (defined by the official *nomenklatura* index) such as district secretary or district-level government posts. As indicated earlier in the chapter, turnover at this level is very great for the district-level posts are regarded as testing grounds. Most of those who are dismissed return, apparently, to manual, or white-collar jobs.

Since the Soviet administrative elite has been stabilized for little more than a generation (since 1938), it is difficult to determine what effects this severe selection process has upon anticipatory socialization. In the late 1930's and 1940's prospects for reaching the top, though certainly never high in a strictly quantitative sense, may have appeared good to ambitious lower officials. The nearly complete turnover of top officials in 1937-38 matched the high rates of turnover at lower levels. A considerable, though reduced, rate of replacement of top officials continued into the early 1950's. Increasingly after 1954, however, the

[50] Fischer, p. 96. We assume that those with Party schooling only acquired it (as discussed below) after service entry.

[51] Stephen Rapawy, "Comparison of U. S. and U.S.S.R. Civilian Employment in Government: 1950 to 1969" (unpublished draft), Foreign Demographic Analysis Division, U. S. Department of Commerce, 1972, pp. 33ff.

body of higher officials began to acquire the features of a self-perpetuating oligarchy.[52]

Various signs indicate that this closing of avenues of advancement caused resentment. In 1961 Khrushchev sought to provide at least the appearance of turnover by instituting rules for changes in some Party offices at fixed intervals, but after his removal these rules were abolished. To some extent Party openings have been created by seconding top officials to diplomatic service, where they nearly monopolize certain branches such as representation to other Communist states.[53]

The second major source of recruits for the Soviet administrative elite consists of lateral transfers from other occupations. During the 1940's some transfers were from political police agencies, but these virtually ceased after 1951. In contrast to the Tsarist practice, transfer of professional military officers to administrative posts has been rigidly avoided in the USSR during the last forty years. A large majority of lateral transfers during these decades have come from technical posts in industry, including engineering and staff specialist jobs. Frequently men with such backgrounds transfer to managerial posts (more rarely to Party posts) at the middle level of the administration—i.e., as managers of small factories, sections of large ones, or directors of ministerial chief administrations (*glavki*). From that point on their roles are primarily generalist administration. For example, the present titular president, N. V. Podgorny, pursued an engineering career until he was thirty-six, then entered state administrative work as deputy people's commissar for food processing in the Ukraine, remaining in similar activities until the age of forty-seven when he temporarily transferred to the Ukrainian Party apparatus.

We know little about how and why some industrial specialists are willing to make this transfer. No doubt the fact that Party officials increasingly have the same type of technical educations (although ordinarily they transferred to administrative work soon after completing higher schools) encourages the trend. There is also little doubt that the Soviet specialist, like his counterpart in the U. S. Federal service, tends to combine his specialized and his administrative role as much as possible. A large majority of Soviet specialists who transfer to administration remain in branches (e.g., ministries concerned with heavy industry) where their specialized knowledge supplements their administrative skills. Resulting role conflict undoubtedly contributes to the oversimplified engineering approach to development which we noted in Chapter Nine.

[52] Armstrong, *Politics of Totalitarianism.*
[53] Vernon V. Aspaturian, *Process and Power in Soviet Foreign Policy* (Boston, 1971), pp. 607ff.

SOVIET MID-CAREER SOCIALIZATION PATTERNS

Very soon after the drastic upheavals of the Great Purge and World War II, the Soviet regime recognized that induction of so many men into top positions posed problems of socialization. Intense achievement motivation could be assumed for lower Party officials who had made their way even to the middle level, for the risk of abrupt demotion—or worse—was extreme. Technical specialists who entered management also had intense achievement values: "Soviet managers spend long hours in their enterprises, they worry about their production and procurement problems, and they take [under Stalin] grave personal risks in pursuit of their goals."[54] What was required, from the regime's standpoint, was a system of mid-career socialization which would inculcate certain administrative skills and a recommitment to the supremacy of Party values. This system was provided, beginning in 1946, by full-time Party schools. Of the three putative "corps" which we identified in Chapter Ten, the economic management group was rarely affected. Central Party officials and state and Party officials at the territorial level, though, were detached to Party schools for periods up to four years. Most of the trainees are middle-level officials being considered for promotion, although (especially in the 1940's) even provincial first secretaries were frequently withdrawn from their major posts for prolonged retraining. Although a secondary level education was required, basic subjects such as logic, international relations, Soviet history, and languages were deemed essential for the haphazardly educated administrative elite of the immediate postwar years. Other subjects (dialectical and historical materialism, for example) had a primary utility as reindoctrination. Practical economic management, utilizing seminar and team approaches, appears, however, to have constituted the core of the program.[55]

The importance of the mid-term retraining program for the territorial Party officials is indicated by the fact that of a group of 181 holding office as provincial first secretary between 1950 and 1966, 42 per cent had attended higher Party schools.[56] Of a group of 306 Party and state officials (1958-62) slightly over one-fourth had acquired their *only* higher education in these Party institutions.[57]

[54] Joseph Berliner, *Factory and Manager in the USSR* (Cambridge, Mass., 1957), p. 321.

[55] Bruno Kalnins, *Der sowjetische Propagandastaat: Das System und die Mittel der Massenbeeinflussung in der Sowjetunion* (Stockholm, 1956), p. 46; Armstrong, *Soviet Bureaucratic Elite*, pp. 35ff.; *Kommunisticheskaia Partiia Sovetskogo Soiuza v Rezoliutsiiakh i Resheniiakh S"ezdov, Konferentsii i Plenumov Ts. K.*, Vol. II (Moscow, 1953), 1,022ff.

[56] Philip D. Stewart, *Political Power in the Soviet Union* (Indianapolis, 1968), p. 144.

[57] Fischer, p. 96.

It may be that the rising proportion of middle-level administrators with technical higher educations will reduce the length of retraining required. As was noted in Chapter Nine, however, Soviet authorities increasingly express dissatisfaction with technical higher educations as a background for administrators. In 1964 a Ukrainian-born member of the Columbia University faculty who had returned to the USSR urged emulation of American business techniques, writing that "the system of our planned economy opens unlimited horizons and presents such tremendous possibilities for applying the science of organization and management as cannot even be dreamed of in the United States of America." By the late 1960's, cybernetics was widely accepted in Soviet institutions for economic planning, although Soviet writers expressed reservations about applying these techniques to social control problems. Mathematic models and the systems approach in social sciences could be fruitfully employed, a *Pravda* writer commented, in conjunction with qualitative Marxist-Leninist sociological analysis.[58]

A recent article coauthored by the vice-chairman of the Russian Republic state planning commission and an academic specialist on administration pointed out that "we still have no adequately developed science of administration, the creation of which was urged by V. I. Lenin." In effect, the authors called for the provision of extensive mid-career courses for economic administrators paralleling the Party schools. After considerable practical experience, but before assuming their first managerial posts, promising lower administrators should spend, they wrote, one or two years in administrative schools, with subsequent refresher courses. Certain general and indoctrination subjects, as well as technical topics like cybernetics, should be included. The main emphasis was to be on case work in economic management taught by high-ranking managers.[59] As yet, there are no clear indications that such a restructuring of the mid-career retraining system will in fact be instituted. Its consequences would be at least as significant as the foundation of the Party schools themselves. It may well be that the present aging, oligarchical Soviet leadership is unwilling to take such a drastic step.

Even with its rather crude selection and retraining procedures, the Soviet system has been markedly more successful in obtaining an ad-

[58] V. Afanasev, "V. I. Lenin and Problems of the Scientific Management of Society," *Pravda*, December 4, 1969, condensed trans. in *Current Digest of the Soviet Press*, XXI, No. 49, pp. 18-20; V. Tereshchenko, "The Effect of 'Trifles,'" *Izvestia*, March 29, 1964, trans. in *Current Digest of the Soviet Press*, XVI, No. 13, pp. 17-18.

[59] V. Lisitsyn and G. Popov, "The Economic Manager's Outlook," *Pravda*, January 19, 1968, condensed trans. in *Current Digest of the Soviet Press*, XX, No. 3, pp. 25-26.

ministrative elite with a strong motivation for initiative in economic development than was the Tsarist system. From this narrow standpoint, we also have little doubt that the Soviet system has been more successful than the U. S. Federal administration. Undoubtedly the prevalence of an intense development interventionist doctrine has been a significant factor. The lengthy mid-career retraining program reinforces the impact of the Leninist doctrine and undoubtedly provides its graduates with high confidence in their ability to assume commanding roles. The drain on personnel resources is very heavy, however, as is the social cost of the immense wastage arising from rapid turnover of middle-level personnel.

Today—in contrast to the 1930's and 1940's when many of the present elite were being socialized—higher education is almost a requisite for promotion to top Soviet positions. At the same time, the proportion of men with advanced educations who are motivated to enter administrative careers may be declining. Under these circumstances it may be impossible for the Soviet regime to continue the prodigal use of personnel resources which our Model 3 (Progressive Equal Attrition Model) implies. In that case, resort to early selection and intensive socialization could economize scarce human resources. Given the high propensity (see Chapter Four) of better-educated Soviet families to produce well-educated children, such a resort would very likely introduce some of the ascriptive elements of the Western European model (Model 2). Certainly there would be no tendency toward aristocratic role models. Even the bourgeois models dominant in France would be substantially altered in the Soviet context. We doubt that any specifically "proletarian" role model has emerged—in the USSR or elsewhere in Europe. What would be likely to dominate role definition if the Soviet administrative system did resort to early recruitment would be the strongly manipulative values which emerged as one element of the bourgeois pattern at the end of the eighteenth century.

CHAPTER TWELVE

Territorial Direction and
Development Initiative

Tʜɪs book is not a study of organizational structures; but one feature of European administrative organization has been so closely linked to the evolution of development role models that we must consider it in detail. Given the primary goal of national integration, preindustrial regimes necessarily emphasized the territorial administration. Even after the peripatetic *commissarius* accompanying the royal armies had been "rooted" by assignment to a specific province, his position remained critical. On the one hand, as the representative of the central authority he was the prime target for recurring cycles of aristocratic reaction. On the other hand, he was tempted to become a particularistic, semi-feudal ruler himself. To avoid these threats to national integration, the monarchical central authority had to provide firm backing for its territorial officials, yet avoid allowing them to control large resources for prolonged periods of time. The French and the Russian response to this problem was designation of a single official to direct governmental activities in a considerable territory. This device, usually termed the "prefectural governor," has persisted in both countries, with strong effects on the general organization of the administration as well as on development role definition specifically.

Evolution of the French Prefectural Governor

Evolution of the prefectural system in France was slow and interrupted; but by the start of Colbert's ministry it was firmly institutionalized by appointment of *intendants de province* to some thirty territorial units. Formally these units were called *généralités*, and their honorific heads *gouverneurs*. For simplicity in comparison we shall at times refer to the *intendants* as "governors" and to the territories as "provinces." The same terms refer to the territorial unit (*guberniia*) which during the eighteenth century became the main Russian territorial division and the director of the unit (*gubernator*).

A fundamental principle in both countries (occasionally disregarded) was that no governor should be appointed to his family's home region. If the governor was to "hold the balance" against the rich and the powerful, intimate ties to the local aristocracy were dangerous.[1] The governor had to be prepared to intervene vigorously against particularistic pretensions, whether by French *parlements* or Russian marshals of nobility. After the French Revolution, the prefects continued the role of the *intendants* as arms of the central authority. During the nineteenth century they were notorious for manipulating elections to support the political status quo, but their primary duty remained suppression of particularistic opposition. The firm support of the prefects was essential to the success of the anticlerical measures at the beginning of the twentieth century. The principal Soviet territorial officials are the first secretaries of the *obkoms* (provincial Party committees) who have ensured success of unpopular measures like collectivization of agriculture and control of non-Russian nationalities.

In both France and Russia, at all periods, the top central authorities have firmly retained the power of appointment. Both Colbert and the Tsarist ministers preferred to rotate governors every two or three years.[2] During all periods, as Table XXI indicates, terms were somewhat longer than that. By the end of the monarchical regimes, terms were much longer. Apparently this phenomenon reflects the tendency to patrimonial regression in preindustrial societies.[3] But it is also related to the need for keeping competent officials in specific posts long enough for them to become thoroughly familiar with the territory. After several years in office, *intendants* frequently became attached to the interests of their provinces, devoting great efforts to improving local conditions. Some *intendants* most intimately involved with "enlightened" social elements resisted the physiocratic doctrines because they precluded intervention to avert widespread economic distress.[4]

Up to a point, central authorities encouraged this concern as a useful corrective to officials' preference for metropolitan life. Louis XIV was so strict in insisting that the provincial "state of affairs demands the whole man" that one *intendant* died of a kidney stone rather than leave his post for surgery.[5] On the other hand, too strong a local attachment might not only lead to patrimonial regression, but to obstruction of

---

[1] Charles de Beaucorps, "Une Province sous Louis XIV: l'Administration des Intendants d'Orléans: De Creil, Jubert de Bouville et de la Baudonnaye (1686-1713)," *Mémoires de la Société Archéologique et Historique de l'Orléanais*, xxxiii (1911), 498.

[2] Maurice Bordes, "Les Intendants de Louis XV," *Revue Historique*, ccxxiii (1960), 62; Pages, "Essai," pp. 128, 133; Got'e, i, 151-53, 217; Demidova, in *Absoliutizm*, p. 213.

[3] See Armstrong, "Old-Regime Governors."

[4] Lhéritier, ii, 12-13, 38; cf. Maurice Bordes, "Les Intendants Eclairés de la Fin de l'Ancien Régime," *Revue d'Histoire Economique et Sociale*, xxxix (1961), 63ff.

[5] J. Ricommard, "Les Subdélégués des Intendants jusqu'à Leur Erection en Titre d'Office," *Revue d'Histoire Moderne*, xii (1937), 356-57; cf. Got'e, i, 140.

vital central resource mobilization. Thus several *intendants* tried to interfere with the exactions of Ferme Générale officials, which bore severely upon the common people of their provinces. Other *intendants* resented the burden of the *corvée* for highway construction imposed on "their" peasants. Conversely, many prefects have welcomed frequent transfer (as Table XXI shows, their terms were slightly lower than our standard) because they feared protracted stays would exhaust their "moral credit" and make it difficult for them to remain impartial among conflicting local interests.[6]

TABLE XXI. CHIEF TERRITORIAL ADMINISTRATORS:
AVERAGE LENGTH OF TERM IN A SINGLE GOVERNING POST (*Years*)[7]

Génération	France, Preindustrial (1661-1773)		Russia, Preindustrial (1762-1855)		France, Industrial (1877-1958)		USSR, Industrial (1943-1966)	
	Average Length of Term	Generation	Average Length of Term	Generation	Average Length of Term	Generation	Average Length of Term	Generation
First Generation	5.3	23	4.6	39	2.7	42.	2.7	13[a]
Second Generation	6.2	32	6.6	25	2.6	22	4.3	17[a]
Third Generation	8.7	58	7.4	30	2.6	14	—	—

[a] Groups overlap—see n. 7.

As long, but only as long, as they retained the confidence of the central authorities, prefectural governors had great powers. These powers included supervision of most other local officials; indeed, centralization of authority at the territorial level is the distinguishing feature of the prefectural organizational principle. Under the French Old Regime, the provincial apparatus was at first rudimentary. Colbert feared subdivision of the provinces would encourage particularism, but the governors on the spot soon found *subdélégués* indispensable to supervise their extensive territories effectively. The *subdélégués* quickly became an established institution (indeed Colbert himself occasionally employed them to report on *intendants*). As a rule, however, the *intendant* was fully responsible for recruiting and training these district officers as well as his staff in the provincial seat: "a more numerous administrative personnel was constituted, notably in the *intendance* bureaus, with a secretary general, bureau chiefs, clerks, etc., devoted to their task . . . the administrative apparatus of modern France; re-

[6] Chapman, *Prefects*, p. 148.
[7] Columns 1 and 2: Armstrong, "Old-Regime Governors," pp. 21-22 (N=65 to 122); column 3 (N's over 100) recalculated from Siwek-Pouydesseau, *Le Corps Préfectoral*, p. 66 (does not include Vichy period); column 4, First Period, Ukrainian *obkom* first secretaries (N=41), Second Period recalculated from Stewart, pp. 170-71, all *obkom* first secretaries (N=377).

gimes succeed one another, the apparatus remains and enables the country to live, to persist—that is the history of the 18th century."[8]

Other governors have had less freedom in choosing subordinate staff members. The *chin* system limited the Russian governor's appointive power, though he had no difficulty in dominating the staff. Except when a strong vice-governor was appointed, the governor was "master and manager [*khoziain*]," responsible for everything.[9] Similarly, the *nomenklatura* system has meant that the Soviet *oblast* first secretary cannot appoint his principal subordinates. Except in the rare circumstances when a strong second secretary has been deliberately installed as a counterweight, however, the first secretary is also "God and Tsar in the *oblast* (province)."[10]

The prefect's authority is more limited geographically and more closely circumscribed legally. Nevertheless, the nineteenth-century French historian, Anatole Leroy-Beaulieu, did not hesitate to equate him to the contemporary Russian governor as a "miniature autocrat."[11] Two generations later a prefect perceived his precarious eminence as follows: "We are in an exciting but precarious, occasionally unjust career. It is the price we pay for the authority we exercise. We must realize it, we must accept the risk that we are acting in the name of the government, which may change its policy and consequently remove us."[12] The perils of the prefectural career were, as noted in Chapter One, as acute during 1940-45 as in the nineteenth century. Like the Soviet *oblast* first secretaries, prefects appointed after the crisis have tended to remain in office. Nevertheless, 70 per cent of all prefects (in the 1950's) had been socialized to the corps by serving in at least one lower grade; and less than half of the lower grades (subprefect and prefectural staff director) had been recruited from outside the Ministry of the Interior. The regular socialization process of the corps has been interrupted since 1948, however, by the fact that the next lower level of posts (subprefect and prefectural staff director) are reserved for E.N.A. graduates.

[8] Phillipe Sagnac, "Louis XIV et Son Administration," *Revue d'Histoire Politique et Constitutionnelle*, III (1939), 36; Ricommard, "Les Subdélégués," pp. 340, 356, 361, 381-82; Douglas Dakin, *Turgot and the Ancien Régime in France* (London, 1939), pp. 38ff.

[9] Torke, p. 179.

[10] By a Soviet defector quoted in Merle Fainsod, *How Russia Is Ruled*, 2nd ed. (Cambridge, Mass., 1963), pp. 225; cf. Torke, pp. 179-81.

[11] Anatole Leroy-Beaulieu, *The Empire of the Tsars and the Russians*, Vol. II (New York, 1894), 89.

[12] Siwek-Pouydesseau, *Le Corps Préfectoral*, p. 114; Association du Corps Préfectoral, p. 18; Chapman, *Prefects*, p. 82.

SCOPE OF PREFECTURAL AUTHORITY IN FRANCE AND RUSSIA

Despite striking general resemblances, differences among prefectural governors in specific spheres of authority have been significant. These differences affect their direct initiatives in development and the feedback influence their roles have had on central administrative elites. The Tsarist governor was unique in commanding regular military units stationed in his province. The fact that he was, more often than not, a seconded military officer facilitated this arrangement. A general was often returned to exercise civil power (either as a regular civil governor or military governor) at the scene of his campaigns. A fairly obvious effect of this practice was to establish the precedence of military requirements over all types of civil activity, including economic development. Since a separate intendancy corps provisioned the military forces, the governor was not always involved deeply even in resource mobilization to support his military units.[13] The Soviet system, on the contrary, has avoided putting civil and military power in the same hands. To facilitate political control and resource mobilization in wartime, Party secretaries have been attached to the staffs of military units operating in their areas, but command is always assigned to a regular officer. The *intendant* was charged with provisioning royal regiments, but their commanders occasionally acted as a significant check on his authority.[14] The prefect ordinarily has no authority over French army units stationed in his *département*.

On the other hand, both the *intendant* and the prefect have supervised the police forces. Under the Fourth and Fifth Republics, the regional prefects (I.G.A.M.E.) have commanded substantial para-military police units assigned to a territory covering several *départements*. Early prefects were threatened by efforts of Napoleon I's minister of police, Joseph Fouché, to construct a parallel network of police agents, keeping the prefects under surveillance by direct reports from subprefects. From the Restoration to the present, however, French regimes have used the prefect as their trusted local police arm. Louis XIV also tended to use the lieutenants of police as a separate chain of command, but by the eighteenth century the *intendants*, like their successors, generally could freely employ provincial police agents for surveillance and enforcement.[15]

---

[13] D. A. Skalon, *Stoletie Voennago Ministerstva, 1802-1902: Glavnoe Intendantskoe Upravlenie* (St. Petersburg, 1903), p. 18; Got'e, I, 325ff.; Ivan E. Andreevsky, *Namestnikakh, Voevodakh i Gubernatorakh* (Dissertation, St. Petersburg University, Law Faculty, 1864), p. 115.

[14] Beaucorps, p. 272; Bordes, "Les Intendants de Louis XIV," p. 52.

[15] Pierre-Henry, p. 53; Savant, pp. 8off.; J. Ricommard, *La Lieutenance Générale*

The relation of Russian governors to the police arm has been less comfortable. By the nineteenth century, a regular separate chain of command linked the St. Petersburg Ministry of the Interior and local police agents. While harsh, the latter often seem to have been more impartial in law enforcement than the local authorities. The practice of a distinct police command was continued under the Soviet regime. During the Great Purge (and in certain limited circumstances until 1951) the political police dominated the provinces. While nominal authority always belonged to the Party first secretaries, the police kept them under surveillance; occasionally secret police chiefs did not even bother to report their actions to responsible Party and state authorities. Between 1951 and 1953 police supremacy was broken, but a separate reporting channel still exists. The significant para-military police units (now mainly in frontier areas) are outside gubernatorial jurisdiction. Lack of either military or police forces at his immediate disposal has always been a potential limitation on the *obkom* first secretary's power. Given the tight central control and the strong doctrinal legitimization of Party supremacy, however, this factor has not significantly restricted his authority as yet.

Because maintenance of order has always been the salient aspect of the prefectural governor's role, a survey of his activity in that field has been necessary. More directly pertinent to our concern is the special relationship which has grown up between the governor and the engineering corps. At no time has the governor exercised complete control over provincial engineers, but his influence has been considerable. The relationship began in eighteenth-century France. *Intendants* provided essential local support for the Ponts et Chaussées corps, partly out of provincial tax resources, more in labor recruitment, and still more in overriding property owners' obstructiveness. In turn, road construction was essential to the *intendants'* prime task of maintaining royal authority: wherever, one reported, wheels could carry cannon and mortars, Huguenots could not hold out.[16] Able *intendants* socialized provincial engineers to a comprehension of practical resource limitations. Working with the engineers made *intendants* appreciate the possibility of fostering economic growth by applying technological advances in constructing a transportation infrastructure. To a striking degree *intendants* eager to promote the welfare of their provinces overcame the traditional upper-class antipathy to participation in ma-

---

de Police à Troyes au XVIIIᵉ Siècle, 1700-1790 (Dissertation, University of Paris, Faculté des Lettres, 1933), pp. 248, 267; Monas, p. 131; Torke, p. 277.

[16] H. Monin, *Essai sur l'Histoire Administrative du Languedoc pendant l'Intendance de Basville (1685-1719)* (Paris, 1884), p. 370.

terial manipulative tasks. Some even mastered the details of road construction and used surveying instruments.[17]

Neither in physical circumstances nor in the ability of their governors were the Russian provinces so fortunate. Nevertheless, outstanding governors took the same interest in constructing a transportation infrastructure as did the *intendants*. After he was dispatched to Siberia as governor-general, Speransky formed a close association with his aide from the Transport corps, a fellow Freemason.[18] For other governors the engineering component or associations in their military background were helpful.

Napoleon's prefects were explicitly ordered to supervise highway construction by Ponts et Chaussées engineers and to make their own arrangements for local roads. Baron Haussmann, the outstanding prefect of the Second Empire, brought the provincial engineer whom he had previously worked with in Bordeaux to help in the reconstruction of Paris.[19]

In later periods the scope and specialized nature of construction activities tended to transcend the confines of the small *département* or even the *oblast*. The specialized transport corps and Ministries still maintained provincial representatives, but their collaboration with the top territorial officer was less intimate. In the Soviet system, Party organizations in major transportation agencies were separated from the ordinary territorial Party system for several decades. Construction and operation of railroads and waterways, like other industrial activities, have always been directed by Moscow ministries.

On the whole, relations between governors and provincial engineers appear to have been harmonious under the old regimes. Nevertheless, the engineer's dual subordination to corps chief and *intendant*, as a contemporary wrote, always posed a delicate problem which could be resolved only by the head of the engineering corps:

> He is obliged to hold the balance in a very difficult equilibrium between the *intendant* who wishes to command at his discretion and the engineer, who wishes to obey only the top authorities to whom he owes his authority, and who takes pride in asserting it. Another kind of contradiction arises between *subdélégués*, supported by the *intendant* whom they represent and engineers who want to take

[17] Lhéritier, II, 130, 135; H. Chéguillaume, "Perronet, Ingénieur de la Généralité d'Alençon (1737-1747)," *Bulletin de la Société Historique et Archéologique de l'Orne*, x (1890), 58ff.

[18] Pypin, p. 472; Karl Ludwig Blum, *Ein russischer Staatsmann: Des Grafen Jakob Johann Sievers* Denkwürdigkeiten zur Geschichte Russlands, Vol. I (Leipzig, 1857), 201, 293.

[19] Savant, p. 51; J. M. and Brian Chapman, p. 87.

precedence over them. Vanity, inseparable from the human heart, gives rise to discord.[20]

Even in this early period, the conflict between staff specialist and line administrator was also apparent. A complaint from an *intendant de province* to the *intendant des finances* in charge of the Ponts de Chaussées corps puts the matter in very modern language:

This [the *corvée*] is not the engineer's business, he has no competence in it. I shall have him only execute what I have decided. I am surprised at his having proposed a solution to you without having informed me of it. . . . Permit me to add, Sir, that while it is convenient to consult an engineer in mechanical operations, it is dangerous to have him do what is not his specialty, since reasoning only by speculation, his lack of experience and the slight knowledge which he has of the government of a country make him put forward schemes which are impracticable of execution or too burdensome on the people.[21]

Despite the great social distance which existed between the engineers on the one hand and the two *noblesse de robe intendants* on the other, Trudaine (head of the corps) backed his technical subordinates. It is interesting to observe a nearly precise parallel in Russia (a century later, but when Russia was still in the preindustrial period). Alexander II supported the engineer officer heading the Chief Transport Administration against the prestigious governor-general of the Baltic provinces, Prince Suvorov.[22]

THE PREFECTURAL GOVERNOR AND RESOURCE LIMITATIONS

Probably the element of give and take in relations between technical corps and governors was valuable in moderating the latter's hierarchical assertiveness. The necessity of working with parallel chains of command led both sides to consider resource limitations with more care than either the professional pride of the engineers or the technical unsophistication of an autocratic governor might have suggested. It is possible, as the following allegations published in the 1950's by the prefects' association imply, that relations between the territorial corps and the technical corps have become less harmonious as well as less intimate:

However, certain jobs in the general administration should not be given to technicians. It would be just as grave an error, for example,

[20] Duclos, p. 54. [21] Chéguillaume, p. 86.
[22] Kislinsky, 1, Sect. 1-2, p. 86.

to assign general direction of hospitals and nursing homes to physicians as to assign the administrative posts in the coal mining basins to the Mines Engineers. A physician is trained to care for the sick, a Mines Engineer to extract coal, an administrator is trained to carry on the administration. By dangerously mixing up types, if they reserve administrative functions for their technicians, certain technical ministries incur the risk of having a poor administration neglecting the general interest in favor of technicians' unbalanced projects. Consequently, in the interest of the general economy of the Nation, it is desirable that the prefectural corps, responsible for general administration, be able to have access to administrative posts in the ministries and in the nationalized sector.[23]

The self-serving nature of this passage is obvious. It is as strong an argument for the "all-rounder" as any Administrative Class officer could make. Equally clear is the readiness of prefects to assume economic managerial tasks which other recent elite administrators have often tended to avoid.

A major obstacle to the *intendant's* development initiative was the narrow margin of resources at his disposal. At no time did he—or any other prefectural governors we consider—control the major tax system operating in his province. For preindustrial and recent regimes alike, centralization of major resource mobilization as well as allocation has appeared vital. Thus the Ferme Générale supervised an army of minor officials throughout France, just as the Financial Inspectorate has during the past century and a half. In Tsarist Russia, the Ministry of Finance had equivalent powers, while basic Soviet revenues are derived from the turnover tax and profits extracted from centrally directed economic enterprises. In the USSR, the predominant economic activity of the first secretaries (at least until very recently) has been mobilization of agricultural resources. The *intendants* and the more able Russian governors also devoted great attention to agriculture, but apart from improving means for getting crops to market and averting mass starvation, not much intervention in the peasant economies was feasible. In post-Revolutionary France, over eighty *départements* fragmented the economy to a degree which made planning at the prefect level hardly feasible. Under the Fifth Republic, ordinary prefects have heightened powers, although less over branches of the finance and welfare ministries than in relation to most other field services. Since 1958 regional prefects designated for unified police control in the 1940's have been assigned considerable power of supervising and planning the economy. In this capacity, however, the regional prefect acts

[23] Association du Corps Préfectoral, p. 45.

not as a hierarchical authority but as the chairman of a committee including a Financial Inspector, an engineer from the technical corps, an economist, and a statistician.[24]

The manifest failure of the Soviet first secretary to control industrial activities when the ministerial system was replaced by provincial councils of national economy (*sovnarkhozy*) appears to reflect on the capacity of prefectural governors to engage in economic development. We think, however, that there were special reasons why the Soviet experiment failed. To begin with there were (during the crucial period between 1957 and 1962) far too many units—over 100, as compared to 18 super-*départements*. Although the Soviet units were comparable in population, territory, and economic level to the French, the unwieldy span of control encouraged autarchy. More important, a majority of the first secretaries lacked either technical or economic training to equip them to deal with industrial development. When *sovnarkhoz* districts were consolidated, technically trained first secretaries appeared able to supervise the managerial personnel; but rather complicated political circumstances made this solution untenable in the 1960's.[25]

FEEDBACK EFFECT OF PREFECTURAL EXPERIENCE
IN DEVELOPMENT

In a curious way, the experience of the prefectural governor recapitulates the movement from engineering to economics in elite higher education. Initially governors shared the regulatory, social control concerns of the administrative elite as a whole. Practical requirements of policing extended territories joined with attachment to the economic welfare of their territories to induce a putative concern for development. Close association with technical corps led the governors to perceive material manipulation as a way to development. Yet they also perceived the limits of the engineering approach. Whether or not they can make a successful transition to participation in complex economic policy-making remains to be seen, just as the ultimate effect of training programs like the E.N.A. and tentative approaches in the USSR remain uncertain.

What is more certain is that the existence of a prefectural governor has had a significant feedback effect upon the central administrations in France and Russia. Recent French analyses have presented two

[24] Ridley and Blondel, p. 115; Pierre Doueil, *L'Administration Locale à l'Epreuve de la Guerre (1939-1949)* (Paris, 1950), pp. 37, 304.
[25] Alec Nove, *The Soviet Economy: An Introduction* (New York, 1961), pp. 67ff.; Hough, pp. 189-91; Armstrong, "Bifurcation," pp. 419ff.

sharply conflicting interpretations of this effect. Michel Crozier, pointing out that the prefect must govern through aloofness, concludes that "in the long run, his role cannot be but conservative with law and order as his central concern."[26] Siwek-Pouydesseau, on the other hand, stresses the dynamism of the role, the prefect's contempt for the routine *fonctionnaire* which we saw in Chapter Four had so heavily influenced bourgeois role models:

> The taste for risk and adventure remain, all the same, profoundly rooted in prefectural psychology. One of the attractions of the post was the chance to utilize all the richness of one's personality, to have to resolve each situation in an original, personal manner.[27]

If Siwek-Pouydesseau's judgment is correct, as we believe it is, the prefect has represented the antithesis of the search for security which (as discussed in Chapter Four) has been a salient element of the model role for the French official, and even the bourgeoisie as a whole. In recent years prefects have often scornfully rejected the appellation of *fonctionnaire* precisely because they see the typical official role as routinizing. During the stalemate period of the Third Republic, groups like the Council of State career officials clung to their static roles and resented the prefects' intrusion. As other elite groups (engineers and Financial Inspectors) groped toward more dynamic roles, the presence of the prefects (even if they were regarded as competitors) provided a significant alternative role model.

A second way in which the prefectural role has been significant is its concern for the *whole* range of problems in a specific area. In 1940 when Khrushchev himself was a high territorial official, he implicitly defined (in a slightly exaggerated way) this generalist role:

> The Party is responsible for everything. Whether it is Army work, Chekist work, economic work, Soviet work—all is subordinate to the Party leadership, and if anyone thinks otherwise, that means he is no Bolshevik.[28]

In administrations deeply imbued with quasi-aristocratic role models, such a generalist outlook can prevent involvement in development. Carried to an extreme (as in the U. S. Federal service) the bourgeois specialization emphasis can also hinder such involvement. Line administration in the field, on the other hand, brings one face to face with concrete needs and limitations. Whether as an alternative to the technocratic tendencies of Soviet industrial ministers and French Poly-

[26] Crozier, *Bureaucratic Phenomenon*, p. 235.
[27] Siwek-Pouydesseau, *Le Corps Préfectoral*, p. 115.
[28] Quoted in Armstrong, *Soviet Bureaucratic Elite*, p. 145.

technicians, or the legalism of the Council of State and the Tsarist State Senate, the territorial generalist role has been significant.

A third important feedback effect of the prefectural role has been on the mix of hierarchy and collegiality in the central administration. From the standpoint of organizational theory, either rigid hierarchy or complete reliance on committee direction is questionable, especially in the field of industrial management and development.[29] In France, the prefectural corps has preserved a tradition of hierarchy of personal command, in contrast to the strictly collegial Council of State. The technical corps and the Financial Inspectorate balance collegial and hierarchical elements.

In postindustrial economic policy, the organizational model of the Commissariat du Plan has been influential. While initial impetus came from individuals like Jean Monnet, the Plan has stressed committees:

> The organization of the Commissariat is flexible and informal. There is no rigid hierarchy and there are few set patterns. The word "team" is frequently used. . . . To a large extent decisions are made at the earliest stage of planning, that is to say by small groups of civil servants with some (though at this stage probably limited) ministerial intervention.[30]

Much of the dynamism as well as the flexibility of the policy process arises from the attachment to Keynesian doctrine and sense of adventure of the young *Grands Corps* members composing these teams.[31] On the other hand, execution depends on ministerial officials—Financial Inspectors actually administering the key resource allocation agencies (nationalized banks, etc.) and engineers managing the nationalized industries. "The Commissariat is merely the spearhead of a pressure group inside the Government; its task is to persuade. The decisive role is that of the departmental officials acting in unison over a wide range of the economy."[32] In their turn, the Commissariat du Plan committee operations combining economic expertise and generalist viewpoints had a feedback effect upon the more hierarchical aspects of the French administrative elite. We have already seen how the emerging regional prefect's role in economic activity is that of a coordinating chairman rather than a commander. Similarly, the Ministry of Finance has been impelled to create a special forecasting section (Direction de la Pré-

[29] See Hans Paul Bahrdt, *Industriebürokratie: Versuch einer Soziologie des industrialisierten Bürobetriebes und seiner Angestellten* (Stuttgart, 1958), pp. 6off.; Herbert A. Simon, *Administrative Behavior* (New York, 1961), pp. 141ff.
[30] Ridley and Blondel, pp. 200-201.
[31] Crozier, "Pour une Analyse," p. 156.
[32] Shonfield, p. 146.

vision), modeled on the Commissariat du Plan, to avoid seeing its resource allocation activities captured by the latter agency.[33]

The effects of the hierarchical territorial role upon the Russian administrative elite have tended to enhance its hierarchical element rather than to act as a balance to collegialism. Whether they arose from the generally harsh atmosphere of human relations or the prevalence of military styles, emphases on unquestioning obedience to superiors and rigid conformity to rules characterized the nineteenth-century Tsarist administration.[34] These characteristics did much to frustrate the acceptance of technological innovation at the center as well as at the periphery. Paradoxically the autocracy itself endeavored to foster collegial elements. Peter I's central agencies were collegial, but their presidents soon united to dominate the other members just as the governors dominated their councils. Speransky tried with very limited success to revive collegiality.[35]

The Soviet counterpart has been *edinonachalie*, "one-man authority." In 1920 Lenin overcame strong arguments for collegial authority to secure Party acceptance of *edinonachalie* as the basic managerial principle.[36] The commanding role of the territorial secretaries is, therefore, matched rather than balanced in the economic hierarchy. The Council of Ministers is a collection of willful department heads rather than a collegial body, and even the Planning Commission has often been dominated by its chairman. Since 1964 (and at brief intervals earlier) "collective leadership" has prevailed at the regime summit. In some measure, however, the oligarchy has allowed greater leeway to high officials in their own bailiwicks than did the one-man dictatorships.

Aside from the strong development interventionist impulse of Leninism, Soviet dynamism in the economic development field has been maintained by a variety of harsh expedients which we can only sketch here. "The institutionalization of mutual suspicion," as Merle Fainsod termed it, has been significant.[37] Apart from maintaining separate channels of surveillance such as the police, the regime has apparently deliberately avoided precise definition of officials' authority. By sub-

[33] Charles Debbasch, *L'Administration au Pouvoir: Fonctionnaires et Politiques sous la Vᵉ Republique* (Paris, 1969), pp. 116-22.

[34] Torke, pp. 178, 242.

[35] F. Dmitriev, "Speranskii i Ego Gosudarstvennaia Deiatel'nost'," *Russkii Arkhiv*, 1868, No. 10, pp. 1,558, 1,600, 1,620; Dukes, p. 224; Raeff, *Michael Speransky*, p. 43; Got'e, II, 283; I. M. Kataev, *Doreformennaia Biurokratiia: Po Zapiskam, Memuaram i Literature* (St. Petersburg, n.d.), p. 15.

[36] Azrael, p. 43.

[37] Fainsod, *How Russia Is Ruled*, p. 388.

jecting officials to dual subordination the regime makes rigid reliance on superior orders difficult. Sudden "raids" by journalists are designed to prevent development of tacit "protective circles" at the local level. Industrial managers have always been somewhat shielded from the impact of such pressures by the clear-cut nature of their goals. As long as they met material targets, they were usually excused other derelictions, except during the most severe purges. Territorial officials, on the other hand, until the middle 1950's were extremely insecure. In both cases the regime apparently hoped that insecurity would lead men to overfulfill their perceived assignments, thus promoting dynamism.[38] Like the engineering approach to resource mobilization, however, these regime techniques were blunt instruments. In an increasingly sophisticated social system as in the more complex economy, they may be counter-productive.

COLLEGALITY VS. PREFECTURAL POWERS IN PRUSSIA

Our confidence in assessing the significance of the prefectural governor's role has been enhanced by a consideration of its evolution over time. Cross-national comparison is even more valuable in this assessment. A superficial observer might conclude that the prefectural model could not be applicable to Germany because of its federal structure. Actually the Prussian portion constituted a thoroughly unitary state, somewhat smaller than France but with more severe problems of national integration. Initial steps toward "rooting" the *commissarius* were similar in both monarchies. Even in the eighteenth century, though, this tendency was hampered in Prussia by the peculiar division between town and countryside. By Frederick II's reign, the town *Steuerrat* office was a real prefectural governorship in miniature. *Steuerräte* were predominantly recruited from the bourgeoisie; their posts were a training ground for the high administration.[39] Three factors were crucial in preventing this office from exerting a lasting influence on administrative elite role definition. Both Frederick William I and Frederick II believed that collegial central administration would avoid dilution of their personal power by setting subordinates against one another.[40] Possibly this was a correct assessment for these dynamic monarchs, but under their weaker successors collegiality, through its

[38] *Ibid.*, pp. 386ff.; Azrael, pp. 98ff., 134; Berliner, pp. 295ff.; Armstrong, *Politics of Totalitarianism*, pp. 310ff.

[39] Reinhold August Dorwart, *The Administrative Reforms of Frederick William I of Prussia* (Cambridge, Mass., 1953), pp. 150ff.; Isaacsohn, III, 103; Hintze, *Staat*, pp. 242ff.; Heffter, p. 31.

[40] Walther Schultze, *Geschichte der preussischen Régieverwaltung von 1766 bis 1786* (Leipzig, 1888), p. 10; Rosenberg, p. 96.

group socializing effect, facilitated the movement toward administrative autonomy. As we have seen, this movement was combined in a complex way with the late eighteenth-century aristocratic reaction. In his compromise with the *Junker* gentry, Frederick II had devolved rural administration to the noble, semi-particularistic *Landrat*. Consequently, the *Steuerrat* directed only a fragment of the territorial administration. His tendency to adopt aristocratic styles was a third factor weakening his significance as a central administrative role model.

The administrative reforms of the Stein-Hardenberg period, permitting a considerable measure of municipal government, eliminated the *Steuerrat*. In rural areas, the *Landrat* remained an aristocratic preserve. The most important territorial unit became the *Bezirk*, with its collegial *Regierung* replacing the old War and Domains Chamber. Concern for tradition was hardly a major factor since both the names and the boundaries of these districts were drastically altered in 1815. Collegiality was mandatory because, it was argued, no one man could justly reach decisions affecting the rights of private persons.[41] It was, in other words, an essential aspect of the *Rechtsstaat* ideology which legitimized the administrative elite's autonomy from royal autocracy.

The considerable degree of equality among all councilors (*Regierungsräte*) with proper juridical backgrounds reinforced internal official solidarity. At the same time, the insistence on the quasi-judicial nature of *Regierung* deliberations effectively excluded officials with other types of training. Group decision-making was slow, inefficient, and uninnovative. The emphasis was on legal restrictions rather than on policy potential. Since each member was also a department head, frequent lengthy meetings interfered with attention to specific local problems.

The inherent inefficiency of the Prussian system was brought into sharp relief by comparison to French prefectural governors in the territories recovered or annexed in 1815 and in Alsace-Lorraine two generations later. Time and again outstanding Prussian officials paid tributes which, in view of the rivalry between the two countries, must have been sincere: "In our conduct of business we three Germans have been the students of the Frenchman [who, as prefect, preceded them], and all of us have, I believe, learned something from him."[42]

The administrative reformers of the Napoleonic period were familiar with the prefectural system. Baron vom Stein and Ludwig von Vincke feared the "tendency to clumsiness, to buck-passing of responsibility from individual to the group" in the collegial body.[43] The more

---

[41] Koselleck, pp. 177-78, 238ff., 281.   [42] Ernsthausen, pp. 295, 342.
[43] Fritz Hartung, "Studien zur Geschichte der preussischen Verwaltung," Zweiter Teil, "Der Oberpräsident," *Abhandlungen der Preussischen Akademie*

enterprising Prussian administrators sought to overcome the limitations of strict collegiality in two ways. The simpler one was to enhance the authority of the *Regierungspräsident*. Faced with the socialist "danger," Bismarck feared collegial dilution of responsibility would make maintenance of order difficult. Consequently, he made the police power strictly hierarchical, with the *Regierungspräsident* responsible only to the minister of the interior for its exercise. In the revenue fields (local taxes, domains, and forests), individual councilors were subordinate to the *Regierungspräsident* instead of to the collegium; indirect taxes, as in France and Russia, were administered directly by the finance ministers. By the end of the Second Reich only education, church affairs, and certain direct taxes remained subject to collegial decisions, and councilors' responsibilities in these fields were more carefully delimited.[44] As a socializing mechanism, however, the *Regierung* remained fundamentally corporate.[45] Its collegial quality was part of the ideological defense of the *Beamten* which permeated the central elite administration. Consequently repeated attempts to eliminate the *Regierung* level, under Weimar as well as the Second Reich, were repelled by the united official stratum.[46]

Abolition of the *Regierung* was urged as a way of making the territorial administrative chain simpler, quicker, and cheaper. While other Continental administrations (except Russia prior to 1775 and France since the institution of the regional prefect) have had two territorial administrative levels, the Prussian system had three. Below the *Regierung* the eighteenth-century bifurcation of town and country administration persisted; between the *Regierung* and the Berlin ministries was the province. In the eighteenth century each of the small number of provinces was administered by a special collegium in the central administration; but territorial expansion made it expedient to assign *Oberpräsidenten* to strategic areas like Silesia and Westphalia. Even in the early nineteenth century, however, these men were regarded as central officials on special coordinating missions.[47] The history of the *Oberpräsident* recapitulated the history of the *commissarius*. First the

der Wissenschaften, 1943, Philosophisch-Historische Klasse, No. 4, p. 9; Koselleck, p. 177.

[44] Otto von Bismarck, *Bismarck: Reflections and Reminiscences*, Vol. 1 (New York, 1899), 15; Hartung, pp. 57, 59; Herbert Jacob, *German Administration since Bismarck: Central Authority versus Local Autonomy* (New Haven, 1963), pp. 14ff.

[45] *Ibid.*

[46] Hartung, pp. 62, 66; *Handbuch der Politik*, 3rd ed., Vol. III: *Der politische Erneuerung* (Berlin, 1921), 139-40.

[47] Hartung, pp. 6-7; Horst Kube, *Die geschichtliche Entwicklung der Stellung des preussischen Oberpräsidenten* (Dissertation, Berlin University, Law Faculty) (Würzburg, 1939), pp. 5, 6, 13, 17; G. Ford, p. 233.

Oberpräsident was designed to overcome the obstructiveness or simple ineffectiveness of particularistic local officials; then, as the extent of problems at the periphery became apparent, he was "rooted" in a specific territory. In a sense the Prussian *Oberpräsident* was a device for overcoming a new cycle of quasi-aristocratic reaction embodied in the *Regierung*, just as the *intendant* was designed to curb the provincial *parlement*.

One must take into account the asynchronous nature of these comparisons, however. Both *parlement* and *Regierung* relied on legalist ideologies, but the latter worked from inside a modern national administration. Once firmly established the *Regierung* system could not be replaced in the old autocratic manner. Consequently, the *Oberpräsident* did not supersede the old territorial administration, but added another layer to it. In number and size, the provinces (between 1818 and 1901 there were 9, as compared to 25 *Bezirke*) were adapted to major economic administration. Yet the *Oberpräsident* could not undertake such tasks without a large staff which would have constituted an intolerable duplication of the *Regierung*'s, both financially and in terms of the resentment and friction generated.

Given the awkwardness of his position, it is not surprising that evaluations of the *Oberpräsident* have varied widely. To the prominent legal scholar, Rudolph Gneist, the *Oberpräsidenten* of the 1860's were as ineffectual as the honorific *gouverneurs* of pre-Revolutionary France. In the Second Reich, according to contemporaries, *Oberpräsidenten* resorted to "mechanical methods which cannot solve the tasks required by modern times." Their retreatist attitude is confirmed by the fact that in 1909 they joined the minister of the interior in arguing against expansion of their own jurisdiction.[48]

Yet other evidence suggests strongly that under favorable circumstances the nature of the office, combining hierarchical authority and contact with the whole range of local problems, could have an important socializing effect on its incumbent.[49] In turn, the latter's perception of a development role at the territorial level occasionally had significant feedback effects on the central administration. In the late eighteenth century, while he was the equivalent of *Oberpräsident* in Westphalia, Stein learned much about economic policy.[50] Vincke, too, was *Oberpräsident* in Westphalia. Two decades later, the dynamic finance minister, Friedrich von Motz, had become involved in the economy and its transportation infrastructure while *Oberpräsident* in Prussian Saxony. Indeed, a leading student of early nineteenth-century Prussian economic policy has contended that (in the general absence

[48] Hartung, pp. 42, 53, 56.   [49] *Ibid.*, pp. 5off.
[50] G. Ford, pp. 23, 30, 32, 33.

of economic training and doctrine) only provincial officials were in a position to learn "satrap" development policies—i.e., could profit from their practical contact with ports, industry, and trade negotiations.[51] One of the few apparently effective Second Reich ministers in World War II economic mobilization, Clemens von Delbrück, had, by his own account, acquired his first serious experience with economic and social affairs at the age of forty-six when he was appointed *Oberpräsident* of West Prussia.[52]

The *Regierung* is still a feature of the West German administrative system. The relatively small states of the Federal Republic have, however, no place for provinces. Hence the potential effect of the *Oberpräsident* role will remain an unfinished story.

IMPERIAL EXPERIENCE AND PREFECTURAL MODELS IN BRITISH ADMINISTRATION

A comparable institution has been out of the question in Great Britain. No territorial governing bodies, whether hierarchical or collegial, directly subordinate to the central authorities have existed in recent centuries. Before the complications of industrialization intervened, justices of the peace in the countryside and lord mayors with their councils were sufficient. Since then, city administration has been made more efficient through devices like the professional Town Clerk, but the tradition of local autonomy is strong.

The basic method of central intervention for promoting universalistic standards has been the system of grants and inspection. Instead of subordinating municipal institutions, the central authorities guide them by advice backed by financial sanctions. Chadwick's great contribution to British administration was the concept of inspection as a substitute for direction. In a vague sense the inspector resembles the peripatetic *commissarius*, but he has never been "rooted" in a locality.

If Chadwick's vision had been realized, the inspector corps might have played a crucial part in economic regulation, if not development. In fact, some groups like the Railway Inspectors (who included a number of military engineers) did begin to play a significant part in rationalizing industry if not promoting its expansion (see Chapter Thirteen). By the 1860's, however, the only inspectors really influential in policy implementation, as contrasted to minor regulation, were H. M. Inspectors of Schools who, as we have seen, furthered the

[51] Carl Brinkmann, *Die preussische Handelspolitik vor dem Zollverein und der Wiederaufbau vor hundert Jahren* (Berlin, 1922), pp. 29ff.

[52] Clemens von Delbrück, *Die wirtschaftliche Mobilmachung in Deutschland 1914* (ed. from His Papers by Joachim von Delbrück) (Munich, 1924), pp. 3, 25.

spread of quasi-aristocratic educational models. Significantly, this was the only corps generally trained at Oxbridge and the only one whose members have frequently transferred to the Administrative Class. The Inland Revenue Inspectors, potentially more concerned with economic affairs, have occupied an intermediate status between Administrative and Executive Class, frequently with university education though it is not required. Taken as a whole, the Inspectors may be the "local selves" of the Administrative Class; but the very fact of their existence shields the latter from contact with concrete problems at the local level. Given the status differential, the Inspectors' experience is unlikely to have major feedback effects on administrative elite role perceptions.[53]

More important for two generations at least was the field experience of the British colonial services. As far as we have discovered, French colonial administration had few feedback effects on the home service. Probably this was due to the integration of the most important areas (e.g., Algeria) into the regular administrative service, and the relegation of others to military administration. Military administration also prevailed in the extensive colonial areas on the periphery of the Russian Empire. The Soviet regime nominally incorporates these areas in the standard administrative framework. For Great Britain, on the other hand, the Indian civil service represented a precedent rather than an offshoot from the main branch of administrative development.

It is significant that the same requirements of defense and integration ("national integration" is hardly appropriate) demanded a systematic territorial administration in India as they had earlier on the European Continent. As Indian governor-general, Lord Dalhousie, "the natural alliance between the Tory gentleman and the scientific Benthamite administrator," set up a hierarchical ("single-seated" to use Bentham's phrase) administrative system. Since Dalhousie had ample experience with the collegial system in the Board of Trade, it is fairly evident that he was giving rein to his own preferences; in fact, he described himself as "a curious compound of a despot and a radical."[54]

The salient official in the nineteenth-century Indian administration (preceding Dalhousie but strengthened by his reforms) was the district officer. The district was small enough for him to know it personally, though critics thought transfers (as often as once a year) were too

[53] H. Finer, p. 83; Kelsall, p. 15; Roberts, *Victorian Origins*, pp. 152ff.; Fry, p. 104; Harvey Walker, *Training Public Employees in Great Britain* (London, 1935), p. 31; Richard Schmidt, *Die Bürokratisierung des modernen England und ihre Bedeutung für das heutige deutsche Behördensystem* (Leipzig, 1932), p. 32.
[54] G. M. Young, *Victorian England*, quoted in Stokes, p. 248; *ibid.*, p. 257.

frequent. Like the *intendant* and the *Oberpräsident*, the district officer frequently went on inspection tours. The breadth of his duties (judicial as well as police, education, public health, and road construction) also resembled the Continental officials'. The district officer had greater responsibility for tax collection, but like them was jealously denied any considerable power of resource allocation. A crucial difference was the district officer's lack of association with an expert staff at his own status level which could have socialized him to the requirements of technological advance. "Every district officer was his own engineer as well as his own policeman." One was "particularly proud of his skill as an engineer, although if his bridges and houses stand up they were really designed by the foreman."[55] As a result (as noted in Chapter Eight), the district officer's experience tended to confirm the "all-rounder" role definition inculcated in the British educational system. On the other hand, both the Indian and the colonial service perpetuated the evangelistic concern for specific practical reforms which had motivated the non-Conformist generation at the end of the take-off period.[56] In contrast to his Whitehall counterpart, even physical manipulative activity (or at least supervision of it) seems to have attracted the colonial official.

As we suggested (Chapter Six), there was probably a considerable element of self-selection among the public school or Oxbridge graduates who chose the risks and adventures of colonial service, just as there was among entrants to the French prefectural corps. Very probably overseas assignments constituted throughout the nineteenth century a much more significant numerical outlet for men with elite educations than did the home service. In 1843-44, 29 per cent of the graduates from two Cambridge colleges were destined for overseas assignments of all types, as contrasted to 3 per cent for home civil service; in 1892-93 the ratio had risen to 30 to 1.[57]

These proportions include military service, which must be taken into account because (as in the rival Russian Empire) half of the colonial governors (131 of 262 in a group from 1830-80) were former army or naval officers. "Hard-core professional" governors, however, were only 35 per cent military by background. The terms (4.5 mean) and entrance age (forty-four) of the latter small sample were also close to the Russian Imperial experience.[58]

There are occasional indications that the feedback effect of colonial service upon British administrative elite role definition was not negligi-

[55] Mason, I, 313, 318; O'Malley, pp. 68-71, 75, 165.
[56] Mason, I, 323ff., 351.   [57] Musgrove, *Migratory Elite*, p. 173.
[58] John W. Cell, *British Colonial Administration in the Mid-Nineteenth Century* (New Haven, 1970), pp. 48, 289-300.

ble. Looking back, Arthur Salter wrote in 1967 that the British civil servant had been at his best as district officer in India. Sir James Dunnett, Permanent Secretary of the Ministry of Transport, pointed out the resemblance of field operations in that managerial department to the Indian service.[59] Given the remoteness of colonial activities and the proximity of the Oxbridge socialization system, however, it could hardly be expected that the Whitehall Administrative Class would be influenced by prefectural governors' experience to the degree that French administrators were. Even Bentham had seen boards or committees as the natural vehicle for his reforms. Probably the British political system is the only one which could be treated in an entire volume as "Government by Committee."[60] Both the public school team spirit and the style of the Oxbridge college make collegial decision-making smooth and attractive.[61] For local problems, Town Clerks and Administrative Class officials join forces to avoid bureaucratic and expert "nonsense."[62] The Treasury's retreat from domination by financial leverage to letting other departments take the initiative in committee was considered "Civil Service democracy."[63] In fact, the committee system emphasizes equality among all fully qualified members (i.e., the Administrative Class) just as the *Regierung* emphasized the equality of legally trained *Räte*. In both systems, the counterpart of internal equality is corporate exclusion of lesser officials outside.

Whether this amounts to "democracy" is a matter of definition. Historically, equality in committee is much more consonant with the aristocratic stress on the essential equivalence of all persons of noble birth, regardless of achievement. From our point of view, what is more important is that *exclusive* resort to committee decision-making has a built-in bias against initiative. We have already noted some of the reasons in examining the *Regierung*. Operating as it does under a democratic regime, the British administrative elite has an additional reason for avoiding initiative by relegating numerous decisions to the category of nondecisions. "The fact surely is that at certain levels only civil servants are in a position to make choices, largely because other agencies are not even aware that a choice is required, or, if aware, are not sufficiently informed to render a verdict."[64] In Andrew Shonfield's view, this shelter is wholly compatible with the postindustrial civil ser-

---

[59] Salter, p. 277; Dunnett, p. 226.

[60] K. C. Wheare, *Government by Committee: An Essay on the British Constitution* (Oxford, 1955).

[61] Weinberg, pp. 106, 108.

[62] Wheare, p. 231.

[63] Professor Austin Robinson, quoted in Beer, p. 75.

[64] J. E. Hodgetts, "The Civil Service and Policy Formation," *Canadian Journal of Economics and Political Science*, XXIII (1957), 469.

vant's role perception, for: "They may be sterilized in terms of overt party politics; but this is regarded as a small price to pay for being almost entirely protected from the rude gaze of outsiders, and even more from the question about what they are doing in the exercise of immense power."[65] All of this intimate corporate seclusion would be threatened by a truly "active" administration in economic as in other spheres.

[65] Shonfield, p. 396.

CHAPTER THIRTEEN

Response to Challenge

IN THE PRECEDING eight chapters converging lines of evidence point to distinctive role definitions. On the whole, these definitions appear to be stable over time but variant among national administrative systems. Yet a nagging question remains. Even if one identifies national tendencies toward defining the administrative role to include or exclude development interventionism, may these not represent corporate styles or fashions? In other words, when they have to face concrete, urgent problems, do not administrative elites—or at least a decisive element among them—react in very much the same ways? While a completely satisfying reply to this question is hardly feasible, it cannot remain wholly unanswered. The way that administrative elites respond to challenges is too important in itself to neglect. Furthermore, because a challenge brings to focus circumstances and testimony which are otherwise diffuse, one may obtain a little more evidence on general distinctions in role definition.

In order to serve our purpose, the challenge must have four characteristics: 1) it must be a problem of great magnitude for all four societies; 2) resource mobilization as well as allocation must be salient; 3) a strong potential for administrative intervention must be evident at least to certain leaders in some of the societies we examine; 4) *either* the inherent physical properties of the challenge *or* its locus in time must be sharply delimited. To these, we may add a fifth practical qualification, that the challenge has been sufficiently discussed and studied to be accessible to our summary examination.

Only two episodes seem to meet all these conditions: construction of railroads in the nineteenth century and mobilization for World War I. Although World War II mobilization would appear equally pertinent, it is unsuitable because it hardly affected one of the four societies (France) while in another (Prussia-Germany) the revolutionary nature of the regime makes it difficult to distinguish a distinct administrative elite response.

We approach these two episodes with diffidence, for their substance is a subject for economic historians. Our conviction that railroad construction is a good subject for examination is bolstered by its use by Bruce Mazlish and his associates as an analogue for anticipating the effects of the space program on American postindustrial economy and society.[1] We do not find any single, focused challenge common to all four societies in the postindustrial period. After examining the two specific challenges more intensively, though, we shall tentatively extend some of our observations to the later period.

RECEPTIVITY OF PREINDUSTRIAL SOCIETIES TO ADMINISTRATIVE INNOVATION

In the preindustrial period challenges were diffuse. One reason (discussed in Chapter Three) was the difficulty of conceiving economic development as a continuous societal factor. Another, discussed there and in Chapter Nine, was the lack of the theoretical and statistical tools required for meaningful administrative intervention. Two lines of development in the preindustrial societies have an immediate relevance for the specific challenge of railroad building, however. One was the receptivity of the administrative systems to foreign developmental assistance. As Raymond Bauer has pointed out, the principal way in which actual technological innovation is diffused is by movement of people, not ideas.[2] This applies to administrative innovation related to technological and economic development as well. Although the phenomenon resembles diffusion of development doctrines, the latter type of diffusion does not necessarily require the acceptance of alien individuals in, or at the periphery of, the elite.

In the preindustrial period Great Britain and France were usually the givers and Russia and Prussia the takers in terms of adapting administration to technology, just as they were in receiving development doctrines. Russia took from Prussia as well, or rather from the whole of Germany. A brief look at the differences between reactions in the Russian and Prussian administrative elites is, therefore, instructive. In the central Russian administration, foreign organizational principles (e.g., collegia) were repeatedly accepted, and as often discarded or modified beyond recognition. In economic fields, foreign innovations, although modified, caught on more readily. For example, the Urals metallurgical industry, crucial to eighteenth-century military needs, was dependent on Saxon mining experts. The Germans and Dutch dominated the administrative council and inspection service in the early part of the century. In the 1730's, led by V. N. Tatishev (a member of an old noble family), newly trained Russian personnel rebelled against the "reign of Germans." Tatishev went so far as to demand the rejection of German technical terms. When the native faction won out

---

[1] Mazlish, p. xiii.   [2] *Ibid.*

(in the 1740's), it retained the major administrative features: the Mining Collegium, a mining inspectorate not subordinated to the local governor, and state initiative in expanding mines.[3]

Xenophobia also characterized Prussian administrators' reactions to their monarchs' importation of foreign personnel. The most famous instance was Frederick II's establishment of the excise *Régie*, which Eckart Kehr presciently compared a generation ago to the way in which twentieth-century "exotic or half-exotic" states call in American financial advisers.[4] After the close of the Seven Years' War, disgusted with the formalist inefficiency of Prussian administrators in resource mobilization—as the story goes they were unable to tell him how many pounds of coffee were consumed in the kingdom—Frederick turned to the Ferme Générale. Between 200 and 500 French financial officials, including a score of experienced high administrators, were imported. Until 1772 the *Régie* operated like the Ferme, with a semi-private, collegial direction. Then it became a state agency under the hierarchical control of the principal French official, Launay. The system was effective both in resource mobilization and impartiality of allocating burdens. Despite the concession of appointing a Prussian as the nominal head, however, native resentment was bitter. After Frederick's death (1786), the *Régie* was dissolved.[5] It appears to have made little lasting impression on Prussian administrative practices; certainly it did not inject a strong hierarchical element. In contrast to the Russian experience, when foreign administrators were ejected from Prussia, their innovations went with them. One reason, undoubtedly, was the great difference in need between backward Russia and a Prussian administration which, by the 1780's, was certainly able to collect taxes in a reasonably efficient manner. But the pattern has been a recurrent one, as the postindustrial rejection of the French training model at Speyer indicates.

The Transportation Infracture as a Lever

The second way in which preindustrial developments are especially relevant to the challenge of railroad construction was the growing inclination of administrators to perceive the transportation infrastructure as a lever to move entire economies. In the final analysis, better

[3] Roger Portal, *L'Oural au XVIIIe Siècle: Etude d'Histoire Economique et Sociale* (Paris, 1950), pp. 61ff., 99, 105, 138ff., 378; F. Ia. Poliansky, "Promyshlennaia Politika Russkogo Absoliutizma vo Vtoroi Chetverti XVIII v. (1725-1740 gg.)," *Voprosy Istorii Narodnogo Khoziaistva SSSR*, 1957, pp. 89ff.

[4] Kehr, "Zur Genesis," in Wehler, p. 39.

[5] W. Schultze, pp. 42ff., 61, 121.

tax administration could only provide more efficient mobilization of limited resources. Apart from special cases like the Urals metallurgical factories, royal manufactures were limited to armaments or luxuries, neither of which could make any direct contribution to development. Roads and waterways, on the other hand, even if originally designed for national integration and defense, had a marked effect on economic development. Colbert personally believed in roads as the principal method by which the state could further commerce and public welfare, and transmitted this concept to his successors. His Languedoc canal was a massive precedent for "regional planning."[6] As we have seen, highway construction played a crucial part not only in nurturing a technological administrative elite, but in socializing elite line administrators to the potential of planned material manipulation.

By the start of the take-off period, as indicated in Table XXII, France was greatly ahead of other Continental countries in serviceable roads. Russian inadequacies were due to the severe climate, vast distances, and general backwardness. Prussian inferiority is harder to explain. Probably a major factor was the irrelevance of a distinctly Prussian highway network to Frederick II's military needs, since the country was frequently occupied by his enemies while his own forces lived off neighboring countries.

Recently, economic historians have presented impressive arguments that extension and perfection of preindustrial means of transportation could have provided an adequate infrastructure for economic growth. More important to our concern are the three ways in which the railroads, as actually constructed, acted as a major challenge to administrations. The railroads captured the imagination of contemporaries to a degree which no incremental improvement of familiar means of transportation could have done. As a result, all groups operating at the societal level were compelled to react, positively or negatively, to the railroads. We can tell much (as in the case of the English educators) about general attitudes toward economic development from the direction and intensity of these reactions.

Second, railroads were technological *systems*, not isolated innovations. Consequently, their construction and operation demanded a complex application of organizational technique to material and human resource mobilization. In industrial Britain as well as in the United States of the take-off period, railroad companies served as the model for large-scale industrial management.[7] The role of professional

---

[6] Lhéritier, I, 105; Lamé and Clapeyron, p. 33.

[7] Alfred D. Chandler and Stephen Salsbury, "The Railroads: Innovators in Modern Business Administration," in Mazlish, pp. 135-42; Payne, p. 538.

engineers (mainly from the military) in managing these private enterprises was not salient. Particularly during the construction stage, however, at least a self-trained technical element was essential in the top management. Eventually even in dominantly laissez-faire societies, this element had a feedback effect on administrative systems. In the crisis of major war, neither the administrative techniques nor the kinds of managerial socialization developed by the railroads was dispensable.

Third, even during the construction period, administrative elites were at least marginally involved because railroads could not escape intrusion on the public sector, limited as the latter was conceived to be

TABLE XXII. MAJOR LAND TRANSPORT NETWORKS [8]
(Kilometers)

Period	France	Great Britain	Germany	Russia
Paved Highways at End of Preindustrial Period (c. 1840)	34,000	35,000	10,000[a]	1,000
Railroads at Beginning of Take-Off Period (c. 1850)	3,000	—	6,000	1,000
Railroads at End of Take-Off Period (France and Germany, c. 1870; Great Britain, c. 1850; Russia, c. 1880)	17,500	10,500	19,500	21,000
Railroads in First Generation of Industrial Society (Western Europe, c. 1890; Russia, c. 1910)	36,500	33,000	43,000	58,500
Railroads in Second Generation of Industrial Society (Western Europe, c. 1910; Russia, c. 1950)	49,500	38,500	61,000	118,000

a Prussia only; for railroads, Prussian component about two-thirds of German total.

in nineteenth-century America and Britain. No railroad could be constructed without resort to the power of eminent domain. Even if unbridled economic competition was encouraged, some attention to standards of public service and safety was inescapable.

[8] Western European figures are from J. H. Clapham, *The Economic Development of France and Germany 1815-1914* (Cambridge, England, 1921), pp. 339, 349, except British turnpikes (1838), in W. T. Jackman, *The Development of Transportation in Modern England*, 3rd ed. (London, 1966), p. 334. Russian figures for paved highway (1834) from V. S. Virginsky, *Vozniknovenie Zheleznykh Dorog v Rossii do Nachala 40 Godov XIX Veka* (Moscow, 1949), pp. 30ff.; for railroads during Take-Off (1855, 1881), N. S. Kiniapina, *Politika Russkogo Samoderzhaviia v Oblasti Promyshlennosti (20-50-e Gody XIX v.)* (Moscow, 1968), p. 158; Chuprov, p. 56; during Industrial period (1913, 1949), Harry Schwartz, *Russia's Soviet Economy*, 2nd ed. (New York, 1954), p. 394.

NONINTERVENTION IN BRITISH RAILROAD DEVELOPMENT

The British experience may be taken as the limiting case of nonintervention. Strictly speaking, there was no administrative elite to become directly involved, but the episode suggests ways in which a development interventionist role might have, but did not, emerge. Since the industrial take-off was nearly accomplished before railroads were introduced, their significance was limited from the economic standpoint. A basic network of toll roads and canals, together with the extraordinary facilities for bulk carriage which the coastal waters provided, had been adequate for supporting industrial development, but this infrastructure was in no sense a "growth sector."[9]

As indicated in Chapter Six, the basic technique for overcoming property-owners' resistance to railroad construction was lavish compensation; when that did not suffice, lines could be rerouted. Parliamentary and judicial proceedings were adequate for arranging these conflict-avoiding measures. By 1840, however, demands for inspection could not be met by nonadministrative devices. As part of a pattern of concern for the abuses of industrialization, the Board of Trade advocated measures like gauge standardization which not only implied a minimal concern for public welfare but would have promoted more efficient resource utilization. A corps of inspectors (including many engineers trained in the military academies) developed more interventionist attitudes as they acquired practical experience. Because their observations were extended and comparative, the railway inspectors' superior expertise became evident even to entrepreneurs who criticized them as men who had "never earned a penny" in practical business.[10]

Several factors prevented this trend from continuing. One was severe interest-group strife reflected in Parliament. The railroad supervisory agencies were reorganized several times in the 1840's and 1850's. For example, Railway Commissioners were disbanded in 1851 as an "extravagance" because they had so little to do. The negative attitude of higher officials (not yet *career* officials) directly concerned was important. The Board of Trade president, for example, objected (in vain) to taking over the Commissioners' duties because he "preferred not to be bothered with railways."[11] Gladstone, already powerful politically (he had been president of the Board of Trade from 1841

[9] Dyos and Aldcroft, p. 71.
[10] Gustav Cohn, *Untersuchungen über die englische Eisenbahnpolitik*, Vol. II (Leipzig, 1875), 226, 229, 604; Henry Parris, *Government and the Railways in Nineteenth Century Britain* (London, 1965), pp. 31, 74, 90.
[11] Roger Prouty, *The Transformation of the Board of Trade, 1830-1885: A Study of Administrative Reorganization in the Heyday of Laissez Faire* (London, 1957), p. 11.

to 1845) was concerned to regulate the excesses of the railroad companies, but was embarrassed by the fact that his family had been engaged in railroad promotion.[12] After the middle 1850's railroad inspectors continued to check safety regulations, but neither their statutory powers nor their status enabled them to influence positive economic policy measures.

The contrast to India is instructive here as on other issues affecting the British administrative elite. To Dalhousie (who had extensive experience in Board of Trade involvement with the British railroads), government intervention was an obvious requirement. He and his associates perceived railroads not merely as conveniences to be regulated and as strategic military assets, but as the motor by which "the whole machinery of society will be stimulated."[13] As early as the 1830's, engineers had advocated construction of a large network; government subsidies were actually provided in 1849. Major publicly guaranteed stock company construction began in the 1850's with Dalhousie's support, and continued throughout the century. By the 1880's, however, one company had been taken over by the Indian Government, which would have nationalized all (in the 1890's) if London had approved. Nationalization was finally completed after World War I.[14]

ADMINISTRATIVE AND PARA-ADMINISTRATIVE INITIATIVES IN FRANCE

Indian developments are suggestive because they parallel Continental experience. Efforts to construct a French railroad system began in the 1820's. It is possible that the very fact that the preindustrial transportation system was so advanced (and that some elements in the Ponts et Chaussées administration were attached to their customary field of activity) hindered rapid progress. According to Isaac Péreire, the official corps was reluctant even to turn to mechanical traction in place of horses. On the other hand, he recognizes that the basic organizational and planning work was done in large part by engineers from the Ponts et Chaussées "to whom we owe our railroads."[15]

[12] Cohn, *Untersuchungen*, I, 156ff.; S. G. Checkland, *The Gladstones: A Family Biography, 1764-1851* (Cambridge, England, 1971), p. 350; Francis E. Hyde, *Mr. Gladstone at the Board of Trade* (London, 1934), pp. 151ff.

[13] Stokes, p. 253.

[14] Mason, II, 110; Clairmonte, p. 130; Daniel Thorner, "Great Britain and the Development of India's Railways," *Journal of Economic History*, XI (1951), 389, 393, 397; Daniel Thorner, *Investment in Empire: British Railway and Steam-Shipping Enterprise in India, 1825-1849* (Philadelphia, 1950), pp. 46, 92, 118, 176; Gustav Cohn, *Zur Geschichte und Politik des Verkehrswesens* (Stuttgart, 1900), p. 91.

[15] Péreire, pp. 69, 101.

The contradiction is only apparent. Three factors prevented effective utilization of state administrations as such for French railroad construction. One was attachment of the higher levels of the corps to customary ways. A second—which some engineers complained was the real impediment to state initiative—was the intrusion of nonprofessional administrators and politicians influenced by pressures from competing means of transportation. A third was the general bias in favor of laissez faire. As we saw in Chapter Four, in the critical decades of the 1830's and 1840's, the status of the French administration was at a low point. The prominent politicians Adolphe Thiers and François Guizot, both ardent advocates of private enterprise, secured the concession for the Paris-Rouen line for a British company, which imported a British engineer staff headed by George Stephenson.

Guizot and Thiers were suspicious of Saint-Simonism. For many development-minded engineers, however, the Saint-Simonian concept of the "omnium" offered a way to use their talents for societal purposes outside the confines of the official administration. Saint-Simon and his principal apostle, Enfantin, had proposed to provide a government subsidy for railroads by diverting military expenditures to a "peaceful army" of construction. Their emphasis on rational planning and central direction associated the Saint-Simonists with the elite engineer corps. Indeed, the Saint-Simonist paper (*Globe*) urged that the Ponts et Chaussées administrators be shielded against private pressures. "If they fell, it would be to the applause of the entrepreneurs, of the speculators who are devouring in advance, like a prey which is theirs by right, the whole network of canals, railroads, and bridges necessary to the viability of the country."[16] To Saint-Simonists a private company was also acceptable so long as it was an embracing, rationally planned enterprise. Consequently, when Péreires advanced their scheme they received enthusiastic cooperation from many of the more adventurous members of the engineer corps.[17]

The results of this transfusion of technical administrators to private enterprise have been debated. The Péreires' holding company ultimately failed, but not until (with government assistance) it had mobilized the large capital sums needed for France to catch up in railroad construction (see Table XXII). Incremental private investment, adequate in Britain, would probably have failed to provide sufficient impetus to construct, by the end of the Second Empire, the infrastruc-

[16] G. Lefranc, "La Construction des Chemins de Fer et l'Opinion Publique vers 1830," *Revue d'Histoire Moderne*, v (1930), 277; cf. Wallon, pp. 36ff., 58.
[17] Lhomme, pp. 95, 96; Pierre Dauzet, *Le Siècle des Chemins de Fer en France (1821-1938)* (Fontenay-aux-Roses, 1948), pp. 62-74; Lefranc, p. 345; W. O. Henderson, *Britain and Industrial Europe, 1750-1870: Studies in British Influence on the Industrial Revolution in Western Europe* (Liverpool, 1954), pp. 67ff.

ture vital for long-haul traffic.[18] By mobilizing resources and solving political problems, the Saint-Simonist bankers (like Stalin a century later) freed technical administrators for material manipulation.

As suggested in Chapter Nine, the Péreires were far from content with the engineers' attitude toward resource allocation. Several of their principal Polytechnician associates were financially ruined when they went off on their own enterprises. Engineers trained in the Ponts et Chaussées corps grossly underestimated costs and delays in construction. Partly, no doubt, this disregard of short-range economic factors reflected the pride that "each of the principal works was sufficient for the glory of an engineer."[19] Although they were sharp critics of the French administration, however, British engineers like Stephenson agreed on construction of lines and bridges to last for generations (in contrast to the American practice of rapidly building railroads which could be replaced as soon as profits made it feasible).

Despite their resentment of the despotic powers of the "sacred congregation" of the Ponts et Chaussées, some British engineers who worked in France discovered advantages in the long-range planning carried out by the French administration in collaboration with the railroad companies. The basic act of 1842 was only a compromise, yet it drastically limited the number of companies, as compared to the 130 operating in Britain as late as 1914. The 1842 act was at least a gesture in the direction of allocating railroad construction where it was needed for economic growth. Forty-one years later, Charles de Freycinet, an engineer who became minister of public works and premier, advanced what Charles Kindleberger has called the last major state economic plan until Jean Monnet.[20] It was based on a "third network" of railroads (eventually constructed by private enterprise) to stimulate agriculture and industry in relatively inaccessible regions. Still later (1908) the state did develop a network for the backward western regions. Joseph Locke, an associate of Stephenson, wrote that the French system would be good for Britain if it had not been so paternalistic. He was especially impressed by the uniformity of guage—which, as noted above, British inspectors desired but had not yet secured. Locke also envied French "freedom from" competition.[21] Like their fellow

[18] Kemp, p. 123; Bert Hoselitz, "Entrepreneurship and Capital Formation in France and Britain since 1700," in *Capital Formation*, pp. 305ff.

[19] Ernouf, p. 50; Bertrand Gille, *Recherches sur la Formation de la Grande Entreprise Capitaliste* (Paris, 1959), pp. 109, 122.

[20] Kindleberger, p. 188; Henderson, *Industrial Revolution*, p. 172; Dauzet, pp. 111, 225.

[21] Joseph Devey, *The Life of Joseph Locke, Civil Engineer* (London, 1862), p. 228; Vignoles, p. 199; Arthur Louis Dunham, *La Révolution Industrielle en France (1815-1848)* (Paris, 1953), pp. 19, 365.

countrymen dealing with Indian development problems, he and other Britons actually confronting the need for rapid railroad construction in unindustrialized areas appear to have rapidly modified their laissez-faire views. One critic even goes so far as to contend (in relation to the Indian subsidies) that avowedly "Manchester liberal" bankers' arguments suggest that laissez faire was a "myth" to fight the "landed oligarchy."[22]

ADMINISTRATIVE OBSTRUCTION IN PRUSSIA

One need not take this extreme position to recognize the ideological elements in the relationship of the Prussian administration to railroad construction. Fortunately, this complex subject has been examined from a wide variety of views, including those of administration apologists, contemporary critics, and (currently) East German Marxist-Leninists. There is general agreement that a strictly political factor, the reluctance of the Prussian royal regime to convoke the Estates, delayed subsidies until 1848.[23] In contrast to the Board of Trade, which simply wanted to keep out of the messy railroad business, Prussian administrators would neither foster new development nor let it go its own way. Where Prussian administration was strongly entrenched in ancillary economic operations like Westphalian coal mining, it resisted innovation proposed by entrepreneurs. Several individual *Oberpräsidenten* and *Regierungspräsidenten* helped the railroad projects. One of the latter even attended university lectures when he realized how inadequate his technical background was for coping with transportation problems.[24] But other high officials and the *Regierung* collegia opposed local initiatives. When railroads were started by private enterprise, the lower officials (especially the *Landräte*, as representatives of the local nobility) secured exorbitant compensation for landowners. Other particularistic interests were evident; for example, one Finance Ministry official did push a Prussian connection to Leipzig, but insisted

[22] Thorner, *Investment*, p. 176.

[23] Dietrich Eichholtz, *Junker und Bourgeoisie vor 1848 in der preussischen Eisenbahngeschichte* (Berlin, 1962), pp. 8ff.; Joseph Hausen, *Gustav von Mevissen, ein rheinisches Lebensbild 1815-1899*, Vol. 1 (Berlin, 1906), 3, 311; Hans Fraenkel, "Dampfschiff und Eisenbahn am Niederrhein: Studien über ihre Anfänge, unter besonderer Berücksichtigung Düsseldorfs," *Düsseldorfer Jahrbuch 1915: Beiträge zur Geschichte des Niederrheins*, XVII (1915), 248; Kech, p. 32; Gustav Cohn, "Die Anfänge des deutschen Eisenbahnwesens," *Zeitschrift für die gesamte Staatswissenschaft*, XLVII (1891), 659, 672; Josef Enkling, *Die Stellung des Staates zu den Privateisenbahnen in der Anfangszeit des preussischen Eisenbahnwesens (1830-1848)* (Dissertation, Cologne University, Economics and Social Science Faculty) (Kettweg, 1935), pp. 13, 60.

[24] Pierre Benaerts, *Les Origines de la Grande Industrie Allemande* (Paris, 1933), pp. 300ff.; R. Delbrück, I, 138.

on its passing through Magdeburg where he had been *Bürgermeister*, rather than Halle; "this man, too, strongly attached as he was to state interests, let his communal office influence him against the general interest on the railroad question."[25] It is curious, but typical, that officials so eager to further the financial interests of their class or local associates had a horror of "speculation," of the "poison tree" of the stock exchange. Some considered all early railroad activity in that light. Even those who supported railroad construction as such tended to reject the only practical method (in the absence of state financing) of major resource mobilization. As late as the 1850's efforts of the Oppenheim banker family in Cologne to collaborate with the Crédit Mobilier were impeded by the Berlin administration.[26]

Several historians draw a distinction between the first fifteen or twenty years after the Napoleonic Wars and the remaining half of the "pre-March" (1848) period. During the first period, the Berlin administration, particularly through the work of finance minister Motz, took a fairly active part in supporting development, mostly through indirect measures such as the German customs union. After 1835 the self-confidence of the administration declined. It appears significant that this coincides with the gradual replacement of older officials trained as cameralists by men fully equipped with *Bildung* and juridical experience. As Reinhart Koselleck has analyzed the situation:

> Every technical-administrative project of the executive branch failed, however, as soon as problems arose which (like the ecclesiastical, the constitutional, and the social problem) required new principles. Here new political decisions were required which constantly became slower within an administration which retreated to purely executive functions, and confined its legislative work to declarative legal projects rather than new initiatives.[27]

In the specific area of our concern the result was that "in no place was there statesman-like initiative (in the sense of a certain abstract theory) which immediately grasped the new technique and utilized it according to plan."[28]

Faced with actual opposition by an administrative elite which believed its role included close control of all spheres of semi-public activity like large-scale enterprise, the entrepreneurs fought back. Essentially it was their forcefulness, and later their political and economic

---

[25] Kurt Wiedenfeld, "Deutsche Eisenbahn-Gestalter aus Staatsverwaltung und Wirtschaftsleben im 19. Jahrhundert (1815-1914)," *Archiv für Eisenbahnwesen*, 1940, pp. 757-58; Eichholtz, pp. 18, 44, 50, 159.

[26] Cameron, *France*, pp. 148-49; Kech, p. 32; Wiedenfeld, "Deutsche Eisenbahn-Gestalter," p. 800.

[27] Koselleck, p. 402.   [28] Cohn, *Die Anfänge*, p. 671.

power, which provided Prussia and Germany with a railroad network at least as effective as the British and the French. A twenty-year struggle was required to establish a new Trade Ministry by detaching the Trade Office from the Finance Ministry. There was a vast difference between the new trade minister and the typical Prussian official. August von der Heydt came from a Westphalian merchant family. He left school for commercial work at fifteen, although, his biographer writes, he continued studying on his own with the assistance of the director of the Wuppertal Latin school (evidently it had not yet been superseded by a *Gymnasium*). Although Heydt was able to expand the basic railroad network, the state operation he advocated was rejected as "undignified" by other officials.[29] His successor, Heinrich von Itzenplitz, was indifferent to state intervention. Not until the late 1860's did Prussia acquire a substantial nationalized sytem by annexing the Hanover state railway system, which she expanded for military reasons later in the century by purchasing privately constructed lines. Until after World War I all heads of the Prussian railroad administration but one (a military officer) were legally trained officials who devoted scant attention to economic considerations.[30]

AMBIGUITIES OF RUSSIAN EXPERIENCE IN RAILROAD DEVELOPMENT

Russian experience in railroad construction was extraordinarily closely linked to the French, but it was also subject to some of the negative administrative elite influences which prevailed in Prussia. The Russian construction occurred slightly later than in Western Europe and was pursued in the face of great physical and economic difficulties. It provides a good opportunity, therefore, to examine the significance, in a sharply different societal context, of several factors identified in France and Prussia. As indicated in Chapter Nine, the Transport Corps was a virtual offshoot of the Ponts et Chaussées. Some French instructors actually drew up plans for a Russian rail network as early as the 1820's, although others—like their Ponts et Chaussées counterparts—apparently continued to prefer more tested means of transportation. According to Soviet sources, this French conservatism was one reason for the sharp xenophobia which affected the first generation of native Russian Transport corps engineers, who were eager to try railroads. In any case, there is no doubt that some of the younger Russian engineers (as in France, mining engineers were at least as important as the Transport corps), together with a few academicians,

---

[29] Alexander Bergengrün, *Staatsminister August Freiherr von der Heydt* (Leipzig, 1908), pp. 7, 25, 165, 267.
[30] Wiedenfeld, "Deutsche Eisenbahn-Gestalter," pp. 810-11.

pressed for introducing the new technique. To them, as to Dalhousie and the French and Rhenish Saint-Simonists, railroads were to be a means of economic development, not just a more convenient form of transportation.[31]

Their great obstacle was neither, as in France, laissez-faire dominance in politics nor divisions within the technical administration. In Russia a more profound current of ideas actively opposed industrialization as such. The current embraced the curious views of Baron Haxthausen and more philosophical Slavophile opinions. To these elements, economic change threatened the sound agrarian substructure which made Russian society superior to Western Europe. The key figure, as in Prussia, was the minister of finance. A career civil administrator, Count G. D. Kankrin was German by parentage and education (the original family name was Krebs), and scarcely a true Slavophile. He also rejected laissez-faire doctrines in favor of a somewhat dated mixture of cameralistics and physiocratic concepts. Basically, however, he reached the same conservative conclusions as the other anti-industrialization forces: that a static agrarian society was safer than capitalist disruption and abuses.[32]

Although this position was widespread among officials and others with vested interests in the status quo, it was also shared by left-wing populists, who hoped to construct a socialist utopia on the basis of peasant institutions. There is little evidence of concerted administrative elite opposition to railroads, or of official complicity (beyond the customary bribery) in landlords' interests. Consequently, in contrast to Prussia, one cannot designate the Russian opposition to railroad construction as ideological, although the opponents employed curious arguments (e.g., that Russian winters were too cold for railroads). Rather, like Dmitri Tolstoi's advocacy of the classics, the position was part of a considered—if not necessarily sound—*Weltanschauung*.

The nonideological basis of the opposition is suggested by the fact that it crumbled quickly in the 1840's after Nicholas I, mainly for military reasons, decided to support railroad construction. From that point until the 1880's the principal cleavage within the administration was between elements which favored private enterprise and those which favored nationalization. The divisions were complicated but rested essentially on two factors: the difficulties of resource mobilization and

[31] Virginsky, pp. 95, 110, 246; Kiniapina, pp. 153-61, 195; Rondo E. Cameron, "The Crédit Mobilier and the Economic Development of Europe," *The Journal of Political Economy*, LXI (1953), 465, 478; Alfred J. Rieber, "Technology and Economic Development in Nineteenth Century Russia: The Formation of La Grande Société des Chemins de Fer Russes" (unpublished MS provided through courtesy of author), p. 7.

[32] Pintner, *Russian Economic Policy*, pp. 10, 22, 25, 95.

the xenophobia of Russian technical administrators. After the Crimean War had demonstrated the incapacity of the Russian highways, the evident need for quick construction led Alexander II and his advisers to concede the main railroad projects to the Grande Société, a branch of the Péreires' grandiose schemes for an all-European rail network. Generally, ministers of finance favored relying on foreign capital, while the Transport corps disliked the Grande Société personnel and favored nationalization. Apparently a key figure was the Mines engineer, K. V. Chevkin, who became converted to state construction after becoming head of the Transport Administration, both because of the Société's financial drain on the government (which guaranteed its obligations) and the need of state direction for military purposes.[33]

As in Prussia and France, private and state lines existed side by side until the 1890's. The dislike of the southwestern railroad company (the "Jew line") indicates the persistence of nativist prejudice. It was there, however, that Sergei Witte gained the railroading experience which he later employed as minister of finance to complete the construction of a basic railroad network. As indicated earlier, he found it necessary to assemble his own staff trained in economic and business methods to overcome the purely engineering bent of the state directors. The original impetus to state construction and nationalization of private lines alike had been military. These considerations remained important (to Witte's dismay), but closer calculation of the utility of the railroads as a stimulus of growth required more refined techniques than the Transport corps could supply.[34]

War Mobilization as Resource Expansion

Railroad construction is an obvious aspect of economic development. War mobilization is hardly as clear a case. Yet the experience of World War I is instructive on several counts. All general elites overtly defined the war crisis as a vital national concern justifying overriding any interests or traditions. For the elite administrator, the demand was atavistic; in devoting himself to mobilizing resources for military needs, he was required to revert to the role of his *commissarius* progenitor. Consequently, the crisis provides an exceptional opportunity to see how strongly the intervening process of socialization had affected administrators' ability to redefine their roles.

[33] Kiniapina, pp. 153-58, 161, 195; Cameron, *France*, p. 276; Kislinsky, I, Section 5, p. 3; II, Section 1, pp. 313ff.; Von Laue, *Sergei Witte*, p. 6; A. P. Pogrebinsky, "Stroitel'stvo Zheleznykh Dorog v Poreformennoi Rossii i Finansovaia Politika Tsarizma (60-90-e Gody XIX v.)," *Istoricheskie Zapiski*, 1954, No. 47, pp. 169-73.
[34] Von Laue, *Sergei Witte*, pp. 72, 187; Von Laue, "Industrialization," pp. 185-87; Gerschenkron, *Economic Backwardness*, pp. 125-31.

Superficially, the crisis was merely the occasion for short-term re-allocation of a fixed supply of resources. However, by 1914 the experience of a century of predominantly laissez-faire growth had shown everyone that economic resources were elastic. As soon as elites adjusted to the surprise of protracted warfare, therefore, the problems of reallocating and expanding resources were inextricably combined. As had been the case for mercantilist planners, short-run military needs and long-run development conflicted, even if one envisaged the "long run" as the four-year duration of hostilities. Nevertheless—as Lenin's copying of them showed—the techniques of planned expansion of production for war needs were the essence of development interventionism.

RUSSIAN FAILURES

The Russian experience can be treated briefly. Despite the construction of a transportation infrastructure and a heavy industrial base two decades earlier, the isolated Russian economy was wholly inadequate to support total warfare. In a sense, therefore, the experience was not a fair test of administrative response. As in other instances of administrators' role adaptation, though, we must take effectiveness of the Russian administrators' response to the crisis as a partial indicator of their role adaptation. Certainly such adaptation required more than a perfunctory, routine response to the challenge. We are not, however, primarily concerned with the ultimate effectiveness of the response, which was doubtless foredoomed to failure by many factors outside the administrators' control.

All sources—Soviet historians, émigré economists, and the few foreign students of the subject—agree that the Tsarist administrative elite performed very poorly. Despite Witte's reorganization and the Transport corps' decades of operational experience, the railroads (outstanding performers in the other three countries) adapted to the crisis very poorly. Not all of the defects appear excusable on the grounds of material deficiencies. For example, the Riga State Railway administration hampered rather than aided evacuation (1915) despite efforts of higher Transport Ministry officials to correct matters on the spot. The Transport Ministry itself was rent by senior officials blaming each other for mistakes. Efforts of the military to improve matters by a joint Army Chief of Communications-Ministry of Transport directorate (1916) were abortive.[35]

[35] Nicholas N. Golovin, *The Russian Army in the World War* (New Haven, 1931), p. 194; Tikhon J. Polner, *et al., Russian Local Government during the War and the Union of Zemstvos* (New Haven, 1930), pp. 275ff.

If the most experienced technical administration proved incapable, it is not surprising that government mobilization of industry was inadequate. The relatively weak private industrial sector and local self-government organizations tried to fill the gap. Their organization (The Union of Zemstvos and Towns—Zemgor) was hampered by the jealousy of career officials. Four major mobilization committees were established in August 1915 to finance industrial expansion and regulate material supplies. They had private-sector representation, but (unlike the German agencies described below) each was attached to a specific ministry. Even so, War Ministry officials bypassed the committees by using prewar "special contacts" with big firms, thus crippling the smaller firms trying to participate in war production. In sum, the rigid hierarchy and routine which characterized Tsarist administration was not essentially shaken by the crisis.

While practical accomplishments were restricted, considerable organizational innovation was undertaken by elements *outside* the civil service. In 1916 the Association of Commerce and Industry prepared a general economic plan which resembled the Soviet Five Year Plans. A year later, P. I. Palchinsky, as de facto chairman of the Central War Industries Committee and deputy minister of trade and industry under Alexander Kerensky, made a last effort to implement these mobilization plans.[36] Later, with other figures active in the war mobilization effort, Palchinsky played a significant role in the early Soviet plan for electrification which Lenin said would (together with "Soviet rule") create socialism.

WARTIME INADEQUACY OF THE PRUSSIAN
ADMINISTRATIVE ELITE

In contrast to the Russian economy, the German—the largest industrial complex in Europe—was at least marginally equipped to cope with the crisis. Consequently, it provided, in some sense, a "fair" test of the role adaptability of the administrative elite. Fortunately for our purposes, the controversy over the reasons for the German defeat provides abundant material for examining this relation. Despite controversy over such aspects as the relative defects of various agencies, and anti-Semitic tendencies of some authors to downgrade Walther Rathenau's contribution, there is surprising agreement on the incapacity of the administrative elite to adapt to war demands.

According to Gustav Schmoller, a forthright critic, the Prussian ad-

[36] *Ibid.*; S. O. Zagorsky, *State Control of Industry in Russia during the War* (New Haven, 1928), pp. 102ff.; Portal, *La Russie*, pp. 155, 161; Azrael, p. 30; Fediukin, *Sovetskaia Vlast'*, p. 18.

ministrative elite had little part in the 1870 victory, though it accepted the reflected glory.[37] Certainly it made little preparation for the 1914 war emergency. The posthumously published memoir of Clemens von Delbrück, the head of the Reich Interior Office, asserts that Chancellor Theobald von Bethmann-Hollweg (both men were career officials) actually hampered early 1914 efforts to prepare for grain mobilization.[38] Other critics pointed out that the administration of the Prussian state coal mines—next to the railroads the largest public-sector element—was particularly ineffective on the eve of war:

> In more than twenty years of parliamentary activity I have watched the Prussian financial administration at work, and belong to those who admire the contributions of the Prussian bureaucracy. But I have never encountered Mr. Financial Administration on the road to moderate prices. "At sea they call them sharks; on land they are called Financial Administration.". . . There is no spot in the whole Prussian Monarchy where prices are higher than in the Saar, where the financial administration had a monopoly, and I believe coal users there would thank God if the financial administration had an energetic competitor in coal mining there.[39]

Also indicative of the Prussian administration's inability to anticipate a new crisis role was the administrators' failure to respond to war mobilization ideas advanced by private entrepreneurial circles. In early 1914 the top management (notably Wichard von Moellendorf) of the Rathenau electrical engineering firm (A.E.G.) was especially active in planning for an emergency. It is probably significant that this firm represented a new type of industrial self-financing, developing without government aid (which to some extent went to the rival Siemens firm) or bank support. Immediately after the war the Rathenau associates suggested to the War Ministry that they be authorized to set up a special organization for industrial mobilization, the War Materials Section (K.R.A.). The Rathenau group believed that the Ministry's lack of commitment to individualistic doctrines and its devotion to the war effort made it potentially more effective than civilian agencies like Delbrück's Reich Interior Office.

> The whole K.R.A. was an alien graft among the many branches of the organizational tree of the Royal Prussian War Ministry, which had been regulated in strict accord with tradition. An industrialist

[37] Schmoller, "Der preussische Beamtenstand," p. 554.
[38] C. Delbrück, pp. 63ff., 78.
[39] Quoted in Oskar Stillich, *Steinkohlenindustrie: Nationalökonomische Forschungen auf dem Gebiete des grossindustriellen Unternehmung*, Vol. II (Leipzig, 1906), 133; cf. Edgar Landauer, "Kapitalistisches Geist und Verwaltungsbürokratie in öffentlichen Unternehmungen," *Schmollers Jahrbuch*, LIV (1930), 506ff.

and a Jew as section chief in the most conservative of all departments! Only awareness of the monstrous danger which the raw material question posed for German conduct of the war could have led the responsible person to underwrite establishment of the K.R.A. at that instant.[40]

The civilian staff of the War Ministry was utterly incapable of operating the new section. Like the Russian officials, they preferred to adhere to established procurement channels. Under token command of a military officer, Rathenau was permitted to recruit a large staff of businessmen, officials, and army officers. The core consisted of A.E.G. engineers. Invalided front officers were found to be more adaptable than legally trained reserve officers, who did not enter into the spirit of getting around legal regulations to accomplish economic purposes. According to staff members writing after the war, the K.R.A. encountered innumerable obstructions from the regular civilian agencies. Apparently the lower territorial administration was particularly unhelpful.[41]

The coordination activities of the K.R.A. vastly exceeded munitions production directly under military control. To control allocation of all major raw materials, War Raw Materials associations were established. Consisting of all private firms in a given branch of manufacturing, the associations were, in effect, universal government-sponsored cartels; they have often been compared to the N.R.A. during the first years of Franklin Roosevelt's New Deal. A kind of public corporation, the associations were an almost unprecedented innovation for bypassing the rigidities of established administrative machinery. Moellendorf, in particular, regarded them as a potentially permanent framework for economic direction—"the genuine construction product of a mechanical engineer."[42]

Apart from criticism from restive private businessmen and from the regular administrative elite, Rathenau's organization was apparently undermined indirectly by the powerful noble landowners, who believed a military dictatorship over the economy would serve their interests better than the "socialistic" activities of the Reich Interior Office.[43] In 1916 Rathenau was displaced by a military officer who had

[40] Otto Goebel, *Deutsche Rohstoffwirtschaft im Weltkrieg einschliesslich des Hindenburg-Programms* (Stuttgart, 1930), p. 22.

[41] Kurt Wiedenfeld, *Die Organisation der Kriegsrohstoff-Bewirtschaftung im Weltkriege* (Hamburg, 1936), pp. 34, 36ff., 56; Wiedenfeld, *Zwischen Wirtschaft,* p. 51; W. Dieckmann, *Die Behördenorganisation in der deutschen Kriegswirtschaft 1914-1918* (Hamburg, 1937), pp. 11ff., 25, 40ff., 80; Alfred Müller, *Die Kriegsrohstoffbewirtschaftung, 1914-1918, im Dienst des deutschen Monopolkapitals* (Berlin, 1955), pp. 14ff.

[42] Wiedenfeld, *Die Organisation,* p. 39; cf. Landauer, p. 508.

[43] C. Delbrück, pp. 37ff. (ed. note).

had considerable peacetime experience in procurement problems. In the meantime, Erich Ludendorff, the chief of staff on the eastern front, was acquiring a great deal of economic experience as a kind of viceroy for occupied Russian territories (the Ober-Ost area). Under the intense pressure of war, his compressed experience recapitulated that of hierarchical territorial governors elsewhere.[44] By 1917 Ludendoff's prestige (as quartermaster general) was so high that he was able to become virtual economic dictator. Much of the Rathenau organizational framework was retained. Without it, an American student writes, Germany would have collapsed years earlier as "the consequence of the German Government's complete and admitted lack of industrial knowledge and foresight in 1914."[45]

ADMINISTRATIVE INNOVATION IN BRITAIN

The Walther Rathenau of Great Britain was David Lloyd George, who transformed economic mobilization by putting ninety experienced businessmen in direct administrative posts in the Ministry of Munitions (March 1915) instead of advisory committee positions as had previously been the custom in war mobilization. Despite some sharp in-fighting, these "men of administrative and business capacity" broke through the routine of civil service operation. The contrast to sporadic prewar planning sponsored by the Board of Trade, but carried on by mixed committees composed of representatives of government departments and private firms, was notable. During the war itself, long-established technical services like H. M. Inspectors of Mines were apparently effective in allocating raw materials and labor. On the other hand, the Railway Executive Committee actually functioned as an executive branch of the largest among the huge number of companies engaged in rail transportation. Apparently this para-governmental organization was as effective as the nationalized or semi-nationalized railroad systems in France and Germany. Nominally, government supervision was provided by the Board of Trade, but the Transport Branch of the Ministry of Munitions (under one of Lloyd George's recruits, a former railroad manager) appears to have been more important.[46]

[44] See especially, Germany, Oberbefehlshaber Ost, Presseabteilung Ober Ost. *Das Land Ober Ost: Deutsche Arbeit in den Verwaltungsgebieten Kurland, Litauen und Bialystok-Grodno* (Stuttgart, 1917).

[45] Ralph H. Bowen, "The Roles of Government and Private Enterprise in German Industrial Growth, 1870-1914," *Journal of Economic History*, x (1950), Supplement, 81.

[46] Thomas Jones, *Lloyd George* (Cambridge, Mass., 1951), pp. 58, 63, 66; Samuel J. Hurwitz, *State Intervention in Great Britain: A Study of Economic Control and Social Response, 1914-1919* (New York, 1949), pp. 150, 169, 177, 288; Sir R.A.S. Redmayne, *The British Coal Mining Industry during the War* (Oxford,

In contrast to Germany, the new organizations set up by Lloyd George and the businessmen, while not as closely coordinated, did not face concerted opposition by the military or civil service agencies. At the local level, as in Prussia, military commanders were occasionally arbitrary in their demands. At a higher level, until Lloyd George's organization took over, War Office officials, like their Russian and Prussian counterparts, tended to rely exclusively on established procurement contacts with large firms.[47] While it did not make a major direct contribution to economic mobilization, the administrative elite apparently functioned smoothly as an auxiliary. Some higher civil servants discovered talents for direct action once the climate of opinion discounted the emphasis on precise procedure and consensus which their in-service socialization had prescribed:

> When the war of 1914-18 came many of the new war-time departments were manned entirely by young civil servants round about thirty years of age, assisted by temporaries. They displayed quite astonishing powers of improvization and initiative.[48]

For disparate reasons (e.g., a decade of exclusively judicial socialization in Prussia; the trauma of defeat, revolution, and reaction after 1905 in Russia), Russian and Prussian administrative elites were at a low ebb of dynamism at the outbreak of war. In contrast, the British administrative elite's self-confidence had been considerably enhanced by the immediate prewar experience of preparing and implementing social legislation on an interdepartmental basis. Such coincidences caution one against attributing too much significance to observations of role perceptions in short-run crisis situations. On the other hand, the generally subordinate if not retreatist position of the British administrative elite within a cohesive general elite facilitated adjustment to an auxiliary role.

For the Third Republic administration the immediate prewar period of legalist dominance was also a kind of low point. No overall pattern of administrative elite initiative in war mobilization is apparent. On the other hand, established administrative agencies appear to have acted more vigorously when directly called upon and to have required less assistance from the private sector than in the other three countries. The scope of French industrial mobilization was more restricted than in Britain and Germany, since France relied more on imported sup-

---

1923), pp. 13, 86; Edwin A. Pratt, *British Railways and the Great War: Organisation, Efforts, Difficulties and Achievements* (London, 1921), pp. 43, 83ff., 302, 327; Parris, *Government*, p. 228.

[47] Jones, p. 58; Pratt, p. 122; cf. C. Delbrück, p. 139.

[48] Lord Chorley, quoted in Greaves, p. 51.

plies than did the other three belligerents. On the other hand, the sudden shock of enemy seizure of a large portion of mining, manufacturing, and transportation resources immediately after outbreak of hostilities was greater even than in Russia.

FRENCH ADMINISTRATIVE ADAPTATION TO WAR

As in Prussia, most of the very limited French prewar preparation was conducted under the aegis of the military: the Historic section [*sic*] of the General Staff and a commission for railroad study in the War Ministry. After war broke out, the railroad networks operated under nominal War Ministry supervision until the end of 1916, when the General Transport Division of the Ministry of Public Works (manned by the technical corps) took over. A general plan of rail operation to redirect the economy to war production purposes was established soon after the outbreak of war. In 1915 General Headquarters established a staff to coordinate war production. The staff was later transferred to the War Ministry, but the main coordination of production and war materials allocation was delegated to a new Ministry of Armaments. This agency corresponded to Lloyd George's ministry, but apparently had more direct military influence.[49] Thus, as the war went on, there was a tendency (precisely opposite to the German development) to have civil administrative agencies take over economic supervisory tasks which the French military had assumed in 1914-15.

Some friction between older civil departments and ones created during the war appeared, but higher officials with common elite training in both types of agencies were apparently able to work out difficulties. The established civilian authorities maintained leading roles at the provincial level. Consultative Committees for Economic Action had been organized in 1915 by the minister of war, General Joseph Gallieni. They were coordinated by an economic section of each army corps region. The prefects became chairmen, however, and the representatives of the other principal administrative branches constituted a majority alongside one or two military representatives and two from the private sector.[50]

French wartime arrangements had a certain lasting influence through the writings of influential advocates of management and ad-

[49] "Les Chemins de Fer Français pendant la Guerre" [J. G.], *Revue des Sciences Politiques*, XLIV (1921), 88-90; Pierre Bruneau, *Le Rôle du Haut Commandement au Point de Vue Économique de 1914 à 1921* (Paris, 1924), pp. 11, 17-19; Marcel Peschaud, "Les Chemins de Fer Français et Allemands et la Guerre," *Revue Politique et Parlémentaire*, 1927, No. 397, pp. 357-59.
[50] Hubert Bourgin, "Administration et Gouvernement," *Revue de Paris*, Nov. 15, 1919, pp. 429-36; Bruneau, pp. 21ff., 51, 77ff.

ministrative reorganization like Henri Fayol. Fayol's disciples believed that Rathenau's innovations could be made less dictatorial by utilizing the more restrained French experience; some even proposed, unsuccessfully, that para-governmental consortiums ("syndicates") be set up after the war to coordinate industrial activity.[51] It is unfortunate that so little intensive study has been devoted to the French World War I administrative experience, especially since (in contrast to that of the other three countries) it had no significant sequel in World War II.

REFLECTIONS ON ADAPTATION TO POSTINDUSTRIAL PROBLEMS

As noted earlier, there is no postindustrial experience involving all four national administrative systems comparable to railroad construction and World War I mobilization. In a tentative way, the organization of European economic cooperation appears to be providing an analogue for these earlier experiences. Since the USSR has held aloof and Great Britain's involvement has been tangential, the comparative utility of this experience is limited. If we were diffident about plunging into the complicated economic history of experiences in the past, we are still more hesitant to assess a development which is still in its formative stage. Our personal impressions, obtained through numerous discussions during the 1960's with officials and advisers of the Western European administrations, agree, however, with the conclusions of more competent observers. Perhaps it will not be amiss to summarize a few of the conclusions concerning negotiations for Western European economic unification which directly bear on our subject.

Since the two countries have been directly involved in the European Economic Community for two decades, the comparison of French and West German administrative performance is most reliable. Some 90 per cent of E.E.C. officials use French, although native German speakers are more numerous in the Community countries than native speakers of French.[52] Certainly French linguistic and stylistic dominance arises in part from prudent self-restraint of German officials who wish to assuage the lingering suspicions of their colleagues. In actual negotiations German representatives appear to be less able than their French counterparts, however. This situation reflects the *Juristenmonopol*, a training experience which handicaps German negotiators on complicated economic questions where the familiar legal

---

[51] Jean-Paul Palewski, *Histoire des Chefs d'Entreprise* (Paris, 1928), pp. 349ff.; Palewski, *Le Rôle*, p. 571.

[52] Armytage, *German Influence*, p. 98.

guidelines do not apply.[53] In contrast, the Keynesian economic training and experience in planning appear to provide optimal equipment for the French. As Shonfield points out:

> In a sense, it was unnecessary for the German authorities to plan the growth of the country's productive capacity as a formal exercise in prediction, in the French manner, because what had to be done was essentially to reconstruct something which had existed before. The guide-lines were provided by the past; there was no need of a German Monnet to invent them.[54]

Under fire for collaboration with the Nazis, the West German administrative elite has tended to retreat to a peripheral position among Federal Republic elites. Domestically, the "economic miracle" could be carried out by the self-confident entrepreneurial elite in a congenial framework arranged by pluralist political elites. But a distinct price has had to be paid at the level of international economic dealings.

British higher civil servants' experience somewhat paralleled the German administrative elite's. During World War II and the immediate postwar years, French administrative reformers were almost unrestrained in their enthusiasm for emulating the British civil service. Seeking to draw lessons from various foreign administrations, particularly the British, a provisional government publication in April 1945 wrote:

> In comparison with these foreign advances, it is useless to talk about French experiments, for one would have to confine oneself to stressing how sporadic and little coordinated these experiments have been. Nevertheless, public rationalization often precedes private rationalization.[55]

Part of the French admiration was for features of stability and responsiveness which do not concern us directly. There was also a high measure of confidence in the efficiency of the British administrative system. The E.N.A. itself was designed to secure the unity which characterizes the Administrative Class.

By 1961, at the latest, a dramatic change in self-appraisal had occurred in both the French and British administrative elites. In his impressive comparative study, Brian Chapman wrote that "the impression an observer obtains is that the highest branches of the French

[53] Hans J. Arndt, *The Politics of Non-Planning* (Syracuse, 1966), pp. 63-65.
[54] Shonfield, p. 275.
[55] "L'Amélioration des Méthodes dans les Administrations," *Gouvernement Provisoire de la République Française, Bulletin d'Information et de Documentation*, No. 8, March-April 1945, p. 83.

civil service have an intellectual capacity, an independence of judgment, a talent for leadership, and a willingness to accept personal responsibility, which their British counterparts do not have."[56] At that time French officials (from the Ministry of Finance and the Commissariat du Plan) negotiating on British entry into the E.E.C. were mainly interested in preserving the existing accords while gaining advantages for France. They had wide discretion on economic details as long as they stayed within the general framework laid down by De Gaulle's government. In contrast, according to the most intensive study of these relations, the Administrative Class negotiators were "reactive and self-limiting," relying for initiative on political direction. British negotiators failed to understand that entrance into the Common Market involved mergers of entire economic systems rather than commercial details. One author attributes this failure of comprehension to the weakness of the Treasury and the Board of Trade staffs in economic expertise. Lacking economic training, they relied on

> tradition and conventional wisdom, . . . practical learning that is a product of long familiarity with their department, interest, group contacts, and recurrent problems. British Treasury officials in particular have compensated for their "amateurism" by grounding their thinking and action on received doctrine.[57]

Apparently the literary training and pragmatic approach of the Administrative Class can compete with the new French training and experience as little as can German legalism. As with other generalizations drawn from postindustrial experience, this one is subject to sweeping revision. Our distrust in the stability of trends which have persisted for less than a generation is enhanced by the sharp turn-about in French and British mutual evaluation in a period of less than two decades. Drastic changes in relationships, whether resulting from intimate British participation in the E.E.C., alterations in administrative elite recruitment, or broader societal currents, are entirely conceivable in the proximate future. Considerable changes are projected, particularly in British administrative organization and recruitment. Keynesian theory is more widely understood in the Treasury. At the moment, though, signs of fundamental alteration in the relative adaptation of administrative elites to economic development are not very convincing.

[56] B. Chapman, *Profession*, p. 92.
[57] Brennan, p. 29.

CHAPTER FOURTEEN

Implications Of Development Interventionist
Role Definition

N ATIONAL differences in administrative elite roles were summarized in the preceding chapter. Four more general aspects of the study require attention. A review of social psychological concepts may make their utility clearer. The historical interpretation implicit in the genetic approach requires brief reconsideration. Most important, the nomothetic implications of the study, its transcendence of particular historical circumstances, remain to be considered. Finally, while this book is not a policy study, brief attention to some major practical implications of its findings can hardly be avoided.

UTILITY OF THE CONCEPTUAL FRAMEWORK

This study has combined a method and a subject matter resembling historical sociology with a conceptual focus derived from social psychology. The key concept of "role" has suggested areas of investigation and provided a set of definitions indispensable for delimiting the research and organizing the exposition. Without the role concept it would have been virtually impossible to proceed through the mass of disparate data in other than a disjointed descriptive manner. Such special concepts as "counter-role" and "role conflict" have illuminated our thinking about the peculiar relationships which emerge as one reads the historical record; we hope they will also contribute to the reader's comprehension. Very exceptionally, we may have been able to add a trifle to the body of concepts associated with role, as in the notion of "fixated peer identification group" (Chapter Seven).

As more profound reflections on the concept have suggested, however, "role theory" is theory only in a rather special sense of the word, since it is difficult to derive precise, empirically testable hypotheses from it. As the example just cited suggests, explicit propositions or even more precise indications of how roles are defined are inseparable from consideration of socialization. Indeed, in a more general sense role theory and socialization theory constitute a single body of theory.[1] Considered separately, socialization propositions are more adaptable

[1] Rocheblave-Spenlé, p. 162.

to empirical verification. For this study, the distinction in ages at which socialization to basic values occurs as contrasted to recombination of values for occupational roles later in life, has been fundamental. Nevertheless, the general emphasis of socialization theory upon the experiences of early childhood (which we could scarcely begin to examine) has limited the utility of the theory for our purposes. So has the tendency of recent studies to concentrate on mass socialization rather than on the particular processes related to elite occupations. We have tried to adapt available conceptual frameworks to the special purposes of our investigation without, we hope, doing excessive violence to their original meaning.

THE GENETIC INTERPRETATION

The genetic approach has been fundamental to our analysis. A perennial problem with cross-national comparison of phenomena like role definition is the tendency to attribute variance to unexplained factors like "national character" or "culture." As Robert Holt and John Turner point out, reliance on psychological characteristics to explain social phenomena is inherently unsatisfactory, unless one can identify the social factors which produced the psychological mediating variable.[2] Without claiming definitiveness for our specific conclusions, we believe examination of the evolution of socialization patterns over a very extended period of time provides a way around this difficulty. The components of the Prussian and British administrators' role definitions which preclude development intervention are traceable to specific patterns of socialization. These patterns originated during relatively brief periods of time scarcely exceeding a generation. At that time the socialization patterns served the interests of determinable groups. Although one may admit a certain inertia for patterns once formed, they persisted over long periods essentially because they continued to accord with the interests of these or other social collectivities. This interpretation does not imply that the interests which originally produced the socialization patterns were necessarily congruent with the role definitions which socialization ultimately produced. Thus the British case suggests that the interests of the educational elite might have been better served by a more interventionist, hence more influential Administrative Class, particularly during the postindustrial period. What we argue is that certain aspects of British elite socialization (scorn for entrepreneurs, emphasis on rural styles, classics predominance in the curriculum, etc.) were in the interest of the educational elite which introduced or strengthened them. The latent, long-range

[2] See the discussion in Holt and Turner, p. 20.

effect of these elements on the elite administrators' role definition was scarcely anticipated and was at most a secondary consideration for the educational elite's interests. Once an administrative elite socialized in accordance with the Oxbridge prescription was firmly established, the administrators themselves acquired an interest in perpetuating the noninterventionist role definition. An interventionist position would have revealed the specific inadequacies of their training, disrupted their corporate solidarity, and reduced their status in the general elite. Each element of the administrative setting (rural nostalgia, oral examinations, etc.) is defended because it is part of the system which perpetuates these interests. At the same time, rejection of disturbing elements (e.g., an elite technical corps) prevents feedback which might alter the system.

In Prussia, social class influence was more direct. The socialization pattern adopted at the end of the eighteenth century was circumscribed by the need to advance a kind of specialization which would legitimize bourgeois status claims yet be acceptable to nobles suspicious of any training which detracted from the "whole man" concept. Neither class consciously envisaged the latent implications of the specialization pattern for the future relation of the administrative elite to development, for economic growth was not a major consideration at that time. Educational elites could play only a marginal part in defining the socialization process suitable for the accommodation of bourgeois and aristocratic values. Once the socialization pattern was established, the closed administrative elite acquired an interest in maintaining it as a means of asserting corporate status superiority. Emerging corporate solidarity was already evident in the *Régie* episode, but became much clearer in reacting against the competition of private entrepreneurial and, later, managerial elites.

The preceding examples are sufficient to indicate the importance of the genetic approach for our interpretation. At the same time, this brief review serves to remind the reader that what we have presented is an interpretation, not a demonstration. As was indicated in Chapter One, the interpretation rests on the assumption that societal collectivities have specific material and status interests which are often in conflict with those of other groups. Moreover, it is assumed that these interests are often latent, i.e., they are not consciously recognized by individual members of the group. As a result of this "false consciousness," arguments are often presented which actually promote group interests while manifestly emphasizing entirely different, instrumental considerations. When these arguments constitute a superficially coherent position, like the Northcote-Trevelyan administrative reform proposals, the justification of the *Juristenmonopol*, or the French *lycée professeurs'* assertion of the superiority of the classics, they constitute an ideology. The kind of ideological position which has interested us is one which is reflected in persistent patterns of socialization, i.e., a set of institutions which is legitimized ideologically.

The concepts of "ideology" and "false consciousness" are ultimately derived from Marx. As indicated in Chapter One, we have deliberately chosen to detach these particular concepts from the general body of Marxist theory. In the Marxist canon, these concepts are inseparable from the historical dialectic, i.e., from the class interpretation of history. For Marx, classes were not collectivities with limited material or status interests, but antagonistic social forces defined by their ineluctable relationship to the production process. As discussed in Chapter Four, our definition of classes is different: we consider them to be both stratification concepts and matters of societal perception. From this standpoint, social classes as salient elements of modern European societies are inescapable. We do not believe that even any realistic partial consideration of those societies is possible without extended discussion of the implications of class divisions. In considering these implications, ideological elements arising from class interests are very important. But we believe that classes are by no means the only collectivities which have latent interests concealed by ideologies. In our investigation, other salient collectivities were occupational groups. For another study, ethnic or religious collectivities might be crucial. A Marxist (and some other grand theorists) would argue that these collectivities might be significant in a limited way but that ultimately they reflect more fundamental social class division. This may be so. If the question can be approached empirically at all, however, it certainly cannot be settled in the scope of this study.

As we have conceived it, our task has been to show how each group's interest has affected our subject. In order to do this, we have analyzed successive layers of arguments. When these clearly shift over time in accordance with the legitimization requirements of the period (e.g., the nineteenth-century classics revival as contrasted to eighteenth-century ecclesiastical emphasis on classics), or when a group abandons a socialization pattern which is no longer in accord with its interests (the diminution of Greek emphasis in mid-nineteenth-century Prussia), we have suspected the presence of ideological arguments. When elites in one society strongly argue for a socialization pattern (e.g., the E.N.A.-type of induction schooling) while those in a contemporary society with superficially similar requirements just as strongly reject or distort the pattern, our suspicion that one or both of the elites is employing ideological argumentation is reinforced. When a series of converging indications of this kind, persisting for decades or generations, is discovered, we have felt justified in presenting an interpretation of the underlying group interest.

Not all of the genetic elements we identify are ideological. The establishment and persistence, for example, of the *tournée* system in the Financial Inspectorate reflects, apparently, persistence for instrumental reasons of a socialization device that may have arisen through historical chance. On the other hand, the Administrative Class's rejection of a similar field induction experience (occasionally explicitly suggested) almost certainly results from 1) the presence of other mechanisms adequate to promote corporate solidarity; and 2) rejection, because of prior socialization, of concern for concrete local problems. The persistence of major territorial experiences in other elements of the French and the Russian administrative elite reflects the instrumental requirement of administering a large area, but the Prussian experience shows that this requirement is not decisive. At the same time, the French and Russian cases show how a pattern like the corps division, once established, may be perpetuated by the interests of the corps as a collectivity.

Many analysts contend that until one has tentatively identified the hierarchy of social causal factors, the kind of special investigation undertaken in this study is not feasible. In other words, a total societal explanation must precede middle-range interpretations of particular societal elements. It has been argued, for example, that administrators' role definitions are interventionist in societies like France and Russia because the societies need to concentrate scarce achievement motivation. In Britain and Germany, on the other hand, achievement motivation is so widely distributed that diffuse private enterprise is feasible. These differences, in turn, reflect basic value patterns inculcated by Protestant as contrasted to Catholic and Orthodox faiths.[3] While such theories have a certain plausibility, they are far from verified. In contrast to Weber's and Tawney's concept of religious motivation for *individual* achievement, these total societal explanations also appear to rest on a teleological assumption, namely that societies respond to a deficiency in one area by compensatory mechanisms. By adhering to the limited conflict model discussed above, our assumptions, on the contrary, admit that groups may misperceive their interests (French nobles probably did so in reducing mobility in the latter part of the eighteenth century). Particular groups may adopt positions which are inimical to the interests of the class with which they are generally identified (as the Third Republic *lycée* instructors may have by insisting on a classics curriculum). Groups may even pursue interests which

[3] McClelland, *The Achieving Society*, p. 419. See also Hoselitz, in *Capital Formation*, pp. 385ff., and the discussion preceding.

are injurious to society as a whole, although we hestitate to specify societal interests in a way that would make this determination possible.

Socialization patterns and role definitions in each national administrative system have been relatively stable over time. Nevertheless, specific alterations in the socialization process may produce considerable changes in role definition. The increasingly legalistic outlook of Third Republic administrative elites has apparently been reversed in considerable measure by the institutional innovation which the E.N.A. represents. The growing importance of committee decision-making in the French administration may lead to equally significant changes in role perception. As recently as the early nineteenth century, British education was generally regarded as unstructured in its socializing effects compared to the French. A relatively minor alteration in the balance of interests in mid-nineteenth-century Britain might—as far as our investigations go—have produced a very different type of socialization from that which actually arose. Today (as noted in Chapter Eight) the Oxbridge educational elite appears to be reducing its interest in the administrative elite. It is wholly conceivable (although we have no reason to predict it) that within a generation the French administration could become thoroughly collegial while the British could be characterized by strict hierarchy. All of this, of course, is another way of saying that a fixed notion of national character or national culture is incompatible with our approach. At the same time, our inability to provide a total-society analysis necessarily restricts our ability to project trends which are influenced by numerous factors beyond the horizon of this investigation.

Constant Factors Contributing to Development Interventionism

Given these limitations, what of the claims for nomothetic significance for this study? Certainly its significance does not reside in prediction of general trends in administration. For reasons just discussed, we cannot even predict with confidence trends in the administrative systems of the societies we have examined. Nevertheless, we do believe that the findings transcend a purely historical interpretation. A reason for avoiding resort to residual cultural explanations was doubt about the intellectual validity of such an interpretation. But resort to cultural variance as an explanation would also have made it impossible for us to be certain that specific factors we identified in all the societies examined were correlated with variation in role definition. By following the approach of first determining the significance of each mechanism within a societal context specific to country and period, we believe that we have been able to identify five factors which have always been positively related to development interventionist role definition, *regardless* of the reasons *why* the factor arose and persisted in a given society.

1) *Metropolitan influence.* Intensive association with upper- and upper-middle-class social groups in a great capital city during some stage of the administrative elite's socialization has been positively related to development interventionist role definition. Metropolitan influence is probably most significant as a linking variable inducing receptivity to development doctrines. These doctrines have been available in all European societies, but are most readily available to men in touch with a broad spectrum of social groups and cosmopolitan influences. Consequently, devices which segregate the administrative elite at any stage of its socialization (see the discussion of Berlin society in Chapter Five; of St. Petersburg closed institutions in Chapter Seven; and of the Administrative Class "bucolic enclave" in London, Chapter Ten) tend to negate the physical location in the metropolis.

2) *Territorial experience.* In contrast to metropolitan influence, which can be significant at any stage of socialization, territorial experience is important only after service entry. Its most important characteristics (defined in detail in Chapter Twelve) include (a) propensity for risk-taking; (b) concern for the whole range of concrete problems in a specific area; (c) hierarchical authority. Only experience in posts like prefectural governorships has all these characteristics although (a) and (b) can be experienced in an attenuated way through training periods like those of E.N.A. students, Financial Inspectors, and the lower ranks of the Soviet territorial administrators. Two important qualifications should be stressed. One is that it is unlikely (and perhaps counter-productive from the point of view of development interventionist role definition) that all of the administrative elite should have the full range of territorial experience. It is sufficient for a salient group among the elite to act as a reference group for other elite administrators. Second, while collegiality may not have adverse effects on some administrative organizations, if applied to the territorial administration it negates the experience by eliminating at least elements (a) and (c) above (see the discussion of the Prussian *Regierung* in Chapters Ten and Twelve).

3) *Administrative integration.* A large measure of organizational unity and homogeneity in socialization among elite administrators has been crucial for development interventionist role definition. At first glance this may appear to contradict the general finding that Prussian and British administrative elites, which were certainly the more homogeneous, have rejected development interventionist roles. It must be understood, however, that we are presenting a five-factor analysis in

which the cumulative effect of the factors is decisive. To exercise effective initiative, an administrative elite must be able to operate as a single unified body. The crucial test for whether integration was essential was the Third Republic, where administrative fragmentation precluded development interventionist roles for most elite administrators. In historical perspective (as noted in Chapter Ten), the corps division of that period may have preserved an option for development interventionism, while the Prussian and British solidarity against that role definition may have precluded such an option. Nevertheless, this option could not be taken up until the French administrative elite had become more homogeneous after 1945. Socialization toward homogeneity can take place either prior to service entry (e.g., through the inculcation to team values), during the induction period (as in the *Regierung*), or even in mid-career (the Higher Party School in the USSR).

4) *Scientific-technological education component.* Appreciation for science, technology, and economics can be achieved through metropolitan influence or territorial experience (factors 1 and 2). Factors 4 and 5, in contrast, are defined as more formally structured experiences. For clarity in presentation we have preferred to define all five factors affecting the elite role definition in a positive manner. It is important to note, however, that the formal presence of such subjects as mathematics and natural science in the secondary school curriculum not only has a positive effect in preparing for development interventionism, but tends to counteract the effect of subjects which *may* be utilized to socialize against development values by instilling the attitude that material manipulation is derogating for upper-class men.

5) *Systematic economics training.* Injection of a systematic consideration of economic factors in the socialization process may take place during higher education (in practice economics has never been a significant secondary education component), service induction, or mid-career training. The definition of "systematic consideration" includes the kind of training provided to beginning Financial Inspectors, but excludes the type of empirical self-training which, for example, an *Oberpräsident* obtained, since that (in our definition) was equivalent to factor 2 above. As was discussed at length in Chapter Nine, the state of economics theory made highly systematic economics training impossible until near the end of the industrial period.

The reservation just made indicates that the significance of the factors varies over time, particularly in relation to stages of industrialization. A development interventionist role could not be defined as explicitly in the preindustrial as in the postindustrial period. Consequently, longitudinal comparison of strength of factors is less satisfactory than cross-national comparison (frequently asynchronous) for the same period. Since, however, this study is primarily concerned with perceptions rather than actual administrative participation or accomplishment, the diachronic comparison appears to be justified.

Table XXIII presents a summary of the relative strength, by national administrative elite and period, of the five factors just defined. Each factor is scaled (1, 2, or 3) as a numerical indication of its relative strength. Factors 1 and 2 are essentially measured by threshold

TABLE XXIII. FACTORS POSITIVELY INFLUENCING DEVELOPMENT
INTERVENTIONIST ROLE DEFINITIONS

Factor and Period	France	Great Britain	Prussia Germany	Russia
(1) Metropolitan Influence				
Period I	3(F,A,H,I)	—	1	2(A,H,I)
Period II	2(A,H)	—	1	3(F,A,H,I)
Period III	3(F,A,H)	1(F,I,S)	1	2(H,I)
Period IV	3(F,A,H,I)	1(F,I,S)	1	—
(2) Territorial Experience				
Period I	3(I,S)	—	1	2(S)
Period II	2(I,S)	—	1	2(S)
Period III	2(I,S)	1	1	3(I,S)
Period IV	3(I,S)	1	1	—
(3) Administrative Integration				
Period I	3(F,A,H,I)	—	2(I,S)	1(A,I)
Period II	1(A,H)	—	3(F,H,I,S)	2(A,H,I)
Period III	1(A,H)	3(A,H,I,S)	3(H,I,S)	3(I,S)
Period IV	2(A,H,I)	3(H,I,S)	2(H,I,S)	—
(4) Scientific-Technological Education Component				
Period I	2(H)	—	1	2(A)
Period II	3(H,I)	—	1	2(A,H,I)
Period III	2(H)	1	1	3(A,H,I,S)
Period IV	2(A,H)	1	1	—
(5) Systematic Economics Training				
Period I	1(I)	—	2(H)	1
Period II	2(H,I)	—	1	2(H,S)
Period III	1(I)	1	1	2(I,S)
Period IV	3(H,I,S)	1	1	—
SUMMARY				
Period I	12	—	7	8
Period II	10	—	7	11
Period III	9	7	7	13
Period IV	13	7	6	—

KEY: For Periods, see Table I (Chapter Two)
Factor Weightings: 1—weak; 2—moderate; 3—strong
Stages of Socialization: F—Familial
                                A—Adolescence
                                H—Higher Education
                                I—Induction to Elite Administration
                                S—Service in Elite Administrative Career

levels. In other words, metropolitan influence and territorial experience were either present or (taking into account offsetting influences) were not effectively present. If present they were strong (weighting 3) or moderate (weighting 2). In practice, much the same trichotomized assessment applies to factors 3, 4, and 5. In principle, factor 3 (administrative integration) can be measured by a single quantitative indicator, homogeneity of career patterns. In practice such refined measurement is unnecessary, for homogeneity is either very high (British Administrative Class), virtually nonexistent (Third Republic corps), or transitional (postindustrial France). Similarly, curriculum weightings can provide more precise quantitative indicators for factors 4 and 5, but intervals between administrative elite systems are so great that gross scalar distinctions are adequate.

Aggregation of the scaled weightings in the summary section of Table XXIII is more questionable. There is, of course, no way to be sure that "metropolitan influence" and "systematic economics training" have had equivalent importance in socializing for development interventionist roles. The fact that the totals do, in a rough way, approximate our qualitative conclusions concerning variation in role definitions makes it seem worthwhile to include the summary totals as a succinct presentation of conclusions we have reached by other lines of reasoning. Even within our framework of analysis only the most recent French and Soviet cases approach the "optimum" weightings for development interventionist role definition. These experiences have persisted for such short periods (approximately a quarter-century in each case) that they must still be regarded as tentative. Since the Soviet factors produce near-optimal roles only for the industrial period (see Chapter Eleven), it is possible that the analysis is already obsolete as far as the USSR is concerned.

A more significant reason why the analysis does not present "one best way" even for development interventionist roles is suggested by the stages of socialization (indicated by the letters beside each numerical weighting) which produce the factor. We have considered (as indicated above) only service experience (induction or later stages) to be relevant to factor 2 (territorial experience) and only those stages plus higher education to be relevant to factor 5 (systematic economics training). Familial socialization is not considered relevant to factor 4 (scientific-technological education component), but for the other two factors all five stages may provide significant socialization.

Because Soviet recruitment has not been ascriptive, familial socialization is not considered relevant for any factors for the Soviet industrial period. Since an enormous majority of secondary school graduates who have entered the elite have attended provincial schools, adolescence is not considered relevant for metropolitan influence. Nevertheless, because of the strong effect of socialization at other stages, Soviet administrative elite role definition is near optimal for all factors. For example, lack of metropolitan experience at early ages is partly compensated for by such devices as Party school mid-career training, frequent convocations to Moscow, and the intense emphasis on attention to political, economic, and technological developments in media published in the capital. Administrative integration is produced by the same mechanisms, in addition to doctrinal emphasis, heightened ethnic homogeneity (as compared to the Tsarist system), and a strong sense of in-group solidarity among the general elite. For France, similar optimal factor levels have required a more extensive reinforcement process during successive socialization stages. If there are several alternative socialization reinforcement patterns by which near-optimal factor combinations are produced, the number of alternative ways in which moderately high combinations of factors (as in Tsarist Russia, preindustrial or take-off France) can be achieved is obviously much greater.

A few words should be devoted to factors mentioned at length in previous chapters which the reader may feel we are neglecting unduly. In Chapter Three we dealt at length with development doctrines, which we concluded were available to all societies and therefore invariant. The only notable difference appeared to be between post-World War I and preceding periods; it is reflected in the strength of factor 4 in the USSR and factor 5 in France. We do not consider this to be a separate variable, however.

What may be more puzzling is the failure to refer to class role models at this point. As we endeavored to show in Chapter Four and the succeeding chapters, the actual effect of these role models depends upon the configuration of interests in specific historical settings. Thus the aristocratic role models had decisive influence on nineteenth-century British and Prussian administrative elite role definitions because of the special position of the administrative elites and educational elites in relation to the noble and bourgeois classes. As a result certain aspects of the aristocratic role (rejection of material manipulation, hence of scientific-technological component in elite education; rural nostalgia as a rejection of metropolitan influence) were mediated to the five factors we identify. On the other hand, the bourgeois role model of specialized achievement provided in some circumstances a basis for the development interventionist definition. In itself, however, specialization was an indeterminate factor. In other historical circumstances types of specialized achievement which were not conducive to development became salient. Achievement measured by specialized accomplishment in literary or legal subjects was more congruent with aristocratic values and styles than were specializations which were instrumental for development. As we pointed out earlier in this chapter, the explanation of how the accommodation between aristocratic and bourgeois role models occurred is crucial to our general approach. In the present abstraction from specific historical circumstances, however, we must prescind from explaining mediating factors.

From the point of view of this study breadth of recruitment is also an indeterminate factor. In the special historical circumstances of two of the societies which have followed the quasi-ascriptive model (Britain and Prussia) restricted recruitment aggravated the tendency to accommodate the aristocratic role aspects which prevented a development interventionist role definition. Without an interest in legitimizing quasi-ascriptive recruitment, the particular elite educational formulas dominant in those societies would not have been adopted. It can be argued that a similar educational formula (classics emphasis) stressed by secondary school teachers under the Third Republic was also adopted because of their social insecurity in a society in which ascriptive status was still salient. Such an interpretation is entirely different, however, from asserting that a narrow recruitment base *in itself* obstructs a development interventionist role orientation. In fact (as discussed in Chapter Seven) precisely because French secondary school teachers were highly mobile they insisted on status symbols which were anachronistic in relation to development requirements. Similarly, the reduced recruitment of upper-class men for the British Administrative Class has not lowered its attachment to aristocratic styles. Indeed, it is quite possible that the decline of the public school element has led the less secure lower-middle-class recruits whose sole legitimizing symbols are derived from Oxbridge to cling more tightly to the literary, antiurban symbols of aristocratic status.

Conversely, the Old-Regime French administrative elite, the most ascriptively recruited of all elites examined in this study, was certainly considerably more concerned with development interventionism than contemporary Prussian and Russian administrative elites. Distinctly more open French administrative recruitment in the first half of the nineteenth century reduced the relative concern for administrative intervention, largely because of the sharp decline in administrative integration. On the other hand, the moderate narrowing of French recruitment in the late nineteenth and early twentieth centuries clearly did not produce a stronger development interventionist orientation. It can be argued that upward mobility of lower-middle-class elements during the nineteenth and early twentieth centuries helped preserve the long-range option for such an orientation among the French administrative elite. When a strong development interventionist role re-emerged after 1945, however, it was apparently accompanied by a slight narrowing of the recruitment base (see Chapter Nine).

As Soviet writers never tire of reiterating, things are different in a society without "exploiting" classes. Certainly it is true that the 1917 Revolution suddenly broadened the Russian administrative elite recruitment base (it had been slowly broadening since the middle of the nineteenth century). The French Revolution also considerably broadened the administrative elite recruiting base, but did not produce, as did the Soviet upheaval, a strong development interventionist orientation. Probably Soviet administrators' orientation has been due at least as much to the intense development interventionist impact of Leninism as to broadened recruitment. It remains to be seen whether either the impact of Leninism or extremely broad elite recruitment will persist throughout the postindustrial period.

Possibly a revolutionary political change does effect a certain opening of the administration to new currents of ideas. More generally, our observations do not suggest that differences in regimes are definitely correlated to administrative role definition in relation to development. Undemocratic regimes like those of Alexander II, Frederick II, and Napoleon III have had relatively interventionist administrations, while the reactionary Prussian regimes of the early nineteenth century as well as those of the Weimar period and the Third Republic have retrogressed in this respect.

In concluding that breadth of recruitment is indeterminate for development interventionist role definition, one should not, of course, overlook the social costs (discussed in Chapters One and Eleven) which accompany either the Maximum Ascriptive Model or the Progressive Equal Attrition Model we outlined. All our conclusions imply is that rational preferences for either recruitment model must be based on considerations other than its relation to development interventionist roles.

Toward a Theory of Socialization for Development Interventionism

Distinguishing the five factors which may be abstracted from specific historical contexts has been an essential preliminary to assessing the nomothetic significance of our exploration. Even if the factors are accepted as valid for the evolution of administrative elite roles in the four European societies examined, the factors can only constitute hypothetical variables for more general investigation. As discussed above, simple threshold levels of effectiveness can be posited for factors 1 and 2, while more precise quantitative indicators can be set for the other three factors. But extension of the universe to other societies would require preliminary investigation in depth of the societal history of the new members. One might find, for example, that what looks like metropolitan experience (say, in Washington) is actually remote from our historical models of Paris, London, and St. Petersburg. What superficially resembles the territorial experience of prefectural governors might, on closer inspection of another society, turn out to be patrimonial sinecures. A considerable mathematical component in secondary education conceivably could indicate an intense socialization toward concern for astrological prediction rather than for applying technology to the economy. In other words, we reject the validity (for the factors which are the concern of this study) of assembling "data books" of cross-national indicators unless and until indicators for each factor have been identified after thorough examination of the societal setting. Something resembling the interdisciplinary study in depth which has characterized the area approach at its best—avoiding the all too common reliance on anecdote and linguistic precosity—is a prerequisite. What this study does demonstrate, we believe, is that the factors presented can be used as variables in operational hypotheses. That is, for any particular societal context, empirical indicators can be identified which would make possible an unambiguous test of the validity of the relationship between the factors and development interventionist role definition.

The relationship of the five factors identified above to role definition constitutes what has been termed "concatenated theory"—"a set of logical empirical generalizations that possess a common focus; however, the logical relationships between such generalizations are not specified."[4] In our case, the focus for the concatenated theory is socialization. Since, in the total societal context the socialization process is an intermediate rather than an independent variable, our theoretical explanation cannot be logically complete. We cannot assert that the five factors we have identified are *sufficient*, although (at least in the cases studied) they appear to be *necessary* for maximizing development interventionist role definitions. For example, we did not find (see Chapter Three) any society in which development interventionist doctrines were unavailable; hence we cannot demonstrate that they constitute an additional necessary factor in producing development interventionist role definitions. Very likely a more extended investigation would find historical periods and non-European societies where un-

[4] Lawrence C. Mayer, *Comparative Political Inquiry: A Methodological Survey* (Homewood, Ill., 1972), p. 62.

availability of development interventionist doctrines precluded appearance of such administrative roles.

Because of its longitudinal dimension, our approach is necessarily limited to studying roles at a distance. All five factors are identified by indicators which do not depend on direct access to the subjects, as is the dependent variable, development interventionist role definition. An approach using interview methods would greatly facilitate identification and measurement of role definitions. An interview approach might very well identify a somewhat different set of variables in the socialization process. To the extent to which the set of factors we have identified can serve as a surrogate for variables requiring direct access to the subjects, however, our set can be advantageous in many circumstances. High administrators are often difficult to interview. Even when they can be approached personally, their recall of biographical data is often inferior to the kind of information which our sources have assembled from official records.[5] Whether or not our variables are really able to substitute can only be determined by applying them hypothetically in a broader empirical context.

POLICY IMPLICATIONS

More than most branches of social inquiry, analysis of administrative phenomena has been influenced by policy considerations. There is nothing wrong with this perspective. Concern for "relevance," far from being an invention of the 1960's, has dominated most fruitful social investigation. It would be absurd to pretend that this study was undertaken in a spirit of pure intellectual curiosity or antiquarian interest. We attacked the problem because we were convinced that administrative elite role definition is crucial for contemporary societies, and our pursuit of the analysis has only strengthened this conviction. An extended treatment of the relevance of the topic for policy would be out of place. Some implications we have treated elsewhere.[6] For the most part the reader will be able to draw his own conclusions. Four types of policy consideration ought at least to be outlined, however.

The first consideration is the delicacy of applying "lessons" derived from administrative experience. Earlier in this chapter five factors

[5] See Blau and Duncan, p. 15, on the inaccuracy of oral informants' autobiographical statements.

[6] John A. Armstrong, "Old-Regime Administrative Elites: Prelude to Modernization in France, Prussia, and Russia," *International Review of Administrative Sciences*, XXXVIII (1972), 38-40.

were presented as hypothetical influences on role definition. From the policy perspective, these factors appear not as hypotheses, but as *prescriptions*; most of the preceding discussion can be readily translated into prescriptive language. The decision-maker concerned with producing development interventionist role definitions might seek to maximize all the factors, although (as we noted earlier) such an effort would not entail "one best way" of administrative socialization, since maximization can be achieved by manipulating different stages of the socialization process. Historically, policy-makers have manipulated this process to influence administrative role definitions. To take only the most outstanding recent example (see Chapter Nine), the E.N.A. represents a deliberate effort to enhance administrative integration (factor 3) and systematic economics training (factor 5). Conscious manipulation of factor 4 (scientific-technological education component) in order specifically to influence administrative roles has been rarer (although Tsarist closed institutions approximated such manipulation) because secondary schooling affects the entire societal elite. Deliberate manipulation of factors 1 and 2 has not been apparent, although it is entirely conceivable. What needs emphasizing is that none of these factors can be applied as prescriptions without careful analysis of the social context in which manipulation must be carried out.

A second, broader policy consideration is the *efficacy* of development interventionist role definitions among high administrators. At the start of this book we cautioned that, because we did not intend to pursue a total societal analysis, we could not demonstrate that variation in role definitions actually affects economic development. Certainly it cannot be claimed that a development interventionist role definition is a *sufficient* condition for development. Even within the administrative context other conditions (e.g., an adequate body of subordinate officials) may be important. Moreover, since development interventionist role definitions have not always been present in the four societies we examine, these roles cannot be a *necessary* condition for economic development. Historically, a very efficacious substitute (discussed in Chapter Three and elsewhere) has been private entrepreneurial initiative.

This conclusion does not mean that the significance of development interventionist role definitions is trivial. Always present to a considerable degree in France and Russia, administrative intervention *may* have been essential for economic development there. As suggested earlier in this chapter, however, the total societal explanations which present this interpretation contain grave methodological difficulties. What is more certain is that economic expansion, as well as reallocation of resources, has become increasingly dependent on central intervention (see Chapter Thirteen). Moreover, improvisations (like the K.R.A. or Lloyd George's businessmen committees during World War I) appear to be increasingly impracticable. Consequently, in the postindustrial period an obstructionist or even a retreatist administrative elite to some extent constitutes a handicap to economic growth, as even the West Germans have found in their E.E.C. involvement.

Obviously an administrative elite with an effective role in development poses certain problems for the political order. For the most part, these problems are related to *maintenance of administrative responsiveness*. While most of this third policy consideration lies outside our scope, at certain points we have been able to approach it obliquely. Will narrowly recruited high administrators socialized to the values of their upper social strata be responsive either to other publics or to political leadership recruited on a different basis? Analysis of the ideological nature of legitimizations commonly presented for narrow recruitment and socialization provides a partial answer to this question. Time and again, the interests of the administrative elite or the upper strata from which it was recruited have taken precedence. It is hardly novel to point out, for example, that the celebration of the *Rechtsstaat* owes as much to administrative elite interests as to abstract concern for the rule of law. To be sure one must not lose sight of the possibility (in this case the probability) that a device like the *Rechtsstaat*, advanced ideologically to further group interests, may embody a more general societal value. The British slogan "Civil Service democracy" and its analogues in other countries appear to have less general utility, even though they are rarely identified as ideological. Assertion of in-group equality may be a most effective protection against pressures from the general public. Every oligarchy has tended toward internal equality as a device for maintaining solidarity against subject populations. There is, of course, a hypothesis (never fully tested) that equality in face-to-face relationships fosters democratic behavior in broader social contexts. Even if this proposition is valid for the relationship of small free associations (churches, schools, neighborhoods) to the great society, it hardly applies when the small group at issue (like the boarding school or the administrative elite) is perceived by its members as a privileged minority. Conversely, hierarchical subordination may be conducive to administrative officials' acceptance of outside authority legitimized by general societal values, whether these are hereditary succession or democratic election. To put the matter another way, easy relationships of equality and mutual accommodation within an administrative elite, far from demonstrating its responsiveness, may indicate that the elite has escaped control of the formally legitimized authorities.

In Chapter Nine the issue of technocracy was briefly raised. Frequently technocracy is seen as another form of administrative irresponsiveness. We doubt that that side of the issue is salient, for the technically oriented administrators we have encountered appear to have acquired little truly autonomous authority. Instead they have depended on strong central regimes, frequently dictatorial. The most that can be said is that the technically trained official is perhaps less sensitive than others to the credentials of the masters he serves. Probably the most serious deficiency of administrators with exclusively technological backgrounds is their tendency—noted repeatedly in Chapters Nine and Ten—to excessive resource expenditure and to neglect of the impact of development projects upon human values.

Today this fourth major policy consideration, the relationship between various types of administrative elite socialization and the *costs of economic development* to the human and the natural environment, is extremely pertinent. According to one currently prominent body of opinion, the very effort to increase material output is wrong. A more extreme opinion contends that "domination of nature" for the purpose of increasing material output has been a fundamental flaw of modern European civilization. If we did not reject both of these positions we would probably not have undertaken the present study, for we readily concede that the direction of research is set by broad assumptions about what is socially valuable. We believe, indeed, that economic development and the transformation of the natural environment rank among the great accomplishments of modern Europe and its progeny. For us—as for so many of the authors we have drawn upon—even peripheral aspects of this high human adventure are fascinating. Nor is it easy to see how this development can be abruptly interrupted without producing calamities infinitely greater than its *controlled* continuation can entail.

Having stated this position frankly, we believe that it is possible to take into account moderate "environmentalist" criticism without rejecting the conclusion that a development interventionist administrative elite is desirable. In the first place, control of any kind of resource utilization requires central planning and supervision. As long as societies dependent on advanced technology exist, any successful attempt to minimize environmental costs will depend heavily upon the activity of administrators. Secondly, rationally directed economic activity may produce enormous growth, even in strictly material terms, with stable or even reduced inputs of scarce raw materials. An obvious consideration, but one which escapes many critics, is that increase in material production need not imply increased output as measured in gross physical categories such as tons of steel, acres of concrete, or millions of automobiles. Miniaturized electric systems consume fewer physical resources than older systems. A highly sophisticated steam-electric generating plant minimizing pollution may require less physical resource input than an old-fashioned one, but by almost any value standard the former represents an increase in material well-being for the population affected. Shifts to types of production which minimize resource depletion and pollution will not occur automatically, however. Reassessment of values to emphasize end products with lower impact on the environment is even less likely to occur without coordinated planning. Recent industrial trends such as the proliferation of non-degradable plastics or destructive mining and forestry practices appear to indicate the inadequacy of market forces as the sole guide to innovation.

On the other hand, environmentalists have rightly suspected that administrative intervention is no panacea. Certainly the Soviet record—marked by gigantomania, lavish expenditure of raw materials, and severe pollution—indicates that unrestrained central administrative control can produce the same results as uncontrolled market mechanisms, or worse. As we saw in Chapters Nine and Eleven, many of the defects of Soviet administration have been due to the one-sided socialization of the administrative elite. A narrow engineering training reinforced by simplistic adherence to production credos like Taylorism and by the rigidities of the command economy mechanism have produced inordinate emphasis on gross categories of physical output. These factors have also produced an extraordinary insensitivity to human values—in the here and now—adversely affected by exaggerated emphasis on material production.

The analysis might lead some to argue that the way to avoid insensitive administrative intervention is to rely on humanistically trained administrators like the Oxbridge B. A. or the German *Jurist*. Attachment to the quaint or the bucolic, devotion to nonmaterialist interests like the classics might appear to condition administrators to reject policies which injure the physical environment. This argument is particularly appealing if one is personally acquainted with the admirable personal values of high administrators from these backgrounds. We must, however, reject this solution. A major reason, explored at length in Chapter Ten, is the impediment which archaic values and styles pose to effective intervention in complex modern economies. Unless one expects it simply to sabotage the technological order, a retreatist elite cannot be expected to solve the problems of runaway economic development. Instead, such an elite becomes an increasingly costly irrelevancy. A somewhat more subtle reason is the fact that inculcation of the type of humanistic values under consideration, like Humboldt's

Bildung, has nearly always depended on elitist socialization. Without questioning these values as goals for individuals, one can doubt that this kind of socialization is suitable as a guide for maximizing values for an entire society.

Rejection of the notion of relying upon top administrators trained in law and letters to control the excesses of economic development does not mean that one need reject participation of such elements in a *balanced* administrative elite. In Chapter Ten we saw how the minor but significant position of the Council of State provides a sense of the value of legal norms and human considerations for contemporary French administration. Similarly, a technically trained component well integrated in the administrative elite may be very useful. On a broader European scale (one day, we hope, from the Atlantic to the Urals) the administrative traditions of each of the four great societies can contribute to the enrichment of a united administrative elite. We believe, nevertheless, that the dominant element in a dynamic but prudent European administration will be men with broad economics training, embracing deep appreciation of technology and the social sciences as well as law and the humanities.

On Quantitative Data

I

T HROUGHOUT this book quantitative data has been presented not as definitive compilations but as approximate indicators for propositions. The data is derived from sources of varying reliability; frequently the sources do not provide saturation coverage for the universes indicated in our table headings, but rely on some portion or "sample." We have not used such "samples" unless we consider them sufficiently representative for our own very approximate purposes, but the reader should consult the original source before endeavoring to use such incomplete data for *his* purposes.

As discussed in Chapter Two, the comparative method demands that one clearly establish (usually through examination of qualitative evidence) the in-system relevance of each quantitative indicator. Comparison of curricula distribution, for example, is meaningful only after one has examined the significance of subjects in each national educational context and for each period.

Most of the data presented in the text or in accompanying tables could be explained reasonably satisfactorily in the footnotes. Because of the large but incalculable error almost inevitable in the data we employ, complicated mathematical analysis has rarely been appropriate. Generally correlation coefficients have not been calculated. Only rarely has calculation of statistical probability appeared useful, for only gross differences can receive serious attention (since most data relates either to universes or to portions of indeterminable universes, statistical significance tests in the narrower sense of the term would in any case be inapplicable). Usually we have simply selected data from the relatively few sources indicated in each footnote, collapsed categories, performed simple recomputations, and standardized by reducing the original numbers to percentages. For those who may find the data attractive for additional manipulation, absolute numbers (N's) are presented in the tables or in the footnotes. Only rarely (in the instances treated in the footnotes) have we made our own estimates or interpolations and then only when the inference appeared obvious.

For two major types of indicators, more complicated reassessment of the source data has been necessary. The general historian (and no doubt other readers) will find our procedures unfamiliar if not suspect. Obtaining approximate series through interpolation and even by informed guesses is, however, a common procedure in economics (and economic history) and in some other branches of the social sciences like demography. In view of the importance of the two indicators to our general conclusions, we have considered similar procedures to be justified. Precise description of all the measures and procedures we have employed would require another volume. In order both to permit replication and to warn the reader against overconfidence in the exactitude of our results, however, a somewhat extended discussion of these procedures appears to be in order. We hope that our tentative estimates will stimulate monographic efforts to generate more precise data.

II

Since we do not consider social class (as defined in Chapter Four) to be necessarily the fundamental factor affecting ideology, occupational groups become salient for the genetic aspect of our investigation. The major indicator of the stability of these occupational groups is identity of occupation between father and son. On the other hand, differences between fathers' and sons' occupations (e.g., between clergyman and educator), as discussed at some length in Chapter Seven, may be an important indicator of group interests. As this example indicates, not all pertinent mobility patterns directly involve administrators, but those which do are particularly important for our consideration. Apart from the effect on group interests, and hence on ideology, parental occupation (as discussed in Chapter Five) may have a major bearing on socialization for the administrative role. Consequently, it has been crucial for us to determine the approximate extent of intergenerational occupational identity among elite administrators (as indicated in Table II) and only slightly less important to determine other occupations of fathers of elite administrators (Table III).

Nearly 50 "samples" providing fairly detailed information on fathers' backgrounds for considerable numbers of elite administrators have been located in the published literature (in many cases a single publication provides several samples). In very few instances are these either "saturation samples" or anything approaching random samples. More commonly, the authors have examined a group of officials for whom biographical documentation was at hand, or who were available for interviews. Some of the samples are smaller than the universe of elite administrators, others somewhat larger (e.g., all German law students). Where portions of the sample were indicated as "unknown," or otherwise indeterminable by fathers' occupations, they were eliminated from consideration. Consequently, sample size (N) is the *known* portion of the group used in each case. Some of these samples are so obviously biased in one dimension (e.g., Saar officials in a predominantly Roman Catholic area would very likely have fewer clergyman fathers than Prussia, on the average, Halle students in a strongly Lutheran area would have more), that adjustments are imperative. Another kind of indispensable adjustment (mainly for recent French and British data) has been interpolation of subcategories (mainly estimated distribution of category "higher cadres and officials" between public and private sectors). As a result, French and British estimates in Table III are generally less reliable than German and Russian figures presented there. For other data groups, distortions are not obvious. Attempts to adjust for those biases which we judge present would inject an undesirable subjective element. Hence, in calculating the figures presented in Table III we have followed two procedures which are logically disparate, but which one may hope will provide the best practical results. All data was attributed to a year approximating the subject's induction into service (usually this meant subtracting twenty from the year for which data was gathered for men in advanced posts, as we did for groups like entrepreneurs at several points in the text). After this procedure, when there are only one or two available samples for a given country and period, we have adjusted figures according to our best judgment. When there are three to six samples, we have aggregated the data by taking the unweighted arithmetic average for each category (after the obvious kind of adjustment indicated above).

For the most important category, the father-son identity as elite administrators presented in Table II, we have added a slightly different procedure. After eliminating extremes which appear due to heavily distorted samples, we have indicated the range within which the data under each category almost certainly falls. We have then used the central tendency of each category as the basis for the graph presented in Figure 6. This procedure has permitted separate estimates (for the Continental countries) of the relationship during the last two preindustrial generations, although other fathers' occupations data is too slight to warrant such separation of these two periods in Table III.

Sources of the data, nature of the sample, and approximate number of administrators (where available) included are as follows:

FRANCE

Preindustrial: Gruder, p. 191 (*intendants de province*, eighteenth century, N=93); Daumard, *La Bourgeoisie*, p. 283 (Paris officials, c. 1810); Daumard, "Les Elèves de l'Ecole Polytechnique," p. 227 (1815-30, N=1,437).

Take-Off: Daumard, "Les Elèves," p. 227 (1831-47, N=2,215).

Industrial, Post-World War I Generation: Lalumière, p. 42 (1919-45, Financial Inspectors, N=c. 200); Lalumière, p. 39 (elite administrators, c. 1932, N=153); Siwek-Pouydesseau, *Le Corps Préfectoral*, p. 30 (c. 1930, N=c. 100); Bresard, p. 534 (c. 1930, N=c. 140); Bottomore, "La Mobilité," p. 174 (Sci Pol students, 1944-50, N=7,126). The last group is on the borderline between industrial and postindustrial, but is placed in the former because of the nature of Sci Pol enrollment in the immediate post-World War II period.

Postindustrial: All groups consist of persons successful in E.N.A. university competition and therefore include a sizeable contingent of persons who eventually enter diplomacy and lower administrative posts. Feyzioglu, p. 178 (1953, N=115); France, Ecole Nationale d'Administration, *Epreuves et Statistiques des Concours de 1953* (Paris, 1954), p. 172 (N=85); France, Ecole Nationale d'Administration, *Epreuves et Statistiques des Concours de 1964* (Paris, 1965), p. 121 (N=79); Henry Parris, "Twenty Years of l'Ecole Nationale d'Administration," *Public Administration*, XLIII (1965), 404 (1963, N=c. 150).

GREAT BRITAIN

Take-Off: Guttsman, *English Ruling Class*, p. 237 (clerkship nominees, 1857, N=493).

Industrial, Pre-World War I Generation: Kelsall, p. 149 (all upper-division clerks, including Indian service, etc., 1911, N=100); Kelsall, p. 150 (attaining grade above assistant secretary, 1909, N=121); Reader, p. 193 (c. 1900).

Industrial, Post-World War I Generation: Kelsall, p. 150 (ultimately attaining grade above assistant secretary, c. 1920, N=179); Kelsall, p. 150, (ultimately attaining grade above assistant secretary c. 1930, N=331).

Postindustrial: Kelsall, p. 150 (open competition entrants, 1949-52, N=223); Fulton Committee, III (1), 52 (ultimately attaining assistant secretary and above, c. 1949, N=211); Fulton Committee, III (1), 52 (assistant principals and principals, including 35 per cent female, c. 1960, N=310).

PRUSSIA

Preindustrial: Ziekursch, p. 4 (inductees in Silesia, c. 1740-1800, N=108); Conrad, p. 51 (Halle law students, 1768-71, N=327); Conrad, p. 51 (1820-22, N=284).

Take-Off: Conrad, p. 51 (1850-54, N=464).

Industrial, Pre-World War I Generation: Conrad, p. 51 (1877-81, N=436); Most, pp. 214-15 (higher officials with sons in same occupation, c. 1860, N=46); Most, pp. 214-15 (Düsseldorf *Bezirksregierung* c. 1895, N=260); Prussia, Königliches Preussisches Statistisches Landesamt, p. 436 (Prussian universities law students, 1886-91, N=738); Prussia, Königliches Preussisches Statistisches Landesamt, p. 436 (1911-12, N=1,702); Jacob, p. 138 (*Regierungspräsidenten*, c. 1904, N=20); Tisch, p. 43 (higher officials, Saarpfalz, 1917, N=369).

Industrial, Post-World War I Generation: Tietjens, p. 190 (German law students, 1930, N=c. 10,000); Zapf, p. 86 (men who eventually became higher officials in Baden-Württemberg, c. 1934); Zapf, p. 93 (men who eventually became higher officials in German Federal Republic, c. 1940, N=738); Zapf, p. 108 (men who eventually became higher state court judges in German Federal Republic, c. 1939, N=836).

Postindustrial: Wagner, p. 137 (judicial inductees, all states of German Federal Republic, 1950, N=620).

RUSSIA

Preindustrial: Walter M. Pintner, "The Social Characteristics of the Early Nineteenth-Century Russian Bureaucracy," *Slavic Review*, XXIX (1970), 435 (St. Petersburg officials, 1798-1800, N=297); *ibid.* (St. Petersburg officials, 1812-24, N=724); *ibid.*, p. 437 (top St. Petersburg officials, early nineteenth century, N=32); *ibid.* (top St. Petersburg officials, mid-nineteenth century, N=159); *ibid.* (St. Petersburg officials [all levels, including top officials just cited, to give greater weight to higher officials], mid-nineteenth century, N=1,131).

III

The procedures for arriving at career circulation patterns are far more complicated even than the procedures just discussed. Consequently, one can indicate only the most crucial steps. Because the estimates are so approximate and the practicability of replicating them is low, we have presented our findings in the text graphically rather than tabularly (Figures 7-10). By using ratios (of persons in age groups) as a basis for calculating the graph abscissas (the age levels shown on the ordinates are reasonably certain), we hope to avoid the spurious appearance of accuracy. In order to provide a maximum degree of comparability, all numbers of persons have been expressed as ratios of the number of officials estimated to obtain top posts in a given year, times ten. Ages indicated in the graphs are those at which persons *enter* a category, arbitrarily assuming that the entire male cohort "enters" the twelfth year with equal chances, and that all secondary school graduates enter higher education and then are reduced to the proportion securing the required higher educational prerequisites for the elite administrative career. On the other hand, only those actually entering the career are shown (at the same age as higher school graduation) as doing so. As indicated in Chapter Eight, these conditions, while simplified for the sake of graphic presentation, substantially reflect the reality of entrance into the administrative elite. For the same reasons, insofar as possible only the *male* component of all statistics has been presented in the graphs and tables in this Appendix.

As indicated in Chapter Eleven, one purpose of the graphs is to indicate career prospects at each age level for those who *might* enter an elite administrative career (i.e., the whole male cohort, progressively reduced to secondary school graduates and graduates of appropriate higher educational programs). For men who actually enter the service, only prospects for those starting at the bottom of the elite career ladder (where it exists) are considered. In other words, *career chances* of lateral transferees are not taken into account in the graphs, but the extent to which they occupy posts at any level must be estimated, since these posts are eliminated as prospects for inductees on the regular career ladder. Aggregate data rarely distinguishes between career officials and those transferred or promoted from outside the elite administrative career pattern. Hence (especially for the complicated French service) we have been obliged to estimate the proportions of each type of official at each level.

There are two ways in which annual appointments to a given category can be determined. The precise method is to determine how many posts are filled each year over a reasonably extended period of time (our "generation" would be suitable). If this is done, one can present both a continuous curve (which probably shows a high degree of fluctuation in annual appointments) and a central tendency for the generation. We did calculate turnover rates in this fashion for Old-Regime French and Russian governors, but omitted the annual fluctuations for the sake of conciseness (see Tables XX and XXI and the source article). In any case, one must calculate a generation-average for age at which the promotion was attained. Since even approximately reliable data was not available in published sources for an entire administrative elite for much less than a generation interval, we were reduced, at best, to calculating generation-averages both for annual promotion rates and age at promotion.

The second, inferior method is to determine approximate promotion ages. From this approximate data one can calculate the average length of time spent in grade. Unfortunately, as noted in Chapter Eleven, aggregate data sources usually give median or average ages for groups *in* office rather than on *entry* to office. In order to get the latter data (i.e., promotion ages) we have been obliged to assume, frequently, that the promotion age falls halfway between the average age of men in top office and the average age of the next highest group awaiting promotion. Neither assumption is likely to be strictly accurate. If one knows the numbers of officials in each grade at the beginning and end of a time interval (a generation or longer), one can estimate the intake by promotion which was required to maintain the number in grade. Obviously the procedure is highly subject to error because of the difficulty of determining what proportion of officials is promoted (at any given age) and what proportion remains in grade until retirement. If, however, one has a good estimate of lateral entry and attrition through resignation or death, one can utilize this procedure to arrive at very rough estimates from fragmentary data. Frequently the range of accuracy of these estimates can be controlled by reference to more accurate data from adjoining time-intervals and partial samples.

Even when fairly high accuracy for generations is attained, the intervals are so wide that precise data on demography and secondary education (which is frequently, though not always, available) would be useless. Consequently, we have used very approximate orders of magnitude for both of these stages.

IV

Both because the Administrative Class career ladder is so precisely defined and because of Roger Kelsall's excellent pioneering work, the British case is the simplest. The principal difficulty in calculating promotion rates, as Tables XXIV and XXV indicate, arises in separating "open competition" entrants (which we consider to constitute career inductees) from the high proportion of promoted men and lateral transferees mentioned in Chapter Eleven.

Lines 1, 2, and 3 present no particular difficulties. Using data in Raymond Poignant, *Education and Development in Western Europe, The United States, and the U.S.S.R.: A Comparative Study* (New York, 1969), pp. 2, 180; Great Britain, Royal Commission on the Civil Service 1953-55, *Report Presented to Parliament by Command of Her Majesty, November 1955* (London, 1955), p. 94; and Perkin, p. 122 (for 1868), one can make a rough estimate of the male cohorts and male graduates (all secondary schools, since public schools, as indi-

TABLE XXIV. CIRCULATION PATTERN: GREAT BRITAIN, INDUSTRIAL PERIOD
(Absolute Numbers)

Stage	Open Competition Entrants			For Men Attaining Next Stage Only		Transferred and Promoted from Other Services	
	Number of Persons per Year	Years in Stage	Age at Completion of Stage	Years in Stage	Age at Completion of Stage	Number of Persons per Year	Age at Completion of Stage
1. Cohort (Male)	400,000	11	11				
2. Secondary School Graduates	10,000	7	18				
3. Oxbridge Honours Graduates	1,500	4 *(For Men Ultimately Attaining Top Posts)*	22				
4. Assistant Principals and Principals	30	15	37	18	40	5	
5. Assistant Secretaries and Under Secretaries	10	15	52			8	45
6. Permanent Secretaries and Deputy Secretaries	6	8	60			4	60

TOTALS FOR LINE 4 varied from approximately 300 to 900 (1911-1939) (Kelsall, pp. 16, 40). LINES 5 and 6 (together): 1911—c. 200; 1929—296; 1939—473 (ibid.).

TABLE XXV. CIRCULATION PATTERN: GREAT BRITAIN, POSTINDUSTRIAL PERIOD
(Absolute Numbers)

Stage	Open Competition Entrants					Transferred and Promoted from Outside	
	Number of Persons per Year	Years in Stage	Age at Completion of Stage	Years in Stage	Age at Completion of Stage	Number of Persons per Year	Age at Completion of Stage
				For Men Attaining Next Stage Only			
1. Cohort (Male)	400,000	11	11				
2. Secondary School Graduates	55,000	7	18				
3. Oxbridge Honours Graduates	2,000	4	22				
		For Men Ultimately Attaining Top Posts					
4. Assistant Principals and Principals	60	16	38	18	40	60	45
5. Assistant Secretaries and Under Secretaries	40	12	50			50	51
6. Permanent Secretaries and Deputy Secretaries	7	10	60			3	

TOTALS FOR LINE 4: c. 550, 1,314.
LINES 5 and 6: 1950—c. 1,045 (Kelsall, p. 198); 1967—1,174 (Fulton Committee, IV, 38).

cated in Chapter Six, were never predominate in civil service recruitment).

For Line 3 only Oxbridge first and second class honours degrees are used (based on Finer, p. 72; Great Britain, Royal Commission on the Civil Service 1953-55, p. 94; Great Britain, *Parliamentary Papers, Sixth Report from the Estimates Committee*; Fulton Committee, III (1), p. 83).

Line 4 utilizes direct information on open competition entrants (Kelsall, p. 39, for 1890-1911; p. 101, for 1909-39; p. 53, for 1938-49; Great Britain, *Parliamentary Papers, Sixth Report from the Estimates Committee*, p. 30; and Fulton Committee, IV, 40, 234, for recent years). Kelsall also provides information on transfers at this level. For age at promotion, see Walker, p. 10 (1935); Ridley, p. 51; Fulton Committee, IV, 234, 562, as well as Kelsall, p. 198. Most of these sources give ages for all men promoted (ranging from thirty-nine to forty-two) which has to be adjusted downward slightly for career officials.

Counting assistant secretaries and under secretaries as the middle-level career group accords with usual British practice. Estimates are based on the same sources as Line 4. The slight drop in promotion age (to top rank) for the postindustrial period is based on Kelsall's calculation (p. 198) of about one-fourth serving (in the interwar period) beyond fifty-two, as compared to the Fulton Committee (IV, 234) indication that that age is high for post-World War II *career* promoted men. *Ibid.*, p. 562, indicates fifty as median promotion age.

The two top ranks are usually considered together. Fulton Committee (IV, 560) anticipates ten years in the levels (permanent secretaries frequently do not serve in the deputy rank at all), with a slight rise in actual retirement age from sixty-one (1950) to sixty-two (1964) (IV, 380). On the other hand, there are some deaths and premature resignations. Actual promotions to these levels in the six years (1960-65) were 77 (with a slight overlap; Fulton Committee, IV, 562).

V

In principle the Prussian calculation is no more difficult than the British, since the Prussian career administrative elite has always been unified. Designation of top positions is not as clear; on the other hand, the very low proportion of promotions from outside the elite or transfers from other types of positions (see Chapter Eleven) facilitates calculation. *Landräte*, as semi-particularistic officials, are disregarded throughout. The main complication is separating officials (*Referendare*, etc.) in the lower stage from inductees to the judicial service. Data is by no means as available (especially for the preindustrial and the postindustrial periods) as for Great Britain and has received little systematic attention from scholars and official analysts. Hence the calculations are more approximate than in the British case.

Lines 1 and 2 in Tables XXVI, XXVII, XXVIII, and XXIX can only be approximations, since the population of Prussia varied drastically through losses and annexations, and the number of secondary school graduates fluctuated even more. The preindustrial estimate of 550 for the latter category is made by taking one-third of the enrollment in the

TABLE XXVI. CIRCULATION PATTERN: PRUSSIA,
PREINDUSTRIAL PERIOD
(Absolute Numbers)

Stage	Number of Persons per Year	Years in Stage	Age at Completion of Stage	Number of Persons per Year
1. Cohort (Male)	60,000	11	11	
2. Secondary School Graduates	550	8	19	
3. Law Faculty Graduates	200	3	22	
		For Men Ultimately Attaining Top Administrative Posts		*Judicial Career*
4. *Auscultatoren, Referendare,* Etc.	13	5	27	60
5. *Räte, Assessoren,* Etc.	12[a]	23	50	15
6. Ministers, Ministerial Directors, Etc.	10	10	60	

[a] Plus 10 transferred from judiciary.

TOTALS FOR LINE 5: Administration: c. 1800—800 (Bonin, p. 149; Brunschwig, p. 331); Justice: c. 1800—c. 400 (major courts only, Bonin, p. 158; cf. Brunschwig, p. 153).

LINE 6: Approximately 100 Ministers and Presidents in Finance and Justice, 1794 (not all appointed from career officials; Bonin, p. 145).

Prussian universities at the end of the eighteenth century, since most secondary graduates entered universities. Blättner (pp. 144-45) provides the very varying Take-Off period figures for *Gymnasium* graduates, nearly all male; 1,600 (c. 1850) appears close to average. The graduation figures for c. 1900 were 5,800, about four-fifths male (Tröger, p. 348); by 1931 graduations had risen to 32,880 in boys' secondary schools (Germany, Länderrat des amerikanischen Besatzungsgebiets, *Statistisches Handbuch von Deutschland, 1928-1944* [Munich, 1949], pp. 619ff.). The male number had dropped (at two-thirds of the total 31,500) about in proportion to population decrease for West Germany up to about 1960.

Conrad (p. 115) gives the figure of 222 students annually taking the government service examination immediately after law school (1841-50), which is one-fifth of the average total Prussian university law enrollment. Not all graduates took the examination, whereas many graduates of non-Prussian universities did take it. Consequently, the pool of relevant law faculty graduates for the 1840's was somewhat higher than Conrad's figure suggests. An annual average of 200 eligible graduates seems reasonable for the preceding two generations. For subsequent periods, graduation data is readily available: Conrad, pp. 114-15; Blondel, p. 81; Zapf, p. 108; Prussia, Königliches Preussisches Statistisches Landesamt, p. 434; Poignant, p. 159; Germany, Federal Republic, Statistisches Bundesamt, *Statistisches Jahrbuch für die Bundesrepublik Deutschland, 1955* (Wiesbaden, 1955), p. 94; Germany, Federal Republic, Statistisches Bundesamt, *Statistisches Jahr-*

TABLE XXVII. CIRCULATION PATTERN: PRUSSIA,
TAKE-OFF PERIOD
(Absolute Numbers)

Stage	Number of Persons per Year	Years in Stage	Age at Completion of Stage	Number of Persons per Year	Age at Completion of Stage
1. Cohort (Male)	200,000	11	11		
2. *Gymnasium* Graduates	1,600	8	19		
3. Law Faculty Graduates	400	3	22		
		For Men Ultimately Attaining Top Administrative Posts		*Judicial Career*	
4. *Auscultatoren, Referendare,* Etc.	40	10	32	215	32
5. *Rate, Assessoren,* Etc.	34[a]	18	50	150	60
6. Ministers, Ministerial Directors, Etc.	15	10	60		

[a] Plus 26 transferred from judiciary.

TOTALS FOR LINE 4: 400 *Regierungsreferendare*, 2,500 total *Referendare* (Conrad, p. 118; cf. Gillis, "Aristocracy," p. 117).

LINE 5: 1,000 (Conrad, p. 117, indicates 1,150 legally trained officials for 1868; Koselleck, p. 438, 1,600 of all types of officials at this level and above for 1835). Judiciary increased from 2,573 (*ibid.*) to 6,845 (1868, Conrad, p. 117).

LINE 6: 150 (Koselleck, pp. 435, 681, indicates 73 permanent top officials in 1842; Albert Lotz, *Geschichte des deutschen Beamtentums* [Berlin, 1906], p. 580, indicates 57 in 1855 at a slightly lower level).

buch für die Bundesrepublik Deutschland, 1970 (Wiesbaden, 1970), p. 78. A moderate adjustment upward has been made to allow for graduates from outside Prussia eligible for the Prussian examination.

Circulation data for the preindustrial period is very approximate because of the enormous fluctuation in numbers of officials from decade to decade. The data in Table XXVI is intended to treat the last two to three decades before the Napoleonic invasions. Figures on inductees are essentially based on the appointments of *Auscultatoren* and *Referendare* given in Brunschwig, p. 153, who considers these categories (for the administration, but not for the judiciary) as generally nonoverlapping. Since the small annual intake of administrative *Referendare* could not meet all provincial and central middle-level posts, many were filled from the juridical career. The second juridical stage (justice *Räte*) is included to indicate the approximate overall promotion chances for beginners in both *Referendare* categories. In fact, during this period it was notorious that induction to the lower judicial ranks was vastly larger than prospective vacancies in both services required. The estimate for top posts assumes that there was a moderate proportion of direct appointees at that level, too. As Bonin indicates (p. 171), ages at appointment to all ranks varied so greatly that averages for successful men are not very meaningful. It appears, however (Brunschwig, p. 150), that six years' preparation for promotion was standard, with perhaps a year less for the favored few who alone could hope for appointment as administrative *Räte* at the corresponding age of twenty-seven. It seems reasonable to assume that, on the whole, these were the men who eventually reached the top.

In many respects it is even more difficult to estimate circulation patterns for officials during the take-off period. A minor problem (too complicated to treat here) arises from calculation of annual *Assessor* turnover. The drastic changes in intake at other levels are harder to estimate adequately. The totals in Table XXVII are reached by considering the fact that judicial positions increased very rapidly after 1860, whereas administrative posts were fairly stable. Hence the proportion of openings in the administration appears, until the 1860's, to be between one-fourth and one-third of the total of judicial and administrative *Räte*. On the other hand, Gillis (*Prussian Bureaucracy*, p. 195) estimates that 26 per year of the administrative middle-level posts were filled from the lower judiciary (1840-60). Thus it seems appropriate to assume that only 15-20 per cent of *Referendare*, etc. were assigned to *Regierungen*, since these were posts which could be filled at discretion. We assume a slightly shorter period in the induction stage than Gillis finds for the Rhineland (approximately 11.5 years, including examination preparation and waiting for promotion after it

—"Aristocracy," p. 118). Other promotion ages are calculated from scattered instances and are very approximate.

Circulation data for the industrial period is more certain. Despite the very long period (1870-1933) involved, as Table XXVIII indicates, totals for all official grades were very stable. As noted in Chapter Ten, the administrative induction stage (*Regierungsreferendare*), which is indicated in the table, existed only during a portion of this period. Law faculty study was lengthened to four years and the *Regierungsreferendare* stage (see Chapter Ten) was also set at that length. The complication for considering the *Assessor* stage is minor, but too intricate to cover in detail here.

TABLE XXVIII. CIRCULATION PATTERN: PRUSSIA,
INDUSTRIAL PERIOD
(*Absolute Numbers*)

Stage	Number of Persons per Year	Years in Stage	Age at Completion of Stage	Number of Persons per Year	Age at Completion of Stage
1. Cohort (Male)	350,000	11	11		
2. Secondary School Graduates	5,000	8	19		
3. Law Faculty Graduates	2,000	4	23		
		For Men Ultimately Attaining Top Administrative Posts		*Judicial Career*	
4. *Referendare*	80	4	27	1,100	26
5. *Räte, Assessoren*	60[a]	24	51	150	50
6. Career Ministers, Ministerial Directors, Etc.	25	10	60		

a Plus about 10 transferred from judiciary.

TOTALS FOR LINE 4: 3,500 (c. 1883-1913, Blondel, p. 56; Prussia, Königliches Preussisches Statistisches Landesamt, p. 481). Of these about 250 were *Regierungsreferendare*, 3,250 were *Gerichtsreferendare*.

LINE 5: 1,700 (see accompanying text).

LINE 6: 250 (see accompanying text).

The estimate for completion of the *Rat* stage (by men who secured promotion) is much more approximate. By the Weimar period there were 410 *Räte* in Reich offices (Arnold Brecht and Comstock Glaser, *The Art and Technique of Administration in German Ministries* [Cambridge, Mass., 1940], p. 26), plus 500 or 600 in Prussian *Regierungen* (cf. for 1900, Lotz, p. 580) and perhaps 400 more in Prussian central agencies. Consequently, an annual promotion to the *Rat* post of about

70 a year (perhaps 60 from *Assessoren* and 10 directly from the judiciary) seems reasonable. The estimate for top posts is derived from a turnover of 9 in top Reich posts (1871-90) estimated from Rudolf Morsey, *Die oberste Reichsverwaltung unter Bismarck, 1867-1890* (Münster, 1957), p. 250, in addition to the yearly turnover among 34 top Prussian provincial officials (1901, Lotz, p. 580), plus about 200 top Prussian central posts. Under the Weimar Republic the proportion of central officials who were career administrators declined, but the overall number of officials increased somewhat.

Because of scarcity of data and the complications introduced by the consideration of state administrations, it is very difficult to arrive at a reasonable circulation pattern for the German Federal Republic. We are, of course, interested only in officials with legal training. Estimates of their proportion in the total state and Federal service vary from 32 per cent (for 1965, Nevil Johnson, in Ridley, p. 138) to 65 per cent for the mid-1950's (Zapf, p. 88, average of Federal and state samples). The proportion of 40 per cent ("Struktur des Bundespersonals: Ergebnis der Personalstrukturerhebung am 2. October 1968," *Wirtschaft und Statistik*, 1970, Heft 3, p. 141, Federal service only, excluding railroads, post office, etc.) seems reasonable. If two-fifths of the 89,347 regular higher service (*Hoheits- und Kammereiverwaltung*) for 1954 (German Federal Republic, Statistisches Bundesamt, *Statistisches Jahrbuch*, 1955, p. 410) is calculated, 36,000 is obtained, of whom about one-fourth are judges (cf. Wagner, p. 129; Rolland A. A. Chaput de Saintonge, *Public Administration in Germany: A Study in Regional and Local Administration in Land Rheinland-Pfalz* [London, 1961], p. 347, for a small sample). It is assumed that the average service is 30 years (for promoted and nonpromoted officials together). Thus average annual entrance to middle-level (*Assessor-Räte*) posts may be estimated at 900 per year, with 300 more for the judiciary. The latter figure coincides with the actual figure of 620 entering judgeships, 1956-57 (Wagner, p. 136). The number of *Gerichtsreferendare* (as indicated in Chapter Ten, this is the only induction stage) was about 9,000, with 2,400 entering and completing during these two years (*ibid.*). These figures would suggest an oversupply of candidates approximating late eighteenth- and mid-nineteenth-century Prussian conditions. In fact, a backlog of aging *Räte* arising from World War II circumstances, plus a rapidly expanding service, appear to have made the high ratio of candidates to openings a transitory phenomenon in the Federal Republic. In order to indicate conditions at the beginning of the postindustrial period, we have adjusted the number of *Referendare* downward, however. Ages are estimated from Zapf, p. 87 (average age for *Räte*) assuming equal distribution of official age categories (from 27 to 60); compare the approximately equivalent distribution for judges (Wagner, p. 134). On the other hand, our estimates on promotion to top posts are from very fragmentary data. An estimate of 150 annual top administrative vacancies could be derived by assuming that the proportion for judges (derived with considerable adjustment from Wagner, p. 134) applies proportionately to administrative officials. Since the total West German top-level officials obtained by this procedure (2,200) is very high in proportion to our other administrative elites, we have arbitrarily restricted annual top vacancies by assuming that the proportion applies only to the *Federal* higher service (about one-tenth of the total West German higher *Beamten* in 1954)

TABLE XXIX. CIRCULATION PATTERN: WEST GERMANY,
POSTINDUSTRIAL PERIOD
(Absolute Numbers)

Stage	Number of Persons per Year	Years in Stage	Age at Completion of Stage	Number of Persons per Year	Age at Completion of Stage
1. Cohort (Male)	330,000	11	11		
2. Secondary School Graduates	21,000	8	19		
3. Law Faculty Graduates	2,400	4	23		
		For Men Ultimately Attaining Top Administrative Posts		*Judicial Career*	
4. *Referendare*	2,000[a]	4	27	2,000[a]	27
5. *Räte, Assessoren*	900	18	45	300	45
6. Career Ministers, Ministerial Directors, Etc.	30	15	60	50	60

[a] All *Referendare* (identical groups).
TOTALS FOR LINE 4: 7,000 (on basis of 3½ years' service).
LINE 5: 22,000 (see accompanying text).
LINE 6: 2,200 (see accompanying text).

plus an equal number for all state services combined (i.e., 20 per cent of vacancies calculated above, or 30 per year).

VI

In contrast to the British and Prussian cases, French experience is divided into three distinct stages (the take-off period presents so many difficulties that we were obliged to abandon efforts to calculate a circulation pattern for it). Male cohorts and secondary school graduates for all periods could be estimated reasonably accurately, since the population was stable both because of low growth rates and territorial stability. See especially E. Levasseur, *La Population Française: Histoire de la Population avant 1789 et Démographie de la France Comparée à Celle des Autres Nations au XIXᵉ Siècle*, Vol. 1 (Paris, 1889), 277; 11 (1891), 261; Gerbod, pp. 10, 12, 141; Liard, 1, 11ff.; Poignant, pp. 60-61.

The unified preindustrial elite (eighteenth century) poses relatively few problems (see Table XXX). We assume that the entrance stage consisted of *fermiers* (for reasons discussed in Chapter Ten) plus the minority of *maîtres des requêtes* who became *intendants de province*.

TABLE XXX: CIRCULATION PATTERN: FRANCE,
PREINDUSTRIAL PERIOD
(Absolute Numbers)

Stage	Number of Persons per Year	Years in Stage	Age at Completion of Stage
1. Cohort (Male)	240,000	11	11
2. Secondary School Graduates	2,500	7	18
3. Law Faculty Graduates and Magistrate Service	800	8	26
		For Men Ultimately Attaining Top Administrative Posts	
4. Maîtres des Requêtes, Apprentice *Fermiers*	12	10	36
5. Intendants de Province, Fermiers	8	12	48
6. Conseillers d'Etat	4	10	58

TOTALS FOR LINE 4: 120, based on 80-90 *maîtres* plus 30-40 *fermiers-adjoints*.
LINE 5: 70–30 *intendants* and 40 *fermiers*.
LINE 6: 37 *conseillers d'état*.
It should be noted that a considerably larger total (about 500) is reached by including all royal central officials listed in the *Almanach Royal* (1705) (H. J. Martin, II, 903). Unfortunately, we have no career pattern data for these other categories.

Gruder, Mousnier, Ardashev, *Les Intendants*, and Armstrong, "Old-Regime Governors," provide information on turnover and ages of appointment in the latter category and Thirion, pp. 517ff., provides information on *fermiers* (1723-89). The number of *conseiller d'état* vacancies is estimated by assuming a rate of attrition (from age or infirmity) equivalent to *intendants* who remained in office as long as they were able to.

Computation of Tables XXXI and XXXII is far more difficult. Stage 3 can be obtained by adding the annual graduates of the Sci Pol and the Polytechnique. Perhaps 300 of the 950 French students in the Sci

TABLE XXXI. CIRCULATION PATTERN: FRANCE, INDUSTRIAL PERIOD
(Absolute Numbers)

Stage	Number of Persons in Stage	Years in Stage	Age at Completion of Stage
1. Cohort (Male)	300,000	11	11
2. Secondary School Graduates	6,000	7	18
3. Sci Pol (and Law Faculty) Graduates *plus* Polytechnique Graduates (and Higher Engineering Schools)	450	6	24
		For Men Ultimately Attaining Top Administrative Posts (Average of Corps)	
OVERALL TOTALS			
4. Beginning Level	58	13	38
5. Intermediate Level	20	10	49
6. Top Level	13	13	61

Stage	Attaining Top Administrative Posts			Successful to Next Stage Only		Recruitment, Promotions, Etc.
	Number of Persons per Year	Years in Stage	Age at Completion of Stage	Years in Stage	Age at Completion of Stage	Number of Persons per Year
COUNCIL OF STATE						
4. *Auditeurs*	3	12	36	16	40	0
5. *Maîtres des Requêtes*	2	12	48	13	53	1
6. *Conseillers d'Etat*	2	15	63			1
FINANCIAL INSPECTORATE						
4. *Inspecteurs-Adjoints, Inspecteurs* Third and Second Class	7	11	35	17	41	0
5. *Inspecteurs* First Class	4	7	43	7	48	0
6. *Inspecteurs-Généraux*, Ministerial Directors, Bank Directors, Etc.	3	18	58			1
PREFECTURAL CORPS						
4. Subprefects, Etc.	20	15	43			7
5. Prefects	2	8	52			
6. *Conseillers d'État*, Ministerial Directors, Etc.	(1)[a]	10	62			[a]
TECHNICAL CORPS						
4. Apprentice and Ordinary Engineers	25	17	40	10	36	10
5. Chief Engineers	10	11	52			4
6. *Inspecteurs-Généraux*, Etc.	5	9	60			2

[a] See Chapters Ten and Twelve for details on prefectural corps career patterns.

TOTAL OFFICIALS BY GRADE AND CORPS

	Council of State	Accounts Court	Financial Inspectorate	Prefectural Corps	Technical Corps
C. 1900					
4. Beginning Level	35	30	50	300	340
5. Intermediate Level	35	25	45	100	110
6. Top Level	35	25	25	–	45
C. 1930					
4. Beginning Level	47	40	65	300	420
5. Intermediate Level	43	35	65	100	137
6. Top Level	39	30	30	–	51

TABLE XXXII. CIRCULATION PATTERN: FRANCE, POSTINDUSTRIAL PERIOD
(Absolute Numbers)

Stage	Number of Persons in Stage	Years in Stage	Age at Completion of Stage
1. Cohort (Male)	300,000	11	11
2. Secondary School Graduates	16,000	7	18
3. E.N.A. (and Law Faculty) Graduates *plus* Polytechnique Graduates (and Higher Engineering Schools)	300	6	25[a]
[a] Slightly lower for engineering graduates			
		For Men Ultimately Attaining Top Administrative Posts (Average of Corps)	
OVERALL TOTALS			
4. Beginning Level	57	10	35
5. Intermediate Level	35	10	45
6. Top Level	16	12	55

	Number of Persons per Year	For Men Ultimately Attaining Top Administrative Posts		For Men Successful to Next Stage Only		Outside Recruitment, Promotions, Etc.
		Years in Stage	Age at Completion of Stage	Years in Stage	Age at Completion of Stage	Number of Persons per Year
COUNCIL OF STATE						
4. *Auditeurs*	7	6	31	7	32	0
5. *Maîtres des Requêtes*	6	9	40	9	41	0
6. *Conseillers d'État*	2	16	56			2
FINANCIAL INSPECTORATE						
4. *Inspecteurs-Adjoints, Inspecteurs* Third and Second Class	8	10	35	20	45	0
5. *Inspecteurs* First Class	7	10	45	10	55	0
6. *Inspecteurs-Généraux*, Ministerial Directors, Bank Directors, Etc.	6	10	55			3
PREFECTURAL CORPS						
4. Subprefects	7	14	39	20	44	0
5. Prefects	3	12	51			3
6. Miscellaneous	uncertain					
TECHNICAL CORPS						
4. Apprentice and Ordinary Engineers	28	16	39	18	41	9
5. Chief Engineers	12	11	50			3
6. *Inspecteurs-Généraux*, Etc.	6	9	59			0

TOTAL OFFICIALS BY GRADE AND CORPS (Mid-1950's)

	Total	Council of State	Accounts Court	Financial Inspectorate	Prefectural Corps	Technical Corps
4. Beginning Level	784	44	36	84	200	420
5. Intermediate Level	495	45	35	91	150	174
6. Top Level	314	48	32	34	130	70

Pol (c. 1930, Sharp, p. 111) were graduated each year. Polytechnique graduation varied from 100 to 200. These figures appear to conform to the high ratio of candidates (six or seven) known to have appeared for each *Grands Corps* vacancy. For calculation of stages 4-6, separate estimates of patterns in each of the four administrative *Grands Corps* and the two elite technical corps is unavoidable. Since our data on the Accounts Court (see Gaston Jèze, "Le Recrutement des Membres de la Cour des Comptes," *Revue de Science et de Législation Financière*, VIII [1910], 233) is extremely limited, we have simply doubled the Council of State estimates. This probably results in a slight overestimation of the totals for the elite corps which we consider to comprise the elite career pattern. In calculating "average of corps" figures for "age at completion" of stage and "years in stage" we have taken the arithmetic average of *five* corps (assuming the figure for the Accounts Court to be the same as for the Council of State). This procedure weights the results in favor of the small *Grands Corps* and against the larger technical corps (the two being combined have only one weight in the average). We believe that this weighting reflects the real importance of the corps and their salience in the perceptions of the whole administrative elite.

Calculations for the Council of State are based on Kessler, pp. 150, 253, and Freedeman, p. 178, for both industrial and postindustrial periods, and on Leon Aucoc, *Le Conseil d'Etat avant et depuis 1789: Ses Transformations, Ses Travaux et Son Personnel* (Paris, 1876), pp. 142ff.; Henri Chardon, *L'Administration de la France: Les Fonctionnaires* (Paris, 1908), pp. 402-405; and Sharp, p. 148, for the industrial period. These varied sources permit a fairly reliable estimate. Lalumière's data on Financial Inspectors for the postindustrial period and the late industrial period is supplemented (for the latter period) by A. Hamon, pp. 222ff., and Sharp, p. 113. Sharp (pp. 30-40, 113) provides most of the technical corps data for the industrial period. Ridley, p. 109, supplemented by Meynaud, *La Technocratie*, p. 53, and Fulton Committee, I, 136, provide information for the postindustrial period, but considerable interpolation has been necessary. Prefectural data is drawn for the most part from Siwek-Pouydesseau, *Le Corps Préfectoral*, pp. 62, 66, 73, supplemented by B. Chapman, *Prefects*, p. 152. As is discussed in Chapters One and Twelve, the prefectural "career" was highly irregular under the Third Republic. Most prefects were appointed from outside (frequently for political reasons) rather than promoted from lower prefectural grades, and the prefect frequently closed his career in another post. For our purposes we are concerned only with those who transferred to another *Grands Corps*, usually as *conseiller d'état* (for which they constituted about one-half of the outside recruitment).

VII

Both the very broad recruitment base of the *chin* system and scarcity of data make calculating Tsarist Russian circulation patterns (see Tables XXXIII and XXXIV) difficult. Male cohorts can be estimated fairly satisfactorily as a little over 1 per cent of populations (Frank Lorimer, *The Population of the Soviet Union: History and Prospects* [Geneva, 1946], p. 11, with adjustments for added territories, suggests about 40,000,000 for 1800). The total 1859 population (*ibid.*, pp. 208-10) was about 71,000,000. Secondary school enrollment for 1800 was about 8,000, reaching 14,000 by 1825 and 17,403 (in regular *gimnazii* alone) by 1838 (Arcadius Kahan, "Social Structure, Public Policy, and the Development of Education in Czarist Russia," in Charles Arnold Anderson and Mary J. Bowman [eds.], *Education and Economic Development* [Chicago, 1965], p. 365; Nicholas Hans, *History of Russian Educational Policy, 1701-1917* [New York, 1964], p. 331; N. P. Eroshkin, *Ocherki Istorii Gosudarstvennykh Uchrezhdenii Dorevoliutsionnoi Rossii* [Moscow, 1960], p. 216). But the proportion graduating was very small. Perhaps 500 is reasonable for the early part of the nineteenth century, including the elite *lycée*-type institutions and men who studied abroad. University graduation (see Chapter Nine) was virtually irrelevant at that time. For 1856, secondary school enrollment was 19,098, rising to 61,000 in 1881. As few as 3 per cent of the enrollees graduated from ordinary institutions (the proportion of *lycée* students graduating in early nineteenth-century France was only 3.5 per cent) but the proportion from elite institutions was high (see Chapter Ten). As late as 1873 only 1,239 students were graduated from regular *gimnazii* (Leikina-Svirskaia, pp. 35, 52) with perhaps half as many more from special military schools, etc. For the take-off period 1,500 seems a reasonable annual approximation. University enrollment rose from 3,659 (1855) to 9,344 (1881; Hans, p. 239), with some influx of foreign (mainly German) university graduates.

The total *chin* figure for the beginning of the nineteenth century (see Table XXXIII) is an estimate (Torke, p. 135). The 1867 figure (Torke, p. 135) is exact (see Table XXXIV), but includes teachers, etc.; it has not appeared feasible to separate administrators except at the top level. Instead, we have simply interpolated rank distribution proportionate to Pintner's ("Social Characteristics") samples. We have increased the relative weight of his small provincial sample by multiplying it by 2.5. The number of officials in *chins* 1-4 (our top level) was, however, estimated separately by using Armstrong ("Tsarist and Soviet Elite Administrators"); Amburger's (p. 517) incomplete list of 2,867 entrants (1727-1917); and Leikina-Svirskaia's (p. 80) figure (c. 2,900) for 1883. All of these estimates indicate a range of slightly under 1 per cent (for the earlier period) to slightly under 2 per cent of all civil *chin* officials in the top four ranks. The estimate of military *chin* officers seconded to civil posts is based on our own data. We have been unable to calculate Transport and Mines engineers (who had military *chin*) separately, although their elite roles correspond to those of civil elite administrators in other societies.

TABLE XXXIII. CIRCULATION PATTERN: RUSSIA, PREINDUSTRIAL PERIOD
(Absolute Numbers)

Stage	Number of Persons per Year	Years in Stage	Age at Completion of Stage	Years in Stage	Age at Completion of Stage	Military Chin Transfers
1. Cohort (Male)	400,000	11	11			
2. Secondary School Graduates	800	8	19			
3. Irrelevant		*For Men Ultimately Attaining Top Administrative Posts*		*For Men Successful to Next Stage Only*		
4. 14th through 9th *Chin*	700	12	31	30	49	
5. 8th through 5th *Chin*	240	12	43	18	46	
6. 4th through 1st *Chin*	16	12	55			20

TOTALS FOR LINE 4: 21,500 (c. 1800), 14,000 14th through 12th *chin*, 7,500 11th through 9th *chin* (see accompanying text).
LINE 5: 4,000.
LINE 6: 200 plus 120 military with shorter terms.

Calculation of age levels and periods in office has been so complicated that we are obliged to forego a detailed explanation here. Essentially they are based on Pintner's sample age distribution; formal minimal time-in-*chin* regulations (not always observed); our own general sample; and our more precise calculations for Tsarskoe Selo graduates discussed in Chapter Ten. There is evidence (also discussed in Chapter Ten) of a special career ladder for graduates of elite schools in the mid-nineteenth century. Since our data on this pattern is incomplete and tentative, we have not felt justified in asserting it as the prime career pattern comparable to career patterns among the administrative elites in Western Europe. In Table XXXIV and Figure 10, there-fore, we have shown both the general *chin* pattern discussed above and the putative elite pattern.

Soviet circulation estimates pose entirely different problems. The in-dustrial period is interrupted by the unparalleled demographic trauma of World War II. The average twenty to twenty-four year old male cohort (1939) was about 1,600,000, but there were only 800,000 survivors in 1959. (USSR, Tsentral'noe Statisticheskoe Upravlenie, *Itogi Vsesoiuznoi Perepisi Naseleniia 1959 Goda: SSSR* [Moscow, 1962], pp. 49-50.) Probably losses among cohort members who had attained important posts were considerably lower; hence 1,300,000 as a realistic estimate of "competitors" for high posts appears reasonable. Secondary school graduates (based on final grade enrollment data) varied enormously in the 1930's, from about 125,000 to 450,000, with

TABLE XXXIV. CIRCULATION PATTERN: RUSSIA, TAKE-OFF PERIOD
(Absolute Numbers)

Stage	Number of Persons per Year		Years in Stage	Age at Completion of Stage	Years in Stage	Age at Completion of Stage	Military Chin Transfers
	General Chin Pattern	Putative Elite Pattern	(Both Patterns)				
1. Cohort (Male)	700,000	700,000	11	11			
2. Secondary School Graduates	1,500	85	8	19			
3. University Graduates	1,000	—[a]	4	23			
			For Men Ultimately Attaining Top Administrative Posts		*For Men Successful to Next Stage Only*		
4. 14th through 9th *Chin*	2,500	80	12	31	30	49	
5. 8th through 5th *Chin*	750	70	12	43	18	46	
6. 4th through 1st *Chin*	65	27	15	58			90

[a] As indicated in Chapter Ten, few men in the elite pattern were graduated from universities. Many, however, attended for special law courses or otherwise prolonged their studies before service entry; hence it appears best to equate their service entrance age to that of the General *Chin* Pattern. All Column 2 figures are included in Column 1 totals.

TOTALS FOR LINE 4: 91,062 (1867); 45,000, 14th through 12th *chin*; 30,000, 11th through 9th *chin* (General *Chin* Pattern). Figures for Putative Elite Pattern not calculated on total basis (see accompanying text).

LINE 5: 13,000.

LINE 6: 1,000 plus 600 military *chin* transfers with shorter terms.

the male proportion dropping to about two-thirds. One-tenth of the cohort appears a reasonable estimate, close to Inkeles' and Bauer's estimate of 7 per cent for both sexes (p. 137). Of the 1,822,000 higher education graduates (1929-50), 68 per cent were male for the median year 1939 (see USSR, Tsentral'noe Statisticheskoe Upravlenie, *Narodnoe Khoziaistvo SSSR* [Moscow, 1956], p. 229; USSR, Tsentral'noe Statisticheskoe Upravlenie, *Zhenshchina v SSSR* [Moscow, 1960], p. 72). About 50,000 male survivors of each year's graduates appears reasonable, since war losses are apt to have been low among this skilled group.

TABLE XXXV. CIRCULATION PATTERN: SOVIET UNION,
INDUSTRIAL PERIOD
(Absolute Numbers)

Stage	Number of Persons per Year	Years in Stage	Age at Completion of Stage	Non-Higher School Graduate Recruitment
1. Cohort (Male)	1,300,000	11	11	
2. Secondary School Graduates	130,000	6	17	
3. University Graduates	50,000	5	22	
4. Beginning Level	30,000	8[a]	36	30,000
5. Intermediate Level	1,500	10	46	1,500
6. Top Level	50	12	58	50

[a] Does not include average of six years in nonadministrative work.
TOTALS FOR LINE 4: 600,000 (see accompanying text).
LINE 5: 30,000.
LINE 6: 1,200.

Chapter Eleven provides a general discussion on Soviet elite administrator categories and an estimate of their size. We consider the half who are university graduates (Fischer, p. 103; Stewart, p. 144) to be a kind of "career pattern" because it appears that higher education requirements have become increasingly important for major categories. The estimate of 450,000 Party apparatus members may be reduced to about 300,000 for the 1940's (Stalin estimated 100,000 to 150,000 for the 1930's, but did not include all primary Party organization secretaries engaged in virtually full-time administrative work). The figure is doubled to allow for economic managers outside the Party apparatus, and divided by ten for the annual intake (turnover is much greater, proportionately, as indicated in Chapter Eleven, for Party personnel; but turnover is much less for foremen, etc., who may spend a lifetime at that level). The intermediate level is reached by taking the approximate number of provincial Party committee members (80 times 150) with a slight increase for officials (police, etc.) left out at this level, and doubling the result to account for central officials.

Stewart (p. 50) provides sample data which suggests an average tenure at this level of four years, but most officials are transferred laterally at least once. Hence ten years seems a reasonable approximation. Complex estimates of numbers of top officials, age levels, and turnover, are based on the more abundant Central Committee studies (Stewart, pp. 156, 165, 168; Hough, pp. 61, 75-77; Armstrong, "Tsarist and Soviet Elite Administrators"; Armstrong, "Bifurcation of the Party Apparatus").

Abbott, Evelyn and Lewis Campbell. *The Life and Letters of Benjamin Jowett, M. A.* London: John Murray, 1897.

Absoliutizm v Rossii (XVII-XVIII vv.). Moscow: Akademiia Nauk SSSR, Institut Istorii, Izdatel'stvo "Nauka," 1964.

Acta Borussica: Denkmäler der preussischen Staatsverwaltung im 18. Jahrhundert. Vol. VI, Erster Hälfte: *Behördenorganisation und allgemeine Staatswerwaltung*. Berlin: Paul Parey, 1901.

Administrative Reform Association. *Official Paper No. 2: The Devising Heads and Executive Hands of the English Government; as Described by Privy-Councillors and Civil Servants Themselves*. London: M. S. Rickerby, 1855.

Afanasev, V. "V. I. Lenin and Problems of the Scientific Management of Society," *Pravda*, December 4, 1969. Condensed trans. in *Current Digest of the Soviet Press*, XXI, No. 49, 18-20.

Allen, G. C. *The Structure of Industry in Britain: A Study in Economic Change*. London: Longmans, 1961.

Amburger, Erik. *Geschichte der Behördenorganisation Russlands von Peter dem Grossen bis 1917*. Leiden: E. J. Brill, 1966.

"L'Amélioration des Méthodes dans les Administrations," *Gouvernement Provisoire de la République Française, Bulletin d'Information et de Documentation*, No. 8, March-April 1945, pp. 82-85.

Ames, Edward. "A Century of Russian Railroad Construction: 1837-1936," *American Slavic and East European Review*, VI (1947), 57-74.

Amiable, Louis. *La Franc-Maçonnerie et la Magistrature en France à la Veille de la Révolution*. Aix: J. Redmonet-Aubin, 1894.

Anderson, Charles Arnold and Mary J. Bowman (eds.). *Education and Economic Development*. Chicago: Aldine Publishing Co., 1963.

Andreevsky, Ivan E. *Namestnikakh, Voevodakh i Gubernatorakh*. Dissertation, St. Petersburg University, Law Faculty, 1864.

Arbois de Jubainville, H. de. *L'Administration des Intendants, d'après les Archives de l'Aube*. Paris: H. Champion Libraire, 1880.

Archer, R. L. *Secondary Education in the Nineteenth Century*. Cambridge, England: Cambridge University Press, 1921.

Ardashev, Pavel. *Les Intendants de Province sous Louis XVI*. Paris: Felix Alcan, Editeur, 1909.

Ardashev, Pavel. "Materialy dlia Istorii Provintsial'noi Administratsii vo Frantsii v Posledniuiu Poru Starago Poriadka," *Uchenyia Zapiski Imperatorskago Iurevskago Universiteta*, x (1902), No. 6, 1-80; xi (1903), No. 1, 81-144; xii (1904), No. 1, 385-480.

Arlt, Erich. *Der Aufbau der Jugendwohlfahrtsbehörden*. Dissertation, Marburg University, Law and State Science Faculty, 1936. Fürstenwald: Bruno Schulze, 1936.

Armstrong, John A. *Ideology, Politics, and Government in the Soviet Union: An Introduction*. Rev. ed. New York: F. A. Praeger, 1967.

———. "Old-Regime Administrative Elites: Prelude to Modernization in France, Prussia, and Russia," *International Review of Administrative Sciences*, xxxviii (1972), 21-40.

———. "Old-Regime Governors: Bureaucratic and Patrimonial Attributes," *Comparative Studies in Society and History*, xiv (1972), 2-29.

———. "Party Bifurcation and Elite Interests," *Soviet Studies*, xvii (1966), 417-30.

———. *The Politics of Totalitarianism*. New York: Random House, 1961.

———. "Sources of Soviet Administrative Behavior: Some Soviet and Western European Comparisons," *American Political Science Review*, lix (1965), 643-55.

———. *The Soviet Bureaucratic Elite: A Case Study of the Ukrainian Apparatus*. New York: F. A. Praeger, 1959.

———. "Tsarist and Soviet Elite Administrators," *Slavic Review*, xxxi (1972), 1-28.

Armytage, W.H.G. *Four Hundred Years of English Education*. Cambridge, England: Cambridge University Press, 1965.

———. *The French Influence on English Education*. London: Routledge and Kegan Paul, 1968.

———. *The German Influence on English Education*. London: Routledge and Kegan Paul, 1969.

———. *The Rise of the Technocrats: A Social History*. London: Routledge and Kegan Paul, 1965.

———. *The Russian Influence on English Education*. London: Routledge and Kegan Paul, 1969.

Arndt, Hans J. *The Politics of Non-Planning*. Syracuse: Syracuse University Press, 1966.

Arnold, David O. (ed.). *The Sociology of Subcultures*. Berkeley: Glendessary Press, 1970.

Arnold, Matthew. *Schools and Universities on the Continent*. London: Macmillan and Co., 1868.

Artaud, A. *La Question de l'Employé en France: Etude Sociale et Professionnelle.* Paris: Libraire Georges Roustan, 1909.

Artz, Frederick B. *The Development of Technical Education in France, 1500-1850.* Cambridge, Mass.: M.I.T. Press and the Society for the History of Technology, 1966.

———. "L'Education Technique en France au XVIIIᵉ Siècle (1700-1789)," *Revue d'Histoire,* XIII (new series VII) (1938), 361-407.

Aspaturian, Vernon V. *Process and Power in Soviet Foreign Policy.* Boston: Little, Brown and Co., 1971.

Association du Corps Préfectoral et des Administrateurs Civils du Ministère de l'Intérieur. *Du Récrutement et des Débouchés des Cadres Supérieurs du Ministère de l'Intérieur: Rapport Présenté au Nom de la Commission du Statut par M. R. Bonnaud Delamare, Préfet de l'Aisne.* N.p., n.d.

Astre, Florentin. "Les Intendants du Languedoc," *Mémoires de l'Académie [Impériale] des Sciences, Inscriptions et Belles-Lettres de Toulouse,* 5th series, III (1859), 7-36; IV (1860), 421-43; V (1861), 102-24; 7th series, III (1871), 31-54.

Aubry, Paul V. *Monge, le Savant Ami de Napoléon Bonaparte 1746-1818.* Paris: Gauthier-Villars, 1954.

Aucoc, Leon. *Le Conseil d'Etat avant et depuis 1789: Ses Transformations, Ses Travaux et Son Personnel.* Paris: Imprimerie Nationale, 1876.

Avenel, G. *Les Revenus d'un Intellectuel de 1200 à 1913: Les Riches depuis Sept Cent Ans.* Paris: Ernest Flammarion, Editeur, 1922.

Aydelotte, William O. "Quantification in History," *American Historical Review,* LXXI (1966), 803-25.

Aylmer, G. E. *The King's Servants: The Civil Service of Charles I 1625-1642.* New York: Columbia University Press, 1961.

———. "Office Holding as a Factor in English History, 1625-42," *History,* XLIV (1959), 228-40.

Aynard, Joseph. *La Bourgeoisie Française: Essai de Psychologie Sociale.* Paris: Libraire Académique Perrin, 1934.

Azrael, Jeremy R. *Managerial Power and Soviet Politics.* Cambridge, Mass.: Harvard University Press, 1966.

Bahrdt, Hans Paul. *Industriebürokratie: Versuch einer Soziologie des industrialisierten Bürobetriebes und seiner Angestellten.* Stuttgart: Ferdinand Enke, 1958.

Bamford, T. W. *Rise of the Public Schools: A Study of Boys' Public Boarding Schools in England and Wales from 1837 to the Present Day.* London: Thomas Nelson and Sons, 1967.

Banton, Michael P. *Roles: An Introduction to the Study of Social Relations.* London: Tavistock Publications, 1965.

Barber, Elinor. *The Bourgeoisie in 18th Century France.* Princeton: Princeton University Press, 1955.

Barbier, Alfred. "Les Intendants du Poitou," *Mémoires de la Société des Antiquaires de l'Ouest*, VI (1884), 1-14.

Bard, Erwin W. (ed.). "Higher Civil Servants: Recruitment-Training," *Les Cahiers de Bruges, Recherches Européenes*, 1957, II.

Barnard, H. C. *The French Tradition in Education: Ramus to Mme. Necker de Saussure.* Cambridge, England: Cambridge University Press, 1970.

Barthélemy, de. *Souvenirs d'un Ancien Préfet, 1787-1848.* Paris: E. Dentu, Editeur, 1885.

Bauer, Max. *Sittengeschichte des deutschen Studententums.* Dresden: Paul Aretz Verlag, n.d.

Beau, Horst. *Das Leistungswissen des Frühindustriellen Unternehmertums in Rheinland und Westfalen.* Cologne: N.p., 1959.

Beaucorps, Charles de. "Une Province sous Louis XIV: l'Administration des Intendants d'Orléans: De Creil, Jubert de Bouville et de la Baudonnaye (1686-1713)," *Mémoires de la Société Archéologique et Historique de l'Orléanais*, XXXIII (1911), 37-500.

Becker, Howard S. *German Youth: Bond or Free.* New York: Oxford University Press, 1946.

———. "Personal Change in Adult Life," *Sociometry*, XXVII (1964), 40-53.

——— and James W. Carpenter. "The Development of Identification with an Occupation," *American Journal of Sociology*, LXI (1956), 289-98.

Beer, Samuel H. *Treasury Control: The Co-ordination of Financial and Economic Policy in Great Britain.* Oxford: Clarendon Press, 1956.

Behrend, Roland. "Der Unternehmer als Erzieher des Juristen," *Preussische Jahrbücher*, CLVII (1914), 247-60.

Benaerts, Pierre. *Les Origines de la Grande Industrie Allemande.* Paris: F. H. Turot, 1933.

Ben-David, Joseph. "The Rise and Decline of France as a Scientific Centre," *Minerva*, VIII (1970), 160-79.

——— and Awraham Zloczower. "Universities and Academic Systems in Modern Societies," *Archives Européenes de Sociologie*, III (1962), 45-84.

Bendix, Reinhard. "Concepts and Generalizations in Comparative Sociological Studies," *American Sociological Review*, XXVIII (1963), 532-39.

———. *Higher Civil Servants in American Society.* Boulder: University of Colorado Press, 1949.

—— (ed.). *State and Society: A Reader in Comparative Political Sociology.* Boston: Little, Brown and Co., 1968.

Bennett, John W. Wheeler. *John Anderson, Viscount Waverley.* London: Macmillan and Co., Ltd., 1962.

Bennis, Warren G. "Leadership Theory and Administrative Behavior: The Problem of Authority," *Administrative Science Quarterly,* IV (1959), 259-301.

Bergengrün, Alexander. *Staatsminister August Freiherr von der Heydt.* Leipzig: S. Hirzel, 1908.

Berger, G. *et al. Politique et Technique.* Paris: Presses Universitaires de France, 1958.

Berliner, Joseph. *Factory and Manager in the USSR.* Cambridge, Mass.: Harvard University Press, 1957.

Bertrand, André and Marceau Long. "L'Enseignement Supérieur des Sciences Administratives en France," *International Review of Administrative Science,* XXVI (1960), 5-24.

Bezard, Yvonne. *Fonctionnaires Maritimes et Coloniaux sous Louis XIV: Les Bégon.* Paris: Albin Michel, 1932.

Biddle, Bruce J. and Edwin J. Thomas. *Role Theory: Concepts and Research.* New York: John Wiley and Sons, Inc., 1966.

Bielawski, J.B.M. *Souvenir d'un Petit Fonctionnaire: Etude Historique, Administrative et Sociale par un Républican-Democrate.* Clermont-Ferrand: G. Mont-Louis, 1894.

Binney, J.E.D. *British Public Finance and Administration, 1774-92.* Oxford: Clarendon Press, 1958.

Bismarck, Otto von. *Bismarck: Reflections and Reminiscences.* Vol. I. New York: Harper and Bros., 1899.

Bize. "Le Problème de la Déformation Professionnelle: Ses Effets sur l'Efficacité," *Revue Administrative,* V (1952), No. 28, 368-76.

Blättner, Fritz. *Das Gymnasium: Aufgaben der höheren Schule in Geschichte und Gegenwart.* Heidelberg: Quelle and Meyer, 1960.

Blau, Peter M. and Otis D. Duncan. *The American Occupational Structure.* New York: John Wiley and Sons, Inc., 1967.

Blondel, Georges. *De l'Enseignement du Droit dans les Universités Allemandes.* Paris: H. Le Soulier, Libraire-Editeur, 1885.

Blum, Karl Ludwig. *Ein russischer Staatsmann: Des Grafen Jakob Johann Sievers* Denkwürdigkeiten zur Geschichte Russlands. 4 Vols. Leipzig: Winter'sche Verlagshandlung, 1857-58.

Blunt, Edward. *The I.C.S.: The Indian Civil Service.* London: Faber and Faber Ltd., 1937.

Boislisle, A. de. *Les Conseils du Roi sous Louis XIV.* Paris: Librairie Hachette, 1884.

Boislisle, A. de. "Les Intendants de la Généralité de Paris," *Mémoires de la Société de l'Histoire de Paris et de l'Isle de France*, VII (1880), 271-98.

Bonin, Henning von. "Adel und Bürgertum in der höheren Beamtenschaft der preussischen Monarchie, 1794-1806," *Jahrbuch für die Geschichte Mittel- und Ostdeutschlands*, XV (1966), 139-74.

Borch, Herbert von. *Obrigkeit und Widerstand: Zur politischen Soziologie des Beamtentums*. Tübingen: J.C.B. Mohr, 1954.

Bordes, Maurice. "Les Intendants de Louis XV," *Revue Historique*, CCXXIII (1960), 45-62.

———. "Les Intendants Eclairés de la Fin de l'Ancien Régime," *Revue d'Histoire Economique et Sociale*, XXXIX (1961), 57-83.

Born, Karl E. "Die soziale und wirtschaftliche Strukturwandel Deutschlands am Ende des 19. Jahrhundert," *Vierteljahrschrift für Sozial- und Wirtschaftsgeschichte*, L (1963), 360-76.

Bottomore, Thomas B. *Elites and Society*. London: C. A. Watts and Co., Ltd., 1964.

———. "Les Hauts Fonctionnaires Français," *Promotions* (1955), No. 33, pp. 15-23.

———. "La Mobilité Sociale dans la Haute Administration Française," *Cahiers Internationaux de Sociologie*, XIII (1952), 167-78.

Boulainville, [Comte] de. *Etat de la France*. Vol. I. London: T. Wood and S. Palmer, 1727.

Bourgin, Hubert. "Administration et Gouvernement," *Revue de Paris*, Nov. 15, 1919, pp. 428-48.

Bowen, Ralph H. "The Roles of Government and Private Enterprise in German Industrial Growth, 1870-1914," *Journal of Economic History*, X (1950), Supplement, 68-81.

Boyer de Sainte Suzanne, Charles de. *L'Administration sous l'Ancien Régime: Les Intendants de la Généralité d'Amiens (Picardie et Artois)*. Paris: Librairie Administrative de Paul Dupont, 1865.

Brabante, Ralph (ed.). *Political and Administrative Development*. Durham: Duke University Press, 1969.

Brecht, Arnold. "How Bureaucracies Develop and Function," *Annals of the American Academy*, CLXIII (1954), 1-10.

——— and Comstock Glaser. *The Art and Technique of Administration in German Ministries*. Cambridge, Mass.: Harvard University Press, 1940.

Brennan, Michael J. *Technocratic Politics and the Functionalist Theory of European Integration*. Ithaca, Center for International Studies, Cornell University, 1969.

Bresard, Marcel. "Mobilité Sociale et Dimension de la Famille," *Population* (Revue Trimestrielle de l'Institut National d'Etudes Demographiques), V (1950), 533-66.

Bridges, Edward. *Portrait of a Profession: The Civil Service Tradition.* Cambridge, England: Cambridge University Press, 1950.

Briggs, Asa. *The Age of Improvement.* London: Longmans, Green and Co., 1959.

Brim, Orville G., Jr. and Stanton Wheeler. *Socialization after Childhood: Two Essays.* New York: John Wiley and Sons, 1966.

Brindillac, Charles. "Les Hauts Fonctionnaires," *Esprit,* XXI (1953), 862-77.

Brinkmann, Carl. *Die preussische Handelspolitik vor dem Zollverein und der Wiederaufbau vor hundert Jahren.* Berlin: Walter de Gruyter and Co., 1922.

Brocher, Henri. *A la Cour de Louis XIV: Le Rang et l'Etiquette sous l'Ancien Régime.* Paris: Librairie Félix Alcan, 1934.

Bronfenbrenner, Urie. *Two Worlds of Childhood: U. S. and U.S.S.R.* New York: Russell Sage Foundation, 1970.

Brown, Bernard E. "The French Experience of Modernization," *World Politics,* XXI (1969), 366-91.

Brun la Valette. *Le Rôle Sociale des Cadres: Enquête sur l'Aristocratie, les Chefs, les Notables, les Elites.* Paris: La Franciade, 1948.

Bruneau, Pierre. *Le Rôle du Haut Commandement au Point de Vue Economique de 1914 à 1921.* Paris: Berger-Levrault, Editeurs, 1924.

Brunschwig, Henri. *La Crise de l'Etat Prussien à la Fin du XVIII⁰ Siècle et la Genèse de la Mentalité Romantique.* Paris: Presses Universitaires de France, 1947.

"Les Cabinets Ministériels et leur Composition," *L'Economie,* No. 495, June 9, 1955, pp. 6-7.

Caillet, J. *De l'Administration en France sous le Ministère du Cardinal de Richelieu.* Paris: Firmin Didot Frères, Fils et Cie, 1857.

Caldwell, Lynton K. "The Relevance of Administrative History," *Revue Internationale des Sciences Administratives,* XXI (1955), 453-64.

Cameron, Rondo E. "The Crédit Mobilier and the Economic Development of Europe," *The Journal of Political Economy,* LXI (1953), 461-88.

————. *France and the Economic Development of Europe, 1800-1914: Conquests of Peace and Seeds of War.* Princeton: Princeton University Press, 1961.

Capital Formation and Economic Growth: A Conference of the Universities-National Bureau Committee for Economic Research. Princeton: Princeton University Press, 1955.

Carré, Henri. *La Noblesse de France et l'Opinion Publique au XVIIIᵉ Siècle.* Paris: Librairie Champion, 1920.

Carstens, F. L. "The Great Elector and the Foundation of the Hohenzollern Despotism," *English Historical Review,* LXV (1950), 175-202.

Caspary, Anna. *Ludolf Camphausens Leben: Nach seinem schriftlichen Nachlass.* Stuttgart: J. G. Cotta'sche Buchhandlung Nachfolger, 1902.

Cell, John W. *British Colonial Administration in the Mid-Nineteenth Century.* New Haven: Yale University Press, 1970.

Chapman, Brian. *The Prefects and Provincial France.* London: George Allen and Unwin, 1955.

————. *The Profession of Government: The Public Service in Europe.* London: George Allen and Unwin, 1959.

————. "Wanted: A Whitehall Revolution," *The Sunday Times,* September 1, 1963.

———— and J. M. *The Life and Times of Baron Haussmann: Paris in the Second Empire.* London: Weidenfeld and Nicolson, 1957.

Chaput de Saintonge, Rolland A. A. *Public Administration in Germany: A Study in Regional and Local Administration in Land Rheinland-Pfalz.* London: Weidenfeld and Nicolson, 1961.

Chardon, Henri. *L'Administration de la France: Les Fonctionnaires.* Paris: Perrin et Cie, 1908.

Charléty, Sebastien. *Histoire du Saint-Simonisme (1825-1864).* Paris: Paul Hartmann Editeur, 1931.

Checkland, S. G. *The Gladstones: A Family Biography, 1764-1851.* Cambridge, England: Cambridge University Press, 1971.

————. *The Rise of Industrial Society in England, 1815-1885.* London: Longmans, Green, 1964.

Chéguillaume, H. "Perronet, Ingénieur de la Généralité d'Alençon (1737-1747)," *Bulletin de la Société Historique et Archéologique de l'Orne,* x (1890), 40-117.

"Les Chemins de Fer Français pendant la Guerre" [J. G.], *Revue des Sciences Politiques,* XLIV (1921), 84-100.

Chéruel, A. *Histoire de l'Administration Monarchique en France depuis l'Avénement de Phillippe-Auguste jusqu'à la Mort de Louis XIV.* Paris: Dezobry, E. Magdeleine et Cie, 1855.

Chouiller, Ernest. *Les Trudaine.* Arces-sur-Aube: Leon Frémont, Imprimeur-Editeur, 1884.

Chuprov, A. I. *Rechi i Stat'i.* Vol. III. Moscow: M. and S. Sabashnikov, 1909.

Clairmonte, Frédéric. *Le Libéralisme Economique et les Pays Sous-Developpés: Etudes sur l'Evolution d'une Idée.* Geneva: Librairie E. Droz, 1958.

Clapham, J. H. *The Economic Development of France and Germany 1815-1914.* Cambridge, England: Cambridge University Press, 1921.

Clark, G. Kitson. *The Critical Historian.* New York: Basic Books, 1967.

Clarke, Martin L. *Classical Education in Britain, 1500-1900.* Cambridge, England: Cambridge University Press, 1959.

Clausen, John A. (ed.). *Socialization and Society.* Boston: Little, Brown and Co., 1968.

Clément, Pierre. *Lettres, Instructions et Mémoires de Colbert.* Vol. IV. Paris: Imprimerie Impériale, 1867.

———— and Albert Lemoine. *M. de Silhouette Bouret; Les Derniers Fermiers Généraux: Etudes sur les Financiers du XVIIIᵉ Siècle.* Paris: Didier et Cie, Libraires-Editeurs, 1872.

Cleveland-Stevens, Edward. *English Railways, Their Development and Their Relation to the State.* London: George Routledge and Sons, Ltd., 1915.

Club Jean Moulin. *L'Etat et le Citoyen.* Paris: Editions du Seuil, 1961.

Cochran, Thomas C. "Cultural Factors in Economic Growth," *Journal of Economic History,* XX (1960), 515-30.

————. *Railroad Leaders, 1845-1890: The Business Mind in Action.* Cambridge, Mass.: Harvard University Press, 1953.

Cohen, Emmeline W. *The Growth of the British Civil Service, 1780-1939.* London: George, Allen and Unwin, Ltd., 1941.

Cohn, Gustav. "Die Anfänge des deutschen Eisenbahnwesens," *Zeitschrift für die gesamte Staatswissenschaft,* XLVII (1891), 655-79.

————. *Ueber die staatswissenschaftliche Vorbildung zum höheren Verwaltungsdienst in Preussen.* Berlin: Julius Springer, 1900.

————. *Untersuchungen über die englische Eisenbahnpolitik.* 3 Vols. Leipzig: Duncker and Humblot, 1874, 1875, 1883.

————. *Zur Geschichte und Politik des Verkehrswesens.* Stuttgart: Ferdinand Enke, 1900.

Conrad, Joh. *Das Universitätsstudium in Deutschland während der letzten 50 Jahre: Statistische Untersuchungen unter besonderer Berücksichtigung Preussens.* Jena: Verlag von Gustav Fischer, 1884.

Le Conseil d'Etat: Livre Jubilaire Publié pour Commémorer Son Cent Cinquantième Anniversaire, 4 Nivose An VIII—24 Décembre 1949. Paris: Recueil Sirey, 1952.

Cooper, William W., H. J. Leavitt, and M. W. Shelly II (eds.). *New Perspectives in Organization Research.* New York: John Wiley and Sons, Inc., 1964.

Cootner, Paul. "The Role of the Railroad in United States Economic Growth," *Journal of Economic History*, XXIII (1963), 477-521.

Copeman, G. H. *Leaders of British Industry: A Study of the Careers of More than a Thousand Public Company Directors.* London: Gee and Co., Ltd., 1955.

Cordier, M. J. *Mémoires sur les Travaux Publics.* 2 Vols. Paris: Carilian-Goeury et Vᵒʳ Dalmonts Editeurs, 1841-42.

Corson, John J. and R. Shale Paul. *Men Near the Top: Filling Key Posts in the Federal Service.* Baltimore: Johns Hopkins Press, 1966.

Coulaudon, Aimé. *Chazerat: Dernier Intendant de la Généralité de Riom et Province d'Auvergne (1774-89).* Dissertation, University of Paris, Faculté de Droit. Paris: Jouve et Cie, 1932.

"La Crise de la Fonction Supérieure," *Le Monde*, March 11-12, 1964.

Croner, Fritz. *Die Angestellten in der modernen Gesellschaft: Eine Sozialhistorische und Soziologische Studie.* Frankfurt: Humboldt-Verlag, 1954.

————. *Soziologie der Angestellten.* Cologne: Kröpeneuer and Witsch, 1962.

Crozier, Michel. *The Bureaucratic Phenomenon.* Chicago: University of Chicago Press, 1964.

————. "Pour une Analyse Sociologique de la Planification Française," *Revue Française de Sociologie*, VI (1965), 147-63.

Curtiss, John Shelton. *The Russian Army under Nicholas I, 1825-1855.* Durham: Duke University Press, 1965.

Dakin, Douglas. *Turgot and the Ancien Régime in France.* London: Methuen and Co., Ltd., 1939.

Dale, Harold E. *The Higher Civil Service of Great Britain.* London: Oxford University Press, 1941.

Danvers, Frederick C., M. Monier-Williams *et al. Memorials of Old Haileybury College.* London: Archibald Constable and Co., 1894.

Dartein, M. de. *Notice sur le Régime de l'Ancienne Ecole des Ponts et Chaussées et sur sa Transformation à Partir de la Révolution.* Paris: E. Bernard Imprimeur-Editeur, 1906.

————. "La Vie et les Travaux de Jean Rodolphe Perronet, Premier Ingénieur des Ponts et Chaussées, Créateur de l'Ecole des Ponts et Chaussées," *Annales des Ponts et Chaussées*, 1906, 4ᵉ trimestre, Vol. XXIV, 8ᵉ série, Première Partie, pp. 5-87.

Daumard, Adeline. *La Bourgeoisie Parisienne de 1815 à 1848.* Paris: S.E.V.P.E.N., 1963.

———. "Les Eleves de l'Ecole Polytechnique de 1815 à 1848," *Revue d'Histoire Moderne et Contemporaine*, v (1958), 226-34.

Dauzet, Pierre. *Le Siècle des Chemins de Fer en France (1821-1938)*. Fontenay-aux-Roses: Imprimerie Bellenand, 1948.

Dean, Maurice. "The Public Servant and the Study of Public Administration," *Public Administration*, xl (1962), 17-28.

Debbasch, Charles. *L'Administration au Pouvoir: Fonctionnaires et Politiques sous la Ve République*. Paris: Calmann-Lévy, 1969.

Delahante, Adrien. *Une Famille de Finance au XVIIIe Siècle: Mémoires, Correspondance et Papiers de Famille Réunis et Mis en Ordre*. 2 Vols. Paris: J. Hetzel et Cie, 1880.

Delbrück, Clemens von. *Die wirtschaftliche Mobilmachung in Deutschland 1914* (ed. from His Papers by Joachim von Delbrück). Munich: Verlag für Kulturpolitik, 1924.

Delbrück, Rudolph von. *Lebenserinnerungen, 1817-1867*. 2 Vols. Leipzig: Duncker and Humblot, 1905.

Delefortrie-Soubeyroux, Nicole. *Les Dirigéants de l'Industrie Française*. Paris: Librairie Armand Colin, 1961.

Demeter, Karl. *The German Officer-Corps in Society and State 1650-1945*. London: Weidenfeld and Nicolson, 1965.

Depping, G. B. *Correspondance Administrative sous le Règne de Louis XIV*. 4 Vols. Paris: Imprimerie Nationale, 1850-55.

Déroche, Henri. *Les Mythes Administratifs: Essai de Sociologie Phénoménologique*. Paris: Presses Universitaires de France, 1966.

Devey, Joseph. *The Life of Joseph Locke, Civil Engineer*. London: Richard Bentley, 1862.

Diamant, Alfred. "Tradition and Innovation in French Administration," *Comparative Political Studies*, i (1968-69), 251-74.

Dibble, Vernon K. "Occupations and Ideologies," *American Journal of Sociology*, lxviii (1962), 229-41.

Dieckmann, W. *Die Behördenorganisation in der deutschen Kriegswirtschaft 1914-1918*. Hamburg: Hanseatische Verlagsanshalt, 1937.

Dimock, Marshall E. "Management in the USSR—Comparisons to the United States," *Public Administration Review*, xx (1960), 139-47.

Dmitriev, F. "Speranskii i Ego Gosudarstvennaia Deiatel'nost'," *Russkii Arkhiv*, 1868, No. 10, 1,527-1,655.

Dodd, C. H. "Recruitment to the Administrative Class, 1960-1964," *Public Administration*, xlv (1967), 55-80.

Dolgorukov ["Comte d'Almagro"]. *Notice sur les Principales Familles de la Russie*. Paris: Didot Frères, 1843.

Dorwart, Reinhold August. *The Administrative Reforms of Frederick William I of Prussia.* Cambridge, Mass.: Harvard University Press, 1953.

Doueil, Pierre. *L'Administration Locale à l'Epreuve de la Guerre (1939-1949).* Paris: Recueil Sirey, 1950.

Dreyfus, Robert. *De Monsieur Thiers à Marcel Proust: Histoire et Souvenirs.* Paris: Librairie Plon, 1939.

Duclos, Charles. *Essais sur les Ponts et Chaussées.* Amsterdam: Chatelain, 1759.

Ducros, L. *La Société Française au Dix-Huitième Siècle.* Paris: Librairie A. Hatier, 1922.

Dukes, Paul. *Catherine the Great and the Russian Nobility.* Cambridge, England: The University Press, 1967.

Dumas, F. *La Généralité de Tours au XVIIIᵉ Siècle: Administration de l'Intendant du Cluzel (1766-1783).* Tours: L. Pericat Libraire, 1894.

Dunham, Arthur L. "How the First French Railways were Planned," *Journal of Economic History,* I (1941), 12-25.

———. *La Révolution Industrielle en France (1815-1848).* Paris: Marcel Rivière et Cie, 1953.

Dunnett, James. "The Civil Service Administrator and the Expert," *Public Administration,* XXXIX (1961), 223-37.

Dupont-Ferrier, Gustave. *Du Collège de Clermont au Lycée Louis-le-Grand (1563-1920): La Vie Quotidienne d'un Collège Parisien pendant plus de Trois Cent Cinquant Ans.* 3 Vols. Paris: E. de Boccard, Editeur, 1921.

Durand, Charles. *Les Auditeurs au Conseil d'Etat de 1803 à 1814.* Aix-en-Provence: La Pensée Universitaire, 1958.

———. *Etudes sur le Conseil d'Etat Napoléonien.* Paris: Presses Universitaires de France, 1949.

Duval, Louis. *Les Intendants d'Alençon au XVIIᵉ Siècle et les Mémoires de J. B. de Pomereu.* Alençon: Librairie Loyer-Fontaine, 1891.

Duyker, H.C.J. and N. H. Frijda. *National Character and National Stereotypes: A Trend Report Prepared for the International Union of Scientific Psychology.* Amsterdam: North-Holland Publishing Co., 1960.

Dvoring, Folke. *History as a Social Science: An Essay on the Nature and Purpose of Historical Studies.* The Hague: Martinus Nihoff, 1960.

Dyos, H. J. and D. H. Aldcroft. *British Transport: An Economic Survey from the Seventeenth Century to the Twentieth.* Leicester: Leicester University Press, 1969.

Early Victorian England, 1830-1865. London: Oxford University Press, 1934.

Eaton, Dorman B. *Civil Service in Great Britain: A History of Abuses and Reforms and Their Bearing upon American Politics.* New York: Harper and Brothers, 1880.

Eckart, Jörg. "Hierarchie von vorgestern," *Die Zeit,* October 1, 1965.

Eckstein, Alexander (ed.). *Comparison of Economic Systems: Theoretical and Methodological Approaches.* Berkeley: University of California Press, 1971.

Egret, Jean. "L'Aristocratie Parlementaire Française à la Fin de L'Ancien Régime," *Revue Historique,* CCVIII (1952) 1-14.

————. *Le Parlement de Dauphiné et les Affaires Publiques dans la Deuxième Moitié du XVIIIᵉ Siècle.* 2 Vols. Grenoble: B. Arthaud, 1942.

Eichholtz, Dietrich. *Junker und Bourgeoisie vor 1848 in der preussischen Eisenbahngeschichte.* Berlin: Akademie Verlag, 1962.

Eisenstadt, Shmuel N. *The Political System of Empires.* Glencoe, Ill.: The Free Press, 1963.

Enkling, Josef. *Die Stellung des Staates zu den Privateisenbahnen in der Anfangszeit des preussischen Eisenbahnwesens (1830-1848).* Dissertation, Cologne University, Economics and Social Science Faculty. Kettweg: F. Flothmann, 1935.

"Enquête sur le Recrutement et le Perfectionnement des Agents du Cadre Administratif Supérieur," *Revue Internationale des Sciences Administratives* (Brussels), X (1937), 423-74.

Erickson, Charlotte. "The Recruitment of British Management," *Explorations in Entrepreneurial History,* VI (1953), 62-70.

Erman, L. K. "Sostav Intelligentsii v Rossii v Kontse XIX i Nachale XX v.," *Istoriia SSSR,* 1963, No. 1.

Ernouf, Alfred A. *Paulin Talabot: Sa Vie et Son Oeuvre.* Paris: Librairie Plon, 1886.

Ernsthausen, A. Ernst von. *Erinnerungen eines preussischen Beamten.* Bielefed: Velhagen and Klasing, 1894.

Eroshkin, N. P. *Ocherki Istorii Gosudarstvennykh Uchrezhdenii Dorevoliutsionnoi Rossii.* Moscow: Uchpedgiz, 1960.

Eschmann, Ernst W. *Die Führungsschichten Frankreichs.* Vol. 1. Berlin: Junker und Dünnhaupt Verlag, 1943.

Esmonin, F. "Les Intendants du Dauphiné des Origines à la Révolution," *Annales de l'Université de Grenoble,* XXXIV (1922-23), 37-90

Etzioni, Amitai. *The Active Society: A Theory of Societal and Political Processes.* London: Collier-Macmillan, Ltd., 1968.

————. *Modern Organizations.* Englewood Cliffs, N.J.: Prentice Hall, Inc., 1964.

Eulenburg, Franz. "Die Frequenz der deutschen Universitäten von ihrer Gründung bis zur Gegenwart," *Abhandlungen der philologisch-historischen Klasse der Königlich-sächsischen Gesellschaft der Wissenschaften*, XXIV (1906), No. 11.

————. "Die Herkunft der deutschen Wirtschaftsführer: Ein Beitrag zur Soziographie," *Schmollers Jahrbuch für Gezetsgebung, Verwaltung und Volkswirtschaft*, LXXIV, Erste Heft (1954), 77-89.

Fainsod, Merle. *How Russia Is Ruled*. 2nd ed. Cambridge, Mass.: Harvard University Press, 1963.

Fayerweather, John. *The Executive Overseas: Administrative Attitudes and Relationships in a Foreign Culture*. Syracuse: Syracuse University Press, 1959.

Fediukin, S. A. *Privlechenie Burzhuaznoi Tekhnicheskoi Intelligentsii k Sotsialisticheskomu Stroitel'stvu v SSSR*. Moscow: Izdatel'stvo VPSh pri AON pri TsK KPSS, 1960.

————. *Sovetskaia Vlast' i Burzhuaznye Spetsialisty*. Moscow: Izdatel'stvo "Mysl'," 1965.

Ferrat, André. *La République à Refaire*. Paris: Gallimard, 1945.

Fesler, James W. "French Field Administration: The Beginnings," *Comparative Studies in Society and History*, V (1962), 76-111.

Feyzioglu, T. "The Reform of the French Higher Civil Service since 1945," *Public Administration*, XXXIII (1955), 69-93, 173-89.

Ficheroulle, Jérome. *Notes et Documents Relatifs aux Intendants de la Flandre, 1672-1790*. Bailleul: Ficheroulle-Beheydt, 1912.

Le Figaro, March 3, 1964.

Finer, Herman. *The British Civil Service*. London: The Fabian Society and George Allen and Unwin, Ltd., 1937.

Finer, Samuel E. *The Life and Times of Sir Edwin Chadwick*. London: Methuen and Co., 1952.

Fischer, George. *The Soviet System and Modern Society*. New York: Atherton Press, 1968.

Flynn, James T. "The Universities, the Gentry and the Russian Imperial Services, 1815-1825," *Canadian Slavic Studies*, II (1968), 486-503.

Fogel, Robert W. *Railroads and American Economic Growth: Essays in Econometric History*. Baltimore: Johns Hopkins Press, 1964.

Foncin, P. *Essai sur le Ministère de Turgot*. Dissertation, University of Paris, Faculté des Lettres. Paris: Librairie Germer-Baillière et Cie, 1877.

"La Fondation Nationale pour l'Enseignement de la Gestion des Entreprises Va Etre Mise en Place," *Le Monde*, February 14, 1968.

Foord, Archibald S. "The Waning of 'The Influence of the Crown,'" *English Historical Review*, LXII (1947), 484-507.

Ford, Franklin L. *Robe and Sword: The Regrouping of the French Aristocracy after Louis XIV*. Cambridge, Mass.: Harvard University Press, 1953.

Ford, Guy Stanton. *Stein and the Era of Reform in Prussia, 1807-1815*. Princeton: Princeton University Press, 1922.

Fouchier, J. de. "Le Rôle de l'Inspection Générale des Finances dans l'Administration Française," *Revue Politique et Parlementaire*, No. 537, August 10, 1939, pp. 61-80.

Fraenkel, Hans. "Dampfschiff und Eisenbahn am Niederrhein: Studien über ihre Anfänge, unter besonderer Berücksichtigung Düsseldorfs," *Düsseldorfer Jahrbuch 1915: Beiträge zur Geschichte des Niederrheins*, XVII (1915), 179-287.

France, Ecole Nationale d'Administration. *Epreuves et Statistiques des Concours de 1953*. Paris: Imprimerie Nationale, 1954.

France, Ecole Nationale d'Administration. *Epreuves et Statistiques des Concours de 1964*. Paris: Imprimerie Nationale, 1965.

France, Ministère des Finances et des Affaires Economiques. Institut National de la Statistique et des Etudes Economique. Direction de la Statistique Générale. *Annuaire Statistique Abrégé*. Vol. 2, 1949. Paris: Imprimerie Nationale, 1950.

Francis, Emmerich. "Beamte—Spezialisten für das Allgemeine," *Frankfurter Allgemeine Zeitung*, March 15, 1966.

Freedeman, Charles E. *The Conseil d'Etat in Modern France*. New York: Columbia University Press, 1961.

Fréville, Henri. *L'Intendance de Bretagne (1689-1790)*. 2 Vols. Dissertation, University of Paris, Faculté des Lettres. Rennes: Plihon, Editeur, 1953.

Fricke, Hermann. "Die Landesdirektoren der Provinz Brandenburg, 1876-1945," *Jahrbuch für die Geschichte Mittel- und Ostdeutschland*, V (1956), 295-325.

Friedrich, C. J. "The Continental Tradition of Training Administrators in Law and Jurisprudence," *Journal of Modern History*, XI (1939), 129-48.

Friedricks, Robert W. *A Sociology of Sociology*. New York: The Free Press, 1970.

Fry, Geoffrey Kingdon. *Statesmen in Disguise: The Changing Role of the Administrative Class of the British Home Civil Service, 1853-1966*. London: Macmillan, 1969.

Die Führungskräfte der Wirtschaft. Eine Untersuchung für Die Welt durchgeführt vom EMNID Institut für Industrielle Market- und Werbeforschung. N.p., n.d.

Gablentz, Otto Heinrich von der. "Industriebürokratie," *Schmollers Jahrbuch*, L (1926), 43-76.

Gaudemet, Paul-Marie. *Le Civil Service Britannique*: *Essai sur le Régime de la Fonction Publique en Grande Bretagne*. Paris: Armand Colin, 1952.

————. "The Teaching of Public Administration in France," *Public Administration*, XXVIII (1950), 87-96.

Gehrig, Hans. *Friedrich List und Deutschlands politisch-ökonomische Einheit*. Leipzig: Koehler and Amelang, 1956.

Geib, Ekkehard. "Die Ausbildung des Nachwuchs für den höheren Verwaltungsdienst unter besonderes Berücksichtigung des Geschichte der Justiz- und Verwaltungsausbildung in Preussen," *Archiv für Öffentliches Recht*, XLI (1956), 307-45.

Gerbod, Paul. *La Vie Quotidienne dans les Lycées et Collèges au XIXᵉ Siècle*. Paris: Librairie Hachette, 1968.

Germany, Federal Republic, Statistisches Bundesamt. *Statistisches Jahrbuch für die Bundesrepublik Deutschland, 1952*. Wiesbaden: W. Kohlhammer for Statistisches Bundesamt, 1952.

Germany, Federal Republic, Statistisches Bundesamt. *Statistisches Jahrbuch für die Bundesrepublik Deutschland, 1955*. Wiesbaden: W. Kohlhammer for Statistisches Bundesamt, 1955.

Germany, Federal Republic, Statistisches Bundesamt. *Statistisches Jahrbuch für die Bundesrepublik Deutschland, 1970*. Wiesbaden: W. Kohlhammer for Statistisches Bundesamt, 1970.

Germany, Länderrat des amerikanischen Besatzungsgebiets. *Statistisches Handbuch von Deutschland, 1928-1944*. Munich: Fritz Ehrenwirth, 1949.

Germany, Oberbefehlshaber Ost, Presseabteilung Ober Ost. *Das Land Ober Ost*: *Deutsche Arbeit in den Verwaltungsgebieten Kurland, Litauen und Bialystok-Grodno*. Stuttgart: Deutscher Verlags-Anstalt, 1917.

Gerschenkron, Alexander. *Economic Backwardness in Historical Perspective*. Cambridge, Mass.: Belknap Press, 1962.

————. *Europe in the Russian Mirror*: *Four Lectures in Economic History*. Cambridge, England: Cambridge University Press, 1970.

Gierke, Otto. "Die juristische Studienordnung," *Jahrbuch für Gesetzgebung, Verwaltung und Volkswissenschaft*, I (1877), 1-32.

Gignoux, C. J. "L'Industrialisme de Saint-Simon à Walther Rathenau," *Revue d'Histoire Economique et Sociale*, XI (1923), 200-17.

Gille, Bertrand. *Recherches sur la Formation de la Grande Entreprise Capitaliste*. Paris: S.E.V.P.E.N., 1959.

Gillis, John R. "Aristocracy and Bureaucracy in Nineteenth Century Prussia," *Past and Present*, XLI (1960), 105-29.

————. *The Prussian Bureaucracy in Crisis, 1840-1860*: *Origins of an Administrative Ethos*. Stanford: Stanford University Press, 1971.

Girard, Alain. *La Réussite Sociale en France*. Paris: Les Presses Universitaires, 1961.

Girard, Louis. *La Politique des Travaux Publics du Second Empire*. Dissertation, University of Paris, Faculté des Lettres. Paris: Librairie Armand Colin, 1952.

Girardet, Raoul. *La Société Militaire dans la France Contemporaine (1815-1939)*. Paris: Plon, 1953.

Göber, Willi and Friedrich Herneck (eds.). *Forschen und Wirken: Festschrift zur 150. Jahr-Feier (Humboldt University, Berlin)*, Vol. III. Berlin: Deutscher Verlag der Wissenschaft, 1960.

Goblot, Edmond. *La Barrière et le Niveau: Etude Sociologique sur la Bourgeoisie Française Moderne*. Paris: Presses Universitaires de France, 1967.

Godard, Charles. *Les Pouvoirs des Intendants sous Louis XIV, Particulièrement dans les Pays d'Elections de 1661 à 1715*. Dissertation, University of Paris, Faculté des Lettres. Paris: L. Larose, 1901.

Goebel, Otto. *Deutsche Rohstoffwirtschaft im Weltkrieg einschliesslich des Hindenburg-Programms*. Stuttgart: Deutsche Verlags-Anstalt, 1930.

Göhring, Martin. *Geschichte der Grossen Revolution*. 2 Vols. Tübingen: J.C.B. Mohr, 1950.

Goldhagen, Erich (ed.). *Ethnic Minorities in the Soviet Union*. New York: F. A. Praeger, 1968.

Goldschmidt, Friedrich and Paul. *Das Leben des Staatsrath Kunth*. Berlin: Julius Springer, 1881.

Golovin, Nicholas N. *The Russian Army in the World War*. New Haven: Yale University Press, 1931.

Goodwin, Albert (ed.). *The European Nobilities in the Eighteenth Century: Studies of the Nobilities of the Major European States in the Pre-Reform Era*. London: Adam and Charles Black, 1953.

Gorchakov, Andrei (ed.). *Aperçu des Chemins de Fer Russes depuis l'Origine jusqu'en 1892*. 2 Vols. Brussels: Paul Weissenbruch, 1897.

Görlitz, Walter. *Die Junker: Adel und Bauer im deutschen Osten*. Blüchsburg am Ostsee: C. A. Starke Verlag, 1957.

Got'e, Iurii. *Istoriia Oblastnogo Upravleniia v Rossii ot Petra I do Ekateriny II*. Moscow: Vol. I, Imperatorskoe Obshchestvo Istorii i Drevnostei Rossii, 1913; Vol. II, Izdatel'stvo Akademii Nauk SSSR, 1941.

Gottfried. "Rang und Gehalt im Justiz und Verwaltung," *Preussische Jahrbücher*, LXXIX (1895), 133-39.

Gould, Jay M. *The Technical Elite*. New York: Augustus M. Kelley, 1966.

Gourdon, A. "Les Grands Commis et le Mythe de l'Intérêt Général," *Promotions* (1955), No. 35, pp. 51-57.

Gournay, Bernard. "Un Groupe Dirigéant de la Société Française: Les Grands Fonctionnaires," *Revue Française de Science Politique*, XIV (1964), 215-42.

Grabowsky, Adolf (ed.). *Die Reform des deutschen Beamtentums.* Gotha: Friedrich Andreas Perthes A. G., 1917.

Granick, David. *Management of the Industrial Firm in the USSR: A Study in Soviet Economic Planning.* New York: Columbia University Press, 1954.

Gras, L. J. *Histoire des Premiers Chemins de Fer Français (Saint-Etienne à Andrezieux; Saint-Etienne à Lyon; Andrezieux à Roanne) et du Premier Tramway de France (Montbrison à Montbrond).* Saint-Etienne: Imprimerie Théolier, 1924.

Great Britain, Civil Service Commissioners. *Report of Her Majesty's Civil Service Commissioners for the Period 1st January to 31st December 1962. Being the Ninety-Sixth Report of the Commissioners.* London: H. M. Stationery Office, 1963.

Great Britain, Committee under the Chairmanship of Lord Fulton. *The Civil Service.* Vols. I, II, III (1), III (2), IV, V (1), V (2). London: H. M. Stationery Office, 1968.

Great Britain, House of Commons. *Parliamentary Papers, 1856. Reports of Commissioners*, XXII, xvii.

Great Britain, House of Commons. *Parliamentary Papers, 1875. Reports from Commissioners*, XXIII, 9, Civil Service Inquiry [Playfair].

Great Britain, House of Commons. *Parliamentary Papers, 1914. Reports of Commissioners*, XV, 5, 841ff. Fifty-Eighth Report of His Majesty's Civil Service Commissioners.

Great Britain, House of Commons. *Parliamentary Papers, 1964-65. Sixth Report from the Estimates Committee. Together with the Minutes of the Evidence Taken before Sub-Committee E and Appendices.* Recruitment to the Civil Service. London: H. M. Stationery Office, 1965.

Great Britain, Ministry of Reconstruction. *Report of the Machinery of Government Committee.* London: H. M. Stationery Office, 1930.

Great Britain, Royal Commission on the Civil Service, 1953-55. *Report Presented to Parliament by Command of Her Majesty, November 1955.* London: H. M. Stationery Office, 1955.

Greaves, H.R.G. *The Civil Service in the Changing State: A Survey of Civil Service Reform and the Implications of a Planned Economy on Public Administration in England.* London: George G. Harrap and Co., Ltd., 1947.

Grech, N. I. *Zapiski o Moei Zhizni*. St. Petersburg: n.p., 1886.

Gretten, R. H. *The King's Government: A Study of the Growth of the Central Administration*. London: G. Bell and Sons, Ltd., 1913.

Gribovsky, Adrian Moiseevich. *Vospominaniia i Dnevniki*. N.p., n.d.

Gross, Llewellyn (ed.). *Symposium on Sociological Theory*. Evanston, Ill.: Row, Peterson & Co., 1959.

Gross, Neal *et al*. *Explorations in Role Analysis: Studies of the School Superintendent*. New York: John Wiley and Sons, Inc., 1958.

Gruder, Vivian R. *The Royal Provincial Intendants: A Governing Elite in Eighteenth Century France*. Ithaca: Cornell University Press, 1968.

Gusfield, Joseph R. "Equalitarianism and Bureaucratic Recruitment," *Administrative Science Quarterly*, II (1957-58), 521-24.

Guttin, Jacques. *Vauban et le Corps des Ingénieurs Militaires*. Dissertation, University of Paris, Faculté de Droit, 1947.

Guttsman, W. L. "Aristocracy and the Middle Class in the British Political Elite, 1886-1916: A Study of Formative Influences and of the Attitude to Politics," *British Journal of Sociology*, V (1954), 12-32.

———— (ed.). *The English Ruling Class*. London: Weidenfeld and Nicolson, 1969.

Hagen, Everett E. *On the Theory of Social Change: How Economic Growth Begins*. Homewood, Ill.: The Dorsey Press, 1962.

———— and Stephanie F. T. White. *Great Britain: Quiet Revolution in Planning*. Syracuse: Syracuse University Press, 1966.

Hall, Richard H. "The Concept of Bureaucracy: An Empirical Assessment," *American Journal of Sociology*, LXX (1964), 32-40.

Halsey, A. H. and M. A. Trow. *The British Academics*. Cambridge, Mass.: Harvard University Press, 1971.

Hamon, Augustin. *Les Maîtres de la France*. 2 Vols. Paris: Editions Sociales Internationales, 1937.

Hamon, Leo. "Les Sciences Administratives et la Diffusion de la Pensée Française à l'Etranger," *Revue Administrative*, VII, No. 39 (1954), 243-47.

Handbuch der Politik. 3rd ed. Vol. III: *Der politische Erneuerung*. Berlin: Dr. Walther Rothschild, 1921.

Hanotaux, Gabriel. *Origines de l'Institution des Intendants des Provinces*. Paris: Champion, Libraire, 1884.

Hans, Nicholas. *History of Russian Educational Policy (1701-1917)*. New York: Russell and Russell, 1964.

Harris, John S. and Thomas V. Garcia. "The Permanent Secretaries: Britain's Top Administrators," *Public Administration Review*, XXVI (1966), 31-44.

Harris, Seymour. *John Maynard Keynes: Economist and Policy Maker.* New York: Charles Scribner's Sons, 1955.

Hartmann, Heinz. *Authority and Organization in German Management.* Princeton: Princeton University Press, 1959.

Hartung, Fritz. "Studien zur Geschichte der preussischen Verwaltung," Zweiter Teil, "Der Oberpräsident," *Abhandlungen der Preussischen Akademie der Wissenschaften,* 1943, Philosophisch-Historische Klasse, No. 4, pp. 1-67.

Haumant, Emile. *La Culture Française en Russie.* Paris: Librairie Hachette et Cie, 1910.

Hausen, Joseph. *Gustav von Mevissen, ein rheinisches Lebensbild 1815-1899.* 2 Vols. Berlin: Georg Reimer, 1906.

Haussmann, Eugène G. *Mémoires du Baron Haussmann.* 2nd ed. 3 Vols. Paris: Victor-Havard, Editeur, 1890.

Haxthausen, Baron von. *The Russian Empire: Its People, Institutions and Resources.* Vol. 1. London: Chapman and Hall, 1856.

Heady, Ferrel. *Public Administration: A Comparative Perspective.* Englewood Cliffs, N. J.: Prentice-Hall, 1966.

Heath, Thomas L. *The Treasury.* London: G. P. Putnam's Sons, Ltd., 1927.

Heer, Georg. *Geschichte der deutschen Bursenschaft.* Vol. IV. *Die Bursenschaft in der Zeit der Vorbereitung des Zweiten Reiches, im Zweiten Reich und im Weltkrieg von 1859 bis 1919.* Heidelberg: Carl Winter, 1939.

Heffter, Heinrich. *Die deutsche Selbstverwaltung im 19. Jahrhundert: Geschichte der Ideen und Institutionen.* Stuttgart: K. F. Koehler Verlag, 1950.

Heinzen, Karl. *Die preussische Büreaukratie.* Darmstadt: Carl Wilhelm Leske, 1845.

Henderson, W. O. *Britain and Industrial Europe, 1750-1870: Studies in British Influence on the Industrial Revolution in Western Europe.* Liverpool: Liverpool University Press, 1954.

———. *The Industrial Revolution on the Continent: Germany, France, Russia 1800-1914.* London: Frank Cass and Co., Ltd., 1961.

———. "Peter Beuth and the Rise of Prussian Industry, 1810-1845," *Economic History Review,* Second Series, VIII (1955), 222-31.

———. "Walther Rathenau: A Pioneer of the Planned Economy," *Economic History Review,* Second Series, IV (1951-52), 98-108.

Henry, William E. "The Business Executive: The Psycho-Dynamics of a Social Role," *American Journal of Sociology,* LIV (1949), 286-91.

Heussler, Robert. *Yesterday's Rulers: The Making of the British Colonial Service.* Syracuse: Syracuse University Press, 1963.

Hicks, W. R. *The School in English and German Fiction.* London: The Soncine Press, 1933.

Hill, Forest G. "Government Engineering Aid to Railroads before the Civil War," *Journal of Economic History,* XI (1951), 235-46.

Hill, George B. *The Life of Sir Rowland Hill.* 2 Vols. London: Thomas de la Rue and Co., 1880.

Hintze, Otto. "Die Hohenzollern und der Adel," *Historische Zeitschrift,* CXII (1914), 494-524.

———. "Preussische Reformbestrebungen vor 1806," *Historische Zeitschrift,* LXXVI (1896), 413-43.

———. *Staat und Verfassung.* 2nd ed. Vol. I. Göttingen: Vandenhoeck and Ruprecht, 1962.

Hochschule für Verwaltungswissenschaften Speyer. *Personal- und Vorlesungsverzeichnis: Wintersemester 1966-1967.*

Hodgetts, J. E. "The Civil Service and Policy Formation," *Canadian Journal of Economics and Political Science,* XXIII (1957), 467-77.

Hoetzsch, Otto. "Adel und Lehnswesen in Russland und Polen und ihr Verhältnis zur deutschen Entwicklung," *Historische Zeitschrift,* CVIII (1912), 541-92.

Hoffmann, Walter. *Bergakademie Freiberg.* Frankfurt a. M.: Weidlich, 1959.

Holt, Robert T. and John E. Turner. *The Political Basis of Economic Development: An Exploration in Comparative Political Analysis.* Princeton: D. Van Nostrand Co., 1966.

Hortleder, Gerd. "Leninismus, Technik und Industrialisierung: Zur Rolle der Technik und des Ingenieurs in der Sowjetunion und der DDR," *Humanismus und Technik,* XII (1968), 1-19.

Hough, Jerry. *The Soviet Prefects: The Local Party Organs in Industrial Decision-Making.* Cambridge, Mass.: Harvard University Press, 1969.

Hsu, Frances L. K. (ed.). *Psychological Anthropology: Approaches to Culture and Personality.* Homewood, Ill.: The Dorsey Press, 1961.

Hubback, David. "The Treasury's Role in Civil Service Training," *Public Administration,* XXXV (1957), 99-109.

Hughes, Edward. "Civil Service Reform 1853-55," *History,* XXVII (1942), 51-83. Reprinted in *Public Administration,* XXXII (1954), 17-51.

———. "Sir Charles Trevelyan and Civil Service Reform, 1853-55," *English Historical Review,* LXIV (1949), 53-88, 206-34.

Humblet, Jean E. *Les Cadres d'Entreprises: France, Belgique, Royaume-Uni.* Paris: Editions Universitaires, 1966.

Hunt, David. *Parents and Children in History: The Psychology of Family Life in Early Modern France.* New York: Basic Books, Inc., 1970.

Hurwitz, Samuel J. *State Intervention in Great Britain: A Study of Economic Control and Social Response, 1914-1919.* New York: Columbia University Press, 1949.

Hyde, Francis E. *Mr. Gladstone at the Board of Trade.* London: Cobden-Sanderson, 1934.

Iablochkov, Mikhail T. *Istoriia Dvorianskago Sosloviia.* St. Petersburg: A. M. Kotomin, 1876.

Iggers, Georg G. *The Cult of Authority: The Political Philosophy of the Saint-Simonians, A Chapter in the Intellectual History of Totalitarianism.* The Hague: Martinus Nihoff, 1958.

Inkeles, Alex and Raymond A. Bauer. *The Soviet Citizen: Daily Life in a Totalitarian Society.* Cambridge, Mass.: Harvard University Press, 1959.

Institut Technique des Administrations Publiques. "La Formation des Dirigéants dans l'Administration et dans les Entreprises Privées." Paris, 1955. Mimeographed.

Irsay, Stephen d'. *Histoire des Universités Françaises et Etrangères.* Vol. II. Paris: Editions August Picard, 1935.

Isaacsohn, Salomon. *Das preussische Beamtentum.* 3 Vols. Berlin: Puttkamer and Mühlbrecht, 1874-84.

Iscoe, Ira and Harold W. Stevenson (eds.). *Personality Development in Children.* Austin: University of Texas Press, 1960.

Jackman, W. T. *The Development of Transportation in Modern England.* 3rd ed. London: Frank Cass, 1966.

Jacob, Herbert. *German Administration since Bismarck: Central Authority versus Local Autonomy.* New Haven: Yale University Press, 1963.

Janowski, Manfred. "Prussian Policy and the Development of the Ruhr Mining Region, 1766-1865." Dissertation, University of Wisconsin, Madison, 1968.

Jenkins, Hester and D. C. Jones. "Social Class of Cambridge University Alumni of the 18th and 19th Centuries," *British Journal of Sociology,* I (1950), 93-116.

Jenks, Leland H. "Business Ideology," *Explorations in Entrepreneurial History,* X (1957), 1-7.

Jèze, Gaston. "Le Recrutement des Membres de la Cour des Comptes," *Revue de Science et de Législation Financière,* VIII (1910), 227-40.

Jones, Thomas. *Lloyd George.* Cambridge, Mass.: Harvard University Press, 1951.

Jungnickel, Friedrich. *Staatsminister Albert von Maybach*: *Ein Beitrag zur Geschichte des preussischen und deutschen Eisenbahnwesens.* Stuttgart: J. G. Cotta'sche Buchhandlung Nachfolger, 1910.

Kalnins, Bruno. *Der sowjetische Propagandastaat*: *Das System und die Mittel der Massenbeeinflussung in der Sowjetunion.* Stockholm: Tidens Förlag, 1956.

Kamm, W. "Minister und Beruf," *Allgemeines Statistisches Archiv.* Jena, XVIII (1928), 3. Heft, 440-52.

Kataev, I. M. *Doreformennaia Biurokratiia*: *Po Zapiskam, Memuaram i Literature.* St. Petersburg: Knigoizdatel'stvo "Energiia," n.d.

Kaufmann, Richard von. *Die Eisenbahnpolitik Frankreichs.* 2 Vols. Stuttgart: J. G. Cotta'sche Buchhandlung, 1896.

Kech, Edwin. *Geschichte der deutschen Eisenbahnpolitik.* Leipzig: G. F. Göschen, 1911.

Keller, Suzanne. *Beyond the Ruling Class*: *Strategic Elites in Modern Society.* New York: Random House, 1963.

Kelsall, Roger K. *Higher Civil Servants in Britain from 1870 to the Present Day.* London: Routledge and Kegan Paul, Ltd., 1955.

Kemp, Tom. *Economic Forces in French History.* London: Dennis Dobson, 1971.

Kern, Ernst. "Berufsbeamtentum und Politik," *Archiv des Öffentlichen Rechts.* Neue Folge, XXXVIII (1951), 107-10.

Kerzhentsev, P. M. *Printsipy Organizatsii.* Moscow: Izdatel'stvo "Ekonomika," 1968.

Kesler, Jean-François. "Les Ancien Elèves de l'Ecole Nationale d'Administration," *Revue Française de Science Politique,* XIV (1964), 243-67.

Kessler, Marie-Christine. *Le Conseil d'Etat.* Paris: Armand Colin, 1968.

Kharvin, A. F. "Captains of Soviet Industry," *Voprosy Istorii,* No. 5, May 1966. Condensed trans. in *Current Digest of the Soviet Press,* XVIII, No. 28, 3.

Khorev, B. S. *Problemy Gorodov*: *Ekonomiko-Geograficheskoe Issledovanie Gorodskogo Rasseleniia v SSSR.* Moscow: Izdatel'stvo "Mysl'," 1971.

Kindleberger, Charles P. *Economic Growth in France and Britain, 1851-1950.* Cambridge, Mass.: Harvard University Press, 1964.

King, James E. *Science and Rationalism in the Government of Louis XIV.* Baltimore: The Johns Hopkins Press, 1949.

Kingsley, J. Donald. *Representative Bureaucracy*: *An Interpretation of the British Civil Service.* Yellow Springs, Ohio: The Antioch Press, 1944.

370—The European Administrative Elite

Kiniapina, N. S. *Politika Russkogo Samoderzhaviia v Oblasti Promyshlennosti (20-50-e Gody XIX v.)*. Moscow: Izdatel'stvo Moskovskogo Universiteta, 1968.

Kirkland, Edward C. *Dream and Thought in the Business Community, 1860-1900*. Ithaca: Cornell University Press, 1956.

Kislinsky, N. A. (ed.). *Nasha Zheleznodorozhnaia Politika po Dokumentam Arkhiva Komiteta Ministrov: Istoricheskii Ocherk*. 2 Vols. St. Petersburg: Gosudarstvennaia Tipografiia, 1902.

Klages, Helmut and Gerd Hortleder. "Gesellschaftsbild und soziales Selbstverständnis des Ingenieurs," *Schmollers Jahrbuch*, LXXXV (1965), 661-85.

Kobeko, Dmitrii. *Imperatorskii Tsarskosel'skii Litsei: Nastavniki i Pitomtsy, 1811-1843*. St. Petersburg: V. O. Kirshbaum, 1911.

Kockjoy, Wolfgang. *Der deutsche Kaufmannsroman: Versuch einer kultur- und geistesgeschichtlichen-genetischen Darstellung*. Strassburg: Heitz Verlag, 1933.

Kogan, Leonard S. (ed.). *Social Science Theory and Social Work Research*. New York: National Association of Social Workers, 1959.

Kohn-Bramstedt, Ernst. *Aristocracy and the Middle Classes in Germany: Social Types in German Literature, 1830-1900*. London: P. S. King and Son, Ltd., 1937.

Kolabinska, Marie. *La Circulation des Elites en France: Etude Historique depuis la Fin du XIᵉ Siècle jusqu'à la Grande Révolution*. Dissertation, Lausanne University, Faculté de Droit et des Lettres. Lausanne: Imprimeries Réunies, 1912.

Kommunisticheskaia Partiia Sovetskogo Soiuza v Rezoliutsiiakh i Resheniiakh S"ezdov, Konferentsii i Plenumov Ts.K. Vol. II. Moscow: Gosudarstvennoe Izdatel'stvo Politicheskoi Literatury, 1953.

König, Helmut. *Zur Geschichte der Nationalerziehung in Deutschland*. Berlin: Akademie Verlag, 1960.

Koselleck, Reinhart. *Preussen zwischen Reform und Revolution: Allgemeines Landrecht, Verwaltung und soziale Bewegung von 1791 bis 1848*. Stuttgart: Ernst Klett, 1967.

Kossmann, Ernst H. *La Fronde*. Dissertation, Leyden University, Faculty of Letters, 1954.

Köttgen, Arnold. *Das deutsche Berufsbeamtentum und die parlamentarische Demokratie*. Berlin: Walter de Gruyter and Co., 1928.

Krutikov, M. "Nachalo Zheleznodorozhnogo Stroitel'stva v Rossii (iz Zapisok P.P. Mel'nikova)," *Krasny Arkhiv*, CIC (1940), 127-79.

Kube, Horst. *Die geschichtliche Entwicklung der Stellung des preussischen Oberpräsidenten*. Dissertation, Berlin University, Law Faculty. Würzburg: Konrad Triltsch, 1939.

Kulischer, Josef. "La Grande Industrie aux XVIIᵉ et XVIIIᵉ Siècles: France, Allemagne, Russie," *Annales d'Histoire Economique et Sociale*, III (1931), 11-46.

———. "Die kapitalistischen Unternehmer in Russland (inbesondere die Bauern als Unternehmer) in den Anfangsstadien des Kapitalismus," *Archiv für Sozialwissenschaft und Sozialpolitik*, LXV (1931), 309-55.

Kuznets, Simon. *Six Lectures on Economic Growth*. Glencoe, Ill.: The Free Press, 1959.

Lalumière, Pierre. *L'Inspection des Finances*. Dissertation, University of Paris, Faculté de Droit, Paris; Presses Universitaires, 1959.

Lambert-Dansette, Jean. *Quelques Familles du Patronat Textile à Lille-Armentières (1789-1914): Essai sur les Origines et l'Evolution d'une Bourgeoisie*. Dissertation, University of Paris, Faculté de Droit. Lille: Emile Raoust et Cie, 1954.

———. "Recrutement et Evolution Sociale d'un Patronat du Nord," *Bulletin de la Société d'Etude de la Province de Cambrai*, XLIII (1954), 3ᵉ Fascicule.

Lamé, G., B.P.E. Clapeyron, and Stéphane and Eugène Flachat. *Vues Politiques et Pratiques sur les Travaux Publics de France*. Paris: Paulin Libraire, 1852.

Landauer, Edgar. "Kapitalistisches Geist und Verwaltungsbürokratie in öffentlichen Unternehmungen," *Schmollers Jahrbuch*, LIV (1930), 505-21.

Landes, David S. "The Structure of Enterprise in the Nineteenth Century. The Cases of Britain and Germany," *International Congress of Historical Sciences, XI, Rapports*, V (1960), 107-28, II, T. 5.

———. *The Unbound Prometheus: Technological Change and Industrial Development in Western Europe from 1750 to the Present*. Cambridge, England: Cambridge University Press, 1969.

"Landsmannschaftliche Herkunft der Bundesbeamten," *Bulletin des Presse- und Informationsamtes der Bundesregierung*, December 2, 1961.

Lane, David, *Politics and Society in the USSR*. New York: Random House, 1971.

Lane, Robert. *Political Ideology: Why the American Common Man Believes What He Does*. New York: The Free Press of Glencoe, 1962.

Langrod, Georges. *Les Problèmes de Formation dans la Fonction Publique en Grande Bretagne*. Extract of No. 2 of *State Sociale*, 1963. Turin: Unione Tipografice-Editrice, 1963.

Lantoine, Albert. *Histoire de la Franc-Maçonnerie Française: La Franc-Maçonnerie dans l'Etat*. Paris: Emile Nourry, Editeur, 1935.

Lanza, Albert. *Les Projets de Reforme Administrative en France (de 1919 à Nos Jours)*. Paris: Presses Universitaires de France, 1968.

LaPalombara, Joseph (ed.). *Bureaucracy and Political Development*. Princeton: Princeton University Press, 1963.

Laski, Harold J. "The Education of the Civil Servant," *Public Administration*, XXI (1943), 13-23.

Lazarsfeld, Paul. "Reflections on Business," *American Journal of Sociology*, LXV (1959), 1-31.

Lederer, Emil. *Die wirtschaftlichen Organisationen*. Leipzig: B. G. Teubner, 1913.

Leendertz, Werner. *Die industrielle Gesellschaft als Ziel und Grundlage der Sozialreform: Eine systematische Darstellung der Ideen Saint-Simons und seiner Schüler*. Dissertation, Cologne University, Economics and Social Science Faculty. Emsdetten: Heinz and J. Lechte, 1938.

Leff, Gordon. *History and Social Theory*. University, Ala.: University of Alabama Press, 1969.

Lefranc, G. "Les Chemins de Fer devant le Parlement Français, 1835-1842," *Revue d'Histoire Moderne*, V (1930), 337-64.

———. "La Construction des Chemins de Fer et l'Opinion Publique vers 1830," *Revue d'Histoire Moderne*, V (1930), 270-79.

Legge-Bourke, Henry. *Master of the Offices: An Essay and Correspondence on the Central Control of His Majesty's Civil Service*. London: The Falcon Press, 1950.

Legrand, Louis. *Sénac de Meilhan et l'Intendance du Hainaut et du Cambrésis sous Louis XVI*. Valenciennes: J. Giard, 1868.

Lehman, Harvey C. *Age and Achievement*. Princeton: Princeton University Press, 1953.

Lehmann, Max. *Freiherr vom Stein*. 3 Vols. Leipzig: S. Hirzel, 1902, 1903, 1905.

Leikina-Svirskaia, V. R. *Intelligentsiia v Rossii vo Vtoroi Polovine XIX Veka*. Moscow: Izdatel'stvo "Mysl'," 1971.

Lekachman, Robert (ed.). *Keynes' General Theory: Reports of Three Decades*. New York: St. Martin's Press, 1964.

Lentin, A. (ed. and trans.). *Prince M. M. Shcherbatov: On the Corruption of Morals in Russia*. Cambridge, England: University Press, 1969.

Leopold, Charlotte. *Auswahl und Anstellung der Verwaltungsbeamten in England*. Leipzig: Theodor Weicher, 1933.

Leroy-Beaulieu, Anatole. *The Empire of the Tsars and the Russians.* Vol. II. New York: G. P. Putnam's Sons, 1894.

Levasseur, E. *La Population Française: Histoire de la Population avant 1789 et Démographie de la France Comparée à Celle des Autres Nations au XIXᵉ Siècle.* 3 Vols. Paris: Arthur Rousseau, 1889, 1891, 1892.

Levet, Georges. *L'Intendance d'Alsace sous Louis XIV, 1648-1715.* Paris: Société d'Edition "Les Belles Lettres," 1956.

Levinson, Daniel J. "Role, Personality, and Social Structure in the Organizational Setting," *Journal of Abnormal and Social Psychology*, LXVIII (1959), 170-80.

Levy, Marion J., Jr. *Modernization and the Structure of Societies: A Setting for International Affairs.* Vol. I. Princeton: Princeton University Press, 1966.

Lévy-Leboyer, Maurice. *Les Banques Européenes et l'Industrialisation Internationale dans la Première Moitié du XIX Siècle.* Paris: Presses Universitaires, 1964.

Lewis, Roy and Rosemary Stewart. *The Managers: A New Examination of the English, German, and American Executive.* New York: Mentor Books, 1961.

Lhéritier, Michel. *L'Intendant Tourny (1695-1760).* 2 Vols. Paris: Librairie Félix Alcan, 1920.

Lhomme, Jean. *La Grande Bourgeoisie au Pouvoir (1830-1880): Essai sur l'Histoire Sociale de la France.* Paris: Presses Universitaires de France, 1960.

Liard, Louis. *L'Enseignement Supérieur en France 1789-1889.* 2 Vols. Paris: Armand Colin et Cie, 1888, 1894.

Liesebach, Ingolf. *Der Wandel des politischen Führungsschicht der deutschen Industrie von 1918 bis 1945.* Dissertation, Basel University, Staatswissenschaft. Hannover: n.p., 1957.

Linton, Ralph. "Culture, Society and the Individual," *Journal of Abnormal and Social Psychology*, XXXIII (1938), 425-36.

———. "A Neglected Aspect of Social Organization," *American Journal of Sociology*, XLV (1940), 870-86.

Lipset, Seymour M. (ed.). *Politics and the Social Sciences.* New York: Oxford University Press, 1969.

Lisitsyn, V. and G. Popov. "The Economic Manager's Outlook," *Pravda*, January 19, 1968. Condensed trans. in *Current Digest of the Soviet Press*, XX, No. 3, 25-26.

Long, Marcel. "Le Régime des Etudes à l'Ecole Nationale d'Administration," *Promotions* (1955), No. 35, pp. 55-60.

Lorimer, Frank. *The Population of the Soviet Union: History and Prospects.* Geneva: League of Nations, 1946.

Lotz, Albert. *Geschichte des deutschen Beamtentums.* Berlin: R. von Decker Verlag, 1906.

Louvel, Albert. "Grands Corps et Grands Commis," *Revue des Deux Mondes,* January, 1959, pp. 130-39.

Lurion, Roger de. "M. [Charles-André] de Lacoré, Intendant de Franche-Comté (1761-1784)," *Académie des Sciences, Belles-Lettres et Arts de Besançon: Proces-Verbaux et Mémoires,* 1897, pp. 207-60.

MacDonagh, Oliver. "The Nineteenth-Century Revolution in Government: A Reappraisal," *The Historical Journal,* 1 (1958), 52-67.

———. *A Pattern of Government Growth, 1800-60: The Passenger Acts and Their Enforcement.* London: Macgibbon and Kee, 1961.

Male, George A. *Education in France.* Washington: U. S. Dept. of Health, Education, and Welfare, Government Printing Office, 1963.

Management Succession: The Recruitment, Selection, Training and Promotion of Managers. London: The Acton Society Trust, 1956.

Mannheim, Karl. *Ideology and Utopia: An Introduction to the Sociology of Knowledge.* New York: Harcourt, Brace and Co., Inc., 1954.

Marchand, J. *Un Intendant sous Louis XIV. Etude sur l'Administration de Lebret en Provence (1687-1704).* Paris: Librairie Hachette, 1889.

Marchet, Gustav. *Studien über die Entwicklung der Verwaltungslehre in Deutschland von der zweiten Hälfte des 17. bis zum Ende des 18. Jahrhunderts.* Frankfurt: Sauer and Auvermann, 1966.

Marsh, Robert. "The Bearing of Comparative Analysis on Sociological Theory," *Social Forces,* XLIII (1964), 188-96.

Martin, Germain. *La Grande Industrie en France sous le Règne de Louis XV.* Paris: Albert Fontemoing Editeur, 1900.

Martin, Henri-Jean. *Livre, Pouvoirs et Société à Paris au XVIIᵉ Siècle (1598-1701).* 2 Vols. Geneva: Librairie Droz, 1969.

Martiny, Fritz. *Die Adelsfrage in Preussen vor 1806 als politisches und soziales Problem: Erläutert am Beispiele des kurmärkischen Adels.* Stuttgart: Verlag W. Kohlhammer, 1938.

Mason, Philip [Philip Woodruff, pseud.]. *The Men Who Ruled India.* 2 Vols. London: Jonathan Cape, 1953.

Matschoss, Conrad. "Vom Ingenieur, seinem Werden und seiner Arbeit in Deutschland," *Beiträge zur Geschichte der Technik und Industrie,* XX (1930), 1-14.

Matthews, George T. *The Royal General Farms in Eighteenth-Century France.* New York: Columbia University Press, 1958.

Mayer, Lawrence C. *Comparative Political Inquiry: A Methodological Survey*. Homewood, Ill.: The Dorsey Press, 1972.

Mazlish, Bruce (ed.). *The Railroad and the Space Program: An Exploration in Historical Analogy*. Cambridge, Mass.: The M.I.T. Press, 1965.

McClelland, David C. *The Achieving Society*. Princeton: D. Van Nostrand Co., Inc., 1961.

———, Alfred L. Baldwin, Urie Bronfenbrenner, and Fred L. Strodtbeck. *Talent and Society: New Perspectives in the Identification of Talent*. Princeton: D. Van Nostrand Co., 1958.

Meier, Ernst von. *Französische Einflüsse auf die Staats- und Rechtsentwicklung Preussens im XIX. Jahrhundert*. 2 Vols. Leipzig: Duncker and Humblot, 1907-1908.

Mendel, Arthur P. *Dilemmas of Progress in Tsarist Russia: Legal Marxism and Legal Populism*. Cambridge, Mass.: Harvard University Press, 1961.

Merton, Robert, *et al. The Student-Physician: Introductory Studies in the Sociology of Medical Education*. Cambridge, Mass.: Harvard University Press, 1957.

Meyer, Alfred G. *Leninism*. Cambridge, Mass.: Harvard University Press, 1957.

Meynaud, Jean. *Technocratie et Politique*. Lausanne: n.p., 1960.

———. *La Technocratie: Mythe ou Réalité*. Paris: Pagot, 1964.

Michaelis, Georg. *Für Staat und Volk: Eine Lebensgeschichte*. Berlin: Furche-Verlag, 1922.

Miliukoff, Peter. "Zur Geschichte des russischen Adels," *Archiv für Sozialwissenschaft und Sozialpolitik*, XLI (1916), 88-109.

Millar, Robert. *The New Classes*. London: Longmans, Green, 1966.

Miller, William (ed.). *Men in Business: Essays in the History of Entrepreneurship*. Cambridge, Mass.: Harvard University Press, 1952.

Mitchell, B. R. "The Coming of the Railway and United Kingdom Economic Growth," *Journal of Economic History*, XXIV (1964), 315-36.

Mitrani, Nora. "Ambiguïté de la Technocratie," *Cahiers Internationaux de Sociologie*, XXX (1961), 101-14.

———. "Attitudes et Symboles Techno-Bureaucratiques: Reflexions sur une Enquête," *Cahiers Internationaux de Sociologie*, XXIV (1958), 148-66.

Mohl, R. "Ueber die wissenschaftliche Bildung der Beamten in den Ministerien des Innern, mit besonderer Anwendung auf Württemberg," *Zeitschrift für die gesamte Staatswissenschaft*, II (1845), 129-84.

Mohl, R. "Ueber eine Anstalt zur Bildung höherer Staatsdiener," *Zeitschrift für die gesamte Staatswissenschaft*, II (1845), 268-93.

Mohnen, Charles-Georges. *La Sociologie Economique de Walther Rathenau*. Dissertation, University of Nancy, Faculté de Droit. Paris: Recueil Sirey, 1932.

Monas, Sidney. *The Third Section: Police and Society in Russia under Nicholas I*. Cambridge, Mass.: Harvard University Press, 1961.

Monin, H. *Essai sur l'Histoire Administrative du Languedoc pendant l'Intendance de Basville (1685-1719)*. Paris: Librairie Hachette, 1884.

Montyon, Auget de. *Particularités et Observations sur les Ministres des Finances de France les plus Célèbres depuis 1660 jusqu'en 1791*. Paris: Le Norman, Imprimeur-Libraire, 1812.

Morsey, Rudolf. *Die oberste Reichsverwaltung unter Bismarck, 1867-1890*. Münster: Aschendorffsche Verlagsbuchhandlung, 1957.

Morstein-Marx, Fritz. "Berufsbeamtentum in England," *Zeitschrift für die gesamte Staatswissenschaft*, LXXXIX (1930), 449-95.

———. "German Administration and the Speyer Academy," *Public Administration Review*, XXVII (1967), 403-10.

Moses, Robert. *The Civil Service of Great Britain. Studies in History, Economics and Public Law, Columbia University*. Vol. LVII, No. 1. New York: Columbia University Press, 1914.

Most, Otto. "Zur Wirtschafts- und Sozialstatistik der höheren Beamten in Preussen," *Schmollers Jahrbuch*, XXXIX (1915), 181-218.

Mounier, Henri. "De la Situation des Anciens Elèves de l'Ecole Nationale d'Administration dans l'Administration," *Promotions* (1955), No. 35, pp. 70-77.

Mousnier, Roland, *et al. Le Conseil du Roi de Louis XII à la Révolution*. Paris: Presses Universitaires, 1970.

Müller, Alfred. *Die Kriegsrohstoffbewirtschaftung, 1914-1918 im Dienst des deutschen Monopolkapitals*. Berlin: Akademie-Verlag, 1955.

Muncy, Lysbeth W. "The Junkers and the Prussian Administration from 1918 to 1939," *Review of Politics*, IX (1947), 482-501.

Mundt, Theodor. *Geschichte der deutschen Stände nach ihrer gesellschaftlichen Entwickelung und politischen Vertretung*. Berlin: M. Semion, 1854.

Munro, Charles K. *The Fountains in Trafalgar Square: Some Reflections on the Civil Service*. London: William Heinemann, Ltd., 1952.

Musgrove, F. "Middle-Class Education and Employment in the Nineteenth Century." *Economic History Review*, Second Series, XII (1959), 99-111.

————. "Middle-Class Education and Employment in the Nineteenth Century: A Rejoinder," *Economic History Review*, Second Series, XIV (1961-62), 320-32.

————. *The Migratory Elite*. London: Heinemann, 1963.

Musson, A. E. and Eric Robinson. *Science and Technology in the Industrial Revolution*. Toronto: University of Toronto Press, 1969.

Myrdal, Gunnar. *An American Dilemma: The Negro Problem and Modern Democracy*. New York: Harper and Bros., 1944.

Napp-Zinn, Anton Felix. *Johann Friedrich von Pfeiffer und die Kameralwissenschaften an der Universität Mainz*. Wiesbaden: Franz Steiner Verlag, 1955.

————. *Verkerswissenschaft*. Heidelberg: Quelle u. Meyer, 1968.

Naroll, Raul. "Two Solutions to Galton's Problem," *Philosophy of Science*, XXVIII (1961), 15-39.

Nathan, Helene. *Preussens Verfassung und Verwaltung im Urteile rheinischer Achtundvierziger*. Bonn: A. Marcus and E. Webers Verlag, 1912.

Necker, M. *De l'Administration des Finances de la France*. 3 Vols. N.p., 1784.

Nettl, J. P. *Political Mobilization: A Sociological Analysis of Methods and Concepts*. London: Faber and Faber, Ltd., 1967.

Neumann, Franz L. "Approaches to the Study of Political Power," *Political Science Quarterly*, LXV (1950), 161-80.

Newcomb, Theodore M. "Role Behaviors in the Study of Individual Personality and of Groups," *Journal of Personality*, XVIII (1950), 273-89.

Newcomer, Mabel. *The Big Business Executive: The Factors That Made Him, 1900-1950*. New York: Columbia University Press, 1955.

Nock, Oswald S. *The Railway Engineers*. London: B. T. Batsford, Ltd., 1955.

Normand, Charles. *La Bourgeoisie Française au XVIIe Siècle: La Vie Publique—Les Idées et les Actions Politiques, 1604-1661*. Paris: Félix Alcan, Editeur, 1908.

"The Northcote-Trevelyan Report," *Public Administration*, XXXII (1954), 1-16.

"Note: Généralité de la Rochelle, 1694," *Recueil de la Commission des Arts et Monuments Historiques de la Charente-Inférieure*, 4e Série, Vol. II (XII), 408.

Novack, David E. and Robert Lekachman (eds.). *Development and Society: The Dynamics of Economic Change*. New York: St. Martin's Press, 1964.

Nove, Alec. *The Soviet Economy: An Introduction.* New York: Praeger, 1961.

O'Malley, L.S.S. *The Indian Civil Service, 1601-1930.* London: Frank Cass and Co., Ltd., 1965.

O'Reilly, E. *Mémoires sur la Vie Publique et Privée de Claude Pellot, Conseiller, Maître des Requêtes, Intendant et Premier Président du Parlement de Normandie (1619-83).* 2 Vols. Paris: H. Champion, 1881.

"Organizers of Production," *Pravda*, November 10, 1969. Condensed trans. in *Current Digest of the Soviet Press*, XXI, No. 45, 27.

Ortlieb, Heinz-Dietrich and Bruno Molitor (eds.). *Hamburger Jahrbuch für Wirtschafts- und Gesellschaftspolitik.* 10th ed. Tübingen: J.C.B. Mohr, 1965.

Padberg, John W. (S. J.). *Colleges in Controversy: The Jesuit Scholars in France from Revival to Suppression, 1815-1880.* Cambridge, Mass.: Harvard University Press, 1960.

Pages, Georges. "Essai sur l'Evolution des Institutions Administratives en France du Commencement du XVIe Siècle à la Fin du XVIIe," *Revue d'Histoire Moderne*, VII (1932), 8-57, 113-37.

———. *La Monarchie d'Ancien Régime en France (de Henri IV à Louis XIV).* Paris: Librairie Armand Colin, 1928.

———. "La Vénalité des Offices dans l'Ancienne France," *Revue Historique*, CLXIX (1932), 477-95.

Palewski, Jean-Paul. *Histoire des Chefs d'Entreprise.* Paris: Gallimard, 1928.

———. *Le Rôle du Chef d'Entreprise dans la Grande Industrie: Etude de Psychologie Economique.* Dissertation, University of Paris, Faculté de Droit. Paris: Les Presses Universitaires, 1924.

Palmade, Guy P. *Capitalisme et Capitalistes Français au XIXe Siècle.* Paris: Armand Colin, 1961.

Parris, Henry. "A Civil Servant's Diary, 1841-46," *Public Administration*, XXXVIII (1960), 369-80.

———. *Government and the Railways in Nineteenth Century Britain.* London: Routledge and Kegan Paul, 1965.

———. "The Nineteenth Century Revolution in Government: A Reappraisal Reappraised," *The Historical Journal*, III (1960), 17-37.

———. "Twenty Years of l'Ecole Nationale d'Administration," *Public Administration*, XLIII (1965), 395-411.

Parsons, Talcott and Robert F. Bales. *Family, Socialization and Interaction Process.* Glencoe, Ill.: The Free Press, 1955.

Paulsen, Friedrich. *Geschichte des gelehrten Unterrichts auf den deutschen Schulen und Universitäten vom Ausgang des Mittel-*

alters bis zur Gegenwart. Vol. II. Leipzig: Veit and Comp, 1897.

Pavlov-Sil'vanskii, Nikolai P. *Gosudarevy Sluzhilye Liudi.* 2nd ed. St. Petersburg: n.p., 1909.

Payne, P. L. "The Emergence of the Large-scale Company in Great Britain, 1870-1914," *Economic History Review,* Second Series, XX (1967), 519-40.

Péreire, Isaac. *La Question des Chemins de Fer.* Paris: C. Motteroz, 1879.

Perkin, H. J. "Middle Class Education and Employment in the Nineteenth Century: A Critical Note," *Economic History Review,* Second Series, XIV (1961-62), 122-30.

Perthes, Clemens Theodor. *Der Staatsdienst in Preussen: Ein Beitrag zum deutschen Staatsrecht.* Hamburg: Verlag von Friedrich Perthes, 1838.

Peschaud, Marcel. "Les Chemins de Fer Français et Allemands et la Guerre," *Revue Politique et Parlementaire,* 1927, No. 397, pp. 349-81.

Petersdorff, Herman von. *Friedrich von Motz: Eine Biographie.* 2 Vols. Berlin: Reimer Hoffing, 1913.

Petot, Jean. *Histoire de l'Administration des Ponts et Chaussées, 1599-1815.* Paris: Librairie Marcel Rivière, 1958.

Peyster, de. "L'Inspection Générale des Finances en France," *Revue Internationale des Sciences Administratives,* 1939, No. 4, pp. 665-85.

Pickering, J. F. "Recruitment to the Administrative Class, 1960-64: Part II," *Public Administration,* XLV (1967), 169-99.

Pierce, Albert. "On the Concepts of Role and Status," *Sociologus,* VI (1956), 29-34.

Pierre-Henry. *Histoire des Préfets: Cent Cinquante Ans d'Administration Provinciale 1800-1950.* Paris: Nouvelles Editions Latines, 1950.

Pinet, Gaston. *Ecrivains et Penseurs Polytechniciens.* Paris: Paul Ollendorff, Editeur. 1898.

———. *Histoire de l'Ecole Polytechnique.* Paris: Librairie Polytechnique, Baudry et Cie, 1887.

Pinot, Robert. "Le Chef dans la Grande Industrie," *Revue de France,* No. 1, 1921, pp. 109-22.

Pintner, Walter M. *Russian Economic Policy under Nicholas I.* Ithaca: Cornell University Press, 1967.

———. "The Social Characteristics of the Early Nineteenth-Century Russian Bureaucracy," *Slavic Review,* XXIX (1970), 429-43.

Pintschovius, K. *Volkswirte als Führer oder als Fachbeamte? Eine Sozialwissenschaftliche Untersuchung.* Munich: Duncker and Humblot, 1930.

Pipes, Richard. *Karamzin's Memoir on Ancient and Modern Russia: A Translation and Analysis.* Cambridge, Mass.: Harvard University Press, 1959.

Plumb, J. H. (ed.). *Studies in Social History: A Tribute to G. M. Trevelyan.* London: Longmans, Green, 1955.

Pogrebinsky, A. P. "Stroitel'stvo Zheleznykh Dorog v Poreformennoi Rossii i Finansovaia Politika Tsarizma (60-90-e Gody XIX v.)," *Istoricheskie Zapiski,* 1954, No. 47, pp. 149-80.

Poignant, Raymond. *Education and Development in Western Europe, the United States, and the U.S.S.R.: A Comparative Study.* New York: Teachers College Press, 1969.

Polanyi, Karl. *The Great Transformation.* New York: Farrar and Rinehart, Inc., 1944.

Poliansky, F. Ia. "Promyshlennaia Politika Russkogo Absoliutizma vo Vtoroi Chetverti XVIII v. (1725-1740 gg.)," *Voprosy Istorii Narodnogo Khoziaistva SSSR,* 1957, pp. 85-137.

Polner, Tikhon J., *et al. Russian Local Government during the War and the Union of Zemstvos.* New Haven: Yale University Press, 1930.

Ponteil, Félix. *Histoire de l'Enseignement en France: Les Grandes Etapes, 1789-1964.* Paris: Sirey, 1966.

Portal, Roger. *L'Oural au XVIIIᵉ Siècle: Etude d'Histoire Economique et Sociale.* Paris: Collection Historique de l'Institut d'Etudes Slaves, 1950.

———. "Das Problem einer industriellen Revolution in Russland in 19. Jahrhundert," *Forschungen zur Osteuropäischen Geschichte,* 1 (1954), 205-16.

———. "La Russie Industrielle de 1881 à 1927." Paris: Centre de Documentation Universitaire "Les Cours de Sorbonne," n.d. (mimeographed).

Porter, Whitworth. *History of the Corps of Royal Engineers.* Vol. 1. London: Longmans, Green and Co., 1889.

Prandy, Kenneth. *Professional Employees: A Study of Scientists and Engineers.* London: Faber and Faber, Ltd., 1965.

Pratt, Edwin A. *British Railways and the Great War: Organisation, Efforts, Difficulties and Achievements.* London: Selwyn and Blount, Ltd., 1921.

Preradovich, Nikolaus von. *Die Führungschichten in Österreich und Preussen (1804-1918) mit einem Ausblick bis zum Jahre 1945.* Wiesbaden: Franz Steiner Verlag, 1955.

Prewitt, Kenneth. *The Recruitment of Political Leaders*. Indianapolis: The Bobbs-Merrill Co., 1970.

Price, John Wilbur. "Education and the Civil Service in Europe," *Western Political Quarterly*, x (1957), 817-32.

Priouret, Roger. *Origines du Patronat Français*. Paris: Bernard Grasset, 1963.

Pritzkoleit, Kurt. *Die Neuen Herren: Die Mächtigen in Staat und Wirtschaft*. Munich: Kurt Desch, 1955.

Prost, Antoine. *Histoire de l'Enseignement en France, 1800-1967*. Paris: Librairie Armand Colin, 1968.

Prouty, Roger. *The Transformation of the Board of Trade, 1830-1855: A Study of Administrative Reorganization in the Heyday of Laissez Faire*. London: William Heinemann, Ltd., 1957.

Prussia, Königliches Preussisches Statistisches Landesamt. *Statistisches Jahrbuch*. Zwölfter Jahrgang. Berlin: Verlag des Königlichen Statistischen Landesamts, 1915.

Prussia, Königliches Statistisches Bureau. *Jahrbuch für die amtliche Statistik des preussischen Staats*. III Jahrgang. Berlin: Verlag des Königlichen Statistischen Bureaus, 1869.

Przeworski, Adam and Henry Teune. *The Logic of Comparative Social Inquiry*. New York: John Wiley and Sons, 1970.

Pypin, A. N. *Russkoe Masonstvo: XVIII i Pervaia Chetvert' XIX. V.* Edited by G. V. Vernadsky. Petrograd: Izdatel'stvo "Ogni," 1916.

Rae, John B. "The Engineer as Business Man in American Industry: A Preliminary Analysis," *Explorations in Entrepreneurial History*, vii (1954), 94-104.

Raeff, Marc. "L'Etat, le Gouvernement et la Tradition Politique en Russie Impériale avant 1861," *Revue d'Histoire Moderne et Contemporaine*, ix (1962), 295-307.

———. "Home, School, and Service in the Life of the 18th Century Russian Nobleman," *Slavonic and East European Review*, xl (1962), 295-307.

———. *Michael Speransky, Statesman of Imperial Russia, 1772-1839*. The Hague: Martinus Nihoff, 1957.

———. *Origins of the Russian Intelligentsia: The Eighteenth Century Nobility*. New York: Harcourt, Brace and World, Inc., 1966.

———. "The Russian Autocracy and Its Officials," *Harvard Slavic Studies*, iv (1957), 77-91.

Rapawy, Stephen. "Comparison of U.S. and U.S.S.R. Civilian Employment in Government: 1950 to 1969." Foreign Demographic Analysis Division, U.S. Department of Commerce, 1972. (Unpublished draft.)

Rashin, A. G. "Gramotnost' i Narodnoe Obrazovanie v Rossii v XIX i Nachale XX v.," *Istoricheskie Zapiski*, 1951, No. 37, pp. 28-80.

Reader, W. J. *Professional Men: The Rise of the Professional Classes in Nineteenth-Century England*. New York: Basic Books, Inc., 1966.

Redlich, Fritz. "The Beginnings and Development of German Business History," *Bulletin of the Business Historical Society*, XXVI (1952). (Special number.)

Redlich, Josef. *Englische Lokalverwaltung: Darstellung der inneren Verwaltung Englands in ihrer geschichtlichen Entwicklung und ihrer gegenwärtigen Gestalt*. Leipzig: Duncker and Humblot, 1901.

Redmayne, Sir R.A.S. *The British Coal Mining Industry during the War*. Oxford: Clarendon Press, 1923.

Regan, D. E. "The Expert and the Administrator: Recent Changes at the Ministry of Transport," *Public Administration*, XLIV (1966), 149-67.

Reinhard, Marcel. "Elite et Noblesse dans la Second Moitié du XVIIIᵉ Siècle," *Revue d'Histoire Moderne et Contemporaine*, III (1956), 5-37.

The Reorganization of the Civil Service: By a Subordinate Therein. London: Smith, Elder and Co., 1855.

Richardson, Nicholas J. *The French Prefectoral Corps, 1814-1830*. Cambridge: Cambridge University Press, 1966.

Richter, Eugen. "Die Vorbildung der höheren Verwaltungsbeamten in Preussen," *Preussische Jahrbücher*, XVII (1866), 1-19.

Ricommard, J. *La Lieutenance Générale de Police à Troyes au XVIIIᵉ Siècle, 1700-1790*. Dissertation, University of Paris, Faculté des Lettres, 1933.

———. "Les Subdélégués des Intendants jusqu'à Leur Erection en Titre d'Office," *Revue d'Histoire Moderne*, XII (New Series, VI) (1937), 338-407.

Ridley, Frederick F. *Specialists and Generalists: A Comparative Study of the Professional Civil Servant at Home and Abroad*. London: George Allen and Unwin, Ltd., 1968.

——— and Jean Blondel. *Public Administration in France*. London: Routledge and Kegan Paul, 1964.

Rieber, Alfred J. "Technology and Economic Development in Nineteenth Century Russia: The Formation of La Grande Société des Chemins de Fer Russes." Unpublished MS. Provided through Courtesy of Author.

Riedler, A. "Zur Frage der Ingenieur-Erziehung," *Volkswirtschaftliche Zeitfragen*, XVI (1895), 1-35.

Riehl, W. H. *Die Bürgerliche Gesellschaft*. 5th ed. Stuttgart: J. G. Cotta'scher Verlag, 1858.

Riemer, Svend. "Sozialer Aufstieg und Klassenschichtung," *Archiv für Sozialwissenschaft und Sozialpolitik*, LXVII (1932), 531-60.

Rigby, T. H. *The Selection of Leading Personnel in the Soviet State and Communist Party*. Dissertation, University of London, 1954.

Ringer, Fritz K. *The Decline of the German Mandarins: The German Academic Community, 1890-1933*. Cambridge, Mass.: Harvard University Press, 1969.

Ritter, Ulrich P. *Die Rolle des Staates in den Frühstadien der Industrialisierung: Die preussische Industrieförderung in der ersten Hälfte des 19. Jahrhunderts*. Berlin: Duncker and Humblot, 1961.

Rivero, Jean. "La Technocratie: Mythe, Epouvantail ou Panacée," *Annales de l'Université de Poitiers*. Nouvelle Série, No. 3, pp. 3-14.

Roach, J.P.C. "Victorian Universities and the National Intelligentsia," *Victorian Studies*, III (1959-60), 131-50.

Roberts, David. "Jeremy Bentham and the Victorian Administrative State," *Victorian Studies*, II (1958-59), 193-210.

―――. *Victorian Origins of the British Welfare State*. New Haven: Yale University Press, 1960.

Robinson, Howard. *The British Post Office: A History*. Princeton: Princeton University Press, 1948.

Rocheblave-Spenlé, Anne-Marie. *La Notion de Rôle en Psychologie Sociale: Etude Historico-Critique*. 2nd ed. Paris: Presses Universitaires de France, 1969.

Roe, Anne. *The Psychology of Occupations*. New York: John Wiley and Sons, 1956.

Rogers, Everett M. *Diffusion of Innovations*. New York: The Free Press, 1962.

Rokkan, Stein and Richard L. Merritt (eds.). *Comparing Nations: The Use of Quantitative Data in Cross-National Research*. New Haven: Yale University Press, 1966.

Roscher, Wilhelm G. F. *Geschichte der National-Oekonomik in Deutschland*. Munich: R. Oldenbourg, 1874.

Rosenberg, Hans. *Bureaucracy, Aristocracy and Autocracy: The Prussian Experience 1660-1815*. Cambridge, Mass.: Harvard University Press, 1958.

Rostow, Walt W. *The Economics of Take-Off into Sustained Growth*. New York: Macmillan, 1963.

Rothblatt, Sheldon. *The Revolution of the Dons: Cambridge and Society in Victorian England.* London: Faber and Faber, 1968.

Rotours, J. A. des. "Le Dernier Intendant de la Généralité d'Alençon," *Bulletin de la Société Historique et Archéologique de l'Orne,* XII (1893), 503-14.

Roux, Pierre. *Les Fermes d'Impôts sous l'Ancien Régime.* Dissertation, University of Paris, Faculté de Droit. Paris: Rousseau et Cie, 1916.

Ruffmann, Karl Heinz. "Russischer Adel als Sondertypus der europäischen Adelswelt," *Jahrbücher für die Geschichte Osteuropas,* Neue Folge, IX (1964), 161-78.

Runge, Wolfgang. *Politik und Beamtentum im Parteienstaat: Die Demokratisierung der politischen Beamten in Preussen zwischen 1918 und 1933.* Stuttgart: Ernst Klett, 1965.

Sacke, Georg. "Adel und Bürgertum in der Regierungszeit Katharinas II. von Russland," *Revue Belge de Philologie et d'Histoire,* XVII (1938), 815-52.

Sagnac, Phillipe. "Louis XIV et Son Administration," *Revue d'Histoire Politique et Constitutionnelle,* III, No. 1 (1939), 23-47.

Salter, Arthur. *Slave of the Lamp: A Public Servant's Notebook.* London: Weidenfeld and Nicolson, 1967.

Sampson, Anthony. *Anatomy of Britain.* London: Hodder and Stoughton, 1962.

Sauvy, Alfred. *Histoire Economique de la France entre les Deux Guerres.* I: *De l'Armistice à la Dévaluation de la Livre.* Paris: Fayard, 1965.

Savant, Jean. *Les Préfets de Napoléon.* Paris: Hachette, 1958.

Sawyer, John E. "The Social Basis of the American System of Manufacturing," *Journal of Economic History,* XIV (1954), 361-79.

———. "Social Structure and Economic Progress: General Propositions and Some French Examples," *American Economic Review,* XLI (1951) (papers and Proceedings of the 65th Annual Meeting of the American Economic Association), 321-29.

Scarrow, Howard A. "The Scope of Comparative Analysis," *Journal of Politics,* XXV (1963), 565-77.

Schäffle. "Zur Frage der Prüfungsansprüche an die Candidaten des höheren Staatsdienstes," *Zeitschrift für die gesamte Staatswissenschaft,* XXIV Erste Hälfte (1868).

Scheibert, Peter. "Marginalien zu einer neuen Speranskij Biographie," *Jahrbücher für Geschichte Osteuropas,* VI (1958), 448-67.

Schelle, Gustave (ed.). *Oeuvres de Turgot et Documents Le Concernant, avec Biographie et Notes.* Paris: Librairie Félix Alcan, Vols. III-V, 1919, 1922, 1923.

Schlesinger, Joseph A. *Ambition and Politics: Political Careers in the United States*. Chicago: Rand McNally and Co., 1966.

Schmidt, Richard. *Die Bürokratisierung des modernen England und ihre Bedeutung für das heutige deutsche Behördensystem*. Leipzig: V. S. Hirzel, 1932.

Schmoller, Gustav. *Grundriss der Allgemeinen Volkswirtschaftslehre*. Vol. I. Leipzig: Duncker and Humblot, 1900.

———. "Der preussische Beamtenstand unter Friedrich Wilhelm I," *Preussische Jahrbücher*, XXVII (1870), 148-72, 253-70, 538-55.

Schnee, Heinrich. *Die Hoffinanz und der moderne Staat*. Vol. I. Berlin: Duncker and Humblot, 1953.

Schneider, Ferdinand Josef. *Die Freimauerei und ihr Einfluss auf die geistliche Kultur in Deutschland am Ende des XVIII. Jahrhunderts: Prologomena zu einer Geschichte der deutschen Romantik*. Prague: Taussig and Taussig, 1909.

Schnier, Roman. "Haben wir die richtigen Beamten?" *Die Zeit*, December 16, 1966.

Schricker, A. *Eduard von Moeller, Oberpräsident von Elsass-Lothringen: Ein Lebensbild*. Cassel: Theodor Kay, 1881.

Schultze, Johanna. *Die Auseinandersetzung zwischen Adel und Bürgertum in den deutschen Zeitschriften der letzten drei Jahrzehnte des 18. Jahrhundert (1773-1806)*. Berlin: Emil Ebering, 1925.

Schultze, Walther. *Geschichte der preussischen Régieverwaltung von 1766 bis 1786*. Leipzig: Verlag Duncker and Humblot, 1888.

Schumpeter, Joseph A. *Imperialism and Social Classes*. New York: Augustus M. Kelley, Inc., 1951.

———. "Die sozialen Klassen im ethnisch homogenen Milieu," *Archiv für Sozialwissenschaft und Sozialpolitik*, LVII (1927), 1-67.

Schwann, Mathieu. *Ludolf Camphausen*. 3 Vols. Essen: G. D. Baedeker, 1915.

Schwartz, Harry. *Russia's Soviet Economy*. 2nd ed. New York: Prentice-Hall, Inc., 1954.

Scott, Harold. *Your Obedient Servant*. London, 1959.

Sears, Marian V. "The American Businessman at the Turn of the Century," *Business History Review*, XXX (1956), 382-443.

Seconde Mission d'Etude du Fonctionnement de l'Entreprise aux Etats-Unis, Octobre 1950-Juillet 1951. Aspects de l'Entreprise Americaine: Environement, Aspect Humain, Aspect Technique. Paris, 1953.

Seleznev, Ivan Ia. *Istoricheskii Ocherk Imperatorskago Byshago Tsarskosel'skago, Nyne Aleksandrovskago Litseia za Pervoe Ego*

Piatidesiatiletie s 1811 po 1861 God. St. Petersburg: V. Bezobrazov and Co., 1861.

Sellow. "Rang und Gehalt in Justiz und Verwaltung," *Preussische Jahrbücher,* LXXVIII (1894), 118-36; LXXIX (1895), 139-45.

Sénac de Meilhan. *Du Gouvernement, des Moeurs et des Conditions en France avant la Révolution avec le Caractère des Principaux Personnages du Règne de Louis XVI.* Hamburg: B. J. Hoffmann, 1795.

Sharp, Walter R. *The French Civil Service: Bureaucracy in Transition.* New York: Macmillan Co., 1931.

Shcherban', A. N. *Nauchnaia Organizatsiia Truda i Upravleniia.* Moscow: Izdatel'stvo "Ekonomika," 1965.

Sheridan, Thomas. *A Plan of Education for the Young Nobility and Gentry of Great Britain, Most Humbly Addressed to the Father of His People.* London: E. and C. Dilly, 1769.

Shonfield, Andrew. *Modern Capitalism: The Changing Balance of Public and Private Power.* New York: Oxford University Press for the Royal Institute of International Affairs, 1965.

Siebel, Wigard. "Soziale Funktion und soziale Stellung des Ingenieurs," *Jahrbücher für Sozialwissenschaft,* XIII (1962), 61-78.

Simon, Herbert A. *Administrative Behavior.* New York: Macmillan, 1961.

Sisson, Charles H. *The Spirit of British Administration and Some European Comparisons.* London: Faber and Faber, 1959.

Siwek-Pouydesseau, Jeanne. *Le Corps Préfectoral sous la Troisième et la Quatrième République.* Paris: Armand Colin, 1969.

———. *Le Personnel de Direction des Ministères: Cabinets Ministériels et Directeurs d'Administrations Centrales.* Paris: Armand Colin, 1969.

Skalon, D. A. *Stoletie Voennago Ministerstva, 1802-1902: Glavnoe Intendantskoe Upravlenie.* St. Petersburg: Berezhlivost', 1903.

Smellie, K. B. *A Hundred Years of English Government.* London: Gerald Duckworth and Co., Ltd., 1950.

Snyders, Georges. *La Pédagogie en France au XVIIᵉ et XVIIIᵉ Siècles.* Paris: Presses Universitaires de France, 1965.

Sokolovskaia, T. *Russkoe Masonstvo i Ego Znachenie v Istorii Obshchestvennago Dvizheniia (XVIII i Pervaia Chetvert XIX Stoletiia).* St. Petersburg: N. Glagolev, n.d.

Sombart, Werner. *Der Bourgeois: Zur Geistesgeschichte des Modernen Wirtschaftsmenschen.* Munich: Duncker and Humblot, 1913.

Spitzer, Alan B. "The Bureaucrat as Proconsul: The Restoration Prefect and the Police Générale," *Comparative Studies in Society and History*, VII (1964-65), 371-92.

Stanley, David T. *The Higher Civil Service: An Evaluation of Federal Personnel Practices.* Washington: The Brookings Institution, 1964.

Stein, Hans Peter. "Der Offizier des russischen Heeres im Leitabschnitt zwischen Reform und Revolution (1861-1905)," *Forschungen zur Osteuropäischen Geschichte*, XIII (1967), 346-507.

Steller, Paul. *Führende Männer des rheinisch-westfälischen Wirtschaftslebens: Persönliche Erinnerungen.* Berlin: Reimar Hobbing, 1930.

Stewart, Philip D. *Political Power in the Soviet Union.* Indianapolis: Bobbs-Merrill Co., 1968.

Stewart, Rosemary G. and Paul Duncan-Jones. "Educational Background and Career History of British Managers, with Some American Comparisons," *Explorations in Entrepreneurial History*, IX, No. 2 (1956), 61-71.

Stillich, Oskar. *Steinkohlenindustrie: Nationalökonomische Forschungen auf dem Gebiete des grossindustriellen Unternehmung.* Vol. 2. Leipzig: Jäh and Schunke, 1906.

Stokes, Eric. *The English Utilitarians and India.* Oxford: Clarendon Press, 1959.

Stolberg-Wernigerode, Otto Graf zu. "Die Nationalbiographien," *Tradition*, VIII (1963), 65-69.

Stölzel, Adolf. *Die Entwicklung des gelehrten Richterthums in deutschen Territorien: Eine geschichtliche Untersuchung.* Stuttgart: J. G. Cotta, 1872.

Sträter, Emma. *Die soziale Stellung der Angestellten.* Dissertation, Bonn University, Law and State Science Faculty. Bochum-Langendreer: Heinrich Pöppinghaus, 1933.

"Struktur des Bundespersonals: Ergebnis der Personalstrukturerhebung am 2. Oktober 1968," *Wirtschaft und Statistik*, 1970, Heft 3, pp. 139-42.

Suhge, Werner. *Saint-Simonismus und junges Deutschland: Das Saint-Simonistische System in der deutschen Literatur der ersten Hälfte des 19. Jahrhunderts.* Berlin: Verlag Dr. Emil Ebering, 1935.

Suleiman, Ezra N. *The French Administrative Elite: Power, Politics, and Bureaucracy.* Princeton: Princeton University Press, 1974.

Sven Stelling, Michaud. "Histoire des Universités au Moyen Age et à la Renaissance au Cours des Vingt-Cinq Dernières Années," *XIe Congrès International des Sciences Historiques, Rapports.* Stockholm, 1960, pp. 97-143.

Swart, Koenrod U. *Sale of Office in the Seventeenth Century*. Dissertation, Leiden University, Faculty of Letters. The Hague: Martinus Nihoff, 1949.

Tarbe de Saint-Hardouin, F.P.H. *Notices Biographiques sur les Ingénieurs des Ponts et Chaussées depuis la Création du Corps en 1716 jusqu'à nos Jours*. Paris: Librairie Polytechnique, Baudry et Cie, 1884.

Tawney, R. H. *Religion and the Rise of Capitalism: A Historical Study*. New York: Penguin Books, 1947.

Tax, Sol. "Selective Culture Change," *American Economic Review*, XLI (1951), 315-20.

"The Teaching of Administrative Sciences in the Higher Educational Establishments of the Union of Soviet Socialist Republics: Report of the Academy of Sciences of the USSR," *International Review of Administrative Sciences*, 1959, No. 4, pp. 453-55.

Tereshchenko, V. "The Effect of 'Trifles,' " *Izvestia*, March 29, 1964. Trans. in *Current Digest of the Soviet Press*, XVI, No. 13, 17-18.

Thiess, Karl and Kurt Wiedenfeld. *Die Preisbildung im Kriege (Volkswirtschaftliche Abteilung des Kriegsernährungsamts, Beiträge zur Kriegswirtschaft)*. Berlin: Reimar Hobbing, 1916.

Thirion, H. *La Vie Privée des Financiers au XVIIIᵉ Siècle*. Paris: E. Plon, Nourrit et Cie, 1895.

Thompson, Victor A. "Hierarchy, Specialization and Organization Conflict," *Administrative Science Quarterly*, V (1960-61), 485-521.

Thomson, Mark A. *The Secretaries of State, 1681-1782*. Oxford: Clarendon Press, 1932.

Thorner, Daniel. "Great Britain and the Development of India's Railways," *Journal of Economic History*, XI (1951), 389-402.

———. *Investment in Empire: British Railway and Steam-Shipping Enterprise in India, 1825-1849*. Philadelphia: University of Pennsylvania Press, 1950.

Tietjens, Wilhelm. "Der akademische Nachwuchs der Beamtenschaft als gesellschaftliches Problem," *Der Beamte*, III (1931), 187-94.

Timoshenko, Stephen P. "The Development of Engineering Education in Russia," *Russian Review*, XV (1956), 173-85.

Tisch, Heinrich. *Das Problem des sozialen Auf- und Abstieges im deutschen Volk dargestellt an hand einer Erhebung über die soziale Herkunft der Beamten in der Saarpfalz*. Dissertation, Heidelberg University, Philosophical Faculty. Speyer: Pilzer-Drückerei, 1937.

Torke, Hans Joachim. "Das russische Beamtentum in der ersten Hälfte des 19. Jahrhunderts," *Forschungen zur Osteuropäische Geschichte*, XIII (1967), 7-345.

Torti, Marcel. "Les Mathématiques à l'Ecole Nationale d'Administration," *Promotions*, 1957, No. 42, pp. 27-29.

Tranchant, Charles. *Notice Sommaire sur l'Ecole Nationale d'Administration de 1848 et sur les Projets Ultérieurs d'Institutions Analogues.* Nancy: Imprimerie Berger-Levrault et Cie, 1884.

Treue, Wilhelm. "Das Verhältnis vom Furst, Staat und Unternehmer in der Zeit des Merkantilismus," *Vierteljahrsschrift für Sozial und Wirtschaftsgeschichte*, XLIV (1957), 26-56.

——. "Zerfall und Einheit: Zum Wandel der europäischen Führungsschicht seit dem 17. Jahrhundert," *Die Sammlung*, VI (1951), 19-29, 111-19.

Trevelyan, G. M. *English Social History: A Survey of Six Centuries, Chaucer to Queen Victoria.* London: Longmans, Green and Co., 1942.

Trevelyan, George O. *The Life and Letters of Lord Macaulay.* 2 Vols. London: Longmans, Green and Co., 1876.

Tröger, Walter. *Elitenbildung: Überlegungen zur Schulreform in einer demokratischen Gesellschaft.* Munich: Ernst Reinhardt Verlag, 1968.

Truchy, H. "L'Elite et la Fonction Publique," *Revue Politique et Parlementaire*, 1927, No. 397, pp. 339-48.

Tucker, Robert C. *The Marxian Revolutionary Idea.* New York: W. W. Norton and Co., 1969.

Tudesq, A. J. "L'Etude des Notables: Inventaire des Sources et Projets d'Enquête," *Bulletin d'Histoire Moderne et Contemporaine*, 1 (1956), 25-61.

Tugan-Baranovsky, Mikhail. *Geschichte der russischen Fabrik.* Berlin: Emil Felber, 1900.

Tumin, Melvin. *Social Stratification: The Forms and Functions of Inequality.* Englewood Cliffs, N. J.: Prentice Hall, 1967.

Turkistanov, Nikolai N. *Gubernskii Sluzhebnik ili Spisok General Gubernatoram, Praviteliam, Poruchikam Praviteliia, Predsedateliam Ugolovnoi i Grazhdanskoi Palat i Dvorianskim Pravoditeliam v 47 Namestnichestvakh (Gubernii), 1777-1796.* St. Petersburg: n.p., 1869.

Turner, Ralph E. "Role-Taking, Role Standpoint, and Reference-Group Behavior," *American Journal of Sociology*, LXI (1956), 316-28.

Twesten, Karl. "Der preussische Beamtenstaat," *Preussische Jahrbücher*, XVIII (1866), No. 1, 1-38; No. 2, 109-47.

Ule, Carl Hermann. *Die Entwicklung des Öffentlichen Dienstes.* Cologne: Carl Heymanns Verlag, 1961.

Ulich, Robert. *The Education of Nations: A Comparison in Historical Perspective.* Cambridge, Mass.: Harvard University Press, 1967.

"Une Enquête sur l'Ecole Nationale d'Administration," *L'Etat Moderne*, XI, No. 6 (1938), 325-84.

USSR, Tsentral'noe Statisticheskoe Upravlenie. *Itogi Vsesoiuznoi Perepisi Naseleniia 1959 Goda: SSSR.* Moscow: Gosstatizdat, 1962.

USSR, Tsentral'noe Statisticheskoe Upravlenie. *Narodnoe Khoziaistvo SSSR.* Moscow: Gosstatizdat, 1956.

USSR, Tsentral'noe Statisticheskoe Upravlenie. *Zhenshchina v SSSR.* Moscow: Gosstatizdat, 1960.

Van Riper, Paul P. "The Senior Civil Service and the Career System," *Public Administration Review*, XVIII (1958), 189-200.

Vernadsky, George V. *Russkoe Masonstvo v Tsarstvovanie Ekateriny II.* Petrograd: Akts. O-va Tipogr. Dela, 1917.

Vignoles, Olinthus J. *Life of Charles Blacker Vignoles.* London: Longmans, Green and Co., 1889.

Vignon, E.J.M. *Etudes Historiques sur l'Administration des Voies Publiques en France aux Dix-Septième et Dix-Huitième Siècles.* 4 Vols. Paris: Dunod, Editeur, 1862.

Virginsky, V. S. *Vozniknovenie Zheleznykh Dorog v Rossii do Nachala 40 Godov XIX Veka.* Moscow: Gosudarstvennoe Transportnoe Zheleznodorozhnoe Izdatel'stvo, 1949.

"Volkswirte im zweiten Glied," *Der Volkswirt*, May 4, 1962.

Vollehim, Fritz. *Die provisorische Verwaltung am Nieder- und Mittelrhein während der Jahre 1814-1816.* Dissertation, Bonn University, Philosophy Faculty. Bonn: P. Hanstein, 1911.

Von Laue, Theodore H. "Factory Inspection under the Witte System: 1892-1903," *American Slavic and East European Review*, XIX (1960), 347-62.

———. "The Industrialization of Russia in the Writings of Sergei Witte," *American Slavic and East European Review*, X (1951), 177-90.

———. *Sergei Witte and the Industrialization of Russia.* New York: Columbia University Press, 1963.

Die Vorbildung zum höheren Verwaltungsdienste in den deutschen Staaten Österreich und Frankreich. Leipzig: Duncker and Humblot, 1887.

Vucinich, Alexander. *Science in Russian Culture.* 2 Vols. Stanford: Stanford University Press, 1963, 1970.

Wagner, Albrecht. *Der Richter: Geschichte, aktuelle Fragen, Reformprobleme.* Karlsruhe: Verlag C. F. Müller, 1959.

Wahl, Adalbert. *Vorgeschichte der französischen Revolution.* 2 Vols. Tübingen: J.C.B. Mohr, 1905, 1907.

Wakeford, John. *The Cloistered Elite*: *A Sociological Analysis of the English Public Boarding School.* London: Macmillan, 1969.

Walker, Harvey. *Training Public Employees in Great Britain.* London: McGraw Hill, Ltd., 1935.

Wallon, Maurice. *Les Saint-Simoniens et les Chemins de Fer.* Dissertation, University of Paris, Faculté de Droit. Paris: A. Pedone Editeur, 1908.

Warner, William Lloyd, *et al. The American Federal Executive*: *A Study of the Social and Personal Characteristics of the Civilian and Military Leaders of the United States Federal Government.* New Haven: Yale University Press, 1963.

"Was lernen die Regierungsräte?" *Die Zeit*, March 5, 1965.

Weber, Max. *Economy and Society*: *An Outline of Interpretive Sociology.* Vol. III. New York: Bedminster Press, 1968.

———. *The Protestant Ethic and the Spirit of Capitalism.* New York: Charles Scribner's Sons, 1958.

Wehler, Hans Ulrich. *Moderne deutsche Sozialgeschichte.* Cologne: Kiepenheuer and Witsch, 1966.

Weinberg, Ian. *The English Public Schools*: *The Sociology of Elite Education.* New York: Atherton Press, 1967.

Weinberger, Eugène. *L'Economie Sociale de W. Rathenau.* Dissertation, University of Paris, Faculté de Droit. Paris: Presses Universitaires, 1924.

Wermuth, Adolf. *Ein Beamtenleben*: *Erinnerungen.* Berlin: August Schere, 1922.

Wheare, K. C. *Government by Committee*: *An Essay on the British Constitution.* Oxford: Clarendon Press, 1955.

White, Hayden V. (ed.). *The Uses of History*: *Essays in Intellectual and Social History.* Detroit: Wayne State University Press, 1968.

Wiedenfeld, Kurt. "Deutsche Eisenbahn-Gestalter aus Staatsverwaltung und Wirtschaftsleben im 19. Jahrhundert (1815-1914)," *Archiv für Eisenbahnwesen*, 1940, pp. 733-824.

———. *Die Organisation der Kriegsrohstoff-Bewirtschaftung im Weltkriege.* Hamburg: Hanseatische Verlagsanstalt, 1936.

———. *Zwischen Wirtschaft und Staat*: *Aus dem Lebenserinnerungen.* Berlin: Walter de Gruyter and Co., 1960.

Wilkinson, Rupert. "Political Leadership and the Late Victorian Public School," *British Journal of Sociology*, XIII (1962), 320-30.

Will, Robert E. "Some Aspects of Railroad Entrepreneurship," *Explorations in Entrepreneurial History*, V (1952-53), 121-25.

Williams, E. N. *The Ancien Régime in Europe: Government and Society in the Major States, 1648-1789.* London: The Bodley Head, 1970.

Winnifrith, John. "The Rt. Hon. Sir Alexander Spearman, Bart. (1793-1874): Gladstone's Invaluable Public Servant," *Public Administration*, XXXVIII (1960), 311-20.

Winter, Georg (ed.). *Die Reorganisation des preussischen Staates unter Stein und Hardenberg.* Erster Teil: *Allgemeine Verwaltungs- und Behördenreform.* Vol. I. *Vom Beginn des Kampfes gegen die Kabinettsregierung bis zum Wiedereintritt des Ministers vom Stein.* Leipzig: S. Hirzel, 1931.

Witte, Sergei. *The Memoirs of Count Witte.* New York: Doubleday, Page and Co., 1921.

Wolfe, Bertram D. "Backwardness and Industrialization in Russian History and Thought," *Slavic Review*, XXVI (1967), 177-203.

Wolitz, Seth L. *The Proustian Community.* New York: New York University Press, 1971.

Wueleresse, Leon. "Les Physiocrates sous le Ministère de Turgot," *Revue d'Histoire Economique et Sociale*, XIII (1925), 314-37.

Young, D. M. *The Colonial Office in the Early Nineteenth Century.* London: Longmans, Green, for the Royal Commonwealth Society, 1961.

Zagorsky, S. O. *State Control of Industry in Russia during the War.* New Haven: Yale University Press, 1928.

Zapf, Wolfgang (ed.). *Beiträge zur Analyse der deutschen Oberschicht.* Munich: R. Piper and Co., 1965.

Zedletz und Neukirch, O. von. "Neueinrichtung der preussischen Verwaltung," *Preussische Jahrbücher*, CVII (1902), 14-43.

Ziekursch, Johannes. *Beiträge zur Charakteristik der preussischen Verwaltungsbeamten in Schlessien bis zum Unterganges des friderizianischen Staates.* Breslau: E. Wohlfarth, 1907.

Ziller, Robert C. "Individuation and Socialization: A Theory of Assimilation in Large Organisations," *Human Relations*, XVII (1964), 341-60.

Zorn, Wolfgang. "Unternehmer und Aristokratie in Deutschland: Ein Beitrag zur Geschichte des sozialen Stils und Selbstbewusstseins in der Neuzeit," *Tradition*, VIII (1963), 241-54.

Zunkel, Friedrich. "Beamtenschaft und Unternehmertum beim Aufbau der Ruhrindustrie, 1849-1880," *Tradition*, IX (1964), 261-77.

———. *Der Rheinisch-Westfälische Unternehmer, 1834-1879: Beitrag zur Geschichte des deutschen Bürgertums im 19. Jahrhundert.* Cologne: Westdeutscher Verlag, 1962.